TIME OF THE DOCTOR

The Unofficial and Unauthorised Guide to
Doctor Who 2012 & 2013

TIME OF THE DOCTOR

The Unofficial and Unauthorised Guide to
Doctor Who 2012 & 2013

Stephen James Walker

First published in the UK in 2016 by
Telos Publishing Ltd
5A Church Road, Shortlands, Bromley, Kent BR2 0HP,
United Kingdom.

www.telos.co.uk

Telos Publishing Ltd values feedback. Please e-mail us with any
comments you may have about this book to: feedback@telos.co.uk

Time of the Doctor: The Unofficial and Unauthorised Guide to Doctor Who
2012 & 2013 © 2016 Stephen James Walker

ISBN: 978-1-84583-944-4 (UK paperback)

CONTENTS

Introduction

Welcome to the latest of Telos Publishing's comprehensive guides to 21st Century *Doctor Who*. Whereas previous books in this ongoing range have dealt with just one year, *Time of the Doctor* spans two – for the simple reason that the BBC chose to split transmission of the show's Series Seven across 2012 and 2013, and it seemed sensible to have the whole series encompassed within a single book rather than covered piecemeal. This has resulted in something of a bumper volume – not least because 2013 was *Doctor Who*'s landmark fiftieth anniversary year, which generated an extraordinary degree of public and media interest in the show, and a whole host of related events. Notable developments during this exceptionally busy two-year period included the return of River Song (played by Alex Kingston), the departure of companions Amy (Karen Gillan) and Rory (Arthur Darvill) and the arrival of their successor Clara Oswald (Jenna-Louise Coleman), the thrilling introduction of the War Doctor (John Hurt), a surprise reappearance by the eighth Doctor (Paul McGann), a team-up with the tenth Doctor (David Tennant), a cameo by the mysterious Curator (Tom Baker) and ultimately the exit of the eleventh Doctor (Matt Smith) and the casting of the twelfth (Peter Capaldi).

All these various comings and goings are recorded in the initial sections of this book. Here you will find a detailed chronicle of the main events, news stories, promotional activities and so forth that occurred in the *Doctor Who* world in 2012 and 2013, in what is designed to serve as an enduring record of the time from the 'outside looking in' perspective of the viewing public. Following this, there are capsule biographies of all the main cast and production team members who worked on the show during this period. Then comes the most substantial section of the book: an in-depth guide to and analysis of all 13 Series Seven episodes, plus the 2012 Christmas special 'The Snowmen', the fiftieth anniversary special 'The Day of the Doctor', and the 2013 Christmas special 'The Time of the Doctor', along with the numerous mini-episodes – otherwise known as 'minisodes' – seen during the course of the two years. Lastly there are six appendices, detailing: the docu-drama *An Adventure in Space and Time*; the humorous anniversary production *The Five(ish) Doctors Reboot*; the viewing figures and fan rankings; the latest entries in BBC Books' original *Doctor Who* novels range; the eleventh Doctor's ongoing appearances in original comic strip stories; and, lastly, other officially-sanctioned original eleventh Doctor fiction published during this period.

After the fairytale influence he brought to Series Five and the ghost-train ride analogy he adopted for Series Six, *Doctor Who* showrunner Steven Moffat decided this time to have each episode of Series Seven take the form a mini blockbuster movie. *Time of the Doctor* looks back and considers how well that idea succeeded. The Dalek Asylum; dinosaurs on a spaceship; a slow invasion; the fate of Amy and Rory; the return of the Ice Warriors; a journey into the heart of the TARDIS; a Victorian mystery; the revival of the Cybermen; Clara's destiny; and the final days of the eleventh Doctor – all these things and more are recalled within this exhaustive guide.

If you are reading this book, the chances are that you are already an avid follower of the good Doctor's adventures, but I hope that in the following pages you will find much to interest, inform and enlighten you, and ultimately to enhance your appreciation and enjoyment of the 2012 and 2013 run of episodes in what is undoubtedly my favourite television series of all time!

Stephen James Walker
May 2016

PART ONE

2012 As It Happened

Chapter One
The Long Wait

For *Doctor Who* fans, 2011 ended with the uncomfortable knowledge that there would be a much longer gap than usual between the recently-transmitted Christmas special and the start of the next full run of episodes.

Karen Gillan made a chat show appearance on the 6 January edition of BBC One's *The Graham Norton Show*, where she spoke briefly about the fact that – as had been made public the previous month – she would shortly be leaving *Doctor Who*. Generally, however, news relating to the show was thin on the ground this month. A rare exception was the announcement, on 12 January, that the BBC would again be running a Script to Screen competition this year. Previously this had been presented as part of *Doctor Who Confidential*, but following the demise of that popular behind-the-scenes tie-in show after its 2011 run, the competition had now been taken over by the long-running children's magazine programme *Blue Peter*. Entries were open to UK pupils aged 9 to 11, who were encouraged to collaborate on a script taking the Doctor on a new adventure in space and time, together with Amy and/or Rory but no other established characters. The closing date was 16 March, and the results would be broadcast in *Blue Peter*'s 24 May edition.[1]

On 18 January, a short video interview with Steven Moffat was placed online. Conducted at the *Radio Times*'s annual covers party, this saw the showrunner enthusing about *Doctor Who*'s forthcoming fiftieth anniversary year: 'I promise you, for so many reasons I can't talk about yet, there will never be a better time to be a *Doctor Who* fan. I absolutely promise that.' He added that Series Seven would begin sometime in the autumn, and would consist of 14 episodes, including the now-traditional Christmas special.

A few early production details about Series Seven had meanwhile

---

[1] For further details, see the entry on 'Good as Gold' in the 'Episode Guide' section below.

started to trickle out, including the news that there would be episodes scripted by Mark Gatiss and by two-time *Torchwood* writer John Fay (although, in the event, Fay's contribution would fall by the wayside).

Toward the end of the month, it was announced that Series Six of *Doctor Who* had won five Virgin Media TV awards: TV Show of the Year (gaining a huge 43.63% of the vote), TV Character of the Year (Rory Williams, as played by Arthur Darvill), Most Explosive TV Moment of the Year (the Doctor getting shot at Lake Silencio in 'The Impossible Astronaut' (2011)), Best Actress (Karen Gillan, for her role as Amy Pond) and Hottest Female (Gillan again). In the more prestigious National TV Awards, broadcast on ITV1 on the evening of 25 January, *Doctor Who* lost out to ITV's own *Downton Abbey* in the Most Popular Drama category, but Matt Smith picked up the Outstanding Drama Performance (Male) award for his performance as the Doctor, and Karen Gillan the Outstanding Drama Performance (Female) one for hers as Amy. Speaking at the awards show, Smith said: 'I'm really pleased with the award. We always try to do the best every day, and try to improve the show as best we can. I wouldn't mind a male companion now that Karen has left. I've always believed me and Karen would have different journeys in *Doctor Who*. I'm sad she's left, but the show is bigger than all the actors who have been in it. I have no plans to leave, though. I've definitely got a year left in the show, and I'll take it from there.'

On 31 January, a short interview with Gillan was broadcast on BBC Radio 1's *Newsbeat* programme. Asked about her forthcoming departure from the role of Amy, she replied: 'It was a mutual decision between me and Steven Moffat, over a lovely dinner actually. We both opened up about where we were at with it, and then came to the conclusion that this was the best time to go … I've had the most fun, so that makes me sad to leave, and I've made my best friends on the show as well. But it's time to go on to other things, and all stories come to their natural end, so I'm excited.'

On 4 February, fans in Australia had a chance to enjoy a selection of *Doctor Who* incidental music performed live, when the show's regular conductor and orchestrator Ben Foster led the Melbourne Symphony Orchestra in an event billed as *Doctor Who – A Symphonic Spectacular*, which took place at the Melbourne Convention and Exhibition Centre. This was similar in format to the *Doctor Who* Proms events previously staged in the UK. It was introduced by actor Mark Sheppard, who had played Canton Everett Delaware III in 'The Impossible Astronaut' / 'Day of the Moon' (2011), and featured an appearance by *Doctor Who*'s regular composer

Murray Gold on piano. A publicity photocall for the event was held at the Melbourne Cricket Ground, featuring a new paradigm Dalek – the orange Scientist variant – along with a Cyberman and a Silent.

On 9 February, the new issue of the official *Doctor Who Magazine* announced the names of two other writers who would be working on Series Seven: Chris Chibnall and Toby Whithouse. Pre-production on the series was by this point well under way, with recording due to begin on 20 February. In a video interview posted on the *Guardian* website on 13 February, Matt Smith commented: 'I'll be shooting sort of now until December on *Doctor Who*. It's a long shoot, but we've got four or five scripts that look in really good shape, and the casting is going very well … Looking forward to it. I love making it.'

Early on in this series, *Doctor Who* would undergo a major behind-the-scenes change, switching from Upper Boat Studios outside Pontypridd, where it had been made ever since 2006, to new facilities at the BBC Roath Lock Drama Village in Porth Teigr, Cardiff Bay. This site was due to have its formal opening in March, and on 13 February the BBC News website reported the Government's Business Minister Edwina Hart as saying: 'Porth Teigr represents a long-term investment by the Welsh government in the future of Cardiff, our capital city, and 2012 promises to be a significant year as we enter the next phase of regeneration and development. The presence of the BBC Wales studios provides a strong focal point around which we want to create a central hub and cluster for the creative industries across South Wales, where companies can work together, share ideas and develop collaborative links with other facilities in the area.' The main walkway connecting all of the facilities at Roath Lock was adorned with a plaque naming it 'Russell's Alley', in recognition of the achievements of Steven Moffat's predecessor as *Doctor Who* showrunner, Russell T Davies.

By the third week of February, with recording on Series Seven now under way, news started to emerge of guest stars who would feature in the forthcoming episodes, the first three to be named being Mark Williams, Rupert Graves and David Bradley. On 22 February, the BBC released the first promotional image for the series: a photograph of Matt Smith, Karen Gillan and Arthur Darvill in costume beside the TARDIS police box prop on set at Upper Boat.

By early March, news reports were starting to emerge of *Doctor Who*'s latest overseas location shoot – this one in Almeria, Spain, at Fort Bravo Studios and an attraction known as 'Mini Hollywood', designed to resemble an American town of the Wild West era.

On 12 March, the 'massively multiplayer' online *Doctor Who* role playing game *Worlds in Time* was officially launched, having been in preview since the previous December. Robert Nashak, Executive Vice President of BBC Worldwide Digital Entertainment and Games was quoted as saying: '*Worlds in Time* offers players a multitude of elements and opportunities to socialise – from introducing beloved characters and progressive storylines to presenting additional guild play, our goal is to become the largest *Doctor Who* community ever assembled, while also being an enjoyable experience for all players.' The game was created for the Adobe Flash forum by Three Rings Design Inc, whose CEO Daniel James added: 'I have been a fan of *Doctor Who* since I was a child, so developing this game with BBC Worldwide is a dream come true. Like the Doctor, we have our own mission: to provide *Doctor Who* fans an experience matched only by the wondrous TV series, and casual gamers a warm opportunity to discover the marvellous world for themselves. It's exciting to see the *Doctor Who* universe come to life in such a unique way.'

Worlds in Time was free to play online for players aged 13 and above, with those between the ages of 13 and 15 needing parental permission to participate, and optional 'enhanced' features were available to purchase. After preparing the TARDIS, players travelled to various immersive worlds (including Ember, Mars and New New York) and worked together to defend civilisation against infamous monsters (including the Weeping Angels, Cybermen, Daleks, Autons, Ood and Zygons) bent on creating chaos and destruction in the universe.

On the evening of 12 March, in a follow-up of sorts to the recent *A Symphonic Spectacular* event in Australia, the BBC National Orchestra of Wales, conducted by Ben Foster, gave two free concerts at the Millennium Centre in Cardiff Bay, close to *Doctor Who*'s new Roath Lock production base, performing Murray Gold's incidental music to the 2011 Christmas special 'The Doctor, the Widow and the Wardrobe' while the special itself was shown on a cinema-sized screen.

The evening of 21 March saw Steven Moffat attending a Royal Television Society awards event. Questioned by a *Radio Times* reporter about the forthcoming series, he said: 'This time we're moving closer to stand-alone stories. At this point, we're not planning any two-parters. So, every week is going to be like a different mad movie. We went quite "arc" last time, and we're going stand-alone this time around. But that doesn't mean that there aren't those things creeping in. You've got to find a way to make the last episode special, and by god that worked ratings-wise last year. We don't want to abandon that idea. Watch out for the title of episode two. I think that's a belter. It's one of my favourite titles ever.'

21 March brought a major announcement from the BBC, revealing the identity of the actress cast to take over as the Doctor's new regular companion following the exit of Amy and Rory: it was 25-year-old Jenna-Louise Coleman, previously best known as a regular in the ITV soap opera *Emmerdale* between 2005 and 2009. The BBC press notice quoted Steven Moffat as saying, 'It always seems impossible when you start casting these parts, but when we saw Matt and Jenna together, we knew we had our girl. She's funny and clever and exactly mad enough to step on board the TARDIS. It's not often the Doctor meets someone who can talk even faster than he does, but it's about to happen. Jenna is going to lead him his merriest dance yet. And that's all you're getting for now. Who she's playing, how the Doctor meets her, and even where he finds her, are all part of one of the biggest mysteries the Time Lord ever encounters. Even by the Doctor's standards, this isn't your usual boy meets girl.'

To mark the announcement, a photocall with Coleman and Moffat was held on the roof of BBC Broadcasting House in central London. Moffat confirmed in interviews that Amy and Rory would be exiting in Series Seven's fifth episode, in an encounter with the Weeping Angels, and that this would be the last to be transmitted in 2012, aside from the usual Christmas special; the remaining eight would be held over to 2013. He went on to say that there would be additional episodes in the fiftieth anniversary year, but gave no further details. Coleman herself was interviewed for BBC One's *One O'Clock News* bulletin, and described how she first found out she had won the role: 'I was in Marks and Spencer's holding an avocado, having the debate of what goes best in a salmon salad, when I got the call from my agent. It was kind of a bewildered excitement, confusion. "Really? Oh, goodness." All sorts of emotions. And I thought, after I'd hung up, "I really can't carry on shopping." So I just put the basket down and left Marks and Spencer's, and just went for a little walk to try to digest!'

As when previous companions had been cast, the whole process had been surrounded by tight secrecy. The actresses in contention had all been instructed to say that they were auditioning for a (fictitious) show called *Men on Waves* – an anagram of *Woman Seven*, alluding to the fact that the character would be debuting in Series Seven. Interviewed on BBC Radio Wales's Roy Noble show on 22 March, Matt Smith said: 'I was part of the audition process, where we met a number of wonderful actresses, but I think that Jenna responded to Steven's writing in the most interesting way. We're very excited to welcome her to the *Doctor Who* family. The Doctor needs a companion – he can't travel alone!'

On 23 March, BBC America released the first *Doctor Who* promotional photo of Coleman, showing her posing in front of the TARDIS police box.

Over the weekend of 24 and 25 March, the first official *Doctor Who* convention of the 21st Century was held at the Millennium Centre. Matt Smith, Karen Gillan and Arthur Darvill were amongst the stars guesting at the sold-out event, along with many behind-the-scenes contributors, including showrunner Steven Moffat, fellow executive producer Caroline Skinner and series producer Marcus Wilson. A press conference was held, which generated considerable media coverage. In their on-stage interviews, the three stars discussed their feelings about the departure of Amy and Rory, while Skinner told the audience that the pair's farewell story would feature sequences recorded on location in New York, USA. The assembled fans were also treated to the first Series Seven trailer – which on the morning of 26 March was also placed on the BBC website and the BBC America website. Opening with the caption 'Coming Soon', it ran for 1' 17" and featured a selection of dramatic clips from the series' first three episodes.[2]

A subject that had given rise to a few press reports during 2011 was the proposal to make a big-screen movie version of *Doctor Who*. This cropped up again on 30 March, when the Bleeding Cool website reported comments made by the movie's proposed director, David Yates, who said: 'Yes, I'm definitely doing a *Doctor Who* movie, but I think where everyone got confused [in 2011] was that we're not making it for five years, or six years – it's a very slow development. I've got projects backed up between now and about 2015, and it's something I'm very passionate and excited about.' Fans remained generally sceptical about the project, having seen many other *Doctor Who* movie proposals fall by the wayside over the years.

On 31 March, an exchange of banter between Steven Moffat and Arthur Darvill on Twitter culminated in Moffat releasing a photo taken during the previous day's studio recording, showing the Doctor and Amy

---

[2] At the time of writing, most of the trailers, promotional videos and similar items detailed in the early chapters of this book are still available to view, and can be found by searching on the BBC's official YouTube channel or elsewhere online.

posing with a cobweb-bedecked Dalek of the same design as the Emperor's guards in 'The Evil of the Daleks' (1967). This effectively broke the news that Series Seven's opening episode would mark the first ever appearance of classic-era-style Daleks in 21st Century *Doctor Who*. John Sheppard, a member of the Real SFX crew working on the special effects, also posted a number of comments on Twitter, including: 'Working late on *Doctor Who* tonight, it was interesting to see all original Daleks since 1960 in one episode.' In addition, eagle-eyed fans spotted from Sheppard's posts that, although *Doctor Who Confidential* had been cancelled, a crew was still recording behind-the-scenes material to be used instead in online video clips – which would also in most cases be included as extras on the show's DVD and Blu-ray releases.

Issue 466 of *Doctor Who Magazine*, published on 5 April, contained the first extensive interview with Jenna-Louise Coleman since the announcement of her casting as the new companion. This quoted her as saying: 'I know what my introduction is, and I have a general idea of where we're going to go. There's definitely a story arc. It sounds really interesting, really exciting. I don't think anything's been done like it before, but there are lots of secrets and intrigue, and I think it's going to throw and confuse a lot of people, and surprise a lot of people.' In his regular column for the magazine, Steven Moffat meanwhile described how he had approached the audition process.

The second week of April saw the *Doctor Who* team carrying out the previously-mentioned New York location recording for the last episode featuring Amy and Rory. Numerous photographs of the recording soon started to appear online, posted by fans who had gathered to watch the proceedings.

After a relatively quiet month for news, Issue 477 of *Doctor Who Magazine*, published on 3 May, brought a small flurry of further casting and behind-the-scenes announcements, and boosted excitement for the forthcoming series, and its first episode in particular, by sporting a special fold-out cover with a digitally-created image of numerous different types of Dalek assembled in the same setting. Inside the magazine, Steven Moffat promised, 'We're going to have the most Daleks we've had on screen ever – but they will be from every era, quite deliberately. We're calling them in from everywhere! All of them! Even the Special Weapons Dalek. They'll all be there …'

11 May marked the last day of recording for *Doctor Who* at Upper Boat Studios, prior to its move to BBC Roath Lock. The following day also had

a special significance as, following a final session of location recording, Karen Gillan and Arthur Darvill were given a farewell party, attended by Matt Smith and many of those involved in the series' production – although, in the event, the pair would have to make unscheduled returns for two further days' studio work in June.

On 19 May, Series Six made its debut on French television when the channel France 4 transmitted the first four episodes, along with the classic-era stories 'Inside the Spaceship' (1964) and 'Genesis of the Daleks' (1975) and numerous interviews with the show's stars and production team members, in a special 'Doctor Who Night' of programming.

On the same date, the Science Fiction and Fantasy Writers of America organisation named writer Neil Gaiman and director Richard Clark as winners of the Ray Bradbury Award for Outstanding Dramatic Presentation in the latest annual Nebula Awards, for their work on the Series Six episode 'The Doctor's Wife' (2011) – the first time Doctor Who had ever won one of these awards, although it had been nominated previously.

Also on 19 May, the Digital Spy website published an interview with Steven Moffat. Asked why the forthcoming series was starting much later in the year than usual, he replied: 'I think that decision actually came from the BBC. But I've been well up for anything that we can do to shake up the transmission pattern, the way we deliver it to the audience and how long we make the audience wait, simply because that makes Doctor Who an event piece. The more Doctor Who becomes a perennial, the faster it starts to die. You've got to shake it up, you've got to keep people on edge and wondering when it will come back. Sherlock is the prime example, as far as that goes. Sherlock almost exists on starving its audience. By the time it came back this year, Sherlock was like a rock star re-entering the building! So keeping Doctor Who as an event, and never making people feel, "Oh, it's lovely, reliable old Doctor Who – it'll be on about this time, at that time of year." Once you start to do that, just slowly, it becomes like any much-loved ornament in your house – ultimately invisible. And I don't want that ever to be the case.'

On 21 May, the official Doctor Who Twitter feed announced that Jenna-Louise Coleman had just completed her first read-through for the show, and two days later she was spotted recording on location at Plas Llanmihangel, Cowbridge, South Glamorgan. It would subsequently emerge, however, that she had in fact already secretly completed some studio recording for the series' first episode, 'Asylum of the Daleks', rather earlier than this.

23 May saw the release of *Doctor Who: The Eternity Clock*, a role playing video game, initially for the Sony PlayStation 3 system. This had been announced back in February, along with a trailer, with a March release date, but had been put back more than once for 'finishing touches', after attendees at the 24 and 25 March official *Doctor Who* convention in Cardiff had been given a first chance to try it out. The game involved players taking on the roles of the Doctor – voiced by Matt Smith – and River Song – voiced by Alex Kingston – as they travel through four different time periods in London and a number of other-worldly locations to save the Earth, and time itself, from monster races including Silurians, Cybermen, Daleks and the Silence. In order to be successful in the gameplay, which offered collaborative multiplayer capabilities, it was necessary to master the complexities of time travel – changes made in one time period would impact another, creating multiple possibilities and challenging players to solve puzzles across the centuries. Matt Smith was quoted as saying: 'I enjoyed working on the game … It's a bit like doing Automated Dialogue Replacement (ADR) for a television project, where you re-record some lines after filming. It's a technique I've used before and one that I enjoy. You've got to make the voiceover and the character on screen match somehow. Obviously you're not moving as you speak and so you've got to apply your voice to the movements of a motion-captured character, which can take a couple of attempts sometimes. But it's a rewarding challenge … Seeing yourself as a computerised character is one of those rare moments that only happens when you're involved in a show like *Doctor Who*.' After several months' further delay, a slightly enhanced version of the game would be extended to the PS Vita system on 10 October, and a PC version would be released on 15 November. It was originally envisaged as the first in a series, but no further titles would be forthcoming.

On 27 May, at BAFTA's annual television awards ceremony held at London's Royal Festival Hall, Steven Moffat was honoured with a special award, presented in the memory of acclaimed playwright Dennis Potter, in recognition of his outstanding creative writing contribution to television. Announcing this the previous week, Tim Corrie, Chairman of BAFTA, had said: 'Steven has had an outstanding year with *Doctor Who* and *Sherlock*, not to mention the feature film *The Adventures of Tintin*, and we are delighted to honour his contribution to television and the arts … He is one of the finest exponents of his craft and his award … is very well deserved indeed.' Russell T Davies had previously won the same award in 2005.

Matt Smith, Karen Gillan and Arthur Darvill were the presenters of a 2' 13" duration video released online by the BBC on 29 May, introducing the new BBC Roath Lock studios. This had been originally shown to visitors on the studios' opening tour, and focused on their role as *Doctor Who*'s new production base.

Meanwhile, questioned on BBC Radio 5 Live's Richard Bacon show about fans' concerns regarding the change in *Doctor Who*'s scheduling, Steven Moffat commented further on this issue: 'You're not getting shorter and shorter seasons; we're just splitting it over Christmas. We're making the same number of episodes as usual – I can tell by the grey hairs on my head – but we delayed it a few months to start it later in the year, that's all that's happened. There's no chance of the BBC giving up on *Doctor Who*. It's a huge money spinner, it's doing better than ever abroad, the global number of people watching *Doctor Who* has just gone up and up and up, it was the most downloaded show on American iTunes last year – not a chance of the BBC giving up on *Doctor Who*, not at all.'

As June began, reports continued to emerge from the ongoing location recording for the forthcoming series, with observant fans spotting that Jenna Louise-Coleman's character would be called Clara. The BBC meanwhile released a series of three official promotional photos of Coleman and Matt Smith together in costume, taken on location at the end of May at Margam Country Park in Margam, Port Talbot for the episode that would later be revealed to be called 'Hide'.

On 15 June, the second (and, to date, last) run of the Punchdrunk theatre company's acclaimed immersive *Doctor Who* production *The Crash of the Elysium* opened at the Ipswich Arts Festival. This was part of a summer-long programme of events nationwide celebrating the London 2012 Olympic Games. There were three types of ticket available – School (for pupils aged 4 to 7), Family (for children aged 7 to 12 accompanied by an adult) and After Dark (for those aged 13 and above) – and the run continued until 8 July.[3]

July saw further details emerging of the forthcoming series, including the titles of the second and third episodes: 'Dinosaurs on a Spaceship' and

---

[3] For further information about *The Crash of the Elysium*, which debuted in Salford in 2011, see the previous book in this series, *River's Run* (Telos Publishing, 2013).

'A Town Called Mercy'. Steven Moffat was quoted as saying: '"Dinosaurs on a Spaceship" – what more do you need? The Doctor will come face to face with some of the most monstrous creatures evolution has ever produced, on some of the most monstrous sets we've ever built. We took one look at Chris Chibnall's brilliant script and said to ourselves: "We're going to need a bigger corridor." And Toby Whithouse's "A Town Called Mercy" takes us into a genre *Doctor Who* hasn't attempted since the '60s – it's a full-blooded Western. We knew from the start we needed some serious location shooting for this one, and given the most iconic American setting imaginable, there was only one place to go – Spain.'

Over the weekend of 14 and 15 July, Matt Smith, Karen Gillan and Arthur Darvill appeared before huge crowds at the annual San Diego Comic-Con in California, USA. They were joined on the Sunday by Steven Moffat and Caroline Skinner for an Inside *Doctor Who* panel, teasing the audience of 6,500 fans with snippets of advance information about Series Seven and discussing a wide range of other topics related to the show.

On 16 July, the BBC's commercial arm, BBC Worldwide, published its latest annual report, for the financial year 2011/12. This listed both *Doctor Who* and the *Torchwood* spin-off as being amongst its most successful brands, with sales to over a hundred overseas markets. Series Six was reported to have helped win BBC America its highest ever ratings, and was also confirmed to be – as Steven Moffat had said in his radio interview a couple of days earlier – American iTunes' most downloaded television series during the year in question.

20 July saw the *Doctor Who Experience* attraction – essentially an exhibition of props and costumes from the show – open its doors for the first time in its new Cardiff venue, very close to the BBC Roath Lock studios. This had been in preparation ever since the 22 February closure of the original version at the Kensington Olympia Two venue in London, where it had been seen by close to a quarter of a million visitors in total. As before, the attraction opened with an interactive walk-through adventure featuring Matt Smith's Doctor and the Daleks, and continued with an exhibition area. Visitors then exited, predictably, via a gift shop.

Further confirming how popular *Doctor Who* was becoming in the USA, the 3 August edition of the 1.8 million-circulation American magazine *Entertainment Weekly*, published the week before its cover date, for the first time accorded the show its front cover photograph, with the headline 'Inside the Cult of *Doctor Who*' – although the accompanying article within the magazine questioned if it was even correct to use the term 'cult', arguing, 'It's not an obscure show anymore. It's not even a "British import". It's just *Doctor Who*.'

In its issue 450, published on 26 July, *Doctor Who Magazine* continued to ramp up anticipation for the start of the new series, with Steven Moffat revealing brief details of all 14 episodes – including the 2012 Christmas special – in the latest instalment of his regular column.

A week later, on 2 August, the BBC released a dramatic image created by digital artist Lee Binding, promoting 'Asylum of the Daleks'. This depicted a battered and bruised Doctor carrying an unconscious Amy in his arms through a fiery scene flanked by seven assembled Daleks of various designs, including the Special Weapons Dalek first seen in 'Remembrance of the Daleks' (1988).

There was further excitement for fans the following evening, as the first broadcast trailer for Series Seven went out on BBC One, and was also placed online. With a 1' 38" duration, this presented a dramatic selection of clips from the five episodes comprising the series' 2012 section – referred to informally as Series Seven A – and ended with a voice-over announcing that the show was returning 'this autumn', though no more precise timing was indicated.

On 4 August, as part of its own build-up to the start of the new series, BBC America gave a debut broadcast to a new, specially produced mini-documentary called *The Science of Doctor Who*. This ran for 44 minutes (in an hour-long slot with commercials), featured a selection of clips from the show, and had various scientists and entertainment personalities giving their views about how the technologies featured in the stories might have a practical application in the real world. This was followed a week later by another documentary in a similar format, this one titled *The Women of Doctor Who*.

As production of the 2012 Christmas special got under way in Cardiff, 6 August brought the announcement that its principal guest star was to be Richard E Grant, who had previously played versions of the Doctor in the 1999 *Comic Relief* skit 'The Curse of Fatal Death' and the 2003 webcast 'The Scream of the Shalka', and who was perhaps best known for appearing opposite eighth Doctor actor Paul McGann in the cult movie *Withnail and I* (1987).

On 9 August, the BBC announced the commissioning of a special BBC Two docu-drama entitled *An Adventure in Space and Time*, for transmission in 2013, recounting the story of *Doctor Who*'s creation fifty years earlier. The BBC's press release read, in part:

> Written by Mark Gatiss, it is executive-produced by current *Doctor Who* showrunner, Steven Moffat, and Caroline Skinner. The single drama was commissioned by Ben Stephenson, Controller, Drama, and Janice Hadlow, Controller of BBC Two.
>
> Mark Gatiss said: 'This is the story of how an unlikely set of brilliant people created a true television original. And how an actor – William Hartnell – stereotyped in hard-man roles became a hero to millions of children. I've wanted to tell this story for more years than I can remember! To make it happen for *Doctor Who*'s fiftieth birthday is quite simply a dream come true.'
>
> Steven Moffat, executive producer, said: 'The story of *Doctor Who* is the story of television – so it's fitting in the anniversary year that we make our most important journey back in time to see how the TARDIS was launched.'

14 August marked a significant development, as 'Asylum of the Daleks' received its premiere screening that evening, to an audience at the British Film Institute's Southbank venue in London. After the episode, BBC Radio 5 Live's Richard Bacon chaired a question-and-answer session with Steven Moffat, Caroline Skinner, Matt Smith, Karen Gillan and Arthur Darvill. A few hours earlier, Moffat had made another appearance on Bacon's afternoon radio show, where he had revealed that in 2013 there would be a special episode broadcast on *Doctor Who*'s fiftieth anniversary date, 23 November. Meanwhile, the titles of the fourth and fifth episodes of the forthcoming series had now been revealed to be 'The Power of Three' and 'The Angels Take Manhattan'.

To coincide with the premiere, the BBC released several further publicity photos from Series Seven's first three episodes, along with an 'Asylum of the Daleks' promotional image in the format of a movie poster. Similar movie poster-type images would in due course be released for all of the other 2012 and 2013 episodes, reflecting the previously-trailed idea that these would be made in the style of mini blockbuster movies.

15 August also saw the BBC publish, primarily for press use, a brief synopsis for each of the first three episodes – a standard part of their publicity effort for forthcoming programmes. Again, similar synopses

would be published for all of the subsequent episodes.

On 17 August, a further BBC press release presented extensive interview quotes from Steven Moffat, Matt Smith, Karen Gillan and Arthur Darvill. Questioned about why he had chosen to kick off Series Seven with a Dalek-filled episode, Moffat explained: 'We've been off the air for longer than usual, so it was an easy decision to come back with *Doctor Who* at its most iconic, and that means Daleks. Lots and lots of scary Daleks. There have been many monsters to face the Doctor over the years, but only one that can sum up the whole series just by being there. Also, it's my first go at writing for them. I *love* the Daleks, and I've held off till now. But I had what I thought was a good idea, and couldn't resist any longer!' Asked if he had a favourite design amongst the Daleks, Smith said, 'Absolutely! The blue and white ones from the 1960s, I think they are from the Troughton era ... They are just kind of groovy, smaller but fantastic. And the lovely Barnaby [Edwards] who operates them. The day we [recorded] with all of those Daleks, there was such an excitable atmosphere on set from cast and crew alike. It was a brilliant few days at work!'

A new teaser trailer for 'Asylum of the Daleks' was released by the BBC on 18 August. With a 20" duration, this featured a sequence of clips of a huge assembly of Daleks chanting 'Save the Daleks!'

20 August brought the eagerly anticipated announcement that the new series would begin its on-air run on 1 September – not only in the UK but also in the USA and Canada. To coincide with the announcement, BBC America released its own exclusive, 1' 01" duration trailer. This was made up of clips from the first five episodes, with a voice-over narration that described *Doctor Who* as 'the global phenomenon'.

A further preview screening of 'Asylum of the Daleks' took place on at the MediaGuardian Edinburgh International Television Festival, which ran from 23 to 25 August. In a question-and-answer session chaired by writer and broadcaster Andrew Collins, Steven Moffat elaborated on his intentions for the style of the forthcoming series: 'I've abandoned fairground rides for movie posters. When we had the pitch meetings for the various stories, I would say, "Tell me the movie poster. Tell me the title, what's on the poster and what's the log-line ... Let's have a blockbuster every single week. No two-parters; every single week is going to be a blockbuster, and let's not have the cheap episode, let's just make them all huge." It has caused some problems, but I think it has worked really well for us. It's the year of the blockbuster.'

On 25 August, 'Asylum of the Daleks' was seen for the first time in the USA, as BBC America hosted its own preview screening at New York's Ziegfeld Theater. The 800 tickets for this had sold out within twenty minutes when placed on sale on 17 August. As with the UK previews, the screening was followed by a question-and-answer session, this one with Caroline Skinner, Matt Smith and Karen Gillan, chaired by Nerdist podcast host Chris Hardwick. Smith and Gillan arrived for the event in a deLorean car similar to that famous for featuring in the movie *Back to the Future* (1985).

Also on 25 August, the BBC unveiled its own full, 40" duration trailer for the Dalek episode.

Released on the BBC website on 27 August was the first of five bonus minisodes making up a story called 'Pond Life'. The subsequent instalments would be made available on a daily basis, and on 1 September – the same day as 'Asylum of the Daleks' went out on BBC One – an omnibus version compiling all five would be broadcast on the BBC Red Button service. In publicity material published the previous week, the story's writer Chris Chibnall was quoted as saying: '"Pond Life" provides us with a lovely opportunity to catch up with Amy and Rory since we saw them at the end of the last series. It opens with the Ponds at home and gives us an insight in to just what happens when the Doctor drops in and out of their lives. Travelling with the Doctor is one of the greatest things you can do, but it's fun to spend a few moments looking at the chaos he can also bring.' Caroline Skinner added: 'Chris has written a beautiful, heartfelt and wickedly funny piece about the adventures the Ponds have been having with the Doctor since we last saw them on screen. It's not long till the series itself will be back with a vengeance – but in the meantime, "Pond Life" is a truly heart-warming piece about our best-loved companions and their madcap relationship with their raggedy Doctor.'[4]

Published on 28 August, the *Radio Times* edition for the week of 1 to 7 September boasted a *Doctor Who* cover, picturing the Doctor, Amy and Rory with two Daleks against a background of explosions, with the headline 'Who's Back!'. Inside, the magazine presented interviews with the three stars, along with a Steven Moffat episode guide and a Dalek wallchart. Other television listings magazines also carried prominent

---

[4] For further details of 'Pond Life', see the relevant entry in the 'Episode Guide' section below.

Doctor Who features.

Two days later, when Issue 451 of *Doctor Who Magazine* hit newsagents' shelves, it offered a choice of three different covers: one promoting each of Series Seven's first three episodes.

The same morning, *Doctor Who* received coverage both on BBC One's *Breakfast* programme and on ITV1's rival *Daybreak*. The former consisted of a 2′ 19″ report by entertainment correspondent Lizo Mzimba, including clips from the forthcoming episodes plus interviews with Matt Smith and Karen Gillan. The ITV1 piece, presented by television reviewer Richard Arnold, likewise saw him talking to Smith and Gillan about the forthcoming series, with Smith confirming that he would be continuing as the Doctor for the fiftieth anniversary year.

30 August also saw the BBC make available the movie poster-style promotional images for the remaining 2012 episodes, to accompany the one for 'Asylum of the Daleks' released a couple of weeks previously.

As excitement reached fever pitch, on 31 August the blastr website published an interview with Arthur Darvill in which he revealed his feelings about leaving *Doctor Who*: 'It does feel like the right time to move on. The worst thing you can do is outstay your welcome on something like this. We've had such a good run and such good stories, but the whole programme is about change. It's about things changing and evolving. So it's sad to leave, but it feels like the right thing to do … It's one of the best things I've ever done in my life. I think people, when they leave a show, they can kind of separate themselves from what they've done. But I'll always be proud of the work that I've done on *Doctor Who*. I've learned so much doing it and had such an amazing time doing it. It's given me such a great start in everything. I still feel fairly early on in my career, and it's a really good foundation'

Karen Gillan meanwhile made a guest appearance on the 31 August edition of BBC One's early evening magazine programme *The One Show*. On giving up the role of Amy, she said: 'Putting my feelings and emotions about it to the side, the most important thing to me is the show and the character, and I just wanted her to leave at the right time and to have maximum impact, and not outstay my welcome. Arthur and I have been the longest companions of the new series now so it's not as if it is happening prematurely. It just kind of feels right.' Recalling the recording of her final scene (prior to the days when she returned for pick-up shots), she said: 'It was weirdly serene, actually. Everyone was really feeling it, and then the last scene was the three of us walking into the TARDIS – this isn't the actual last scene – and we were all in the darkness, and then we all just started hugging, and it was this really weird moment. And then I cried a lot … probably [for] two weeks, actually, in total!' The actress also revealed that, at the end of her and Arthur Darvill's leaving party on the same day, everyone ended up in *Torchwood* star John Barrowman's flat!

The 1 September edition of the *Daily Mirror* newspaper carried a *Doctor Who* item with the sensationalist headline 'I Quit!', suggesting that Matt Smith had decided to leave the show. However, the accompanying article on page three made clear that the actor was under contract until November 2013, and quoted an unnamed 'source' as saying: 'Next year is the fiftieth anniversary, so it seems right to have a regeneration. Matt is a brilliant Doctor, so we will keep him for the run, but a Christmas regeneration would be incredible and guarantee huge ratings.'

The BBC meanwhile released online a short video in which Matt Smith, Karen Gillan and Arthur Darvill introduced 'Asylum of the Daleks' via on-camera interviews combined with various clips. Similar videos would later be made available for each of the other 2012 episodes. In addition, Amazon Instant Video and iTunes Store subscribers were able to access an exclusive 'Asylum of the Daleks' prequel video, the synopsis for which read: 'The Doctor receives a message from a mysterious hooded stranger – a woman called Darla Von Karlsen wants to meet him.'[5]

Finally, at 7.22 pm on 1 September, over eight months since the 2011 Christmas special 'The Doctor, the Widow and the Wardrobe' was transmitted, and a full 11 months since 'The Wedding of River Song' brought Series Six to an end, the long wait for a new run of *Doctor Who* came to an end, as 'Asylum of the Daleks' made its highly-anticipated BBC One debut.

---

[5] For further details, see the relevant entry in the 'Episode Guide' section below.

Chapter Two
Series Seven – Part One

Immediately after the transmission of 'Asylum of the Daleks', the BBC released online the first of the weekly behind-the-scenes featurettes that would accompany this series' episodes, as a replacement of sorts for the much more substantial *Doctor Who Confidential* programmes broadcast in previous years. Entitled 'Life Cycle of a Dalek', it had a 3' 34" duration[6] and focused, naturally, on the on-screen presentation of the Daleks – featuring far more shots of the classic-era versions than seen in 'Asylum of the Daleks' itself! Also made available was a 30" long trailer for the next episode, 'Dinosaurs on a Spaceship'.

The following day, as the BBC released some promotional images of Jenna-Louise Coleman in her surprise 'Asylum of the Daleks' appearance as Oswin Oswald, aka 'Soufflé Girl', overnight figures showed that a healthy 6.4 million British viewers had tuned in to watch the episode live. Press and media reviews of the episode also started to appear – not only in the UK but overseas too – and others followed on 3 September. The overall reaction was overwhelmingly positive, with many commenting on Coleman's unexpected early debut. In Australia, the episode was reported to have set a new record of 75,900 plays on the ABC's iView internet television service; it would not actually be transmitted by the ABC until 8 September. The viewing figures had also been exceptionally good in both the US and Canada, as revealed in press releases from broadcasters BBC America and Space respectively. BBC America said:

---

[6] The durations given here and in subsequent chapters are generally a few seconds shorter than those of the versions of the behind-the-scenes featurettes commercially released on *The Complete Seventh Series* DVD and Blu-ray box set (where applicable). This is due to the fact that the latter generally had longer blank lead-ins and lead-outs. The actual programme content was unchanged.

[The episode] delivered the channel's highest-rated, most-watched telecast ever in Live + Same Day. *Doctor Who* delivered 1.555 million viewers and 723,000 A25-54. The series ranked #1 in cable, excluding sports, among A25-54 in the Saturday 9.00 pm to 10.00 pm time slot. The *Doctor Who* premiere and the third episode of BBC America's first original series *Copper* helped BBC America achieve its highest-rated weekend ever.

Space's press release read in part:

He did it again! The Season Seven premiere of *Doctor Who* drew an earth-shattering 620,000 viewers, making it the second-highest rated episode in series history on Space and the most-watched programme on Canadian television in its timeslot Saturday night. Featuring zombies, break-ups, make-ups, and more Daleks than you can shake a sonic screwdriver at, 'Asylum of the Daleks' made Space the #1 network – conventional or speciality – Saturday night at 9.00 pm ET with total viewers and in the key demos A25-54 and A18-49. Peaking with 746,000 viewers, in all 1.1 million Canadians watched some or all of the episode.

2 September meanwhile brought the news that the Series Six episode 'The Doctor's Wife' had picked up another award; this one, a Hugo in the Best Dramatic Presentation, Short Form category for 2015, other nominees for which had included Tom McCrae's 'The Girl Who Waited' and Steven Moffat's 'A Good Man Goes to War'. The presentation ceremony took place at Chicon 7, the seventieth World Science Fiction Convention, held at the Hyatt Regency hotel in Chicago, and in accepting his award – *Doctor Who*'s sixth Hugo overall – writer Neil Gaiman revealed that he was currently working on the third draft of another script for the show.

On 6 September, the BBC released online two preview clips from the following Saturday's episode, 'Dinosaurs on a Spaceship'. Entitled 'The Doctor and Nefertiti' and 'Meet Riddell!', these ran for 37″ and 38″ respectively. Similar brief extracts from subsequent episodes would be released on a weekly basis thereafter.

On 8 September, following transmission of 'Dinosaurs on a Spaceship', the accompanying behind-the-scenes video went online. With a 4′ 12″ duration, this one was called 'Raptors, Robots and a Bumpy Ride'. The BBC also made available a gallery of production design artwork for the episode, and two galleries of storyboards for key action sequences. Again, press reaction to the episode was largely positive. Dan Martin of the *Guardian* commented, 'Well, that was fun, wasn't it? The only way this could have been more of a riot is if Samuel L Jackson had turned up … Yes, it was flimsy and, yes, it was pretty much a story built around a title. The producers have admitted as much. But second episodes are supposed to be fun – and you only have to think back to "The Curse of the Black Spot" to realise that this is the finest episode two from *Doctor Who* in some time.'

'Asylum of the Daleks' meanwhile received its debut Australian transmission. Ratings were good: the episode averaged 549,000 viewers in the five major capital cities and, despite being up against popular football finals, was the highest-rated drama of the day, and the eighth highest-rated programme of the day overall.

On 10 September, in an interview published on the *SFX* magazine website, writer Toby Whithouse explained that it was Steven Moffat who had come up with the Western theme for the following Saturday's episode, 'A Town Called Mercy'. The writer added, 'He said he wanted to do a Wild West episode because this year, certainly for the first half of the series, it's these big kind of movie marquee ideas. The pitch he gave was just, "There's a town that is being terrorised by some kind of robot." I thought about what it was in the town that the robot wants. What if it's a person? Then the idea kind of fell out from there.'

Also on 10 September, *Doctor Who* was honoured again when, for the third year running, it won the Best Family Drama category in the annual *TV Choice* Awards, voted for by the listings magazine's readers. Steven Moffat attended the ceremony to accept on the show's behalf.

13 September saw 'Asylum of the Daleks' kick off New Zealand broadcaster Prime's Series Seven screenings, reportedly gaining 171,690 viewers – making it the highest-rated programme of the day on the channel, and the second highest-rated eleventh Doctor episode after the 2011 Christmas special, 'The Doctor, the Widow and the Wardrobe'.

Following the 15 September transmission of 'A Town Called Mercy', the latest online behind-the-scenes featurette, 'Wild, Wild … Spain?', had a 4' 11" duration and focused on the location recording carried out in Spain.

Matt Smith was amongst the guests on the 21 September edition of Channel 4's *Alan Carr: Chatty Man* evening chat show, in an appearance recorded three days earlier. *Doctor Who* was naturally a main topic of discussion, with Carr raising the old question of whether or not the Doctor would ever be played by a woman.

22 September saw the transmission of 'The Power of Three'. This week's accompanying behind-the-scenes featurette, released online immediately afterwards, had the shortest duration yet, at 3' 06". Entitled 'A Writer's Tale', it was introduced by Chris Chibnall and focused mainly on the episode's scripting. Chibnall had also been the subject of an interview published a few days earlier on the *SFX* magazine website, where he had given his perspective on the story: 'It's *Doctor Who* from Amy and Rory's point of view. We're in the last days of the Ponds, as everybody keeps saying, and it was really a chance to see where they've got to in their lives since "The Eleventh Hour" [2010], and to see what it's like to be them ... They're living at home, and the Doctor pops in and goes, "Shall we go somewhere?", and they're off. That's very new, because they're not permanently with him, and I wanted to see what that would mean. I think it's very different from pretty much any other episode of *Doctor Who* ever, which is both wonderful and terrifying.'

On the evening of 26 September, the mid-series finale, 'The Angels Take Manhattan', received a preview screening arranged by BAFTA Cymru at Cineworld in Mary Ann Street, Cardiff. As usual with such screenings, a question-and-answer session followed, this one chaired by broadcaster Matthew Sweet – a long-time *Doctor Who* fan, who had previously contributed to several extras on the show's DVD range and written a number of the Big Finish audio dramas – with a the panel consisting of Steven Moffat, fellow executive producer Caroline Skinner, director Nick Hurran (standing in for the originally-advertised series producer Marcus Wilson) and production designer Michael Pickwoad. Moffat – who had recently been ranked at 87 in the MediaGuardian's annual list of the 100 most powerful figures in UK media, up from 92 the previous year – was subsequently quoted as saying: 'After showing Amelia Pond in the garden as a young girl in "The Eleventh Hour", Karen [Gillan]'s first episode, the final shot in ... "The Angels Take Manhattan" is a punchline I have been waiting to tell for two and a half years. This weekend's episode is more devastating for the Doctor. At certain points he becomes useless and emotional. It was torment and hell trying to write the episode. I struggled for ages to work out a fitting ending and changed my mind until I finally got it right. I must have rewritten it twenty odd times. I kept changing my mind about the exact way they'd leave. Alive or dead? One or both of them? Their fates kept changing every five minutes until I hit on what I thought was right. Hopefully, there are scares *and* emotion.'

In the US, Karen Gillan made a guest appearance on the 27 September edition of the TBS network's *Conan* chat show – but, proving that she had well and truly moved on from *Doctor Who* now, her role as Amy was not even mentioned.

In addition to the usual trailer, preview and introductory clips released by the BBC, BBC America made available its own online interview teasers for 'The Angels Take Manhattan': a 2' 08" 'sneak peak' titled 'Weeping Angels in Central Park!' and a 58" snippet called 'Karen Gillan on Rory: the Stud?!' Immediately before its 29 September transmission of 'The Angels Take Manhattan', BBC America also repeated the exclusive *Doctor Who* mini-documentary *Doctor Who in America*, originally shown after the previous year's episode 'Day of the Moon'. This time it went out under the slightly revised title *Doctor Who in the U.S.*

Straight after that evening's UK transmission of 'The Angels Take Manhattan', the BBC placed online a video with the rather cumbersome title-cum-descriptor 'The *Doctor Who* Team on Angels and What's in Store for the Doctor ...' Lasting 4' 29", this consisted of extracts from the panel discussion at the recent BAFTA preview screening in Cardiff, and came in addition to the usual behind-the-scenes video – which on this occasion was released two days later, on 1 October, under the title 'A Fall With Grace', with a 4' 09" duration. Also made available on the evening of 29 September were small galleries of production artwork – five images in total – and behind-the-scene photographs – only four. By far the most substantial online accompaniment to the episode, however, was a mini-documentary, of 11' 45" duration, called 'The Last Days of the Ponds'. This presented an emotional look back at the history of Amy and Rory, and featured interview contributions from Matt Smith, Karen Gillan and Arthur Darvill, sharing their memories of working together and of recording their final scenes.[7]

The whole of the 2012 section of Series Seven had been transmitted within the single month of September, and – as had been the case the previous year, with the first section of Series Six, the only other series to have been split in this way – it seemed to fans that no sooner had *Doctor Who* returned to their screens than it had gone away again ...

---

[7] Unlike the usual weekly behind-the-scenes clips and 'The Last Days of the Ponds', 'The *Doctor Who* Team on Angels and What's in Store for the Doctor ...' was not subsequently included as an extra on *The Complete Seventh Series* DVD and Blu-ray box set.

Chapter Three
The Snowmen Cometh

As the mid-series finale, not to mention the final appearance of two very popular companion characters, 'The Angels Take Manhattan' was the subject of an even greater number of media reviews than most *Doctor Who* episodes. This time, though, the reaction was rather more mixed than usual. Maureen Ryan writing for the *Huffington Post* expressed some typical reservations:

> I wish I had liked [it] more than I did, but there was a lot of throat-clearing before we got to the meat of the story. We met a couple of characters (the rich guy and the hard-boiled detective) who didn't matter in the end, and River simply took up too much space, plot-wise and emotionally. She got in the way. And normally, I love film noir, but the big and operatic tone the director was clearly going for clashed with the mood of film noir, which is all about bittersweet cynicism. The scene in Central Park was fun, but it felt like it was from a different episode. 'Angels' simply didn't cohere.
>
> Part of the reason the episode didn't fully work for me was because I dislike the kind of timey-wimey machinations on display here. It's just a personal dislike; I'm willing to concede that others may not share it (and yes, I get that this kind of thing is somewhat baked into the premise). The detective novel, the Angels, the apartment building, the clues – I more or less understand how all that worked, but the episode featured yet another Moffat-style house-of-mirrors plot that buried the emotional beats in time math. Trying to figure out how it all worked and what it all meant stopped me from being able to fully bask in the Ponds' exit.

On 30 September, *Doctor Who* picked up another award, this one a BAFTA Cymru for 'The Gunpowder Plot' (2011), one of *The Doctor Who Adventure Games* series of online adventures. However, both *Doctor Who* itself and its spin-off *The Sarah Jane Adventures* lost out in the categories in which they had been nominated.

With recording of the 2013 episodes getting under way on 8 October, the next couple of months saw the appearance of the usual spate of guest casting and behind-the-scenes announcements and fan location reports. One of the few other developments of any note came on 12 October, when the BBC released online a largely animated minisode entitled 'P.S.', which served as a kind of coda to 'The Angels Take Manhattan'. Caroline Skinner was quoted as saying: 'We're delighted we can present this lovely scene written by Chris Chibnall. People took Rory's dad, Brian, to their hearts very quickly, so it's fitting we can give the character a degree of closure in this poignant piece.'[8]

On the same date, Skinner's fellow executive producer, showrunner Steven Moffat, joined Matt Smith at the *Doctor Who Experience* venue, where they both had their hand prints preserved in cement, to go on display there. This coincided with the unveiling of several other new exhibits, consisting mainly of props and costumes from the recently-concluded run of episodes.

Matt Smith took a further break from recording on 26 October, when he and Caroline Skinner appeared at the MCM London Comic-Con. This was partly in order to promote the *Series 7 Part 1* DVD and Blu-ray box set, advance copies of which were made available for a signing session at the event, three days ahead of the official release date. The half-hour panel interview given by Smith and Skinner was streamed live, and on 9 November made available to view in two parts on the BBC's YouTube channel.

On 7 November, the BBC announced that an old foe of the Doctor's would be featuring in one of the forthcoming episodes. Their press release read, in part:

> We can confirm that the Cybermen will be menacing the universe once again when *Doctor Who* returns for a run of eight epic episodes in spring 2013. The iconic enemies will feature in an adventure directed by Stephen Woolfenden and written by the

---

[8] For further details, see the relevant entry in the 'Episode Guide' section below.

acclaimed Neil Gaiman whose previous episode was the Hugo Award-winning 'The Doctor's Wife'.

Starring Matt Smith as the Doctor and Jenna-Louise Coleman as the new companion, the episode co-stars Warwick Davis (*Life's Too Short* and *Harry Potter*), Tamzin Outhwaite (*EastEnders* and *Hotel Babylon*) and Jason Watkins (*Being Human* and *Lark Rise to Candleford*) as a band of misfits on a mysterious planet …

Steven Moffat, lead writer and executive producer, told us, 'Cybermen were always the monsters that scared me the most! Not just because they were an awesome military force, but because sometimes they could be sleek and silver and right behind you without you even knowing.' He added, 'And with one of the all-time classic monsters returning, and a script from one of our finest novelists, it's no surprise we have attracted such stellar names as Tamzin, Jason and Warwick.'

At the Writers' Guild of Great Britain Awards on 14 November, Steven Moffat picked up the Special Award for Outstanding Writing – although for his role as part of the scripting team on *Sherlock* rather than on *Doctor Who*. *The Sarah Jane Adventures* also picked up the Best Children's TV Script award for Phil Ford's 'The Curse of Clyde Langer' (2011).

On 16 November, the BBC's annual *Children in Need* charity telethon as usual featured a *Doctor Who* item: in this case, 'The Great Detective', a prequel to the forthcoming Christmas special, the title of which was announced here to be 'The Snowmen'. A short trailer for the special was shown an hour later, when it was seen by 8.6 million viewers – out-rating that evening's episode of *Coronation Street* opposite it on ITV1.[9]

The following day, BBC America stole something of a march on the BBC, putting out a full press release about the Christmas special. This read in part:

A new companion, a new look for the Doctor, plus a new monster will all be introduced in this movie-scale episode. Starring Matt Smith as the Doctor and introducing Jenna-Louise Coleman as new companion Clara, 'The Snowmen' follows their adventures as they embark on a mission to save Christmas from the

---

[9] See the entry on 'The Snowmen' in the 'Episode Guide' section below for further information on 'The Great Detective'.

villainous Dr Simeon (Richard E Grant, *The Iron Lady*, *Dracula*) and his army of icy snowmen. This year's *Doctor Who* Christmas special premieres Tuesday 25 December, 9.00 pm ET/PT on BBC America ...

Steven Moffat, lead writer and executive producer, said: 'The Doctor at Christmas is one of my favourite things – but this year it's different. He's lost Amy and Rory to the Weeping Angels, and he's not in a good place: in fact, he's Scrooge. He's withdrawn from the world and no longer cares what happens to it. So when all of humanity hangs in the balance, can anyone persuade a tired and heartbroken Doctor that it's time to return to the good fight? Enter Jenna-Louise Coleman ...'

Matt Smith ... commented: 'For this year's Christmas special we have the wonderfully villainous Richard E Grant as Dr Simeon. As well as lizards, Victorian assassins and deranged warriors from the future, who all return to convince the Doctor that he should board the TARDIS again and save the world. Add to that Jenna-Louise Coleman and so begins the Christmas Special 2012. I hope everyone enjoys it!'

The ABC meanwhile made known this week that the Australian premiere of 'The Snowmen' would come on Boxing Day – a day behind the UK, the US and Canada. It would later be announced that Prime in New Zealand would also give the special a Boxing Day slot.

On 27 November, the BBC released a promotional image for 'The Snowmen' in the same movie poster style as those it had previously put out for the Series Seven episodes, plus a screen-shot of a group of the Snowmen themselves, complete with shark-like pointed teeth and snarling expressions. The same evening, BBC One broadcast its first trailer for its Christmas programming line-up, with an 'It's Showtime!' theme, including a number of very brief clips from the *Doctor Who* special.

1 December saw the BBC's official *Doctor Who* website launch its by now traditional Adventure Calendar feature, in which each day would see a different treat made available for the show's fans. The first of these this year was a 2' 20" duration video in which Jenna-Louise Coleman described how she had won the role of Clara, accompanied by clips illustrating her debut appearance as Oswin in 'Asylum of the Daleks' and giving a tantalising foretaste of 'The Snowmen'. A second instalment of

this interview would be presented as the 7 December treat.

The *Radio Times* edition for the week of 8 to 14 December, which started to appear in shops at the beginning of the month, continued another tradition by giving over its front cover to the *Doctor Who* special. The Doctor was pictured in the same Victorian garb as seen in 'The Great Detective' prequel, standing next to Clara in front of a snow-laden Christmas tree. The accompanying feature inside the magazine previewed 'The Snowmen', along with the BBC's other main family programming for the festive season. Matt Smith was quoted as saying, 'I've got a whole new Christmassy outfit and the best hat! A bit Artful Dodger meets the Doctor. There's a lot of purple this year, which is nice. I've always wanted something purple, but they were always reluctant. It's taken three years to get a jaunty hat and a purple coat!' Questioned about the connection between Clara and Oswin, Jenna-Louise Coleman commented: 'The connection is that it's me playing both. I'm not Oswin: I'm a different person who looks and sounds like Oswin.'

In the US, the similarly iconic *TV Guide* listings magazine also devoted the cover of its 10 to 23 December double issue to *Doctor Who*, favouring an image of Matt Smith in his original eleventh Doctor costume complete with tweed jacket. This was the first time *Doctor Who* had ever graced the magazine's cover, and was the result of it having won a poll in which readers had been asked to choose which of ten cult shows they would most like to see featured – the other nine all being American productions. This cover would later be voted the magazine's best of 2012.

On 5 December, BBC One's Christmas Day schedule was announced, revealing that 'The Snowmen' would go out in an unusually early 5.15 slot.

6 December saw the unveiling of both a teaser and, given a debut broadcast just before that evening's edition of *EastEnders*, a first 'episode' in BBC One's ongoing series of 'It's Showtime!' trailers. Instead of presenting programme clips, these were specially shot, with a storyline in which comic actor Rob Brydon supposedly took on the job of producing the BBC's Christmas programming, assisted by actress Sarah Alexander and meeting along the way various celebrities who would be featuring in shows over the festive season. This first episode included a brief sequence of comedian Brendan O'Carroll, in his Mrs Brown persona from the hit series *Mrs Brown's Boys*, mistaking the TARDIS police box for a dressing room and getting whisked off into time and space. A further video in this campaign was released two days later, this one involving viewers being

wished a merry Christmas by various celebrities – including Matt Smith, in his Victorian-style costume from 'The Snowmen', standing in front of the police box. Signs reading 'Light Up Christmas With BBC One 11/12/2012' were also shown, advertising the fact that 11 December was to be a day of further promotion for the BBC's festive fare.

8 December also saw the BBC giving further publicity specifically to 'The Snowmen', releasing a full press pack including interviews with Steven Moffat, Matt Smith, Jenna-Louise Coleman and guest stars Richard E Grant and Tom Ward. Moffat was quoted as saying: 'The Christmas episode is *Doctor Who*, only more so, and this year we're going for more epic. The Doctor, when we meet him, isn't in a good place. A bit like when we first encountered William Hartnell as the Doctor in 1963 – or indeed Christopher Eccleston in 2005 – this is a cold and withdrawn Time Lord, wanting no part of the world around him. It's going to take a lot of Christmas spirit to get him back out of those TARDIS doors.' Asked how she was finding her time in *Doctor Who* so far, Coleman replied: 'Every day is really surprising. For the last two years, I have mainly been doing period dramas, so to be thrown into this world with loads of CGI is very different. Whole new sets are built in the space of a couple of weeks. For this episode, we had snow machines, and it does make you feel like a big kid!'

Also issued on 8 December were a number of further images from the special, including one showing part of a redesigned TARDIS interior, the accompanying press release for which read:

> The BBC's *Doctor Who* has revealed a sneak peek at a brand new TARDIS that will debut in this year's Christmas special, 'The Snowmen'. The second TARDIS for Matt Smith, it will be the first TARDIS for new companion Clara (Jenna-Louise Coleman), who makes her entrance on Christmas Day at 5.15pm on BBC One.
>
> The new set was designed by Michael Pickwoad, the show's production designer, and will be home to the Doctor and Clara as they travel through space and time when the adventure continues in spring 2013 with eight epic episodes.

Meanwhile, a *Radio Times* preview of 'The Snowmen', which went online on this date, revealed another impressive guest star name, reporting that the distinguished Ian McKellen would be lending his vocal talents to the special.

10 December's treat in the official *Doctor Who* website's Adventure Calendar feature was a short video interview with Richard E Grant, incorporating various preview clips from 'The Snowmen', and the following day's was a similar interview with Dan Starkey, who would be reprising his role as the Sontaran Strax from the previous year's episode 'A Good Man Goes to War'.

As foreshadowed by the 'Light Up Christmas' signs the previous week, 11 December was a significant date in BBC One's 'It's Showtime!' promotional campaign. During that day's edition of the early evening magazine programme *The One Show*, a special light-show sequence of images relating to the BBC's Christmas programming was projected onto the side of Television Centre, including a virtual TARDIS apparently breaking its way out of the building. This was unfortunately slightly marred by the weather during the programme's live transmission, as Television Centre was shrouded in mist at the time, but the BBC later uploaded to its YouTube channel a clearer version recorded during rehearsals. The programme was immediately followed by a second 'episode' in the 'It's Showtime!' running story, this one featuring Matt Smith as the Doctor being chased by comedienne Miranda Hart with a sprig of mistletoe, and ending with Mrs Brown reappearing in the TARDIS and telling a worried Rob Brydon, 'Relax, I've just been to the future – it all turns out fine, Rob!' The opening section of this, with Smith and Hart, would also be broadcast as a separate, shorter trailer several times over the coming days.

The Christmas double issue of *Radio Times*, which went on sale around this time, presented interviews with Matt Smith and Jenna-Louise Coleman. Asked about the influences on his portrayal of the Doctor, Smith gave the revealing response: 'When I started as the Doctor I watched loads of [1970s BBC sitcom] *Some Mothers Do 'Ave 'Em*, loads of Peter Sellers and loads of [1980s BBC sitcom] *Blackadder* – and somewhere betwixt the three lies my Doctor. I love how grumpy but brilliant Blackadder can be. Frank Spencer [in *Some Mothers Do 'Ave 'Em*] is slightly unaware of how ridiculous he is and I think the Doctor is too. [Sellers' character] Clouseau and Blackadder have massive egos and the Doctor has a massive ego. Frank Spencer is kinder and gentler.'

On 12 December, a full, 37″ duration trailer for 'The Snowmen' debuted on BBC One, and also featured as that day's Adventure Calendar treat. A few days later, BBC America began broadcasting two trailers of its own; each having a 30″ duration, these featured a different selection of clips from the BBC's.

Published on 13 December, Issue 455 of *Doctor Who Magazine* was a bumper 100-page edition presenting, amongst other things, an extensive preview of 'The Snowmen'. It also revealed that the second section of Series Seven would begin transmission in April 2013, though no exact date was specified.

15 December saw *Doctor Who – A Symphonic Spectacular* return to Australia, this time presented at the iconic Sydney Opera House with Ben Foster conducting the Metropolitan Orchestra. Six further performances followed, on 16, 18, 19, 20 (matinee and evening) and 21 December. The presenters on this occasion were Alex Kingston, known to *Doctor Who* fans as the Doctor's wife River Song, and Mark Williams, who had been introduced as Rory's dad Brian in 'The Power of Three'; and, as usual, the auditorium was invaded by various monster-costumed extras during the course of the show. On 17 December, the Sydney Opera House promoted the event with its own YouTube video, featuring Kingston, Williams and composer Murray Gold; and on 19 December, that evening's performance was attended by special guest Dudley Simpson, who had been responsible for many *Doctor Who* scores during the 1960s and 1970s.

Meanwhile, back in the UK, the BBC revealed on 17 December that 'The Snowmen' would mark the debut of a new Murray Gold theme music arrangement, plus new opening and closing title sequences. The announcement read:

> We can't give too much away about the new-look titles except to say they are wonderfully dramatic and striking, with a couple of unexpected touches. In short, they're a perfect way to welcome back the Doctor!
>
> And fans of the famous *Doctor Who* theme tune needn't worry … This new arrangement remains true to the original, written by Ron Grainer back in 1963, but on Christmas Day you'll hear it as it's never sounded before. This latest version is more thrilling and powerful but retains that slightly scary quality that remains stirring no matter how many times you catch it.

Also on 17 December, Steven Moffat made a promotional guest appearance on BBC Radio 2's early evening *Simon Mayo Drivetime* show, and the BBC released a second prequel to 'The Snowmen', this one entitled 'Vastra Investigates', which formed the latest Adventure

Calendar treat.[10]

The next day, the Adventure Calendar presented a 1' 19" duration video entitled 'The Matt Smith Christmas Show', of Matt Smith humorously interviewing Jenna-Louise Coleman in a break during recording of the Christmas special. Smith and Coleman also guested on that morning's edition of the BBC Radio 1 *Breakfast Show*, presented by Nick Grimshaw, following which Smith quickly relocated to ITV1's studios to appear on their *This Morning* show.

Of greater significance, though, the evening of 18 December saw 'The Snowmen' receive a UK press preview screening[11], followed by a question and answer session with Smith, Coleman and Steven Moffat, chaired by television reviewer Boyd Hilton. Asked about the kiss the Doctor and Clara share in the special, as seen in some of the trailers, Smith commented: 'I think always with this show, and always with this relationship in this show, it will constantly evolve. And it should. And hopefully over the course of the next eight or nine episodes … it will evolve even further. We're excited about next year now, and getting into that and actually going, "Well, now we know what we know about each other, and the way we work and who we are and all the rest of it …" I kind of likened it … earlier, in an interview, to an arranged marriage. Not that I know what an arranged marriage is like. But it's like, "You're married, have chemistry." Do you know what I mean?' Moffat, meanwhile, commented on the thinking behind the new TARDIS interior set: 'It was mainly saying to [production designer] Michael Pickwoad, 'What would you do with the TARDIS? But we had a notion, because I thought we'd been getting progressively whimsical with the interior …, and I started to think, "Well, why is that? It's not a magical place, it's actually a machine." So we did say "machine"; and actually, potentially, as you'll see more spectacularly later, quite a scary place sometimes. We make a lot of use of that. And it's also a lot easier to shoot [than the previous set], I have to say.'

The following day, the preview screening gave rise to a number of previews of 'The Snowmen' on media websites. Catherine Gee of the *Telegraph* opined: 'For all its new features, this is an episode filled with knowing nods to please *Who* fans, including a reference drawn from elsewhere in the Moffat catalogue, and the return of some of the Doctor's

---

10 See the 'Episode Guide' entry on 'The Snowmen' for further details.

11 There had also been an American press screening a few days earlier.

old friends in the shape of Strax, Vastra and Jenny. Dr Simeon's ominous warning that "Winter is coming" also suggests that Moffat may be a *Game of Thrones* fan ... Sadly [Richard E] Grant's emotionless stiff face makes him less menacing than hoped – it seems more like you could stop his evil doings with a quick slap to the face with a leather glove. But fortunately, our CGI adversaries more than hold their own in the scary stakes. It's not quite as action-packed as previous specials, but compared with the other sedate period Christmas Day offerings of *Call the Midwife* and *Downton Abbey*, or the impending apocalypse-free episodes of *The Royle Family* and *Strictly Come Dancing*, this festive instalment of the sci-fi series will give the post-dinner snoozers a much-needed boost.'

19 December also brought another exciting development, as the BBC unveiled the first promotional image of the redesigned TARDIS interior set, depicting Matt Smith as the Doctor stood in front of the control console with his arms outstretched in a welcoming pose.

As anticipation for the Christmas special continued to build, with a slew of other media reports and previews appearing in the run-up to the big day, 20 December saw the 'Vastra Investigates' prequel receive a television broadcast on the BBC Red Button service.

On 21 December, a humorous 'Songtaran Carols' video formed the latest Adventure Games treat.[12] In addition, Matt Smith was one of the guests on that evening's edition of BBC One's *The Graham Norton Show*, recorded at the end of the previous month; this would also be broadcast by BBC America, immediately after 'The Snowmen' on Christmas Day. The actor was tight-lipped about the plot of the special, ruefully admitting to Norton, 'As always, I can't tell you anything. This is the tragedy of the show I'm in: that you come on and you can't actually promote it!' However, fans were at least given another exclusive clip, this one featuring the Doctor, Clara and Strax.

21 December 2012 also saw an announcement made that the *Worlds in Time* game had been extended to three additional platforms: Kongregate, Newgrounds.com and Armor Games. Robert Nashak of BBC Worldwide Digital Entertainment and Games said: 'We are excited to extend the game's reach to a wider audience and bring the beloved *Doctor Who* brand to more players. Distribution deals with companies like Newgrounds.com, Kongregate, and Armor Games are mutually beneficial for both parties, and provide players with an avenue to expand

---

[12] See the 'Episode Guide' entry on 'The Snowmen' for further details.

their gaming options.'

The 22 December Adventure Calendar treat was a 51" teaser clip from 'The Snowmen', of a group of children in Victorian garb playing in the snow, and one solitary young boy being observed with concern by his parents and then reacting in surprise as his snowman speaks to him. The following day, a second teaser clip was presented, this one of 33" duration, showing Dr Simeon being confronted on a snowy street by Madame Vastra and Jenny.

On Christmas Eve, the BBC publicity machine again went into overdrive. Jenna-Louise Coleman was a guest on that morning's BBC One *Breakfast* show, and also featured with Matt Smith in a pre-recorded preview piece contributed by entertainment correspondent Lizo Mzimba; the latest Adventure Calendar treat was another, 1' 16" duration video interview with the two stars; and the *Independent* newspaper also had an interview with Smith, in which he commented: 'The Doctor under Amy and Rory eventually became like their pet. He was just this sort of strange pet that could talk, that would sweep in every now and then. He's meeting someone new [now] because he presents himself in a new light and she forces him to be a different version of himself slightly. As always with *Doctor Who*, the essence and heartbeat of the show is the same – old alien, hot chick travel through the universe and get into capers. That will always be the heartbeat of the show, and it's whether it's more flirtatious, whether there's more attraction, whether there's more zing. You'll have to wait and find out. I'm sure we'll cover all that territory.'

Of the Doctor's state of mind at the start of 'The Snowmen', the actor said: 'There's a great deal of time that's passed in cunning story terms. It's great because you kind of go, "500 years later ...", but the burden of that loss will always be with him. Like the burden of losing Rose Tyler, or whoever it is, is always with him to some extent. But I think particularly for my Doctor it is. Amy and Rory were so significant. But what I would say as well is I always think it's important for the show for that grieving to have its place but move on. I felt it affected Martha's journey quite a lot that he was always talking about Rose, which is completely understandable, because the tenth Doctor and Rose had such a wonderful connection; but the show has to propel forward, back into adventure mode.'

The abundance of trailers, preview clips and teasers for 'The Snowmen' – more numerous, it seemed, than for any previous episode – had led some fan commentators humorously to suggest that there might be little new material left to see on Christmas Day, but fortunately there was still plenty to enjoy when the special at last reached Britain's television screens at 5.14 pm; and when the media reviews started to appear online later that evening and the following day, the majority were complimentary. Dan Martin of the *Guardian* wrote: 'Welcome back, Merry Christmas, and wow. "The Snowmen" was easily the finest Christmas special under this regime. After last year's dog's giblets of an episode, it needed to be, but this poetic romp was actually the best since "The Christmas Invasion" [2005], and possibly better. It had everything we like about *Doctor Who* (frights, romance, running, a menacing baddie, lizard people) while being just sentimental enough to tick off a lot of things we like about Christmas.' Some reviewers had reservations, however. The *Mirror's* Jon Cooper opined: 'Where this year's *Who* snowtacular fails is appealing to the dinner-bloated and mildly [uninterested] middle viewer. It'll totally pass by family members who, at 5.15 in the afternoon, just want to sleep for a bit until they feel the need to attack the cold cuts. Through sprout-engorged eyes and a brandy befuddle, it's a great piece of entertainment, but it doesn't hold up to much sober fanboy scrutiny. It's miles better than anything else on, but for the casual Christmas viewer there's little to hold the interest besides noticing how gorgeous the new companion is, and well ... maybe the ending.'

On Boxing Day, the BBC released online the by now standard behind-the-scenes featurette to accompany 'The Snowmen'. Entitled 'Clara's First Christmas', this ran for 3' 27".[13] The following day, they made available another video, this one under the title 'A Christmas Q&A', consisting of 3' 44" of highlights from the question and answer session that had followed the 18 December press preview screening of the special.

2012 drew to a close with no other significant *Doctor Who* developments to report. However, anticipation amongst the show's fans remained high. A 'Coming Soon' trailer of clips at the end of 'The Snowmen' had whetted appetites for the 2013 section of Series Seven, and the coming months promised much excitement as the show approached its golden jubilee.

---

[13] When included as an extra on the *Complete Seventh Series* DVD and Blu-ray box set, this would be given the slightly revised title 'Clara's White Christmas'.

PART TWO

2013 As It Happened

Chapter Four
The Celebrations Begin

Doctor Who's landmark fiftieth anniversary year opened relatively quietly. The remaining Series Seven episodes were now in post-production, recording having been completed a month earlier, so there was a lull in news emerging from Cardiff.

Issue 456 of *Doctor Who Magazine*, published on 10 January, had a round-up of some of the merchandise and events planned for the coming months, plus an interview with production designer Michael Pickwoad, giving an insight into the creation of the new TARDIS interior set that had debuted in 'The Snowmen'.

12 January saw *Doctor Who*'s first ever story '100,000 BC' (1963) being shown to a 450-strong capacity audience at BFI Southbank in London. This was the first of a series of celebratory one-story-per-Doctor screenings that would take place throughout the year, each of them followed by a question-and-answer session with guests appropriate to the chosen story.

On 23 January, the BBC announced that *Doctor Who* would return to BBC One on 30 March – a couple of days earlier than the expected April start previously indicated by *Doctor Who Magazine*. This would also be the date on which the second section of Series Seven began in the US and Canada, as confirmed by BBC America and Space respectively.

27 January saw BBC America kick off its own celebrations for the anniversary year by airing the classic-era story 'The Aztecs' (1964), along with an exclusive half-hour documentary about the first Doctor, as part of a new strand called *The Doctors Revisited*. Further stories and accompanying documentaries, one per Doctor, would be shown monthly throughout the rest of the year, and the documentaries would later be collected for release in DVD sets in the US and Australia, although not in the UK.

Released online by the BBC on 31 January was a promotional video in which Matt Smith appeared in his original costume as the Doctor along with a number of other celebrities telling viewers what they planned to do to help raise money for the forthcoming *Comic Relief* telethon, due to take place on 15 March. In a brief clip recorded in front of the TARDIS police box, he said, 'I'll decide what I'm gonna do when I've got my fundraising kit.'

As February began, recording got under way on *An Adventure in Space and Time*, the previously-announced BBC Two docu-drama about *Doctor Who*'s 1960s origins, and associated casting and location reports began to appear.

11 February brought two exciting announcements. The first was that popular classic-era monsters the Ice Warriors would be making their new-era debut in the forthcoming run of episodes, in a Mark Gatiss-scripted story set on board a submarine. This news came courtesy of an online report on the website of *SFX* magazine, which quoted executive producer Caroline Skinner as saying: 'We wanted to bring them back because they're wonderful! In the mix of stories that we were planning for this year it felt as if doing something very bold with a monster that hadn't been seen for a while would be really cool. Mark is an enormous fan of the Ice Warrior stories and came up with the idea. The sense of a monster of that scale and that size trapped in a really small, contained environment such as a submarine was a really brilliant story to be able to tell.'

The second announcement, buried away within a more general BBC press release about Controller of Drama Ben Stephenson's plans for the future, was that *Doctor Who*'s fiftieth anniversary would be marked by its first major 3D broadcast.[14] Steven Moffat was quoted as saying: 'It's about time. Technology has finally caught up with *Doctor Who* and your television is now bigger on the inside. A whole new dimension of adventure for the Doctor to explore.'

Published the following day, the *Radio Times* edition for the week of 16 to 22 February launched the magazine's own celebrations of the anniversary year, each copy including one of two different sets of four free postcards picturing past *Doctor Who* covers.

---

[14] The two-part *Doctor Who* skit 'Dimensions in Time', produced for the 1993 *Children in Need* telethon, had previously been broadcast in a rudimentary form of 3D, and Series Five – Matt Smith's first as the Doctor – had been promoted with a 3D trailer shown in cinemas and released online.

Mark Williams presented another performance of the *Doctor Who – A Symphonic Spectacular* incidental music concert on 27 February, this one in Liverpool and with attendance restricted to some 700 international television buyers present at a BBC Worldwide Showcase sales event being held in the city that week. As another part of its efforts to promote *Doctor Who* to the assembled buyers, BBC Worldwide also unveiled at the event, and made available to view online, a 3' 15" duration video publicising the fact that the show had already been sold to over 200 territories, as illustrated by way of a clip from 'The Wedding of River Song' (2011) with sections of dialogue dubbed into Brazilian Portuguese, French, German and Italian, and in the original English.

On 1 March, the BBC started to ramp up its pre-publicity for the new run of *Doctor Who* episodes, issuing the following press release:

Doctor Who is to return to BBC One on 30 March in a modern day urban thriller announced today as 'The Bells of Saint John', as the first official image is revealed giving fans a sneak peak at what to expect from the epic new series.

Written by Steven Moffat, 'The Bells of Saint John' will mark the official introduction of the Doctor's newest companion, Clara Oswald, played by Jenna-Louise Coleman. [Coleman] having already made two appearances last year, the opening episode will be the first time fans get to see the Clara that will accompany the Doctor across the series' eight adventures.

Set in London against the backdrop of new and old iconic landmarks, the Shard and Westminster Bridge, 'The Bells of Saint John' will also establish a new nemesis, the Spoonheads, who will battle the Doctor as he discovers something sinister is lurking in the wi-fi.

Steven Moffat, executive producer and lead writer, said: 'It's the fiftieth year of *Doctor Who* and look what's going on! We're up in the sky and under the sea! We're running round the rings of an alien world and then a haunted house. There's new Cybermen, new Ice Warriors and a never before attempted journey to the centre of the TARDIS. And in the finale, the Doctor's greatest secret will at last be revealed! If this wasn't already our most exciting year it would be anyway!'

Featuring a movie a week, from a ghost story to an underwater siege to a period drama, the new series will also introduce new monsters, as well as bringing back fan favourites the Ice Warriors and Cybermen.

Meanwhile the series' stellar list of guest stars include Celia Imrie, Richard E Grant, Warwick Davis, Jessica Raine, Dougray Scott and Tamzin Outhwaite, as well as for the first time on screen together, mother and daughter Dame Diana Rigg and Rachael Stirling.

The promotional image referred to in the press release was a digital composite of the Doctor on a motorbike, with Clara riding pillion, crashing through a sheet of glass, presumably intended to represent the side of the Shard skyscraper.

The following day, BBC One gave two airings to a very brief promotional teaser, consisting solely of a caption advertising the 30 March date for *Doctor Who*'s return.

On 5 March, *SFX* magazine followed up its earlier exclusive about the return of the Ice Warriors by publishing on its website the first image of one of the creatures as it would appear, with a slightly modernised design, in the forthcoming episode.

BBC Worldwide announced on 7 March that, following on from the successful official convention held in Cardiff the previous year, London's ExCel centre would be the venue for a three-day *Doctor Who* Celebration event, beginning on 22 November, to mark the show's anniversary, with 15,000 tickets available.

As the second week of March began, Matt Smith was the subject of one of the regular Meet the Star events staged at London's Apple Store, where he confirmed to interviewer Boyd Hilton that there was to be a *Doctor Who* fiftieth anniversary special, for which he had just read the script. A video of their discussion would later be made available to view for free on Apple's iTunes platform.

13 March brought a surprise development, as the BBC issued a press release announcing that Caroline Skinner had stepped down from her role as one of *Doctor Who*'s executive producers. This read in part:

Caroline Skinner says: 'It has been an honour to have been a part of *Doctor Who*, and a privilege to have worked with Steven Moffat and Matt Smith on this extraordinary show. I have hugely enjoyed my time in BBC Wales and would like to thank Faith Penhale and our wonderful production team for their unending commitment and brilliance. I will miss them all enormously, but I'm leaving *Doctor Who* in fine form, with the new series starting at Easter and the fantastic plans for the fiftieth anniversary already underway. I am delighted to be now returning to BBC Drama Production in London as an executive producer, and the new opportunities and projects that will bring.'

Faith Penhale, Head of Drama BBC Wales, adds: 'I would like to take this opportunity to thank Caroline for her contribution to *Doctor Who* since taking on the role in 2011, on behalf of both the BBC and the show. She leaves the show in good shape – there's a brilliant new series starting on Easter Saturday that will see the official arrival of the Doctor's new companion! And the fiftieth anniversary plans are on track to deliver audiences an unmissable event! I wish her all the very best for the future.'

Faith Penhale will take over as the executive producer on the fiftieth anniversary with immediate effect.

Caroline will continue working on BBC Two's one-off drama *An Adventure in Space and Time*, which forms part of the BBC's celebrations to mark the fiftieth anniversary.

The recruitment process for a new executive producer for the next series will start shortly.

The following week, the latest issue of the satirical and current affairs magazine *Private Eye* gave some apparent context to Skinner's departure when it alleged:

Skinner had in fact been absent from the programme's offices since the end of February, after she and showrunner Steven Moffat had an extremely noisy and public falling-out during a party at the BBC Worldwide Showcase, a programme sales festival in Liverpool, which ended with Moffat being led away by colleagues while bellowing at Skinner, 'You are erased from *Doctor Who!*'

The bust-up came as a surprise to colleagues, who had noted the very close working relationship that had developed between Skinner and Moffat since she joined the programme in 2011.

Meanwhile, the 14 March edition of the CBBC show *Cracking the Code* featured a 7′ 05″ duration item called '*Doctor Who* and Visual Effects', looking in particular at how the CGI effects for 'Asylum of the Daleks' had been created by regular *Doctor Who* contributors The Mill. This came only two weeks before The Mill would announce via Twitter that its UK visual effects office would be closing at the end of April, due to a downturn in business. By the beginning of June, however, a successor company, Milk, would be formed, and would continue to meet most of *Doctor Who*'s CGI requirements.

14 March also gave fans in Australia and New Zealand a chance to enjoy a big-screen double bill of the two-parter 'The Impossible Astronaut' / 'Day of the Moon' (2011), given a simultaneous showing in numerous cinemas across the continent.

On 15 March, Matt Smith guested on the *Chris Evans Breakfast Show* on BBC Radio 2, where he promoted the fact that he would be making a contribution to that evening's *Comic Relief* telethon on BBC One. This contribution came initially in the form of a roughly minute-long cameo cross-over appearance by the Doctor with the TARDIS in a sketch featuring some of the stars of the hit drama series *Call the Midwife*. Unfortunately the dialogue Smith was given to deliver included some rather inappropriate sexual innuendo, and was not particularly funny. The actor then made an in-costume appearance live in the *Comic Relief* studio, in a brief humorous exchange with hosts Dermot O'Leary and Claudia Winkleman.

The following day, the BBC released a 40" duration trailer of clips to promote *Doctor Who*'s forthcoming run – referred to informally as Series Seven B. Then, that evening, Matt Smith made a further primetime television appearance, when he was amongst the guests on the latest edition of ITV1's *The Jonathan Ross Show*. Asked how long he saw himself continuing as the Doctor, the actor said: '*Doctor Who* is one of those jobs that you have to take year by year. It's ten months a year, it's all-consuming, so I don't think you can plan five or six years ahead, or even two years ahead. It's a year by year thing, and at the moment it's 2013 and we'll see what 2014 holds.'

On 18 March, the BBC issued a press pack for the first four of the upcoming episodes, confirming the titles as 'The Bells of Saint John', 'The Rings of Akhaten', 'Cold War' and 'Hide', giving a brief synopsis of each, and presenting some promotional pictures for them, including the now routine movie poster-style images. Also included were interview extracts from Matt Smith, Jenna-Louise Coleman and Steven Moffat. Smith was quoted as saying: 'I think it is going to be very exciting to introduce Clara to the world, and Steven has hit a real vein of form.' Asked how she found working with Smith, Coleman replied: 'Just a joy, it really is. He is the most perfect leading man and sets such a lovely tone on set, making the atmosphere so wonderful. There's not much more you could ask for in your co-star.' Questioned about the urban thriller theme chosen for 'The Bells of Saint John', Moffat commented: 'It was [producer] Marcus Wilson's idea. We were discussing how the first episode of the second run would probably be a contemporary Earth adventure, so the Doctor could meet the modern day Clara – and anyway, I wanted to do wi-fi monsters – and Marcus suggested we do a proper urban thriller. The Doctor can never be Bond or Bourne – but if he tried, it might look a bit like this.'

Also on 18 March, in the US, that evening's edition of CBS's *The Late Late Show with Craig Ferguson* – the Scottish presenter of which was a long-time *Doctor Who* fan – featured a guest appearance by Jenna-Louise Coleman, talking about her role as Clara and various other subjects. This was recorded during a week-long US visit by Coleman and Smith, which also saw Coleman tape some promotional segments for the weekday entertainment news programme *Access Hollywood*.

The *Radio Times* edition published on 19 March for the week of 23 to 29 March ran a two-page behind-the-scenes feature on the recording of a scene near London's iconic St Paul's Cathedral for 'The Bells of Saint John'. In the US, meanwhile, the 21 March edition of *Entertainment Weekly* again featured *Doctor Who*, on a choice of two covers: one depicting the Doctor with a Cyberman, the other showing the Doctor and Clara beside the TARDIS, with a Dalek in the background.

The 22 March edition of *The Sun* newspaper ran another report suggesting that Matt Smith would be leaving *Doctor Who* in the 2013 Christmas special, and that the BBC already had in mind a potential replacement. However, a BBC spokesperson said, 'Sorry folks but even we don't know what's going to happen at Christmas. It's not been written yet! But Matt loves the show and is to start [recording] the unmissable fiftieth anniversary [special], and the new series [is] starting on Easter Saturday.'

22 March also brought an evening of programmes, starting with *The One Show* on BBC One and continuing on BBC Four, marking the imminent and much lamented closure of the BBC's iconic Television Centre studios, where many *Doctor Who* episodes had been made from the 1960s to the 1980s – as acknowledged in a guest appearance by former Doctors Colin Baker and Sylvester McCoy in the BBC One programme.

The famous landmark would subsequently be demolished to make way for the building of homes, offices, cinemas and restaurants, although some new television studio facilities would also remain on the site.

Also on 22 March, BBC America released online the latest of its irregular series of 'Doctor Who Insider' videos, this one of 1' 00" duration and entitled 'Meet Jenna-Louise Coleman', featuring snippets of an interview with Coleman and Matt Smith recorded during their US visit, illustrated by various clips. The same date saw the Nerdist podcast promote its tie-in BBC America programme, which would go out after Doctor Who on 30 March, with a 2' 00" duration YouTube video in which presenters Matt Mira and Jonah Ray challenged the two stars to a game of darts.

With just a week to go before transmission of 'The Bells of Saint John', 23 March saw the BBC release online a short prequel to the episode.[15] On the same date, BBC One broadcast a pre-recorded edition of *Pointless Celebrities* – the celebrity version of the popular *Pointless* quiz programme – with a *Doctor Who* theme, the guest contestants being former stars of the show, in four teams of two: Sylvester McCoy (seventh Doctor) and Sophie Aldred (Ace); Frazer Hines (Jamie) and Louise Jameson (Leela); Bernard Cribbins (Wilf Mott) and Jacqueline King (Sylvia Noble); and Nicola Bryant (Peri) and Andrew Hayden-Smith (Jake Simmonds from 'Rise of the Cybermen' / 'The Age of Steel' (2006)). K-9 – as usual, voiced by John Leeson and operated by Mat Irvine – was also on hand to help presenters Alexander Armstrong and Richard Osman. Debuted immediately prior to the programme was a dedicated 30" trailer for 'The Bells of Saint John'.

Another BBC America video appeared online on 24 March, this one of 1' 27" duration, with Jenna-Louise Coleman posing questions to Matt Smith. This was followed up the next day with a 59" video in which the tables were turned and Smith interviewed Coleman. Again, these videos were recorded during the recent US promotional visit made by the two stars.

25 March also saw the release of a minisode entitled 'The Battle of Demon's Run: Two Days Later', which effectively served as a belated additional prequel to 'The Snowmen'. Initially this could be viewed only in North America as part of the Series Seven Part Two subscription offered on the Amazon and iTunes digital platforms, but eventually it would be given a commercial release on *The Complete Seventh Series* DVD

---

[15] See the 'Episode Guide' entry on 'The Bells of Saint John' for further details.

and Blu-Ray box set.

Published on 26 March, the *Radio Times* edition for the week of 30 March to 5 April boasted a cover photograph of the Doctor and Clara, with assorted monsters in the background. Inside, the magazine presented interviews with the two stars, a *Doctor Who* monster wallchart and a Steven Moffat Series Seven B guide, which amongst other things revealed the titles of a further three episodes: 'Journey to the Centre of the TARDIS', 'The Crimson Horror' and 'Nightmare in Silver'. However, still kept under wraps was the title of the closing episode, which was listed simply as 'The Finale'.

The same date saw the BBC release online a 47" duration teaser clip from 'The Bells of Saint John', showing the Doctor in the TARDIS console room changing out of a monk's habit and into the Victorian-style purple outfit first seen in 'The Snowmen'. The prequel placed online three days earlier was meanwhile made available to view on the BBC Red Button service.

Also on 26 March, the Royal Mail marked the anniversary year by issuing a special set of *Doctor Who* postage stamps. These had been first announced the previous December, and there had reportedly been an unprecedented level of pre-registration demand for them. There were first class (60p) stamps picturing each of the eleven television Doctors with an appropriate title sequence background and logo, and second class (50p) varieties showing images of a Dalek, a Cyberman, an Ood and a Weeping Angel. Various items of associated merchandise were also made available, including first day covers. The release was publicised with numerous photographs taken at a prestigious launch event hosted by the Royal Mail a few earlier at BAFTA in London. The specially-invited guests for this had included former Doctors Tom Baker, Peter Davison and Paul McGann, William Hartnell's grand-daughter Jessica Carney, Jon Pertwee's son Sean, and Jenna-Louise Coleman. Matt Smith was unable to attend in person, but instead sent a video message, which was introduced by Steven Moffat, who also gave a short speech, as did the Royal Mail's Chief Executive Moya Greene. Each of the Doctors was pictured holding an enlarged copy of the stamp bearing his image.

The flurry of pre-publicity for 'The Bells of Saint John' continued on 27 March. The BBC released two more teaser clips – one of 37" duration introducing the character Miss Kizlet, played by Celia Imrie, and the other of 1' 13" showing the Doctor and Clara materialising the TARDIS on board a plane to try to prevent it crashing – and Matt Smith and Jenna-

Louise Coleman were interviewed by entertainment correspondent Richard Arnold on that morning's edition of ITV1's *Daybreak*. Further *Doctor Who* covers also appeared at around this time on, amongst others, the *TV and Satellite Week* listings magazine and the *Big Issue* street newspaper sold by homeless people to raise money; and numerous magazine and newspaper preview pieces saw print, often including quotes from Steven Moffat and/or the show's stars.

On the morning of 30 March, the major news broke that the fiftieth anniversary special would see David Tennant reprising his role as the tenth Doctor, that the highly distinguished actor John Hurt would be starring alongside him and Matt Smith, and that Billie Piper, famous for her portrayal of companion Rose Tyler, would also be appearing. The BBC had not intended to release this information until it appeared in the new issue of *Doctor Who Magazine* the following week, but their hand was effectively forced when a distribution error resulted in many of the magazine's subscribers receiving their copies several days ahead of schedule.

That evening, an exciting day for *Doctor Who* fans was capped when 'The Bells of Saint John' made its eagerly-awaited debut at 6.14 pm on BBC One, launching the on-air run of Series Seven B.

Chapter Five
Series Seven – Part Two

As usual, media reviews for the opening instalment of *Doctor Who*'s new run started to appear online almost as soon as the closing credits had faded away – and certainly by the time the BBC placed online that evening the 3' 52" accompanying behind-the-scenes featurette and the 30" television trailer for the following episode, 'The Rings of Akhaten'. As with 'The Angels Take Manhattan' and 'The Snowmen', the critics' response was somewhat mixed. The piece by Jon Cooper of the *Mirror* was fairly typical in tone: 'While "The Bells of Saint John" certainly had its moments, as a whole it didn't reach the heights of previous episodes. Arguably the two biggest set pieces … (concerning a crashing plane and the Doctor driving up the side of the Shard on a motorbike) were impressive enough – you could even say Hollywood impressive. The only problem is, that isn't much of compliment. Yes, they were big and bold and doubtless expensive, but they felt shoehorned in. Showy and a bit spectacle for spectacle's sake. Let's face it – *Doctor Who* has never been about Hollywood special effects, big bangs and crashing planes. From its humble beginnings to the present day, [it] is at its most charming when it is at its most creaky, when its creativity is fully on show.'

Following on from Saturday's unexpectedly early casting announcement, 1 April saw the BBC release, initially via Twitter, two promotional behind-the-scenes images for the fiftieth anniversary special, both coming from the script read-through that had taken place that morning. The first was of Matt Smith and David Tennant standing together holding their respective scripts – which gave no clue as to the story's title, as they were marked simply '50th Anniversary Special'. The second was a group shot of Smith, Tennant, Jenna-Louise Coleman and previously-unannounced guest star Joanna Paige, best known for her role as Stacey Shipman in the previous decade's hit BBC romantic sitcom *Gavin & Stacey*.

The following day, as recording of the anniversary special got under way in the grounds of the Ivy Tower in Tonna, Neath, a further promotional image was released, this one a location-taken shot of a menacingly-posed Zygon, confirming that this popular classic-era monster race would be making its first reappearance in the 21st Century show.

Meanwhile, this week saw the BBC begin the recruitment process for *Doctor Who*'s new executive producer, following Caroline Skinner's abrupt departure the previous month. The post was advertised on a twenty-month fixed-term contract basis, with a 14 April closing date for applications.

In the light of much press and fan speculation as to whether or not ninth Doctor actor Christopher Eccleston would be seen alongside his successors in the anniversary special, with some media outlets alleging that he had pulled out at the last minute, on 5 April the BBC disclosed that the actor had actually never agreed to appear – a statement that brought enormous disappointment to many fans. A spokesman was quoted as saying, 'Chris met with Steven Moffat a couple of times to talk about Steven's plans for the *Doctor Who* fiftieth anniversary episode. After careful thought, Chris decided not to be in the episode. He wishes the team all the best.'

Following transmission of 'The Rings of Akhaten' on 6 April, the BBC placed online the usual behind-the-scenes featurette, this one of 3' 55" duration, and a 30" television trailer for 'Cold War'.

Two days later there came an announcement that the anniversary special would feature a return appearance by Jemma Redgrave, who in the 2012 episode 'The Power of Three' had taken over the role of UNIT's Kate Lethbridge-Stewart, daughter of the iconic classic-era character Brigadier Lethbridge-Stewart. This news was quickly updated to add that the new character of UNIT scientist Osgood, played by Ingrid Oliver, would also be seen. On 9 April, both actresses featured, along with Jenna-Louise Coleman, in a 1' 16" duration video released online by the BBC, showing some snippets of the location recording that had taken place the previous day at the Tower of London. Another video released on the same date was the first of what would prove to be a series of humorous 'Strax Field Report' clips. Entitled 'Doctor at Trafalgar Square', this had a 1' 25" duration and highlighted the location recording carried out earlier that day in London's Trafalgar Square.[16]

Meanwhile, in Australia, 9 April also brought a joint guest appearance by Colin Baker, Sylvester McCoy and Paul McGann (incorrectly referred to as Paul McCann) on Channel 9's breakfast show, *Today*, to talk about the fiftieth anniversary.

In what was by now a well-established pattern, the transmission of 'Cold War' on 13 April was immediately followed by the appearance online of the accompanying behind-the-scenes featurette, this one lasting 3' 48". This time, though, the BBC offered no television trailer for the following week's episode, 'Hide'; and the same would be true for each of the next three episodes (although, in the US, BBC America would continue to run its own 30" trailers).

Meanwhile, on 17 April, further location recording for the anniversary special took place at Chepstow Castle in Chepstow, Monmouthshire, and John Hurt was pictured in media reports wearing a distinctly Doctorish costume, heightening speculation amongst fans as to the nature of the his role in the story.

On 18 April, the BBC released – in both portrait and, for the first time, landscape formats – the latest of Series Seven's movie poster-style promotional images, for 'Journey to the Centre of the TARDIS', 'The Crimson Horror' and 'Nightmare in Silver'. The latter showcased a dramatic shot of one of the redesigned Cybermen that would feature in the episode.

The following day, the equivalent image for the series finale was made available, finally revealing its title to be 'The Name of the Doctor'. The poster also carried the tagline 'His Secret Revealed' and disclosed the fact that Alex Kingston would be guest-starring.

The behind-the-scenes featurette that went online immediately after the 20 April transmission of 'Hide' was of 3' 34" duration. The one for 'Journey to the Centre of the TARDIS', a week later, ran for 3' 39".

On 30 April, the BBC announced that, following the recent recruitment exercise, the post of *Doctor Who*'s new executive producer had gone to Brian Minchin – who, in addition to his other accomplishments, had previously worked as a script editor on the show, and as a producer on the spin-offs *Torchwood* and *The Sarah Jane Adventures*. However, Minchin would not receive his first credit in his new capacity until the 2013

---

[16] See the 'Episode Guide' section for further details of the 'Strax Field Report' videos.

Christmas special; BBC Wales Head of Drama Faith Penhale, who had been acting as a temporary stand-in pending his appointment, would be credited alongside Steven Moffat on the anniversary special.

The behind-the-scenes featurette for 'The Crimson Horror', placed online on 4 May, had a 4' 16" duration. The one for 'Nightmare in Silver', on 11 May, ran for 2' 54". For the first time in several weeks, 11 May also saw the release of a 30" trailer for the next episode – the series finale, 'The Name of the Doctor'. In addition, a prequel to 'The Name of the Doctor' was made available to view online and on the BBC Red Button service; entitled 'She Said, He Said: A Prequel', this ran for 3' 32".[17]

On 12 May, this year's BAFTA television awards ceremony at the Royal Festival Hall in London, televised on BBC One, paid tribute to *Doctor Who*. Steven Moffat was quoted in advance as saying: 'This is a massive and exciting year for *Doctor Who*, so I'm thrilled that BAFTA are including a special tribute to the show. So thrilled, in fact, we're sending the Doctor's best friend, Jenna Coleman, to present an award. We're also sending the Doctor's worst enemy, the Daleks, to exterminate lots of innocent people. Sorry, it's just what they do. Let us know if it's a health and safety issue.' As revealed in this statement, Coleman had by this point decided to drop the 'Louise' part of her name for professional purposes; from the anniversary special onwards, she would be credited simply as 'Jenna Coleman'. Shown on the big screen at the awards ceremony was a video consisting of a montage of exciting clips from *Doctor Who*'s whole fifty year history, followed by a specially-recorded segment of about 50" duration in which Clara patiently explains to the Doctor that the golden 'face on a stick with its eye poked out' that he has found in the TARDIS is not an alien artefact resembling an Axon (from the classic-era story 'The Claws of Axos' (1971)) but a BAFTA award. The segment ends with Clara heading off with the award, asking the Doctor to wish her luck – immediately after which, host Graham Norton welcomed Coleman onto the stage at the Royal Festival Hall with celebrity scientist Professor Brian Cox to present the BAFTA for Best Comedy Programme, which was won by BBC Three's *The Revolution Will Be Televised*. The BBC subsequently made the *Doctor Who* video available to view online, but it has not been given a commercial release.

Only six weeks after the error that had led to the premature release of casting news for the anniversary special, a similar blunder saw the US

---

[17] See the 'Episode Guide' entry on 'The Name of the Doctor' for further details.

edition of the *Series 7 Part 2* Blu-ray set being sent out early to 210 fans who had bought it through the BBC America online shop, enabling them to view 'The Name of the Doctor' a week before its transmission date. On 13 May, the BBC posted online a plea from Steven Moffat: 'We respectfully ask those fans not to divulge information or post content publicly, so that fellow fans who have yet to see the episodes do not have their viewing pleasure ruined. If everyone keeps the secrets safe until next Saturday we will release a special new clip featuring material of the tenth *and* eleventh Doctor!' This was echoed in an e-mail sent out by the BBC America shop to the customers concerned.

Published on 14 May, the *Radio Times* edition for the week of 18 to 14 May boasted a *Doctor Who* cover, with a picture of Clara in the foreground and the Doctor in the background and the headline 'Who Am I?' Interviewed inside the magazine, Jenna Coleman – still named here as Jenna-Louise Coleman – gave a few intriguing hints about 'The Name of the Doctor', saying: 'In the beginning we see a Clara in the '60s, the '70s and the '80s, so there are a lot of costume changes, which I love. Always one for a bit of dressing up, me. Love a red carpet. Richard E Grant is back with his evil Great Intelligence, the Doctor's greatest secret is revealed, all of his friends rally round to protect him and we finally understand why the Doctor has met Clara so many different times.'

On 15 May, the BBC surprisingly released online a second behind-the-scenes video for 'Nightmare in Silver', this one of 2' 38" duration and called 'Neil Gaiman on "Nightmare in Silver"', based around an interview with the scriptwriter. Uniquely amongst the Series Seven behind-the-scenes featurettes, this has not received a commercial release.

16 May brought another two online videos from the BBC: one of them a 1' 09" duration piece of Matt Smith and Jenna Coleman introducing 'The Name of the Doctor', the other the second of the 'Strax Field Report' series. These were followed on 17 May by a 25" duration teaser extract from the episode, of Clara receiving a letter from Madame Vastra. Another 'Strax Field Report' appeared on 18 May – the day when 'The Name of the Doctor' received its debut transmission, its surprise closing revelation of John Hurt as a previously unknown incarnation of the Doctor finally bringing Series Seven to a end, some eight and a half months after it had kicked off with 'Asylum of the Daleks' back on 1 September.

Meanwhile, on 16 May, the *TV Magazine* supplement of *The Sun* ran an interview with Matt Smith in which he appeared to indicate that, contrary to the newspaper's assertion back in March, he would be staying with *Doctor Who* for Series Eight in 2014. The actor was quoted as saying: 'I'm on a break for a couple of months while I'm in Detroit making [the movie] *How to Catch a Monster*. We come back and shoot the Christmas special over the summer, then we go on to the next series, which will either start filming at the end of this year or at the start of 2014.' It would soon become apparent, however, that these remarks had been somewhat disingenuous ...

Chapter Six
Big News

Immediately following transmission of 'The Name of the Doctor', the *Guardian* website ran a short message in which Steven Moffat thanked *Doctor Who* fans for their co-operation:

Well that was all a bit Keystone Cops, wasn't it? Our biggest surprise, our most secret episode, a revelation about the Doctor that changes everything …

… and we'd have got away with it too, if we hadn't accidentally sent Blu-ray copies of 'The Name of the Doctor' to 210 *Doctor Who* fans in America. Security-wise, that's not *good*, is it? I mean, it's not top-notch; it's hard to defend as professional-level, hard-line secrecy.

My favourite fact is that they're Blu-rays. Listen, we don't just leak any old rubbish, we leak in high-def – 1080p or nothing, that's us. Every last pixel in beautifully rendered detail. It's like getting caught extra naked.

But here's the thing. Never mind us blundering fools, check out the fans. Two hundred and ten of them, with the top-secret episode within their grasp – and because we asked nicely, they didn't breathe a word. Not one. Even *Doctor Who* websites have been closing their comments sections, just in case anyone blurts. I'm gobsmacked. I'm impressed. Actually, I'm humbled. And we are all very grateful.

Now you might be thinking, what does all this matter? It's a plot development in the mad old fantasy world of *Doctor Who*, why is that important? Well of course, it's not important, and in the scheme of things, it doesn't matter at all. Just as it doesn't matter when you're telling a joke, and some idiot shouts out the punchline before you finish. It's irritating, that's all. It's bad manners.

Well, no bad manners here! Two hundred and ten *Doctor Who* fans kept the secret, and many, many more fans helped. I wish I could send you all flowers, but I don't know where you live (and, given our record, you really shouldn't be sharing private information with us). So instead, if we can get our act together – and I forgive you for thinking that's a big if – there will be a little video treat released on the *Doctor Who* site later tonight.

Ten plus 11 gives you ...

Shortly afterwards, the promised video treat did indeed appear on the *Doctor Who* website – but those fans who had been hoping to see a preview extract from the anniversary special itself were slightly disappointed to find that it consisted instead of a 1' 26" duration behind-the-scenes clip of Matt Smith and David Tennant, both in costume, sitting together and chatting about their association with the show. The evening of 18 May also saw the expected posting online of the behind-the-scenes featurette for 'The Name of the Doctor', this one with a 4' 09" running time.

As usual, the series finale provoked an exceptional level of media reaction. 'And so the mystery of Clara is finally resolved,' wrote Dan Martin on the *Guardian* website. 'Your demented theories as to her true nature have been fantastic, but I always thought it would be something much more simple than her being Susan or Romana or the Rani. She chases the Great Intelligence into the grave, fracturing herself through time and space, in endless copies and versions: sometimes Clara the governess, sometimes Oswin, usually Soufflé Girl. The Clara we meet now is the real one, with different facets of her saving the Doctor in different eras. The pre-credits sequence, with all the Doctors, actually made me fall over. The solution is both straightforward and mindbending.' Simon Brew of the Den of Geek website was highly impressed: '"The Name Of The Doctor" was ..., for our money, the most satisfying, brilliant finale in Steven Moffat's run on *Doctor Who*, the kind of episode you rewatch for fun as much as to solve mysteries (and we'll be hunting for clues). Much better than "The Wedding of River Song" [2011] and a real rival to "The Big Bang" [2010], this was, for large parts, really gripping stuff, surrounded by an air of mystery, and a real sense that something big was going to be revealed. Fortunately, on this occasion, that was very much the case. And while Series Seven, in both parts, has been a bumpy ride (with Jenna-Louise Coleman's Clara our highlight), Steven Moffat and his team pulled quite a rabbit out at the end. Just brilliant.'

A BBC press release meanwhile gave an indication of what lay in store for fans in the months ahead:

We're delighted to confirm a new series of *Doctor Who* has been commissioned, and the show's lead writer and executive producer, Steven Moffat, has revealed he's already plotting a brand new run of adventures for the Doctor.

But way before that hits our screens we have a huge amount to look forward to. Your calendars should already have a big red circle around 23 November, because that's when the TARDIS returns in the frankly Earth-shattering adventure that celebrates half a century of *Doctor Who*. This 3D special stars Matt Smith and Jenna Coleman with David Tennant and John Hurt, seen briefly at the end of 'The Name of the Doctor'. Billie Piper returns alongside Jemma Redgrave, Joanna Page … and the Zygons!

…

Later this year the BBC also premieres *An Adventure in Space and Time*, the brilliant drama written by Mark Gatiss that looks at the genesis of *Doctor Who* …

And given that this year's Christmas special will be rounding off such a spectacular year, we're sure it will kick off the Doctor's next half century in style! But that's not all. Big plans are being put in place that will well and truly celebrate the Doctor's half-centenary. Make sure you check back for some exciting announcements!

It was now clear that, Series Seven having come to an end, fans would have to wait some six months until the next new *Doctor Who* – the anniversary special itself – reached the screen. During that period, however, there would be plenty of associated developments and events to keep everyone interested, as anticipation slowly built to fever pitch. Indeed, it seemed that barely a day would go by without some *Doctor Who*-related story hitting the media. In short, *Doctor Who* was now big news.

On 20 May, Steven Moffat, Matt Smith and Jenna Coleman were all present in New York, USA to accept a highly prestigious Institutional

Award presented to *Doctor Who* at the ceremony for the seventy-second Peabody Awards. Named after American businessman and philanthropist George Peabody and administered by the Grady College of Journalism and Mass Communication at the University of Georgia, these recognise excellence in radio, television and online media. The citation for *Doctor Who*'s award, which had been announced back at the end of March, read: 'Seemingly immortal, fifty years old and still running, this engaging, imaginative sci-fi/fantasy series is awarded an Institutional Peabody for evolving with technology and the times like nothing else in the known television universe.'

In a major development, 1 June brought the announcement that – contrary to what he appeared to have told *The Sun* the previous month – Matt Smith would be making his exit from *Doctor Who* in the 2013 Christmas special. The press release read, in part:

> Matt first stepped into the TARDIS in 2010 and will leave the role at the end of this year after starring in the unmissable fiftieth anniversary [special] in November and regenerating in the Christmas special.
>
> During his time as the Doctor, Matt has reached over 30 million unique UK viewers and his incarnation has seen the show go truly global. He was also the first actor to be nominated for a BAFTA in the role.
>
> Matt quickly won over fans to be voted Best Actor by readers of *Doctor Who Magazine* for the 2010 season. He also received a nod for his first series at the National Television Awards, before winning the Most Popular Male Drama Performance award in 2012.
>
> Matt has played one of the biggest roles in TV with over 77 million fans in the UK, USA and Australia alone!
>
> [He] says: '*Doctor Who* has been the most brilliant experience for me as an actor and a bloke, and that largely is down to the cast, crew and fans of the show. I'm incredibly grateful to all the cast and crew who work tirelessly every day, to realise all the elements of the show and deliver *Doctor Who* to the audience. Many of them have become good friends and I'm incredibly proud of what we have achieved over the last four years.
>
> 'Having Steven Moffat as showrunner write such varied, funny, mind-bending and brilliant scripts has been one of the

greatest and most rewarding challenges of my career. It's been a privilege and a treat to work with Steven; he's a good friend and will continue to shape a brilliant world for the Doctor.

'The fans of *Doctor Who* around the world are unlike any other; they dress up, shout louder, know more about the history of the show (and speculate more about the future of the show) in a way that I've never seen before. Your dedication is truly remarkable. Thank you so very much for supporting my incarnation of the Time Lord, number eleven, who I might add is not done yet; I'm back for the fiftieth anniversary and the Christmas special!

'It's been an honour to play this part, to follow the legacy of brilliant actors, and helm the TARDIS for a spell with "the ginger, the nose and the impossible one". But when ya gotta go, ya gotta go, and Trenzalore calls. Thank you guys. Matt.'

Steven Moffat, lead writer and executive producer, says: 'Every day, on every episode, in every set of rushes, Matt Smith surprised me: the way he'd turn a line, or spin on his heels, or make something funny, or out of nowhere make me cry, I just never knew what was coming next. The Doctor can be clown and hero, often at the same time, and Matt rose to both challenges magnificently.

'And even better than that, given the pressures of this extraordinary show, he is one of the nicest and hardest-working people I have ever had the privilege of knowing. Whatever we threw at him – sometimes literally – his behaviour was always worthy of the Doctor.

'But great actors always know when it's time for the curtain call, so this Christmas prepare for your hearts to break, as we say goodbye to number eleven. Thank you Matt – bow ties were never cooler.

'Of course, this isn't the end of the story, because now the search begins. Somewhere out there right now – all unknowing, just going about their business – is someone who's about to become the Doctor. A life is going to change, and *Doctor Who* will be born all over again! After fifty years, that's still so exciting!'

While fans were still digesting this huge bombshell – which immediately prompted the usual rash of speculation and bookmaker odds-making regarding the possible identity of the new Doctor – 1 June also gave those in Australia and New Zealand a chance to enjoy another big-screen *Doctor Who* double bill, following on from the one back in March. This time the episodes chosen were 'Asylum of the Daleks' and 'The Angels Take Manhattan', which were shown in 48 different cinemas simultaneously. To coincide with this, a *Doctor Who* light-show consisting of a series of specially-created 3D-mapped images was projected onto the façade of the Customs House building in Circular Quay, Sydney. This was created by the Spinifex Group as part of the 18-day Vivid Sydney festival, organised by the New South Wales Government's tourism and major events agency, Destination NSW.

On 7 June, the Queen opened the BBC's new, extended Broadcasting House in central London, and amongst the stars presented to her was Jenna Coleman. This took place in front of a TARDIS police box, and there was also a Dalek lurking nearby. Coleman told BBC News: 'The Queen and I had a conversation about time travel, and I told her I am the Doctor's assistant and we get to travel anywhere in all of time and space, to which she replied, "That must be fun" – to which I replied, "It really is, it's marvellous, not knowing where you're going to be from one week to the next."'

21 June saw the BBC release a 1' 50" duration video in which Matt Smith, standing on a street in Detroit, Michigan, USA, with his hair shorn for his role in the movie *How to Catch a Monster*, thanked Steven Moffat, the *Doctor Who* cast and crew and particularly the show's fans for all of their support over the past four years.

On 3 July, as part of a week's tour of Wales, the Prince of Wales and the Duchess of Cornwall paid an official visit to BBC Roath Lock. They were given a tour of the studios, including the TARDIS control room set, introduced to the Daleks – prompting the Prince to give his own rendition of their famous cry 'Exterminate! – and given displays by the show's costume designer, locations manager, graphic artist, set decorator, and special effects team. They also met some of the apprentices currently in training at the studios, as well as stars Matt Smith and Jenna Coleman. Afterwards, Smith was quoted as saying: 'It was great to welcome the Prince of Wales and the Duchess of Cornwall to set today. Showing them how to fly the TARDIS was a real treat and something I never thought I would be doing when I first took on the role. The Prince of Wales said he remembers watching the show when he was 15 and seemed very knowledgeable on the *Who* history, so it's nice to think they are watching.'

Over the weekend of 6 and 7 July, a faithful recreation of the original 1960s TARDIS control console and roundel-patterned walls, constructed for use in *An Adventure in Space and Time*, went on public display for the first time, at Comic-Con France in Paris, prior to being permanently installed amongst the exhibits at the *Doctor Who Experience* attraction in Cardiff. Writer Mark Gatiss was also present at the event, appearing on a panel and introducing a trailer for the docu-drama. Further interest in the production was generated the following week when the BBC released the first promotional photograph of its star, David Bradley, in costume as William Hartnell playing the Doctor in the recording of *Doctor Who*'s first episode.

On the evening of 13 July and the morning of 14 July, *Doctor Who* returned to the BBC Proms at the Royal Albert Hall in London for the first time since 2010, for two performances of Murray Gold's incidental music from the show, plus some classical pieces, played by the National Orchestra of Wales with the London Philharmonic Choir, conducted by Ben Foster, with soloists Elin Manahan Thomas, Allan Clayton and Kerry Ingram. There was also a special section of electronic music from the classic-era stories, played by original members of the BBC Radiophonic Workshop. As usual at such events, appropriate clips montages were played on big screens, and a host of monsters invaded the auditorium at suitable points. On-stage introductions were made by Matt Smith, Jenna Coleman, Neve McIntosh in costume and prosthetic make-up as Madame Vastra, Dan Starkey in costume and prosthetic make-up as Strax, fifth Doctor actor Peter Davison and Susan Foreman actress Carole Ann Ford. Classic-era composer Dudley Simpson was in the audience for the 13 July performance, as were Steven Moffat and numerous other people connected with the show. There was a live BBC Radio 3 broadcast of that performance, which was also recorded for later BBC One television transmission – which ultimately occurred on 26 August, followed some months later by a commercial release on the *50th Anniversary Collector's Edition* DVD and Blu-ray box set. During the twenty-minute interval, Radio 3 broadcast a documentary called *The Soundworld of Doctor Who*, in which broadcaster Matthew Sweet interviewed the show's sound designers and voice artist Nicholas Briggs.

Other notable features of the Proms event, which attracted much media interest, were the debut performance of 'Song for Fifty', a song specially composed by Gold to mark *Doctor Who*'s fiftieth anniversary, although this piece received only a lukewarm audience reaction; an exclusive 'Strax Field Report' video in which the Sontaran reported to his home planet that he was in a large room full of 'human scum' celebrating the Doctor; and another specially-recorded video in which the Doctor and Clara plan to infiltrate the concert using 'bodyswap' tickets that will allow them to replace two audience members, but this goes wrong and they are instead substituted for two of the orchestra members – this serving as a lead-in to Matt Smith and Jenna Coleman making their first on-stage appearance, still in costume as their respective characters, with the incongruity of Smith's now shorn hair being blamed on the Doctor having bought the bodyswap tickets from a man from 'Space Vegas'.

Two additional pieces of music played at the event were 'You're Going to Have to Take Those Clothes Off' by Gabe Stone and Matthew Owen of Cirencester Deer Park School in Gloucestershire, and 'I Never Know Why, I Only Know Who' by William Davenport and Jordan Picken of the Biddulph High School in Stoke-on-Trent. These were the winning entries in the 14-16 and 11-14 age categories respectively of a BBC Learning competition for schools, which was effectively the successor to the Script to Screen ones held in previous years. The competition had entailed composing a new soundtrack to one of a choice of 'clean' clips from 'The Snowmen', the entries being judged by a panel of music education experts appointed by BBC Proms, taking account of a number of criteria: musical idea, originality, creative use of soundtrack methods, and interpretation of action through soundtrack. The results had been announced at the end of June, and the winners had also had the opportunity to attend a workshop with Ben Foster and *Doctor Who* orchestration coordinator Samuel Thompson, held at the BBC Radiophonic Workshop's original Maida Vale Studios. Stone and Owen were quoted as saying, 'This is an amazing experience and a fantastic opportunity, particularly working with Ben and Sam to gain a real insight into this side of the music world. This experience has inspired us to work in this wonderful field of music-making and we are so looking forward to hearing our piece at the Proms.'

16 July saw the launch of a further anniversary-themed event, this time at London's Heathrow Airport, where visitors over the coming weeks could enjoy appearances by Cybermen and displays of props and memorabilia and have photographs taken in TARDIS photobooths. On 16 July itself, the airport hosted an incidental music performance by the London Philharmonic Orchestra, and *Doctor Who* novelist Jenny T Colgan was on hand to sign books. *Doctor Who* 'passports' were given out,

providing access to a free episode download, information about the airport's *Doctor Who* activities and a free digital copy of the *Doctor Who Adventures* comic. The event was organised by BBC Worldwide in conjunction with the airport authorities. Terminal 5 Operations Director Susan Goldsmith was quoted as saying: 'I am delighted that Heathrow has been chosen to host this much-loved British iconic series. With visitors from over 180 destinations worldwide, as the UK's only hub airport, Heathrow offers a fantastic opportunity to bring the *Doctor Who* experience to an international audience this summer.'

BBC Worldwide's *Annual Review 2012/13*, published this week, again highlighted the extent to which the BBC's commercial revenue depended on *Doctor Who's* success. The show was said to be amongst the 'superbrands' that contributed 27% to the organisation's headline sales – which were 14% down on the previous year, partly due to the fact that, owing to the split series, fewer *Doctor Who* episodes had been produced during this period.

On 22 July, the BBC issued a press release and accompanying publicity photos announcing the fact that the fiftieth anniversary special would feature an appearance by the Doctor's greatest foes, the Daleks. The release read in part:

> The Doctors, Matt Smith, David Tennant and John Hurt, will battle the deadly Daleks, the BBC announces today, in the show's fiftieth anniversary special.
> Returning to BBC One on 23 November, the highly anticipated adventure will star: Matt Smith; Jenna Coleman; David Tennant; Billie Piper; John Hurt and Joanna Page. In a surprise twist in the recent series finale it was revealed John Hurt would be playing a Doctor, alongside Smith and Tennant.
> The Daleks are the second monster to be announced for the [special] and will join the shape-shifting Zygons, which have only appeared in the show once before in 1975. The Daleks were one of the first monsters to terrify audiences in 1963 … cementing their place in British popular culture.
> Steven Moffat, lead writer and executive producer, said:
> 'The Doctor once said that you can judge a man by the quality of his enemies, so it's fitting that for this very special episode, he should be facing the greatest enemies of all.'

The fiftieth anniversary episode was shot earlier this year at

BBC Cymru Wales' Roath Lock Studios in Cardiff and across South Wales. Filming also took place in iconic London locations the Tower of London and Trafalgar Square for a huge stunt, which saw Matt Smith dangling from a TARDIS alongside Nelson's Column.

The latest of the huge San Diego Comic-Con events took place from 18 to 21 July, and again there was a strong *Doctor Who* presence, with Matt Smith, Jenna Coleman, Steven Moffat, Marcus Wilson, Mark Gatiss and David Bradley appearing on a panel hosted by Craig Ferguson. Exclusive video trailers were shown of both the fiftieth anniversary special and *An Adventure in Space and Time* – the first time that footage from either production had been aired publicly. For no apparent reason, the BBC refused to make these trailers available online for fans elsewhere to view, predictably provoking much disgruntlement. Questioned about this in a guest appearance on the 24 July edition of *The Late Late Show with Craig Ferguson*, Matt Smith could only offer the fans his apologies.

On 26 July, BBC Worldwide announced plans for the anniversary special to be broadcast simultaneously by numerous channels around the world. A spokesperson was quoted as saying: 'It's always been our ambition to work with our broadcast partners so that international *Doctor Who* fans can enjoy the fiftieth anniversary special at the same time as the UK. We'll have more details soon about our very exciting global plans for November.' BBC One was expected to broadcast the special in a typical early evening slot, but time zone differences would mean that viewers outside the UK would see the 'simulcast' at various other times of day – in some cases, in the early hours of 24 November.

2 August marked the opening of a three-month-long exhibition at the Museum of London to celebrate the *Radio Times*'s ninetieth anniversary in September, with a special section dedicated to the magazine's many *Doctor Who* covers from the past half-century. Amongst the other exhibits was a life-size Dalek placed against a photographic backdrop of the Houses of Parliament, effectively recreating the award-winning 'Vote Dalek!' cover that the magazine had run back in April 2005. Promoting the exhibition, the latest *Radio Times* edition, published on 30 July, included a two-page feature explaining how *Doctor Who*'s first episode had narrowly missed out on being accorded the prime cover spot back in November 1963, illustrated by a specially-created mock-up of what such a cover might have looked like.

Also on 2 August, it was announced that the identity of the actor cast to play the twelfth Doctor would be revealed the following Sunday, 4 August, in a live programme broadcast at 7.30 pm on BBC One. The BBC released a 20″ duration trailer for the programme, which would be simulcast in America, Canada and Australia. The bookies' favourite for the role was 55-year-old actor Peter Capaldi, who had previously appeared as Caecilius in the *Doctor Who* episode 'The Fires of Pompeii' (2008) and as John Frobisher in the *Torchwood* mini-series 'Children of Earth' (2009), but who was best known to the general viewing public as the foul-mouthed spin doctor Malcolm Tucker in the BBC's political sitcom *The Thick of It* (2005-2012). Indeed, so strong a favourite was Capaldi that by 3 August the betting had been closed.

Sure enough, when *Doctor Who Live: The Next Doctor* went out on 4 August, Capaldi was confirmed as the actor chosen to play the twelfth Doctor. Presented by Zoe Ball, the 31′ 18″ duration programme featured contributions from, amongst others, Capaldi's predecessors Peter Davison, Colin Baker and Matt Smith. Capaldi made his on-stage entrance to rapturous applause, and gripped his lapels in intentional homage to a pose often adopted by the first Doctor, as played by William Hartnell. Interviewed by Ball, he revealed that his agent had broken the news to him that he had won the much-coveted role by greeting him 'Hello, Doctor.'

Supposedly – although the betting suggested otherwise – the advance knowledge of the new Doctor's identity had been confined to only ten people. One of these was the renowned photographer Rankin, who had been commissioned to take an official promotional portrait of the actor for release to the media immediately after the live transmission – which was later revealed to have had an audience of 6.1 million, a 29.8% share of the total viewing audience, peaking at 6.9 million for the actual moment of the big reveal.

Many of the show's past and current stars and production team members quickly joined other celebrities in taking to Twitter to offer Capaldi their congratulations and best wishes. The BBC later claimed that there had been a total of 542,000 tweets reacting to the news, averaging 9,000 a minute and peaking at over 22,000 a minute during the live programme. Rankin's portrait had also been re-tweeted over 25,000 times.

The casting announcement generated a phenomenal volume of press and media coverage, with a number of the UK's national daily newspapers – including *The Times*, the *Daily Telegraph*, the *Guardian*, the

Daily Mail and the *Daily Express* – featuring Rankin's portrait or another photograph of Capaldi on the front page of their 5 August edition. The *Guardian*'s Mark Lawson wrote: 'His primary quality as an actor is danger; during his most vicious riffs as the sewer-mouthed Malcolm Tucker in *The Thick of It*, there frequently seemed a threat that his pulsing facial veins might burst. He was also memorably menacing as the new boss in the second series of the TV newsroom drama *The Hour*. In that sense, Capaldi might have seemed more natural casting for the Time Lord's nemesis, the Master. So the main interest in his portrayal of the Doctor will be whether showrunner Steven Moffat ... encourages him to maintain his signature screen-bursting energy or explore a gentler part of his range. As Capaldi is not only in demand as an actor but also writes and directs, he is giving up a significant amount to fulfil the show's brutal shooting schedules in Cardiff. His casting confirms that, like James Bond, the Doctor has become a role serious actors are happy to take on.'

Steven Moffat was meanwhile asked in a *Radio Times* website interview if he had had a shortlist for the role. He replied: 'Yes. The list went "Peter Capaldi". It was a very short list. [He came on the radar] a fair amount of time ago. I happened to know he's a big fan. There's something very seductive about an utterly brilliant, arresting-looking leading-man actor – one of the most talented actors in Britain – who you happen to know is a big fan of the show. You start to think "Maybe we should so something about that."'

On 15 August, a celebratory *Doctor Who* exhibition opened at the ABC Ultimo Centre in Sydney, Australia. Boasting a large display of props and costumes from the show, including national treasure Kylie Minogue's costume from her role as Astrid in 'Voyage of the Damned' (2007), this free attraction was organised by the Australia and New Zealand branch of BBC Worldwide in partnership with the ABC channel, and would remain open until the end of the following January.

3 September saw Matt Smith attending the *GQ* Men of the Year Awards ceremony at the Royal Opera House in London. Interviewed at the event, he revealed that he would begin recording the 2013 *Doctor Who* Christmas special the following Sunday, 8 September, and that he would have to wear a wig as the Doctor, owing to the fact that his own hair had still not grown back since it was cropped for his *How to Catch a Monster* movie role. The actor then travelled to Cardiff, where the following day he took part in the read-through for the Christmas special. A photo of him holding his copy of the script was posted by the BBC on Twitter.

Doctor Who was named Best Family Drama Series for the fourth year running when the latest *TV Choice* Awards were presented on the evening of 9 September. In addition, the show was given a special Outstanding Achievement Award to mark its fiftieth anniversary. Steven Moffat was on hand to accept the awards, the Outstanding Achievement one being handed to him on stage by Peter Davison. Another former Doctor, Davison's son-in-law David Tennant, was also present at the event, having been named Best Actor for his role in the ITV1 drama *Broadchurch*. When questioned by the media, Moffat, Davison and Tennant were all careful to give away nothing of any significance about the *Doctor Who* anniversary special. On 10 September, however, a prematurely released and quickly withdrawn item on the BBC News website did disclose some further details of the BBC's plans, revealing the special to be called 'The Day of the Doctor', with a 75-minute running time[18], and listing a number of other celebratory programmes in preparation. The following day, a lengthy official BBC press release put meat on the bones of this news leak, giving full details of the anniversary programmes lined up for broadcast across all of the BBC's main channels.[19] Matt Smith was quoted as saying: '"The Day of the Doctor" is nearly here! Hope you all enjoy. There's lots more coming your way, as the countdown to the fiftieth begins now.' Danny Cohen, Director of BBC Television, added: '*Doctor Who* is a titan of British television and I'm incredibly proud to have it on the BBC. It's an astonishing achievement for a drama to reach its fiftieth anniversary. I'd like to thank every person – on both sides of the camera – who has been involved with its creative journey over so many years.'

Eagle-eyed fans spotted that one item included in the original news leak had been omitted from the next day's press release: a BBC Four repeat screening of the very first *Doctor Who* story, '100,000 BC' (1963). This was due to the fact that objections had been raised by Stef Coburn, the son of the story's scriptwriter, the late Anthony Coburn, who was in dispute with the BBC over his belief that his father ought to have owned the rights to the TARDIS. Fortunately, these objections would be eventually disregarded, allowing the repeat to go ahead.

To accompany the press release, the BBC also made available the by-now-expected movie poster-style promotional image for 'The Day of the Doctor'. This showed the tenth and eleventh Doctors standing back to

---

[18] The actual duration would be 76' 38".

[19] Details of all these programmes are given later in the next chapter.

back, with a smaller inset of the John Hurt incarnation walking away from a battle scene including some destroyed Daleks, a police box door and a wall bearing 'Bad Wolf' graffiti.

On 28 September, BBC One ran some 10" duration teasers for 'The Day of the Doctor', featuring the caption '#Save the Day' – a Twitter hashtag that would be used in much of the BBC's subsequent promotion for the special.

The following day, at the annual BAFTA Cymru Awards ceremony, *Doctor Who*'s anniversary was marked by the showing of a video clips montage, although the show failed to win any awards on this occasion.

BBC One's long-running satirical current affairs quiz show *Have I Got News for You* jumped on the *Doctor Who* bandwagon on 30 September when the 4 October start of its forty-sixth series was promoted by way of the release of a television trailer in which team captains Paul Merton and Ian Hislop, each wearing a fourth Doctor-style long, muticoloured scarf, emerged from the TARDIS outside the Houses of Parliament in the year 2063, before deciding to return to 2013.

On 1 October, further details emerged of the planned international simulcast of 'The Day of the Doctor', when the BBC issued a press release that read in part:

From Canada to Colombia, Brazil to Botswana and Myanmar to Mexico, fans in at least 75 countries spanning six continents will be able to enjoy the episode in 2D and 3D at the same time as the UK broadcast, with more countries expected to be confirmed within the next month. The US, Australia and Canada have also signed up for the simulcast, which will be shown in numerous countries across Europe, Latin America and Africa …

On top of the worldwide TV broadcast, hundreds of cinemas in the UK and across the world also plan to screen the hotly-anticipated special episode simultaneously in full 3D, giving fans the opportunity to make an event of the occasion and be part of a truly global celebration for the iconic British drama series. Details about tickets for the anniversary screening will be announced in due course.

Tim Davie, CEO of BBC Worldwide, comments: 'Few TV shows can still lay claim to being appointment viewing but *Doctor Who* takes this to another level. In its fiftieth anniversary year we wanted to create a truly international event for *Doctor Who* fans in as many countries as possible, and the simultaneous broadcast and cinema screening of the special across so many countries will make for a fitting birthday tribute to our Time Lord.'

Steven Moffat ... adds: 'The Doctor has always been a time traveller – now he's travelling time zones. On 23 November, it won't be the bad guys conquering the Earth – everywhere it will be "The Day of the Doctor"!'

The free-to-air 3D coverage will be available to those with access to a 3D TV set and to the BBC's HD Red Button service. This is part of the BBC's two-year trial experimenting with 3D production and distribution, which has also included selected coverage from Wimbledon 2012 and the London 2012 Olympic Games.

5 October was the last day of recording on the 2013 Christmas special (with only some model filming to follow). Alluding to the fact that this marked not only Matt Smith's departure from *Doctor Who* but also his own, series producer Marcus Wilson took to Twitter to tweet: 'So it's goodnight from me, and it's goodnight from him. That's a wrap. Christmas 2013. Thank you all.'

On 10 October, BBC Worldwide held a London press conference, attended by Mark Gatiss and classic-era companion actors Frazer Hines and Deborah Watling, to announce the fantastic news that nine previously missing *Doctor Who* episodes had been recovered from the town of Jos in Nigeria and returned to the BBC by Philip Morris of the Television International Enterprises Archive (TIEA) organisation. The episodes in question – five from 'The Enemy of the World' (1967/68) (completing that story) and four from 'The Web of Fear' (1968) (leaving only the third part of that story missing) – were made available to buy from iTunes from midnight that night, with subsequent DVD releases promised. This amazing news naturally generated much media coverage.

12 October saw Steven Moffat appearing at the *Radio Times*-hosted Cheltenham Literature Festival in a session called 'Sherlock, the Doctor and Me', discussing his work on the two hit shows.

On 15 October, the Australia and New Zealand branch of BBC Worldwide announced that the simulcast of 'The Day of the Doctor' would include some 87 cinema screenings in the former country and some 19 in the latter, all in 3D.

A promotional image of all 11 Doctors standing in line was issued by the BBC on 19 October, accompanying a press release that read in part:

> A specially-created trailer celebrating the last fifty years of *Doctor Who* will air tonight on BBC One, as an exclusive image is revealed today featuring the 11 Doctors.
>
> Travelling through time, fans will be taken on a journey from the very beginning using state-of-the-art technology. The special trailer is set to show all of the Doctors as they first appeared on screen, including William Hartnell in high-res colour for the very first time, as celebrations ramp up to 23 November.
>
> The minute-long trailer will air after *Strictly Come Dancing* tonight on BBC One and will also be available on www.bbc.co.uk/doctorwho

The impressive trailer opened in black and white outside the 76 Totter's Lane junkyard gates seen at the start of the very first episode back in 1963, then quickly switched to colour, presenting a kaleidoscopic CGI montage of images featuring all 11 Doctors (some seen only briefly, and one, the third, represented rather too obviously by a lookalike instead of Jon Pertwee), the Master, K-9, Sarah Jane Smith, Clara, Daleks and various other items closely associated with *Doctor Who*, including a number of different models of the sonic screwdriver. This was accompanied by a voice-over from Matt Smith as the Doctor: 'I've been running all my lives. Through time and space. Every second of every minute of every day for over 900 years. I've fought for peace in a universe at war. Now the time has come to face the choices I have made in the name of the Doctor. Our future depends on one single moment of one impossible day. The day I've been running from all my life. The day of the Doctor.' The final words of this were delivered by Smith direct to camera, then the trailer ended with the anniversary date, '23.11.63', the '11' being substituted by the 'DW' *Doctor Who* logo in a burst of light, and the '#Save the Day' hashtag.

On 22 October, a week after the announcement of the cinema simulcast screenings of 'The Day of the Doctor' 'down under', BBC Worldwide gave details of some 216 screens that would be showing the special in the UK. Two days later, BBC America made a similar announcement, listing 11 major city cinemas that would be joining the simulcast, with many others following on two days later, on 25 November.

Meanwhile, 23 October saw Big Finish release the limited edition CD box set and digital download versions of their own anniversary special audio adventure, 'The Light at the End', featuring a team-up by all five surviving classic-era Doctors: Tom Baker, Peter Davison, Colin Baker, Sylvester McCoy and Paul McGann. The standard CD version and a vinyl album version would follow later.

As the last week of October drew to a close with the BBC giving further advance publicity to *An Adventure in Space and Time*, issuing several promotional images and a press release of interview quotes from the docu-drama's key cast members and writer Mark Gatiss, everything was set for the start of the month that would bring, in *Doctor Who* terms, the party to end all parties.

Chapter Seven
Party Time!

The first day of the anniversary month brought further news about the official *Doctor Who* Celebration event planned for 22 to 24 November. Dozens of guests from all eras of the show's history were lined up to attend, and 'The Day of the Doctor' was due to be screened as part of the Saturday evening simulcast – although, to the consternation of many fans who had booked to attend on that day, it was stated that tickets for the screening would be allocated on a first come, first served basis, as not everyone could be accommodated.

By the end of the week, BBC America had announced that it would show *An Adventure in Space and Time* on 21 November, and had released extensive information about the background to the docu-drama. Back in the UK, 6 November saw the Royal Welsh College of Music and Drama in Cardiff host *An Evening with Steven Moffat*, in which the showrunner, interviewed on stage by Boyd Hilton, gave the packed audience his thoughts on *Doctor Who*'s long history. A 20' 39" duration video of highlights from this event would be made available to view on the BBC iPlayer a week later.

On 7 November the BBC put out further publicity for 'The Day of the Doctor' in the form of short video interviews with Steven Moffat, Matt Smith, David Tennant, Jenna Coleman and Joanna Paige. On the same date, they also released a new, 40" duration video of Matt Smith as the Doctor speaking straight to camera, enthusing about hashtags and encouraging people to use '#Save the Day'. This tied in with the launch of a new BBC-created website, www.doctorwhosavetheday.com, on which fans could submit their own *Doctor Who* messages, pictures and videos. 7 November also saw the debut of a 25" duration trailer for an upcoming BBC Two factual programme, *The Science of Doctor Who*.

The following day, another new video was released; this one a 13" duration teaser clip from 'The Day of the Doctor', of a large painting being unveiled before the eleventh Doctor and Clara in a gallery, and Clara saying 'But that's not possible.' It was also announced that on the anniversary date, BBC Three would be showing another *Doctor Who Live* programme, this one called *The Afterparty*, although no further details were provided at this stage.

In the fortnight leading up to the anniversary date, a TARDIS police box model would be making background appearances in various BBC programmes, the first of which was the 8 November edition of *The Graham Norton Show*, where the model was positioned behind the host as he chatted to his guests.

On 9 November came the first full television trailer for 'The Day of the Doctor'. Lasting 40", this presented an exciting collection of clips and ended with a caption of the anniversary date and the '#Save the Day' hashtag.

The programme introduction to the 10 November edition of BBC One's *Strictly Come Dancing* was briefly interrupted by a video clip of Matt Smith as the Doctor in the TARDIS control room, tapping his wristwatch and saying 'The clock's ticking.' This would be repeated during a number of other programme introductions over the coming days, and a 'clean' version was also placed online by the BBC. Between *Strictly Come Dancing* and the next programme, *Atlantis*, viewers were then treated to another trailer for the anniversary special. This one lasted a full 1' 19" seconds, and featured many previously unseen clips.

On 12 November, *An Adventure in Space and Time* was given a preview screening at BFI Southbank in London, with many of its cast and behind-the-scenes contributors present, along with various other *Doctor Who* luminaries. The audience were sufficiently impressed by the docu-drama to give it a standing ovation at its conclusion, prior to an on-stage question-and-answer session chaired by Matthew Sweet. A 10' 04" duration video of highlights from the question-and-answer session would be uploaded to the BFI's YouTube channel the following month.

14 November brought the most significant anniversary-related events yet. First, the minisode 'The Night of the Doctor' was made available to view on the BBC iPlayer and also released online, delighting fans with the surprise return of Paul McGann as the eighth Doctor.[20] Then, at 9.00 pm that evening, the first of the televised anniversary tie-in programmes, the

---

[20] See the relevant entry in the 'Episode Guide' section below for further details.

59' duration *The Science of Doctor Who*, went out on BBC Two.[21] This took the form of a presentation delivered from the lecture theatre of the Royal Institution in London by Professor Brian Cox – who had made a cameo appearance in the Series Seven episode 'The Power of Three', and had also appeared in *Doctor Who Live: The Next Doctor*. Aided by celebrity guests in the audience, Cox looked in a light-hearted way at some of the questions raised by the Doctor's adventures in time and space, such as: Can you really travel in time? Does extraterrestrial life exist in our galaxy? And how do you build something as fantastical as the TARDIS? The programme opened with a short, specially-recorded drama segment of Cox entering the TARDIS, mistakenly believing it to be his make-up room, and being greeted by the Doctor. Continuations of this storyline then appeared at intervals during the programme, with the Doctor taking Cox on a trip in the TARDIS, showing him a Silent on one of its monitors and discussing with him its bigger-inside-than-out dimensions and black hole power source. The programme closed with the Doctor fixing Cox's make-up, and Cox then exiting the ship. Cox naturally wrote all the factual science material himself, but the *Doctor Who* drama segments were written by Steve Thompson and directed by Ashley Way. The programme, which was executive produced by Andrew Cohen and produced by Milla Harrison-Hanley, was later included on the *50th Anniversary Collector's Edition* DVD and Blu-ray box set, in slightly edited form and retitled *A Night With the Stars: The Science of Doctor Who*.

The transmission of *The Science of Doctor Who* also provided the opportunity for the debut airing of a 30" duration trailer for *An Adventure in Space and Time*.

This year's *Children in Need* telethon, broadcast on BBC One on the evening of 15 November, again had some *Doctor Who* involvement. A 2' 00" duration clip from 'The Day of the Doctor' was shown, concluding with the eleventh Doctor's first meeting with the tenth and the caption 'The Doctors Will Return – 23rd November 2013', and a *Doctor Who* set visit was put up for auction on eBay to raise money for the charity.

Also on the evening of 15 November, BBC Three launched a *Doctor Who: Greatest Monsters & Villains* weekend. This took the form of a series of repeat screenings of ten 21st Century *Doctor Who* episodes, each preceded by a short introduction in which comedian and actor Joel

---

[21] This programme is not to be confused with the BBC America documentary of the same title, broadcast on 4 August 2012.

Dommett spoke about the featured monster or villain.

16 November marked the start of a week-long promotional tour of Wales by the TARDIS police box. Starting in Holyhead, it would conclude in Cardiff on the anniversary date itself. The show's new executive producer Brian Minchin was quoted as saying: 'Doctor Who fans across Wales will get a unique opportunity to get up close to the Doctor's time machine and be part of our anniversary celebrations. Look out for it in a town near you.'

As the BBC continued to promote the forthcoming transmission of 'The Day of the Doctor', releasing a number of batches of publicity images from the special, the 18 November edition of the street magazine *The Big Issue* boasted a *Doctor Who* cover, with pictures of all eleven Doctors and a trio of Daleks. Inside the magazine were details of a prize draw to win £1,800-worth of *Doctor Who* merchandise. *Doctor Who* was also featuring increasingly heavily in the local and national press, with coverage appearing in the *Independent*, the *Daily Mirror* and the *Daily Mail*, amongst others.

Also on 18 November, BBC One's *Breakfast* programme presented a 3' 55" duration report by entertainment correspondent by Lizo Mzimba, giving a behind-the-scenes glimpse of the making of 'The Day of the Doctor', with interview contributions from Matt Smith, David Tennant, John Hurt and Jenna Coleman. Later in the day, the Queen's daughter-in-law, Sophie, Countess of Wessex, hosted a highly prestigious anniversary reception for *Doctor Who* in Buckingham Palace's Bow Room, in which a police box and some Daleks had been installed for the occasion. Guests included Doctors Tom Baker, Peter Davison, John Hurt and Matt Smith, Steven Moffat, Catherine Tate, Jenna Coleman and BBC Director General Tony Hall and Director of Television Danny Cohen. They were joined by children from two Cardiff schools, Gladstone Primary and Mount Stuart Primary, who had won a local competition to design a TARDIS for the Queen. The event was later mentioned in a *Doctor Who* report included in BBC One's *The Six O'Clock News*.

The same day, Steven Moffat was interviewed on BBC Radio 4's *Today* programme, and BBC Radio 1 ran a report on *An Adventure in Space and Time*, including interviews with some of the cast. The BBC also released online a 1' 18" duration teaser clip from the docu-drama. BBC America got in on the act too, making available two videos: one, duration 18", of Arthur Darvill, Series Six guest star Mark Sheppard, Karen Gillan and Alex Kingston all wishing *Doctor Who* a happy fiftieth; the other, duration

30", of 'The Bells of Saint John' guest star Sir Ian McKellen expressing his affection for the show in general, and for Matt Smith in particular.

That evening saw the debut transmission of the BBC Three documentary *Doctor Who: The Ultimate Guide*.[22] This 118' duration programme, produced and directed by Tom Cohen for BBC Events Production in London, presented an overview of *Doctor Who* by way of clips from all eras of the show's history coupled with interview contributions from many of its past and present stars and various celebrities. Like *The Science of Doctor Who*, the programme also included some specially-recorded drama sequences. In this case there were just two, bookending the main content. In the first, lasting about two minutes, the standard *Doctor Who* opening title sequence is followed by Clara entering the TARDIS console room with her bags packed for a promised holiday, only to find that the Doctor has accidentally erased his own memory. In order to help him remember who he is and all about his life, she retrieves his 1,200 Year Diary from beneath the console. In the second segment, lasting about one and a half minutes, the Doctor tells Clara that he now remembers everything: 'It's like seeing it all for the first time. Seeing me. Me. The Doctor. Eleven faces, hundreds, thousands of years of space and time.' At first, he wonders how he can go on, when he has encountered so much death and lost so many friends, but Clara reassures him that he has saved billions of lives and always helps people wherever he goes. They set off for their holiday, the TARDIS spinning away through the time vortex. This documentary was subsequently given a commercial release on the *50th Anniversary Collector's Edition* DVD and Blu-ray box set.

On 19 November, Jenna Coleman was a guest on ITV1's *Daybreak* programme, being interviewed about 'The Day of the Doctor' in a roughly four-minute slot. The BBC meanwhile released two further promotional videos: a 30" duration sneak peak clip of 'The Day of the Doctor', of Clara being greeted by the Doctor on joining him in the TARDIS at the start of the adventure; and a very jokey 1' 11" piece of David Tennant supposedly introducing the special. Also published on this date, the latest issue of *Radio Times*, covering the week of 23 to 29

---

[22] Not to be confused with the *Doctor Who Confidential* special of the same title, broadcast just before 'The Parting of the Ways' on 18 June 2005, or with the BBC America documentary of the same title, broadcast on 4 April 2010 with a view to introducing US fans to the show.

November, came with an astonishing choice of 12 covers, one for each Doctor (including John Hurt as the War Doctor) – by far the most cover variants ever offered for a single issue. Inside the magazine there were 26 pages of *Doctor Who* features, including interviews with Matt Smith, David Tennant and John Hurt, pieces by Steven Moffat and BBC Director General Tony Hall, a guide to all the Doctors, and a gallery of all fifty of *Radio Times*'s *Doctor Who* covers over the years. The rival *TV Times* listings magazine also got in on the act, although in their case the eleven Doctors (omitting John Hurt) were grouped onto a relatively modest four cover choices.

Jenna Coleman was on interview duty again on 20 November, when she and John Hurt promoted 'The Day of the Doctor' on that evening's edition of BBC One's *The One Show*, which was a *Doctor Who* special. Steven Moffat was also interviewed, speaking live from the TARDIS console room set in Cardiff, and the revived Radiophonic Workshop, featuring composer Mark Ayres and one-time members of the famous BBC electronic sound studio, were on hand in *The One Show* studio to play the programme out with a rendition of the *Doctor Who* theme music.

Earlier in the day, the BBC had released via iTunes another minisode effectively serving as a prequel to 'The Day of the Doctor'. Entitled 'The Last Day', this was available to view free of charge – although, due to an error on the part of iTunes, the UK store initially listed it as costing £2.49.[23] Anyone who had paid this charge later received a refund. The minisode would later be included on the anniversary special's DVD and Blu-ray releases.

Meanwhile, ITV1's *This Morning* had run an item on *Doctor Who* memorabilia, and Mark Gatiss had been interviewed on BBC Radio 2's *Simon Mayo's Drivetime* programme, speaking about the fiftieth anniversary and *An Adventure in Space and Time*.

Many of the BBC's regional radio stations had also been featuring *Doctor Who* content over the past week, and on 21 November there were reports on BBC Radio Manchester, BBC Radio Sheffield, BBC Radio Solent, BBC Radio Norfolk and BBC Radio Scotland. BBC Radio Wales dedicated a significant portion of its daytime schedule to the show, with two of its regular programmes, presented by Jason Mohammad and Eleri Siôn respectively, coming live from *The Doctor Who Experience* in Cardiff.

---

[23] See the relevant entry in the 'Episode Guide' section for further details of 'The Last Day'.

BBC Radio Wales Editor Steve Austins was quoted in advance as saying: 'I'm thrilled we're going to celebrate this truly Welsh success story with the Radio Wales *Doctor Who* Day. [The show's] return in 2005 marked the start of BBC Cymru Wales's drama success story, with programmes like *Doctor Who* now viewed by millions all over the world. It's fitting therefore that we pay tribute not only to the Doctor but also to all those involved in making the series from our Roath Lock studios in Cardiff Bay. I'd say it's one of the great Welsh success stories of recent years.' Jenna Coleman and Steven Moffat were amongst the guests featured from 10.00 am on the show presented by Mohammad, who had previously made several cameo appearances as a newsreader in both *Doctor Who* and *The Sarah Jane Adventures*. Siôn's show, which went out from 1.00 pm, had a discussion with *Doctor Who* location manager Iwan Roberts and an exclusive look behind the scenes at the BBC National Orchestra of Wales's recording of the incidental music for 'The Day of the Doctor', including interviews with composer Murray Gold and conductor Ben Foster.

On BBC Radio 1, Jenna Coleman was a guest on Nick Grimshaw's morning show, and Steven Moffat was interviewed on Richard Bacon's afternoon one. 21 November was also the date on which BBC Radio 2 broadcast two *Doctor Who*-related programmes. The first was *The Blagger's Guide to Doctor Who*, in which broadcaster David Quantick gave a quick-fire summation of the show, aiming to provide answers to questions such as: Why do Americans think Tom Baker still plays the Doctor? How many Doctors have there really been? And were the Daleks really named after an encyclopaedia volume? The second was the more substantial 90-minute anniversary documentary entitled *Who is the Doctor?*. Written and produced by Malcolm Prince and presented by Russell Tovey – who had played Midshipman Frame in 'Voyage of the Damned' (2007), and had also been heard narrating BBC Two's *Doctor Who: The Ultimate Guide* three days earlier – this gave a good overview of *Doctor Who*'s fifty year history, featuring newly-recorded interviews with numerous stars, production team members and BBC executives, along with archive audio clips and incidental music extracts. A CD and digital download release of the documentary was at one point planned for 27 November, but this unfortunately fell through, owing to the fact that AudioGo, the company responsible for the commercial release of BBC audio product at that time, had gone into administration at the end of October.

Also on 21 November, the BBC placed online a 59" duration video introduction to 'The Day of the Doctor', including comments from Jenna

Coleman, David Tennant and Matt Smith. Meanwhile, on television, CBBC's *Blue Peter* presented the first of two live *Doctor Who* specials. This featured the launch of a competition to design a new sonic device for use by Strax, Madame Vastra or Jenny, with the promise that the winning gadget would actually feature in *Doctor Who* the following year. There were three age categories in the competition – six to eight years, nine to 11 years and 12 to 15 years – and all entries would be considered by a panel of judges including *Blue Peter* editor Ewan Vinnicombe and series producer Ellen Evans, CBBC presenter Chris Johnson and *Doctor Who* showrunner Steven Moffat, producer Nikki Wilson, production designer Michael Pickwoad and brand manager Edward Russell. The results were due to be announced in *Blue Peter*'s Christmas show on 19 December, and the winning designer would be invited to Cardiff to see his or her gadget being used on the *Doctor Who* set, with three runners-up each receiving a framed picture including their competition entry and a signed picture of the actor for whom they designed their device.

Arguably, though, the most significant of all the many *Doctor Who*-related events of 21 November came at 9.00 pm, when BBC Two broadcast *An Adventure in Space and Time*, which had been promoted earlier in the day with an appearance by its star, David Bradley, on BBC One's *Breakfast* programme.[24] The broadcast was immediately followed by an extra programme called *William Hartnell – The Original*, a 5' 00" duration mini-documentary about the actor who had brought the first Doctor to life. Online, the BBC released a 10' 52" duration video, presented by Carole Ann Ford, giving a behind-the-scenes look at the making of the docu-drama. Both the mini-documentary and the behind-the scenes video were later included on the docu-drama's DVD release, and again on the *50th Anniversary Collector's Edition* DVD and Blu-ray box set.

The same evening, on BBC Four, the promised repeat screening of all four episodes of '100,000 BC' took place (although the dispute between the BBC and the late scriptwriter Antony Coburn's son Stef meant that, unlike most programmes, they sadly could not be made available to view on the iPlayer service afterwards); and on BBC Three there was a repeat of the *Doctor Who* Proms broadcast originally shown in August.

On 22 November, the ambitious official *Doctor Who* Celebration event got under way at London's Excel Centre. Over the course of the Friday,

---

[24] See Appendix A for more information on *An Adventure in Space and Time*.

Saturday and Sunday, attendees would be able to enjoy a plethora of activities, displays, presentations, screenings, autograph and photo opportunities, merchandise stalls and guest panel interviews, with appearances by a whole host of production personnel and stars, including no fewer than five Doctors: Tom Baker, Peter Davison, Colin Baker, Sylvester McCoy and Matt Smith. The event was designed such that the same activities and panels were generally repeated on each of the three days, meaning that fans who attended on only one would still get to see most of what was on offer – although some guests, such as Tom Baker, were able to participate only on certain dates. While the event was still in progress, the BBC placed online a couple of short videos recorded at the venue, giving a flavour of some of the activities and including comments from attendees.

Meanwhile, the incredible intensity of anniversary-related media interest in *Doctor Who* continued. Radio coverage today included an appearance by Matt Smith on Nick Grimshaw's BBC Radio 1 show, and guest spots for numerous former *Doctor Who* actors and production team members throughout the day on both BBC Radio Essex and BBC Radio Norfolk. On television, BBC One's *Breakfast* programme had a *Doctor Who* feature by arts editor Will Gompertz and a brief interview with Matt Smith, speaking from the Celebration event, and ITV1's rival *Daybreak* programme also had a *Doctor Who* report and a preview of 'The Day of the Doctor'. A rare sour note was sounded by the *Sunday Mirror*'s television critic Kevin O'Sullivan when, during his regular *Talking Telly* slot in Channel 5's *The Wright Stuff* show, he ventured the opinion that *Doctor Who* had been accorded too much media attention over the previous fortnight. Then, that evening's pre-recorded edition of BBC One's *The Graham Norton Show* had both Matt Smith and David Tennant in conversation with the host.

The most significant of this day's broadcasts, though, was BBC Two's 9.30 pm debut screening of *Me, You and Doctor Who*. A BBC Scotland production, directed by Jude Ho and written and presented by Matthew Sweet, this 59' 12" duration special edition of the channel's flagship arts round-up *The Culture Show* took an in-depth look at *Doctor Who* from the standpoint of its importance within British popular culture. Highlighting the contributions of some of the often unsung talents who pioneered *Doctor Who*'s innovative storytelling, music and design, it incorporated numerous clips from the fifty years' worth of adventures, along with a selection of specially-conducted and archive interviews with stars, production team members and celebrity fans. At the time of writing, this insightful programme has sadly not received a commercial release.

22 November also brought the news that the *Radio Times*'s famous 'Vote Dalek!' composite from the end of April 2005 had been judged the best of ten magazine covers nominated for the Professional Publishers' Association's Cover of the Century award – perhaps unsurprisingly, as it had previously topped the same organisation's Best Magazine Cover of All Time poll back in 2008.

As 23 November – the anniversary day itself – began, the latest of Graham Norton's three-hour BBC Radio 2 morning shows was broadcast live from the Celebration event, where in between the music selections the presenter chatted with some of the assembled fans and stars, including Tom Baker. Another familiar face present at the ExCel Centre was entertainment correspondent Lizo Mzimba, delivering live reports for BBC One's *Breakfast* programme, which also featured in-studio discussions about *Doctor Who*. The Saturday editions of most of the national daily newspapers also carried *Doctor Who* items of one sort or another within their pages.

In another development that morning, a special *Doctor Who* display opened at the National Media Museum in Bradford. This had been originally planned to run from 26 October to 3 November, when it would have begun with a week of family fun activities coinciding with school half-term holidays, but had been delayed until the anniversary date, and would remain open until 9 February 2014. Exhibition curator Toni Booth was quoted in advance as saying: 'Over the past few weeks it has become very apparent that the influence of the Doctor extends into many parts of people's lives – I have heard about marriage proposals at a *Doctor Who* exhibition in Blackpool and another fan confessing to me, that in life, "I often ask myself: WWTDD? (What would the Doctor do?)" The stories and objects in the exhibition will show just how intertwined into their everyday lives the Doctor has become for so many people. We have visited a number of superfans at home and they have simply incredible collections of *Doctor Who*-related objects. We hope to give a real insight into this ultra-dedicated few, as well as display the objects that mean the most to them from the hundreds of items they have amassed.'

In the afternoon, the BBC released a 32" duration video of Steven Moffat acknowledging the huge impact *Doctor Who* had made on his life and wishing the show a happy anniversary. Then, at 4.00 pm on BBC Radio 4 Extra, the highlight of a week-long season of *Doctor Who* programming – which consisted mostly of broadcasts of selected Big Finish audio dramas and other pre-existing material – was the specially-produced three-hour-long documentary *Who Made Who*. Presented by Tracy-Ann Oberman, who had played Torchwood's Yvonne Hartman in 'Army of Ghosts' / 'The Parting of the Ways' (2006), this looked back to *Doctor Who*'s roots in 1960s Britain and presented archive audio clips and newly-recorded interviews, including with William Hartnell's grand-daughter Jessica Carney and writer Charlie Higson, whose *Doctor Who* short story 'The Beast of Babylon' had been published by Puffin in e-book back in September. Although it has not so far been given a commercial release, this documentary was subsequently made available to listen to on the BBC's YouTube channel.

Over on television, CBBC's *Blue Peter* that morning presented the second of its two *Doctor Who* special editions. Presenters Barney Harwood, Lindsey Russell and Radzi Chinyanganya were joined by aliens and monsters in the studio, and the audience were challenged to design their own alien live on air. Viewers' questions were answered by Matt Smith and Jenna Coleman, and instructions were given on how to make cushions (to hide behind when watching scary bits) and Dalek cupcakes.

Another CBBC show devoting its 23 November edition to *Doctor Who* was *12 Again*, the premise of which involved celebrity guests recalling what life was like when they were 12 years old. Beginning at 2.30 pm, this 28' 11" duration programme featured contributions from CBBC presenter and *Doctor Who* fan Chris Johnson, impressionist Jon Culshaw, Tommy Knight (Luke Smith in *The Sarah Jane Adventures*), Warwick Davis (Porridge in 'Nightmare in Silver'), Neve McIntosh (Madame Vastra), Dan Starkey (Strax), Louise Jameson (classic-era companion Leela) and seventh Doctor Sylvester McCoy.

At approximately 5:15 pm on the Saturday, an announcement was made over the public address system at the ExCel event: 'Ladies and gentlemen. Boys and girls. Doctors, monsters and companions, past, present and future. At precisely 5.16 and 20 seconds, fifty years ago today a BBC announcer said the words: "… and now the first of a new series". Ladies and gentlemen, the moment is upon us. *Doctor Who* is fifty years old. Happy Birthday *Doctor Who*!' At which point everyone present at the event paused to applaud and cheer in celebration. It was a lovely moment.

The main event of the day was, of course, the worldwide simulcast and multi-cinema screening of 'The Day of the Doctor' at 7.50 pm UK time.[25] Immediately after this ended, BBC One promoted the 2013 Christmas special with a 10" duration teaser trailer featuring the Doctor, Daleks, a Cyberman, a Silent and Weeping Angels, and captions reading, 'This Christmas Silence Will Fall'. More substantially, the BBC Red Button service broadcast two follow-up programmes: first *Behind the Lens*, a behind-the-scenes look at the making of 'The Day of the Doctor', and then the humorous tie-in *The Five(ish) Doctors Reboot*[26]. More substantial than the similar videos that had accompanied the Series Seven episodes, with a 13' 09" running time, *Behind the Lens* was also made available to view online, as was an 18" duration deleted scene from 'The Day of the Doctor'. *The Five(ish) Doctors Reboot* was subsequently made available to watch via the BBC iPlayer. *Behind the Lens* and *The Five(ish) Doctors Reboot* would later be released commercially – the first on both the special's individual DVD and Blu-ray releases and then as extras on the *50th Anniversary Collector's Edition* DVD and Blu-ray box set, the second on just the latter – but strangely the deleted scene would go unreleased.

BBC Three meanwhile presented *Doctor Who Live: The Afterparty*. This 59' 16" duration BBC Events production, produced by Russell Minton and directed by Victoria Simpson, was broadcast from BFI Southbank and featured guest appearances by a huge gathering of *Doctor Who* stars, production team members and fans, who had just viewed 'The Day of the Doctor' at the venue, having in most cases travelled across there from the Celebration event earlier in the day. The general party atmosphere of the occasion, coupled with the pitfalls of live broadcasting, unfortunately made for a rather shambolic programme. Many of the guests, including a large number of former companion actors and actresses, were given little or no chance to speak, and sometimes referred to only by their character names, and the questions posed by presenters Zoe Ball and Rick Edwards were very much skewed toward soliciting reactions to the anniversary special. While this did afford Tom Baker his first opportunity to speak freely about his surprise cameo appearance at the end of the story, the overall impression given was of a lack of respect toward the show's earlier eras. The absolute nadir came with a live satellite link-up with two members of the popular boy band One Direction in Los Angeles. As the band members had not seen 'The Day of the Doctor', there was little they

---

[25] See the relevant 'Episode Guide' entry below for further details.
[26] See Appendix B for further details.

could say about it, and the link-up was plagued by technical problems, which at one point led to Steven Moffat being seen holding his head in his hands in mock despair. No commercial release of the programme was forthcoming.

This rather unfortunate conclusion to the day's events could not, however, spoil things for *Doctor Who*'s legion of fans worldwide who, through the hugely ambitious and groundbreaking simulcast of 'The Day of the Doctor', had been given an unprecedented opportunity to come together and share in their celebration of an anniversary that, to those who had seen or been involved in the show's relatively humble launch way back in 1963, would surely have seemed like pure fantasy.

Chapter Eight
End of Eleven

The slew of media and fan reviews that appeared in the wake of 'The Day of the Doctor' were overwhelmingly positive. The Den of Geek website's Simon Brew commented: 'In 2013, Steven Moffat promised us a story that would change the Doctor forever. And that's pretty much what we got. From the off, it was clear that this had labour of love stamped throughout it, with the old titles (adorable touch) contrasting neatly with the more modern subsequent sight of Matt Smith hanging off the TARDIS – courtesy of the always-welcome UNIT – whilst being flown over London. Then, by the time the new-style end credits and reworked theme tune were over, it turned out we were going to get more Doctors than we were originally promised. It was impossible to feel short-changed.'

Equally enthusiastic was the *Los Angeles Times*'s television critic Robert Lloyd, who wrote in his 24 November piece: 'It was a great episode, I thought, silly and lovely by turns, full of great lines, most of which would wither out of context ("Regeneration, it's a lottery" – classic!), with the temporal chutes and ladders and four-dimensional farce that have marked current showrunner Steven Moffat's scripts since he was writing for former showrunner and *Who* re-originator Russell T Davies. (Here he thinks up clever things to do with Time Lord paintings). There were riffs on Tennant's skinniness, Smith's chin, Eccleston's ears, sonic screwdrivers, timey-wimeyness, big red buttons and the roundels in the walls of the TARDIS. And there was Billie Piper too, not in her old role as tenth Doctor companion Rose Tyler, exactly, but the living expression of a weapon so advanced that it had developed a conscience … And most miraculously, there was Tom Baker, who played the fourth Doctor, walking in at the end, when the hurly burly was done, possibly as the Doctor's older self, and possibly as his younger, and maybe neither.'

One of the few dissatisfied voices was the *Daily Mail*'s Christopher Stevens, who wrote in his 25 November piece: 'Really, I should have known better. The perennial small boy in my head, the one who still watches scary telly through the cracks between his fingers, had been hopping with excitement for months: David Tennant was to return for one episode as the Doctor. Better still, this mega-budget, feature-length show celebrating half a century of *Doctor Who* would co-star John Hurt as another, darker incarnation of the character. It promised to be fabulous. And, of course, it wasn't. It was patchy, it was cobbled together and, despite some excellent moments, it was a rotten disappointment.'

With the anniversary special now out of the way, and just over a month to go before the Christmas special went out, media coverage of *Doctor Who* understandably quietened down considerably from the extraordinary level it had reached during the first three weeks of November. There were still however occasional developments to interest the fans.

On 24 November, BBC Radio Norfolk's midday programme included a collection of *Doctor Who* anecdotes from around the county, while BBC Radio 6's evening *Freak Zone* programme, presented by Stuart Maconie, ran an item on the BBC Radiophonic Workshop, with a strong *Doctor Who* element. The following evening, BBC Radio 1 was a little late to the party in presenting its own contribution to the *Doctor Who* anniversary celebrations. Originally pencilled in for transmission the previous week, the 60' 22" duration documentary *The Story of Trock* looked at the phenomenon of Time Lord Rock (Trock); that is, rock music with lyrics inspired by *Doctor Who*. At the time of writing, this programme has not received a commercial release, but it has been made available to listen to on the SoundCloud audio distribution website by its independent producers, 2ZY.

Also on 24 November, the BBC issued a slightly tweaked version of the promotional image, originally made available on 19 October, of all 11 Doctors standing in line, plus a new version incorporating John Hurt's War Doctor into the line-up. Speaking at a press conference on the final day of the official *Doctor Who* Celebration event, Steven Moffat addressed the question of how the War Doctor's introduction affected the numbering of the Doctors: 'He's just the Doctor. Matt Smith's Doctor is the eleventh Doctor, however there is no such character as the eleventh Doctor – he's just the Doctor – that's what he calls himself. The numbering doesn't matter, except for those lists that you and I have been making for many years. So I've given you the option of not counting John Hurt numerically – he's the War Doctor.' Moffat also spoke about Tom

Baker's cameo appearance in 'The Day of the Doctor', and the absence of the other classic era Doctors: 'Tom didn't want to come and do a long thing and he didn't want to put the old costume on. He didn't want to do any of that, but his agent said that he wasn't against the idea of doing a short appearance ... You can't have scenes with around 11 or 12 people – you can't do it. To have the longest-standing Doctor make an appearance and be the one who briefs the new Doctor on where to go ... well, it's irresistible, isn't it? You get to hear that voice again! It was just wonderful.'

The final day of the Celebration event also saw two guest panels take place on which Matt Smith, Jenna Coleman, Steven Moffat and director Nick Hurran were interviewed by Matthew Sweet about the anniversary special – something they had been unable to discuss freely on the first two days, prior to its transmission. A 30' 29" video compiled from these two panels would be placed online by the BBC on 20 December.

27 November saw the launch of a new, free-to-play match-3 mobile role playing video game, *Doctor Who: Legacy*. This was developed by Tiny Rebel Games and Seed Studio for both Android and iOS operating systems. Players were invited to build a team of their favourite companions and allies drawn from the whole history of the show, to face the Doctor's most notorious enemies and relive his greatest triumphs. Initially the game focused on episodes and characters from the two most recent series, but more would be added as time went on. A new score by acclaimed video game composer Chris Huelsbeck accompanied the action, although the Murray Gold theme arrangement was retained. Lee Cummings, Creative Director and Co-Founder of Tiny Rebel Games, said: 'With decades of epic adventures to draw from, *Doctor Who: Legacy* is a loving homage created by loyal Whovians, and is rich in the show's creative legacy and fun. Combining easy to learn, hard to master mechanics with beloved characters and cunning villains, *Doctor Who: Legacy* will be a treat for fans, casual players and even the most hard-core gamers alike. The game also has a Twitter account, @DoctorWhoLegacy for updates.'

On 30 November, the latest *Radio Times*, detailing programmes for the week of 7 to 13 December, boasted a *Doctor Who* cover – only a fortnight after the fiftieth anniversary special issue with its 12 variant covers. This one, previewing the forthcoming Christmas special, presented an image of the Doctor being confronted by two new paradigm Daleks – a red one and a blue one – with snowflakes falling around them. The headline was

'Exterminate!', and inside the magazine was what was described as 'The Doctor's last stand – Matt Smith's final interview.'

In the first week of December, the BBC released further details and promotional photos for the Christmas special, the title of which was now confirmed as 'The Time of the Doctor'. 4 December saw the debut of a 35" duration trailer for some of the BBC's Christmas programming highlights, including a couple of *Doctor Who* clips, and 5 December brought the release of several variants of the movie poster-style image for the special. Then, on 11 December, there followed a full 30" duration trailer.

11 December also saw the advent of *Say What You See*, a new *Doctor Who* game app created by Big Ideas Digital and published by BBC Worldwide. This consisted of 150 cryptic pictures suggesting *Doctor Who*-related words or phrases that could be characters, gadgets, episode titles or monsters. Solving a puzzle rewarded players with a trivia-filled fact file. Available on iOS, Android, and Kindle Fire, the app boasted retina-quality screens painted by concept artist Ryan Firchau, with the artwork taking players on a journey through three iconic *Doctor Who* locations: Gallifrey, Totter's Lane and inside the TARDIS. Big Ideas Digital director Jon Hamblin was quoted as saying: 'There have been many *Doctor Who* games in the past but this is the first that covers the entire span of the show's history, referencing episodes, characters and monsters from every one of its fifty years. If this isn't the first game to appeal to old-school, hard-core fans just as much as younger fans of modern *Who* then I'll eat my Tom Baker scarf!'

The following day, the BBC issued a full media pack for 'The Time of the Doctor'. This included interview quotes from Steven Moffat, Matt Smith, Jenna Coleman and guest star Orla Brady. Asked how it felt to be making his final appearance as the Doctor, Smith – whose interview was also presented in video form – said: 'It felt very emotional to be doing my final episode. My mother is mortified. Honestly, she was at the front of campaigning for me to stay, and wasn't happy when I said I was going to leave. But, when you've got to go, you've got to go. Of course, it's very sad for me in many ways because everything is the last time. It's the last read-through, the last time I put on the bow tie and the last scene in the TARDIS. But the show is about change, and I had lunch with Peter Capaldi shortly after the announcement and I think he's just going to be incredible. He has the most brilliant ideas. As a fan, I'm genuinely excited to see what he's going to do, because I think he's going to do something extraordinary.' Setting the scene for the eleventh Doctor's swansong,

Moffat said: 'It's his final battle and he's been fighting it for a while. The Doctor is facing the joint challenge of a mysterious event in space that has summoned lots of aliens to one place and helping Clara cook Christmas dinner. There are also elements from every series of Matt's Doctor, which will come to a head in this special. Things that we've laid down for years are going to be paid off.'

On 17 December the BBC put out another Christmas trailer, this one running 35" and focusing specifically on the main Christmas Day programming. Again some *Doctor Who* clips were included.

18 December saw a press screening of 'The Time of the Doctor' take place at the usual venue of BFI Southbank in London. In America, meanwhile, BBC America unveiled an extended, 1' 00" trailer for the special.

The following day's edition of CBBC's *Blue Peter* brought the announcement of the winners of the competition launched on 21 November. These were named as 13-year-old Connor from Somerset, who had designed a sonic guantlet for Jenny to use; 11-year-old Arthur from Hampshire, who gadget was a sonic lorgnette for Strax; and seven-year-old Amber from Kent, who came up with a sonic hatpin for Madame Vastra. The winning entries and runners-up were made available to view in an online gallery.

Also on 19 December, the latest 'Strax Field Report' video was placed online by the BBC. Subtitled 'The Doctors', this addressed the issue of regeneration and, in line with Steven Moffat's recent comments regarding the numbering of the Doctors, had the Christopher Eccleston incarnation still referred to as 'the ninth', and the John Hurt incarnation as 'the warrior'. This was followed the next day by a 27" duration preview clip from 'The Time of the Doctor', of Clara seeking the Doctor's help with cooking her Christmas turkey. On 23 December came a second preview clip, this one of 57" duration, with Clara phoning the TARDIS to talk to the Doctor, and on 24 December a third, of 39" duration, showing the Doctor and Clara with Orla Brady's character, Tasha Lem. 23 December also saw the release of a 1' 16" duration video in which Steven Moffat introduced 'The Time of the Doctor'.

Meanwhile, Brady had been busy promoting the special, discussing it with Clive Anderson on his early evening BBC Radio 4 Extra *Loose Ends* show on 21 December, and with guest presenter Colin Paterson on Richard Bacon's afternoon BBC Radio 5 Live show on 23 December. Jenna Coleman had also been on the interview circuit, chatting on the sofa on

BBC One's Breakfast on 23 December and talking to Colin Paterson on BBC Radio 5 Live the following afternoon.

On Christmas Day, the BBC made available online a 22" duration video of Orla Brady speaking in character as Tasha Lem from the TARDIS console room set, conveying seasons greetings to all *Doctor Who* fans worldwide, and a 57" duration video of Matt Smith and Jenna Coleman giving their own introduction to 'The Time of the Doctor'. Then, at 7.30 pm, the Christmas special itself went out as planned on BBC One, bringing the era of the eleventh Doctor to a dramatic end. In another milestone, it was *Doctor Who*'s eight-hundredth televised episode.

Following the transmission, a farewell message from Matt Smith was posted on the official *Doctor Who* Twitter feed: 'To the Whoniverse, thanks a million. You're the best. I'll miss you. And I'll miss the madness.' The BBC meanwhile made available several further online videos: another 'Strax Field Report', titled 'The Doctor Has Regenerated!'; a 1' 17" duration piece called 'The Secrets of Making Christmas', in which production designer Michael Pickwoad discussed the location recording of the special's Christmas town scenes; and an 18" snippet in which child actor Jack Hollington, who portrayed a character called Barnable, wished all *Doctor Who* fans a merry Christmas.

Just before their own broadcast of 'The Time of the Doctor' that evening, BBC America debuted another of their *Doctor Who* documentaries. This one had the self-explanatory title *Farewell to Matt Smith*, ran for 43' 30" (in an hour-long slot with commercials) and was narrated by Alex Kingston. It was also screened in Canada, where Space had picked up the rights, and was later included as an extra on the *50th Anniversary Collector's Edition* DVD and Blu-ray box set.

On 26 December, the BBC released online a *Behind the Lens* behind-the-scenes video for 'The Time of the Doctor'. Like the equivalent one for 'The Day of the Doctor', this was a relatively substantial offering, with a 12' 41" running time, and also covered the Doctor's regeneration. BBC America meanwhile made available an exclusive 34" duration deleted scene from the special. Again, both of these items turned up later on the *50th Anniversary Collector's Edition* set.

Also on 26 December, at midday, BBC Radio Tees broadcast *The TARDIS in Teeside*, a programme looking at the area's links to *Doctor Who*, including interviews with local fans and actor Mark Benton, who had appeared in 'Rose' (2005). Then, that evening, BBC Radio Norfolk put out a revised repeat of some of its pre-anniversary *Doctor Who* coverage, while BBC Radio 2 had a repeat of its *Who is the Doctor?* documentary.

Meanwhile, there was plenty of media reaction to 'The Time of the Doctor'. Patrick Mulkern, in his review on the *Radio Times* website, seemed to be in rather Scrooge-like mood: '"The Time of the Doctor" is – extraordinarily – the ninth Christmas special since the series returned in 2005. Of course there's immense kudos in being central to BBC One's Christmas Day schedule, but with the slow-down in production rate, this works out as the Time Lord's third Christmassy outing in a run of 17 episodes. I may be in the minority, but *Doctor Who* doesn't say "Christmas" to me. Never has. And does each special need to be so blooming Christmassy?'

Jim Shelley, of the *Mail* website, was more impressed, commenting: 'As for Matt Smith, generally he's brought a lot of humour to the role – in the vein of a Sylvester McCoy – but Steven Moffat's story "The Time of the Doctor" showed he should come back in 30 years' time. It meant we saw Smith in a variety of unexpected guises – naked, bald and, more pertinently, aged. This was as a result of a compelling, classic Christmas Day *Doctor Who* plot that was a sister piece to Moffat's previous episode (the more convoluted, pompous "The Day of the Doctor").'

As had now become commonplace, journalists outside the UK also made their views known. On 27 December, for instance, Robert Smith of the *New Zealand Herald* wrote: 'After the bombastic blow-out of last month's fiftieth anniversary special, Matt Smith's final appearance in *Doctor Who* cut back on the epic storytelling and concentrated on the smaller pleasures in life. Instead of striving to save his home planet from being annihilated in a vast cosmic war, the Doctor spends almost all of "The Time of the Doctor" slowly growing old in one small town somewhere in the infinite landscape of the universe. He still fights the monsters every now and then, but spends most of his time fixing toys for the local children. It's an apt way to farewell the eleventh Doctor – Smith was the youngest actor to ever play the enigmatic character, but he was also fantastic at conveying the sheer age of the character, and he deserved a long, slow retirement before the inevitable end.'

On 28 December, it was reported that 'The Time of the Doctor' had become the most watched programme in BBC America's history, attracting 2.47 million viewers overnight, just breaking the 2.40 million record set the previous month by 'The Day of the Doctor'. On Twitter, the Christmas special was also the most tweeted programme of the day, with 183,550 tweets.

One final piece of notable BBC local radio coverage came on 30 December, when BBC Radio Kent broadcast a belated *Doctor Who Anniversary Special*, covering amongst other things the involvement in the show's creation by writer Anthony Coburn, who had lived in the local seaside town of Herne Bay.

And so *Doctor Who*'s landmark fiftieth anniversary year drew to a close. Including the three specials – 'The Snowmen', 'The Day of the Doctor' and 'The Time of the Doctor' – only 16 new episodes in total had been transmitted over the course of 2012 and 2013 – fewer than over any equivalent period since the show's return to television in 2005. But while this downturn in production was lamented by many fans, who felt that it made disingenuous at best the prior promises by Steven Moffat and others to the effect that the anniversary year in particular would bring a veritable feast of *Doctor Who*, the disappointment was at least partly offset by the fact that the on-screen adventures had been accompanied by an extraordinary profusion of tie-in programmes, minisodes, celebratory events, media coverage and other related activities, the like of which had never been seen before, and perhaps never would be again.

PART THREE

Bio-Data

Chapter Nine
Principal Cast

MATT SMITH (THE DOCTOR)

Matt Smith was born in 1982 in Northampton. He initially hoped to have a career as a professional footballer, and played for the youth teams of Northampton Town, Nottingham Forest and Leicester City, but a back injury forced him out of the sport. Encouraged into acting by his school drama teacher, he joined the National Youth Theatre in London. Then, after leaving school, he studied drama and creative writing at the University of East Anglia. His first notable role as a professional actor came at London's National Theatre in a production of the Alan Bennett play *The History Boys* (2005-2006). He made his television debut in the Billie Piper-starring BBC One dramatisations of Philip Pullman's books *The Ruby in the Smoke* (2006) and *The Shadow in the North* (2007), and appeared opposite Piper again in an episode of the first series of ITV2's *Secret Diary of a Call Girl* (2007). However, his first major television role came in the BBC Two political drama series *Party Animals* (2007). He also made a successful return to the stage, taking a leading role in the Polly Stenham play *That Face*, initially at the Royal Court Theatre Upstairs in Chelsea in 2007 and then at the Duke of York's Theatre in London's West End the following year. The play was critically acclaimed, and Smith's performance won him the *Evening Standard*'s Best Newcomer award. Smith was one of the first actors to audition for the role of the eleventh Doctor, and was quickly recognised by showrunner Steven Moffat as an ideal candidate. Since leaving *Doctor Who* in 2013, he has gone on to numerous other projects, including a role in the movie *Terminator Genisys* (2015).

KAREN GILLAN (AMY POND)

Karen Gillan was born in 1987 in Inverness in Scotland. She became interested in acting from a young age, and performed in plays at her school and in local youth theatres. She studied drama at Telford College in Edinburgh from age 16, and at the Italia Conti stage school in London from age 18. However, she dropped out of the Italia Conti course to begin working professionally, both as an actor and, for a time, as a fashion model. Her first notable television work was as a regular performer in the Channel 4 comedy sketch vehicle *The Kevin Bishop Show* (2007-2009). Another minor television role at that time was under heavy make-up as a Soothsayer in the Series Four *Doctor Who* episode 'The Fires of Pompeii'. She then successfully auditioned to play Amy Pond, which was her first leading television role. She has gone on to make her professional theatre debut in *Inadmissible Evidence* (2011) at London's Donmar Warehouse, and to star as 1960s supermodel Jean Shrimpton in the BBC Four television movie *We'll Take Manhattan* (2012). Other projects have included taking a regular role in the American sitcom *Selfie* (ABC, 2014) and writing and directing her own short film, *Coward* (2015), which won the award for Best Independent Short at the Independent Film-makers Showcase at the Beverly Hills Film Festival 2015.

ARTHUR DARVILL (RORY WILLIAMS)

Thomas Arthur Darvill was born in 1982 in Birmingham. His mother was involved in the theatre and his father was a professional keyboard player, so he was introduced to the performing arts from an early age. He joined the Stage2 youth theatre company in 1991, and remained with them until 2000, when he gained a job doing in-vision links on the ITV children's programming strand CITV. He studied acting at London's RADA from age 18. His professional stage debut came in the play *Terre Haute*, initially at the Assembly Rooms during the Edinburgh Festival Fringe in 2006, then on tour, and finally at the Trafalgar Studios in London in 2007. Another notable stage role came alongside Matt Smith in *Swimming with Sharks* at London's Vaudeville Theatre, also in 2007. He made his television debut in a minor role in the ITV1 crime drama *He Kills Coppers* (2008), and then appeared as Edward 'Tip' Dorrit in a BBC One serialisation of Dickens' *Little Dorrit* (2008). However, *Doctor Who's* Rory Williams is his most major television part to date. In addition to his acting work, Darvill is an accomplished musician and award-winning composer, having worked in this capacity on shows including *Frontline* (2008) at the Globe

Theatre and *Been So Long* (2009) at the Young Vic. He has the unusual hobby of collecting taxidermy.

JENNA-LOUISE COLEMAN (OSWIN OSWALD / CLARA OSWIN OSWALD / CLARA OSWALD)

Jenna-Louise Coleman – credited simply as Jenna Coleman from 'The Day of the Doctor' onwards – was born in Blackpool, Lancashire on 27 April 1986. She started acting at a young age, joining the In Yer Space theatre company and then, in 2005, winning the regular role of Jasmine Thomas in the ITV1 soap opera *Emmerdale*. Further television work came as a regular in the 2009 series of the drama *Waterloo Road* (BBC One), and with roles in the mini-series *Room at the Top* (BBC Four, 2012), *Titanic* (ITV1, 2012) and *Dancing on the Edge* (BBC Two, 2013), amongst others. Since her time as a *Doctor Who* regular from 2012 to 2015, she has gone on to take the starring part as Queen Victoria in the mini-series *Victoria* (ITV1, 2016).

ALEX KINGSTON (RIVER SONG)

Alex Kingston was born in 1963 in Epsom, Surrey. She became interested in acting while at school, and performed for the Surrey County Youth Theatre. Later she trained at London's RADA. She went on to become a member of the Royal Shakespeare Company, but it is for her long and distinguished film and television career that she is best known. Her earliest screen appearances came in 1980, when she had a small, uncredited part in the movie *The Wildcats of St Trinian's* and played a character in three episodes of the long-running BBC One children's show *Grange Hill*. More notable film roles came in *The Cook, the Thief, His Wife & Her Lover* (1989), *A Pin for the Butterfly* (1994), *Croupier* (1998), *Essex Boys* (2000) and *Crashing* (2007). However, her greatest success came on television, as Dr Elizabeth Corday in some 160 episodes of NBC's medical drama series *ER* from 1997 to 2004. Her performances in this hit US show gained her numerous awards and widespread public recognition. It led on to many other memorable roles, on both sides of the Atlantic, including as *Doctor Who*'s River Song, who was introduced in the Series Four story 'Silence in the Library' / 'Forest of the Dead' (2008) and then brought back as a semi-regular from the start of Series Five. Other notable television credits include *Lost in Austen* (ITV1, 2008), *Hope Springs* (BBC One, 2009), *FlashForward* (ABC, 2009), *Law & Order: Special Victims Unit* (Universal, 2009), *Marchlands* (ITV1, 2011), *Upstairs, Downstairs* (BBC One, 2012) and *Chasing Shadows* (ITV1, 2014).

Chapter Ten
Principal Creative Team

STEVEN MOFFAT (SHOWRUNNER, EXECUTIVE PRODUCER, LEAD WRITER)

Steven Moffat was born in 1961 in Paisley, Scotland. He had gained a degree in English and begun working as a teacher when a chance encounter between his father and a television producer led to him being commissioned to write the children's series *Press Gang* (ITV, 1989-1993), which quickly acquired cult status. He went on to create and write the sitcom *Joking Apart* (BBC Two, 1993-1995), which was inspired by the breakdown of his first marriage and won the Bronze Rose of Montreux award, and the less-well-received *Chalk* (BBC One, 1997). One of his biggest early successes came with the sitcom *Coupling* (BBC Two/BBC Three, 2000-2004), which was also the subject of a short-lived American remake (NBC, 2003). Later he wrote the acclaimed drama *Jekyll* (BBC One, 2007) as a modern take on Robert Louis Stevenson's *Strange Case of Dr Jekyll and Mr Hyde* (Longmans, Green & Co, 1886). He was the only writer other than Russell T Davies to contribute episodes to each of the first four series of the new *Doctor Who*, and these scripts earned him numerous Hugos, BAFTAs and other awards. He took over from Davies as showrunner in 2009. His other projects around that time included scripting the movie *The Adventures of Tintin* (2011) for director Steven Spielberg; he was due to write a follow-up as well, but declined that opportunity in favour of working on *Doctor Who*. He co-created with Mark Gatiss the BBC One show *Sherlock* (2010-), a modern-day retelling of the Sherlock Holmes stories, which he works on concurrently with *Doctor Who*. In January 2016 it was announced that he would be quitting his *Doctor Who* showrunner role after production of Series Ten.

CAROLINE SKINNER (EXECUTIVE PRODUCER)

Caroline Skinner – Caro to her friends – started out in television as a script editor, on shows including *The Last Detective* (ITV, 2003-2007), *William and Mary* (ITV, 2003-2005), *Bleak House* (BBC One, 2005), *Jane Eyre* (BBC One, 2006) and *House of Saddam* (BBC Two, 2008) and the television movies *The Ruby in the Smoke* (BBC One, 2006) and *The Shadow in the North* (BBC One, 2007). She progressed to the role of producer on *Five Days* (BBC One, 2007-2010) and the BAFTA award-winning *The Fades* (BBC Three, 2011) before moving on to become executive producer on *Doctor Who*, starting from the Christmas special 'The Doctor, the Widow and the Wardrobe'. After completing her work on Series Seven, she moved on to be executive producer on other BBC projects, including the spin-off docu-drama *An Adventure in Space and Time* and the series *Our Girl* (BBC One, 2014-).

FAITH PENHALE (EXECUTIVE PRODUCER)

Faith Penhale gained a degree in drama at Bristol University, then a postgraduate degree in journalism at City University. After a brief spell as a journalist, she joined BBC television, initially as a researcher for the Features and Events Department. Moving on to the Drama Department, she became a script editor on *Doctors* and then *EastEnders*. In 2001, she left the BBC for a time, joining Kudos Film and Television as script editor on the second and third series of *Spooks*, their acclaimed spy drama produced for BBC One. During her ten years at Kudos she rose through a succession of jobs, eventually becoming Creative Manager. In 2011, she joined BBC Wales as Head of Drama. In addition to her duties in that post, she has been executive producer on a number of projects, including 'The Day of the Doctor' for *Doctor Who* and a dramatisation of the Tolstoy classic *War And Peace* (BBC One, 2016).

BRIAN MINCHIN (EXECUTIVE PRODUCER)

Brian Minchin was born in Aberystwyth, Wales, in 1987. Early in his career he worked for several Welsh independent production companies and served as assistant producer or producer on a number of low-budget films, mainly for Sgrin Wales and ITV Wales, including *Down* (2003), which he also co-wrote, *Work in Progress* (2004) and *Dead Long Enough*

(2005). He was script editor on BBC Wales's *Belonging* in 2005 before moving on to work in the same capacity on *Torchwood* Series One and Two in 2006 and 2007. He gained his first *Doctor Who* script editor credits on Series Four in 2008, before having a longer stint in that role on Series Five in 2010. He was assistant producer on the *Torchwood* mini-series 'Children of Earth' (2009) and UK producer of the follow-up 'Miracle Day' (2011). He also produced Series Four and Five of *The Sarah Jane Adventures* (2010-11). He subsequently served as an executive producer on *Dirk Gently* (2012), *Wizards vs Aliens* (2013) and the Cold War spy thriller *The Game* (2014), before taking up that post on *Doctor Who* in time to work on the 2013 Christmas special, 'The Time of the Doctor'.

MARCUS WILSON (SERIES PRODUCER)

Born in 1973, Marcus Wilson began his television career as an assistant grip on the ITV soap opera *Emmerdale*. He then became, in fairly rapid succession, a third assistant director, a locations manager and a first assistant director. He worked in the latter capacity throughout the early 2000s on a number of different shows, including BBC One's *Cutting It*, ITV1's *At Home with the Braithwaites*, *Heartbeat* and *The Royal* and Channel 4's *No Angels*. In 2004 he became line producer on *Cutting It*, and in 2007 he gained his first full producer job on the BBC One drama *True Dare Kiss*. Further producer credits followed on BBC One's *Life on Mars* (2006) and *Paradox* (2009) and ITV1's *Whitechapel* (2009) and *Taggart* (2010). An avid viewer of *Doctor Who* since the Tom Baker era of the late 1970s, he was delighted to have the chance to produce the show during Series Six and Seven. He has since gone on to produce further BBC One dramas, including *Our Zoo* (2014) and *The A Word* (2016).

DENISE PAUL (SERIES PRODUCER)

Denise Paul started out as a script editor, working in that capacity at the Scottish ITV company STV on over two dozen episodes of *Taggart* between 2005 and 2010 and on several episodes of *Rebus* in 2006 and 2007. She joined *Doctor Who* as its associate producer for most of Series Six, and produced the single episode 'Closing Time'. For Series Seven she produced four further episodes – 'The Bells of Saint John', 'The Rings of Akhaten', 'Nightmare in Silver' and 'The Name of the Doctor' – as well as various minisodes and similar content.

CHRIS CHIBNALL (WRITER)

Chris Chibnall was raised in Lancashire and began his television career as a football archivist and occasional floor manager for Sky Sports. He then took a succession of administrative jobs with different theatre companies including, between 1996 and 1999, the experimental group Complicite. He subsequently became a full-time writer, initially for the theatre, with credits including *Gaffer!* – a single-actor piece about homophobia in football, first staged in 1999 – and *Kiss Me Like You Mean It* – which premiered at the Soho Theatre in 2001 and has also been staged in a number of European venues, including Paris under the title *Un Baiser, Un Vrai*. On the strength of his play scripts, he was invited by the BBC to develop a period drama series for them. This became *Born and Bred* (2002-2005), which he not only created but also contributed to as consultant producer and lead writer throughout its four seasons. His other television writing credits include episodes of *All About George* (2005) and *Life on Mars* (2006). During 2005, he was charged with developing the fantasy show *Merlin* for BBC One, but this was ultimately farmed out to the independent company Shine Productions. He was lead writer on Series One and Two of *Torchwood* in 2006 and 2007, and in the latter year also gained his first *Doctor Who* script credit on the Series Three episode '42'. He became showrunner on the first series of the ITV1 show *Law and Order: UK* (2008), helped Russell T Davies to storyline the *Torchwood* mini-series 'Miracle Day' (2011) and took on the showrunner role on the Starz historical fantasy drama *Camelot* (2011). He then achieved great success with the ITV1 crime drama series *Broadchurch* (2013-), which he created, wrote and executive produced. In January 2016, it was announced that he would take over from Steven Moffat as *Doctor Who*'s showrunner from Series Eleven.

TOBY WHITHOUSE (WRITER)

Toby Whithouse hails from Southend. He began his career as an actor, and had a regular role in the BBC One drama *The House of Eliott* (1991-1994). He also appeared in the theatre – including in a 1996-1997 Gene Wilder-starring production of *Laughter on the 23rd Floor* in London's West End – and worked as a stand-up comedian. Frustrated by what he saw as a lack of quality in the scripts he was being offered, he took to writing in his spare time. He gained his first television commission on a 1999 episode of ITV's *Where the Heart Is,* and his play *Jump Mr Malinoff* was performed as the opening production at London's Soho Theatre in 2000, winning him that venue's annual Verity Bargate Award. He then became involved with the independent production company World Productions, and developed for them the successful Channel 4 hospital drama *No Angels* (2004-2006). His first *Doctor Who* credit came on the Series Two episode 'School Reunion', and he also wrote 'Greeks Bearing Gifts' for Series One of *Torchwood*, both transmitted in 2006. Perhaps his most notable achievement to date has been devising and writing the hit BBC Three supernatural drama show *Being Human* (2008-2013), on which he also served as executive producer. He still makes occasional appearances as an actor, but is now focused primarily on his writing career, which saw him script further *Doctor Who* episodes for Series Five, Six and Seven.

NEIL CROSS (WRITER)

Neil Cross was born in Bristol on 2 September 1969. He started his writing career as a novelist, beginning with *Mr In-Between* (Jonathan Cape, 1998), but then diversified into television. He wrote an episode of the BBC One spy drama *Spooks* in 2006 and became the show's lead writer for the following two years. His biggest success to date came with the creation of the BBC One crime show *Luther* (BBC One, 2010-), for which he was also the sole writer. For the cinema, he co-wrote the script of the hit horror movie *Mama* (2013). The following year, he then co-created, co-wrote and executive produced the pirate series *Crossbones* for America's NBC network. Throughout this period, he also continued to write novels, including the *Luther* tie-in *The Calling* (Simon & Schuster, 2011). The Series Seven episodes 'The Rings of Akhaten' and 'Hide' were his debut *Doctor Who* contributions. Although he writes primarily for UK and US television, he lives in Wellington, New Zealand, with his wife and two sons.

MARK GATISS (WRITER)

Mark Gatiss was born in 1966 in Sedgefield, County Durham. He was a *Doctor Who* fan from a young age. In the 1990s he authored a number of original novels based on the show for Virgin Publishing and BBC Books and scripted and acted in the *P.R.O.B.E.* series of independent video dramas from BBV featuring Caroline John as the Doctor's former companion Liz Shaw. Also in the same decade he got together with fellow performers Reece Shearsmith, Steve Pemberton and Jeremy Dyson to form the League of Gentlemen comedy team. They made their first stage appearances in 1995, with Gatiss and Dyson writing most of their material. In 1997 they were given their own show on BBC Radio 4, and in 1999 this transferred to television on BBC Two. Later they made the movie *The League of Gentlemen's Apocalypse* (2005). Throughout this period Gatiss gained many further credits both as a scriptwriter and as an actor. He contributed two stories – 'Phantasmagoria' (1999) and 'Invaders from Mars' (2002) – to Big Finish's range of audio *Doctor Who* dramas, before graduating to write for the television show itself, initially with 'The Unquiet Dead' (2005). He also made an on-screen appearance in the show, as Professor Lazarus in 'The Lazarus Experiment' (2007). His other accomplishments included writing a trilogy of Simon and Schuster-published novels about a bisexual British secret agent called Lucifer Box: *The Vesuvius Club* (2004), *The Devil in Amber* (2006) and *Black Butterfly* (2008). He co-created and produced with Steven Moffat the BBC One show *Sherlock* (2010-), for which he has also written numerous episodes and appeared in the role of Mycroft Holmes. Further *Doctor Who* script contributions came in Series Five, Six and Seven.

STEVE THOMPSON (WRITER)

Steve Thompson, sometimes credited as Stephen Thompson, was born in 1967. He trained on the RADA playwrights' course, and his first play, *Damages*, was produced at the Bush Theatre in Shepherd's Bush in 2004, winning him the Arts Council's Meyer-Whitworth Award for new writing. A number of other successful plays followed, including *Whipping it Up* (2006) at the Bush Theatre, *Roaring Trade* (2009) at the Soho Theatre and *No Naughty Bits* (2011) at the Hampstead Theatre. By 2005 he had broken into television scriptwriting on BBC One's daytime drama *Doctors*. He also wrote a 2007 episode of ITV1's *The Whistleblowers*. In 2010 he did his first work for Steven Moffat, writing 'The Blind Banker' episode of *Sherlock*. This led to him being commissioned to write 'The Curse of the Black Spot' for Series Six of *Doctor Who* and 'Journey to the Centre of the TARDIS' for Series Seven.

NEIL GAIMAN (WRITER)

Neil Gaiman was born in 1960 in Porchester, Hampshire but now lives in the USA, near Minneapolis. In the 1980s he worked as a freelance journalist, contributing interviews and reviews to numerous publications, and wrote some short fiction and biographies of rock group Duran Duran and author Douglas Adams. An avid interest in comic books also prompted him to move into that area of writing, in which he has since enjoyed considerable acclaim and success, perhaps most notably on the groundbreaking title *The Sandman* for DC's Vertigo imprint between 1988 and 1996. In 1990 he collaborated with author Terry Pratchett on the novel *Good Omens*, and in 1996 he wrote both the BBC Two series *Neverwhere* and a novel based on it. This led on to further highly successful solo novels: *Stardust* (1999), the multi-award-winning best-seller *American Gods* (2001) and *Anansi Boys* (2005). The multi-talented Gaiman also turned his hand to movie scriptwriting, starting with *MirrorMask* (2005). A number of his original stories have since been adapted as films scripted by other writers, including *Stardust* (2007) and *Coraline* (2009). Another multi-award-winning project was *The Graveyard Book* (2008), aimed at teenage readers. Gaiman continues to write occasionally for television on shows that particularly appeal to him, contributing the 'Day of the Dead' episode to Season Five of the US show *Babylon 5* and 'The Doctor's Wife' (2011) and 'Nightmare in Silver' to *Doctor Who*.

SAUL METZSTEIN (DIRECTOR)

Saul Metzstein was born on 30 December 1970 in Glasgow. He worked as a runner on the iconic Danny Boyle movies *Shallow Grave* (1994) and *Trainspotting* (1996), but first came to prominence as director of the comedy *Late Night Shopping* (2001). Further movie work followed on *Guy X* (2005) and *Dredd* (2012), but increasingly he turned his attention to the small screen, his first major project for television being the one-off BBC Four docu-drama *Micro Men* (2009). Having directed a 2010 episode of BBC Wales's revival of the drama series *Upstairs, Downstairs*, he was invited to work on *Doctor Who*. He handled four Series Seven episodes – more than any other director – plus the 2012 Christmas special 'The Snowmen'.

STEPHEN WOOLFENDEN (DIRECTOR)

Stephen Woolfenden's career in television and films stretches back over two decades. He started out as a runner, then became a second assistant director, initially on the series *We Are Seven* (ITV, 1991). Before long he had progressed to first assistant director, his credits in that capacity including episodes of *The Lifeboat* (BBC One, 1994), *Murder Most Horrid* (BBC Two, 1996), Neil Gaiman's *Neverwhere* (BBC Two, 1996), *Big Bad World* (ITV, 1999), *Happiness* (BBC Two, 2003) and *State of Play* (BBC One, 2003). Since the late 1990s, however, most of his work has come as a second unit director, both on television series, such as *Echo Beach* (ITV, 2008) and *Strike Back: Vengeance* (Sky 1, 2012), and on movies, including notably a number of the *Harry Potter* franchise. His first credits as a full director came on several episodes of the BBC children's programme *The Mysti Show* in 2004 and 2005. Others followed, including on episodes of *Echo Beach* and *Trinity* (ITV2, 2009). Series Seven's 'Nightmare in Silver' marked his debut as a *Doctor Who* director.

MAT KING (DIRECTOR)

Mat King started out producing and directing his own short films in the early 2000s before getting his first real break as a director on the television movie *Star Runners* (Sci-Fi Channel, 2009). For the BBC he then directed numerous episodes of the children's series *M. I. High* between 2009 and 2011, and five episodes of another, *Spirit Warriors*, in 2010. Other credits came on episodes of the Australian series *Underbelly* in 2011 and of the ITV1 series *DCI Banks* in 2012. He made his *Doctor Who* debut on Series Seven's 'Journey to the Centre of the TARDIS'.

NICK HURRAN (DIRECTOR)

Born in London in 1959, Nick Hurran started out in television in the mid-1980s as a floor manager at Thames TV on shows such as *Dramarama* (ITV, 1983-1989), *Lytton's Diary* (ITV, 1985-1986) and *Chance in a Million* (Channel 4, 1984-1986). He then turned his hand to directing, gaining credits on shows including *Never the Twain* (ITV, 1981-1991), *Boon* (ITV, 1986-1992) and *Outside Edge* (ITV, 1994-1996). His 1998 feature film *Girls' Night* won him the Silver Spire award at the San Francisco International Film Festival. In 2003 he had a change of role when he was appointed as producer of *The Last Detective* (ITV, 2003-2007), starring fifth Doctor actor Peter Davison. After that show ended, however, he returned to directing, including on the remake of *The Prisoner* (ITV, 2009). Aside from his work on Series Six and Seven of *Doctor Who*, the early 2010s also saw him direct for the comedy series *Me and Mrs Jones* (BBC One, 2012), *Sherlock* (BBC One, 2014), *Fortitude* (Sky Atlantic, 2015) and *Childhood's End* (Syfy, 2015).

DOUGLAS MACKINNON (DIRECTOR)

Douglas Mackinnon was born in Scotland and grew up on the Isle of Skye. After working as a newspaper photographer, he cut his directorial teeth in 1992 on the short film *Sealladh*, which he also wrote. He went on to gain numerous television credits, including as assistant director on a number of 1994 and 1995 episodes of *The Bill* (ITV1) and some 1996 episodes of *Soldier, Soldier* (ITV1), and as director on *The Grand* (ITV1, 1997), some 1999 episodes of *The Vice* (ITV1), *Nice Guy Eddie* (BBC One, 2002), *Murder in Suburbia* (ITV1, 2004), some 2004 episodes of *Silent Witness* (BBC One) and some 2004 and 2005 episodes of *Bodies* (BBC Three). He made his feature film debut on *The Flying Scotsman* (Verve/MGM 2006). In 2007, he was lead director on Steven Moffat's *Jekyll* (BBC One). The Series Four two-parter 'The Sontaran Stratagem' / 'The Poison Sky' (2008) was his first contribution to *Doctor Who*. Before returning to the show for the Series Seven episodes 'The Power of Three' and 'Cold War', he also directed, amongst things, the comedy series *Happy Hollidays* (BBC Scotland, 2009), some episodes of the 2012 series of the drama series *Line of Duty* (BBC Two) and some docu-dramas for STV.

COLM McCARTHY (DIRECTOR)

Colm McCarthy was born in Edinburgh, Scotland on 16 February 1973. Having no formal training, he started out making short films, music videos and the like with friends. He broke into television at the end of the 1990s, gaining his initial director credits on the Sky 1 series *Dream Team* in 1997 and the RTE series *No Frontiers* in 2001. More substantial projects followed, including several episodes of ITV's *Footballers' Wive$: Overtime* in 2005 and two of BBC One's *Hustle* the following year. Over the next decade, he continued to work regularly as a freelance television director, including on shows such as BBC One's *Murphy's Law* in 2006 and 2007, ITV1's *Injustice* in 2011 and BBC Two's *Peaky Blinders* in 2014. Season Seven's 'The Bells of Saint John' is his sole *Doctor Who* credit to date.

FARREN BLACKBURN (DIRECTOR)

Like Matt Smith, Farren Blackburn started out with hopes of becoming a professional footballer, being on the books of Cambridge United and playing for England at youth level. However, after attending film school in the late 1990s, he made five short films in the early 2000s that won him a number of awards and achieved success on the international festival circuit. This led him into a career as a television director. Following a brief stint on the BBC's long-running documentary series *Panorama* in 2004, he directed episodes of shows including *Footballers' Wives: Extra Time* (ITV2, 2005-2006), *Doctors* (BBC One, 2000-), *Holby City* (BBC One, 1999-) and *Survivors* (BBC One, 2008-2010). His biggest success to date came as director of *The Fades* (BBC Three, 2011), which won a BAFTA for Best Drama Series. When Caroline Skinner moved from being producer of *The Fades* to work alongside Steven Moffat as executive producer on *Doctor Who*, she recommended Blackburn for the job of directing the 2011 Christmas special 'The Doctor, the Widow and the Wardrobe'. He returned to the show for the Series Seven episode 'The Rings of Akhaten'.

JAMIE PAYNE (DIRECTOR)

Jamie Payne started out producing and directing his own short films at the end of the 1990s. His first credits as a television director came on several 2002 episodes of the ITV police series *The Bill*. Many others followed, including on the science fiction dramas *Primeval* (ITV1) in 2007 and 2008 and *Survivors* (BBC One) in 2008 and 2010, and episodes of hit shows such as *Ashes to Ashes* (BBC One) in 2010 and *Call the Midwife* (BBC One) in 2012. The Series Seven episode 'Hide' marked his *Doctor Who* debut, which he followed up with the 2013 Christmas special – and Matt Smith's swansong – 'The Time of the Doctor'.

PART FOUR

Credits

DOCTOR WHO

GOOD AS GOLD (minisode) (2012)
POND LIFE (Parts 1-5) (minisodes) (2012)
SERIES SEVEN 7.01-7.05 (2012)
P.S. (minisode) (2012)
THE SNOWMEN (2012)
THE BATTLE OF DEMON'S RUN: TWO DAYS LATER (minisode) (2013)
SERIES SEVEN 7.06-7.13 (2013)
THE INFORARIUM (minisode) (2013)
CLARA AND THE TARDIS (minisode) (2013)
RAIN GODS (minisode) (2013)
THE NIGHT OF THE DOCTOR (minisode) (2013)
THE DAY OF THE DOCTOR (2013)
THE TIME OF THE DOCTOR (2013)

CREDITS[27]

Series Producer: Marcus Wilson (7.06, 7.07, 7.12, 7.13)
Producer: Marcus Wilson (all except 7.06, 7.07, 7.12 and 7.13)[28], Denise Paul (7.06, 7.07, 7.12, 7.13)[29]

MAIN CAST
Matt Smith (The Doctor)[30]
David Tennant (The Doctor) (TDotD)

---

[27] Where an episode number (or more than one) appears in brackets after a person's name in the listing, this means that they were credited only on the episode (or episodes) indicated. Otherwise, the person concerned was credited on all episodes, apart from the minisodes, which generally had no production credits. The 2012 Christmas special, 'The Snowmen', is denoted as 'TS', 'The Day of the Doctor' as 'TDotD' and the 2013 Christmas special, 'The Time of the Doctor', as 'TTotD'.

[28] Also uncredited producer of 'The Inforarium'.

[29] Also producer of 'Pond Life' and 'The Night of the Doctor', and uncredited producer of 'The Battle of Demon's Run – Two Days Later', 'Rain Gods' and 'Clara and the TARDIS'.

[30] Also appears in 'Good as Gold', 'Pond Life', 'P.S.', 'Rain Gods' and 'The Inforarium'.

John Hurt (The Doctor) (7.13[31], TDotD)[32]
Paul McGann (The Doctor)[33]
Karen Gillan (Amy Pond) (7.01-7.05, TTotD[34])[35]
Arthur Darvill (Rory Williams) (7.01-7.05)[36]
Jenna-Louise Coleman[37] (Oswin) (7.01[38]), (Clara[39]) ('TS' to 'TTotD')[40]
Billie Piper (Rose[41]) (TDotD)

PRODUCTION TEAM
Stunt Co-Ordinator: Crispin Layfield (all except 7.03), Gordon Seed (7.01-7.03, 7.05, TS, 7.09, 7.10, 7.12, TDotD), Jo McLaren (TS, 7.06, 7.13, TDotD), Daniel Euston (7.11)
Stunt Performer: Will Willoughby (7.02, 7.03), Rob Cooper (7.02), Mike Lambert (7.02), Matthew Stirling (7.05, 7.13), Stephanie Carey (7.05), Annabel Canaven (TS, TDotD), Andy Godbold (7.06), Dani Biernat (7.06, 7.07, 7.13, TDotD, TTotD), Gordon Seed (7.07, 7.13, TTotD), Amy J Smart (7.07), David Newton (7.08, TDotD), Marcus Shakesheff (7.08), Tom Aitken (7.08), André Layne (7.10), Lewis Young (7.10), Ryan Stuart (7.12), Tracey Caudle (TDotD), Rob Hunt (TDotD), Ian van Temperley (TDotD), Christian Knight (TDotD), Kim McGarrity (TDotD), Daz Parker (TTotD), Lloyd Bass (TTotD), Stephen Walsh (TTotD)
Choreographer: Ailsa Berk (7.12)
First Assistant Director: Fay Selby (7.01, 7.05, 7.12, TDotD), Nick Brown (7.02, 7.03, TS, 7.06, 7.11, 7.13), Sarah Davies (7.04), David Mack (7.07), Ken Cumberland (7.08), John Bennett[42] (7.09, TTotD), Jonathan Farmer (7.10)

---

[31] Cameo appearance – credited only on closing credits.
[32] Also appears via archive footage in 'The Night of the Doctor', but credited as 'The War Doctor'.
[33] 'The Night of the Doctor' only.
[34] Cameo appearance – uncredited.
[35] Also appears in 'Good as Gold', 'Pond Life' and 'P.S.'.
[36] Also appears in 'Pond Life' and 'P.S.'.
[37] Credited as 'Jenna Coleman' on TDotD and TTotD.
[38] Credited only on closing credits.
[39] Full name of the version seen in 'The Snowmen' is 'Clara Oswin Oswald', and that of the version seen in subsequent episodes is simply 'Clara Oswald'.
[40] Also appears in 'Clara and the TARDIS'.
[41] Although credited as 'Rose', Billie Piper actually plays the Moment in TDotD.
[42] Credited as 'John Bennet' on 7.09

CREDITS

Second Assistant Director: James DeHaviland (7.01-7.05, 7.08, 7.09), Heddi-Joy Taylor-Welch (TS-7.07, 7.10-7TTotD)
Third Assistant Director: Heddi-Joy Taylor-Welch (7.01-7.05, 7.08, 7.09), Delmi Thomas (TS, 7.10, 7.11), Danielle Richards (7.06, 7.07, 7.12, 7.13, TTotD), Marie Devautour (TDotD)
Assistant Director: Danielle Richards (7.01-TS, 7.08-7.11), Gareth Jones (TS-7.07, 7.10, 7.12-TTotD), Louisa Cavell (7.06, 7.07, 7.12-TTotD)
Utility Stand In: Ian William George (TDotD, TTotD)
Location Manager: Nicky James (7.01, 7.05-7.10, 7.13), Iwan Roberts (7.02-7.04, TS, 7.11, 7.12, TDotD, TTotD), Thomas Elgood (7.06)
Location Assistant: Iestyn Hampson-Jones (7.04, TS-7.13)
Unit Manager: Geraint Williams (7.01-7.05, 7.08, 7.09), Monty Till (TS-7.07, 7.10-7.13, TTotD), Nick Clark (TDotD)
Production Manager: Phillipa Cole (all except 7.08 and TTotD), Claire Hildred (7.11, 7.12)
Production Manager (Spain): Pere Agullo (7.03)
Production Manager (New York): Moe Bardach (7.05)
Production Co-Ordinator: Claire Hildred (7.01-7.07, 7.09, 7.10, 7.13), Gabriella Ricci (7.08, 7.11, 7.12, TDotD, TTotD)
Assistant Production Co-Ordinator: Gabriella Ricci (7.01-7.07, 7.09, 7.10, 7.13), Sandra Cosfeld (TDotD, TTotD)
Production Secretary: Sandra Cosfeld (all except TDotD and TTotD), Rachel Vipond (TDotD, TTotD)
Production Assistant: Rachel Vipond (all except TDotD and TTotD), Samantha Price (all except 7.13-TTotD), Katie Player (TDotD, TTotD)
Assistant Production Accountant: Rhys Evans (all except TDotD and TTotD), Justine Wooff (7.01, 7.04, 7.05, 7.08, 7.09, 7.11, 7.12), Bethan Griffiths (TDotD, TTotD)
Art Department Accountant: Simon Wheeler (TTotD)
Assistant Script Editor: John Phillips (all except 7.02, 7.03 and TDotD)
Script Supervisor: Steve Walker (7.01, 7.05, TS, 7.06, 7.08, 7.09, 7.11, 7.12, TDotD, TTotD), Lindsay Grant (7.02, 7.03), Rory Herbert (7.04, 7.07, 7.10, 7.13)
Camera Operator: Joe Russell (all except TTotD), Mark Mcquoid (TTotD), Martin Stephens (TTotD)
Focus Puller: James Scott (all except TTotD), Julius Ogden (7.01, 7.04-TS, 7.08, 7.09, 7.11, 7.12, TDotD), Steve Rees (7.02, 7.03), Chris Walmsley (7.06, 7.10), Chris Reynolds (7.07, 7.13), Berndt Wiese (TTotD), Rich Turner (TTotD)

Grip: Gary Norman (all except TTotD), Damian Roberts (TTotD)
Camera Assistant: Meg de Koning (all except TTotD), Sam Smithard (all except TDotD and TTotD), Cai Thompson (7.01-7.03, TS-7.07, 7.13, TDotD), Evelina Norgren (7.04, 7.05, TS, 7.08-7.12), Chris Johnson (TDotD), Pete Lowden (TTotD), Kyle Brown (TTotD), Natalie Davies (TTotD)
Assistant Grip: Owen Charnley (all except TTotD), Ryan Jarman (TTotD)
Stereo DIT: Jay Patel (TDotD)
Stereo Sculptor: Adam Sculthorp (TDotD)
Sound Maintenance Engineer: Ross Adams (all except 7.02, 7.03, TDotD and TTotD), Chris Goding[43], Jeff Welch (7.02, 7.03), Tam Shoring (TDotD, TTotD)
Gaffer: Mark Hutchings (all except TDotD), Scott Napier (TDotD)
Best Boy: Stephen Slocombe (all except TDotD), Colin Price (TDotD)

Electrician: Bob Milton (all except TDotD), Gareth Sheldon (all except TDotD), Matt Wilson (7.01, 7.02, 7.04, 7.05), Alan Tippetts (7.03), Nick Powell (TS-7.07, 7.10, 7.13), Gafin Riley (TS-7.08, 7.10-7.13, TTotD), Bob Fernandes (7.08), Steve Guy (7.09), Jordan Brown (TDotD), Gareth Crean (TDotD), James Foy (TDotD), Billy Harron (TDotD, TTotD), Thomas Rhodri Moses (TDotD), Andrew Williams (TDotD, TTotD)
Board Operator: Jon Towler (TDotD)
Supervising Art Director: Paul Spriggs (all except TTotD), Lucienne Suren (TTotD)
Set Decorator: Adrian Anscombe (all except TS), Joelle Rumbelow (TS)
Production Buyer: Charlie Lynam (7.01-7.05, 7.06, 7.07, 7.09), Adrian Greenwood (all except 7.02, 7.03, TDotD and TTotD), Holly Thurman (TS-7.08, 7.10-7.13), Sarah Frere (TDotD), Jayne Davies (TTotD), May Johnson (TTotD), Helen O'Leary (TTotD)
Art Director: Lucienne Suren (7.01, 7.05, 7.07), Amy Pickwoad (all except 7.01, 7.05, TDotD and TTotD), Carly Reddin (7.08), Joelle Rumbelow (7.11, 7.12), Daniel Martin (7.13)
Standby Art Director: Nandie Narishkin (TS, 7.07, 7.08, 7.10-7.12), Helen Atherton (7.09), Jim McCallum (TDotD), Amy Pickwoad (TTotD)
Assistant Art Director: Richard Hardy (all except TTotD)
Draughtsperson: Kartik Nagar (TDotD, TTotD)

---

[43] Credited as 'Christopher Goding' on TTotD.

Art Department Coordinator: Donna Shakesheff (all except TDotD and TTotD)

Prop Master: Paul Smith

Prop Chargehand: Bernie Davies (7.01-7.03, 7.05), Ian Griffin (7.04, TS-7.13)

Set Dresser: Jayne Davies (all except 7.09, TDotD and TTotD), Austin J Curtis (TS), Ian Griffin (TDotD), Mike Elkins (TDotD), Jamie Farrell (TDotD), Jamie Southcott (TTotD)

Prop Hand: Austin J Curtis (all except TS, TDotD and TTotD), Jamie Southcott (TS-7.07, 7.10, 7.13), Jamie Farrell (7.06, 7.10, 7.13, TTotD), Liam Collins (TDotD, TTotD), Ian Davies (TDotD, TTotD), Ian Griffin (TTotD), Kyle Belomont (TTotD), Roger Hendry (TTotD), Ryan Milton (TTotD)

Standby Props: Phill Shellard (7.01-7.05), Helen Atherton (all except 7.09, TDotD and TTotD), Rob Brandon (TS-7.07, 7.09, 7.10, 7.13), Garry Dawson (7.08, 7.11, 7.12)

Dressing Props: Mike Elkins, Ian Griffin (7.01-7.03, 7.05), Tom Belton (7.02, 7.03), Paul Barnett (7.04, TS-7.13), Jamie Farrell (TS), Rob Brandon (7.08, 7.11, 7.12), Jayne Davies (7.09, 7.13)

Storeman: Jamie Southcott (TDotD)

Graphic Artist: Christina Tom

Graphic Designer: Chris Lees[44]

Concept Artist: Bryan Hitch (7.10)

Storyboard Artist: Andrew Wildman (TS-7.08, 7.10-7.13)

Petty Cash Buyer: Helen O'Leary (7.01-7.03), Florence Tasker (7.04-7.13)

Standby Carpenter: Will Pope (all except TDotD), Tim Jones (TDotD), Paul Jones (TTotD)

Standby Rigger: Bryan Griffiths

Practical Electrician: Christian Davies (TS-TTotD)

Props Maker: Penny Howarth (all except TDotD and TTotD), Alan Hardy, Jamie Thomas (7.01-7.05, 7.08-7.10, TDotD, TTotD), Tom Belton (7.01)

Props Driver: Gareth Fox

Construction Manager: Terry Horle

Construction Chargehand: Dean Tucker

Scenic Artist: John Pinkerton (TS-7.13), Clive Clarke (TDotD, TTotD)

Assistant Costume Designer: Fraser Purfit (all except TDotD and TTotD), Carly Griffith (TDotD, TTotD)

---

[44] Credited as 'Chris J Lees' on 7.03.

Costume Supervisor: Carly Griffith (all except TDotD and TTotD), Claire Lynch (TDotD, TTotD)

Costume Assistant: Katarina Cappellazzi, Gemma Evans, Florence Chow (TS), Lauren Kilcar (TDotD), Charlotte Bestwick (TTotD)

Make-Up Supervisor: Steve Williams (TDotD), Claire Pritchard-Jones (TTotD)

Make-Up Artist: Sara Angharad (7.01-7.05, 7.06-7.09, 7.11-7.13), Vivienne Simpson (all except 7.09, TDotD and TTotD), Allison Sing (7.01-7.05, 7.06-7.08, 7.11-7.13), Katie Lee (TS, 7.10), Elin Rhiannon (TS), Julie Fox Pritchard (7.09), Kathryn Newsome (TDotD), Jenny Jones (TDotD), Clare Golds (TDotD, TTotD), Emma Cowen (TTotD), Danny Marie Elias (TTotD)

Casting Associate: Alice Purser

Post Production Coordinator: Samantha Price (7.12-TTotD)

Assistant Editor: Becky Trotman (all except TDotD and TTotD), Katrina Aust (7.12-TTotD)

VFX Editor: Joel Skinner

Stereo 3D Consultant: David Wigram (TDotD)

Dubbing Mixer: Tim Ricketts (all except 7.04), Darran Clement (7.04)

ADR Editor: Matthew Cox (all except 7.04)

Dialogue Editor: Darran Clement (all except 7.04), Paul McFadden (7.04)

Sound Effects Editor: Paul Jefferies (all except 7.04), Tom Heuzenroeder (7.04)

Foley Editor: Jamie Talbutt

Graphics: Peter Anderson Studio (all except 7.01, 7.02 and TDotD)

Additional VFX: BBC Wales Visual Effects (TS-7.08, 7.10-7.13), Blue Bolt (TDotD), Jellyfish (TDotD)

Additional Editing: Matthew Cannings (TS)

Online Conform: Mark Bright (7.01, 7.02, 7.05)

Online Editor: Jeremy Lott (7.01), Geraint Pari Huws (7.02, 7.04, TS, 7.07-7.12, TDotD, TTotD), Matt Mullins (7.03), Jon Everett (7.05, 7.06, 7.13)

Colourist: Mick Vincent (7.01, 7.02, 7.05-7.11, TDotD), Gareth Spensley (7.03, 7.04, 7.12, 7.13, TTotD)

With Thanks To: The BBC National Orchestra of Wales (all except TS)

Conducted (all except TS) and Orchestrated by Ben Foster

With Thanks To: Crouch End Festival Chorus (TS, 7.07)

Conducted by David Temple (TS, 7.07)

Recorded (7.01, 7.05, TS, 7.07) and Mixed by Jake Jackson

CREDITS

Recorded by Gerry O'Riordan (all except 7.01, 7.05, TS and 7.07)

Original Theme Music: Ron Grainer
Original Theme Arranged By: Delia Derbyshire (TDotD)
Casting Director: Andy Pryor CDG
Production Executive: Julie Scott
Script Editor: Richard Cookson (TDotD), Derek Richie (TTotD)
Post Production Supervisor: Nerys Davies
Production Accountant: Jeff Dunn
Sound Recordist: Deian Llŷr Humphreys
Costume Designer: Howard Burden
Make-Up Designer: Barbara Southcott (all except TDotD and TTotD), Lin Davie (TDotD, TTotD)
Music: Murray Gold
Visual Effects: The Mill (all except 7.03 and 7.12-TTotD), Space Digital (7.03, 7.04), Stargate Studios (7.05, 7.12, 7.13), Milk (TDotD, TTotD), BBC Wales Visual Effects (TDotD, TTotD)
Special Effects: Real SFX
Miniature Effects: The Model Unit[45] (7.08, TDotD, TTotD)
Prosthetics: Millennium FX
Editor: Jamie Pearson (7.01, 7.05), Tim Porter (7.02, 7.03), Mike Hopkins (7.04), William Oswald (TS, 7.08), Mark Davis (7.06), Sam Williams (7.07), Nick Arthurs (7.09), Selina Macarthur (7.10), Matthew Cannings (7.11, 7.13[46]), Ian Erskine (7.12), Liana Del Giudice (TDotD), St John O'Rorke (TTotD)
Production Designer: Michael Pickwoad
Director of Photography: Neville Kidd (7.01, 7.05, 7.13-TTotD), Stephan Pehrsson (7.02, 7.03, TS, 7.11), Gavin Struthers (7.04), Simon Dennis (7.06), Dale McCready (7.07), Suzie Lavelle (7.08), Mike Southon BSC (7.09), Jake Polonsky (7.10), Tim Palmer BSC (7.12)
Script Producer: Denise Paul (7.01, 7.03-7.05, 7.08-7.11)
Associate Producer: Denise Paul (7.02)
Line Producer: Diana Barton (7.01-7.05, 7.09, 7.11), Des Hughes (TS-7.07, 7.10, 7.12-TTotD), Phillipa Cole (7.08)
Line Producer (New York): David Mason (7.05)

---

[45] Incorrectly credited as 'The Modelo Unit' on TTotD.
[46] Credited as 'Matt Cannings' on 7.13.

125

Executive Producer: Steven Moffat[47], Caroline Skinner (all except TDotD and TTotD) [48], Faith Penhale (TDotD)[49], Brian Minchin (TTotD)

BBC Wales

---

[47] Also uncredited executive producer on all minisodes.
[48] Also uncredited executive producer on all minisodes except 'The Night of the Doctor'.
[49] Also uncredited executive producer on 'The Night of the Doctor'.

PART FIVE

Episode Guide

Readers who have yet to see the episodes may wish to bear in mind that this guide is a comprehensive one that contains many plot 'spoilers'.

Good as Gold (minisode)

Writer: The Children of Ashdene School
Director: Saul Metzstein[50]

<u>DEBUT TRANSMISSION DETAILS</u>

CBBC
Date: 24 May 2012.

Duration: 2′ 59″

<u>ADDITIONAL CAST (UNCREDITED)</u>

Elliot Barnes-Worrell (Athlete), Sarah Louise Madison (Weeping Angel)

<u>PLOT</u>

The Doctor and Amy go in search of adventure, but the TARDIS malfunctions and materialises on an Olympic running track. An athlete runs into the console room carrying a flaming torch, and the Doctor realises that he is a torch-bearer from the London 2012 Olympic games. The athlete explains that something was chasing him. Suddenly a Weeping Angel appears behind him, and the torch instantly transfers into its hand. The Doctor disintegrates the Weeping Angel with his sonic screwdriver, and the athlete catches the torch as it falls. The athlete then leaves to go and light the Olympic flame, throwing the Doctor a gold medal in thanks. The Doctor and Amy turn to the TARDIS console, intending to resume their quest for adventure, but behind them, the Weeping Angel suddenly reconstitutes …

---

[50] Uncredited.

QUOTE, UNQUOTE

- Amy: 'Oh my god, Doctor, what's it doing?'
  Doctor: 'It's trying to steal the Olympic flame, and destroy the very spirit of respect, excellence and friendship it represents.'

- Athlete: 'Good as gold, you are, Doctor.'

CONTINUITY POINTS

- When the Doctor puts the TARDIS controls on 'adventure setting', the ship starts to malfunction, and the cloister bell sounds.

- In the Series Two story 'Fear Her', the Doctor himself was seen to take on the task of lighting the Olympic flame at the London 2012 games. The events in 'Good as Gold' are difficult to reconcile with that, suggesting that time has been rewritten in the interim, probably by the Series Five 'cracks in time' or by the Doctor's rebooting of the universe in 'The Big Bang' (2010).

PRODUCTION NOTES

- This minisode was recorded on 8 May 2012 at BBC Roath Lock. The script was the winning entry in the 2012 Script to Screen competition held by the long-running CBBC children's magazine series Blue Peter. The competition was open to British schoolchildren aged 9-11.

- The competition was launched in January 2012 with a two-minute-duration video performed by Matt Smith in character as the Doctor, speaking to camera against a white background. The Doctor explains that he, Amy and Rory are trapped in the Land of Fiction (as introduced in the 1968 television story 'The Mind Robber'), and that the only way they can escape is for primary schoolchildren to think up an adventure for them – as happened the previous year when he met Albert Einstein (a reference to the 2011 Script to Screen competition winner 'Death is the Only Answer'). He suggests incorporating the theme of the Olympic Games – although not the 2012 ones, as he has been there already, and does not want to bump into himself. The closing date for entries was 16 March 2012, and further details were given on the Blue Peter website.

- Karen Gillan also performed a 40" duration video piece in character as Amy to promote the competition. Speaking to camera in front of a police box prop, she reiterated the premise, explaining that she, the Doctor and Rory were still trapped in the Land of Fiction. This was broadcast during the 8 March 2012 edition of Blue Peter, only eight days before the competition's closing date.

- The competition entries were judged by Steven Moffat, Caroline Skinner and BBC Learning executive producer Katy Jones, with Doctor Who series producer Marcus Wilson also helping out. Skinner commented: 'We loved reading all of the scripts from schools across the UK, and the standard of entries was truly outstanding. It was a difficult but a tremendously fun task to choose a winner, and it was just brilliant to see so many children being creative in developing an adventure for the Doctor. We hope all fans enjoy this special one-off mini episode!'

- 'Good as Gold' had its debut broadcast as part of a nine-minute-long feature on the 24 May 2012 edition of Blue Peter on CBBC, repeated the following day on BBC One. Although credited to the children of Ashdene School in general, the script was actually written by three in particular; they introduced themselves on screen as Rebecca, Ruby and Emily, and their surnames were not given, although Emily's is known to be Gaskin. The feature opened with some behind-the-scenes coverage of the production of the minisode, centring around a studio visit made by the three winners as part of their prize.

- The minisode begins with a shortened version of the usual Doctor Who opening titles.

- Unlike 'Death is the Only Answer', 'Good as Gold' was given a commercial DVD and Blu-ray release. This was on The Complete Seventh Series box set – but only the UK version.

CRITICAL REACTION

'Let's take this in the spirit in which it was intended, i.e. some fun for primary school kids who love Doctor Who, the Olympics, and presumably, making their teachers happy.' Louisa Mellor, Den of Geek website, 24 May 2012.

ANALYSIS

'Good as Gold' is a brief but fun interlude, with a script cleverly combining a *Doctor Who* monster story with contemporary interest in the then forthcoming London 2012 Olympic games – even though this was actually the one Olympic games that entrants were advised to avoid featuring when the competition was launched (see 'Production Notes' above). There is one major plot problem – the Weeping Angel should not have been able to chase the athlete in a stadium packed with spectators, as it would always have been observed (a fact unfortunately highlighted when the Doctor and Amy warn the athlete 'Don't blink!') – but, all in all, this is a very good effort by the three young competition-winners.

Pond Life (Parts 1-5) (minisodes)

Writer: Chris Chibnall
Director: Saul Metzstein

<u>DEBUT TRANSMISSION DETAILS</u>

BBC Red Button
Date: Part 1: 27 August 2012; Part 2: 28 August 2012; Part 3: 29 August 2012; Part 4: 30 August 2012; Part 5: 31 August 2012

Duration: Part 1: 0' 54"; Part 2: 1' 12"; Part 3: 0' 54"; Part 4: 1' 26"; Part 5: 1' 33"

<u>ADDITIONAL CAST (UNCREDITED)</u>

Paul Kasey (Ood), Silas Carson (Voice of the Ood)

<u>PLOT</u>

Part 1: April: Amy and Rory raise their wine glasses in a toast to the Doctor, after listening to an answerphone message in which he gives them a brief update on his activities: making a perilous escape from a troop of Sontarans; having a close encounter with Mata Hari in a Paris hotel room; laying down some backing vocals in a recording studio; and accidentally colliding with ancient Greece in the TARDIS.

Part 2: May: Amy and Rory are asleep in their bedroom when the TARDIS materialises outside and the Doctor bursts in, exhorting them to hurry and get dressed as everyone on Earth is in danger. Realising that they don't know what he is talking about, the Doctor then deduces that he has arrived too early. Giving his friends an unconvincing assurance that the future is 'really, really safe', he rapidly departs again.

Part 3: June: Amy and Rory are taken aback to discover an Ood sitting on the toilet seat in their bathroom, asking if it may be of any assistance.

Part 4: July: In a phone call between their home and the TARDIS, Amy and Rory learn that the Ood was inadvertently left behind by the Doctor during his recent night-time visit. He had been *en route* to return it to the Ood-Sphere, after rescuing it from the Androvax conflict. Conditioned to serve, the Ood becomes the Ponds' 'butler', attending to all their household chores.

Part 5: August: The Doctor is leaving another answerphone update for Amy and Rory while apparently changing the light bulb on the TARDIS's police box roof. He tells them that he has dropped the Ood home, and briefly recounts a number of other exploits, ending by telling them that he came to visit them but found them out. Seeming to sense that something is wrong, he has second thoughts about leaving the message, and uses his sonic screwdriver to delete it. Meanwhile, Rory has left home, after a fierce argument with Amy ...

QUOTE, UNQUOTE

- Amy: 'We need you, raggedy man ... I need you ...'

CONTINUITY POINTS

- The Doctor refers to the TARDIS's helmic regulator, a component mentioned in a number of previous stories, the earliest being 'The Ark in Space' (1975)

- Although each episode of 'Pond Life' is set in a particular month, no year is specified. The incidents depicted must, however, post-date the Doctor's visit to Amy and Rory at the end of the 2011 Christmas special, 'The Doctor, the Widow and the Wardrobe', as he did not know until then that they were aware he had survived his apparent death at Lake Silencio in 'The Impossible Astronaut' and 'The Wedding of River Song' in Series Six. That visit probably took place at Christmas 2012 or Christmas 2013 (as it was said to be 'two years' since the Time Lord had last seen his companions, and the incident at Lake Silencio occurred in April 2011), so the earliest the events of

'Pond Life' could take place is between April and August 2013.

- The Doctor mentions in his August phone call that he might have accidentally invented pasta.

PRODUCTION NOTES

- Originally released on the BBC's *Doctor Who* website in the form of five separate episodes over five consecutive days, 'Pond Life' was then compiled into an omnibus version, total running time 6' 12", and broadcast on the BBC's Red Button service on 1 September 2012 – the same day that Series Seven's opening episode, 'Asylum of the Daleks', had its debut transmission. The omnibus version was also given a commercial release on *The Complete Seventh Series* DVD and Blu-ray box set.

- 'Pond Life' was made at the same time as 'The Power of Three', as part of Block Three of Series Seven's production schedule. The scenes inside the Ponds' house were taped at 7 Church Road, Penarth, on 6 June 2012. The sequence of the Doctor outside the house was taped the following day at the usual location of Bute Esplanade in Cardiff. The brief shots of Amy and Rory arguing outside the house, presented in the form of a silent flashback, were recorded at the same location but somewhat earlier, on 5 April, as they were originally intended for inclusion in 'Asylum of the Daleks'.

- Each episode (and the omnibus version) opens with a shortened version of the *Doctor Who* opening titles, not including the series' logo.

- Part 2 features two brief montages of very short clips from the forthcoming episode 'Dinosaurs on a Spaceship'.

ANALYSIS

'Pond Life' is a well-written series of five amusing vignettes, nicely reflecting the madcap nature of the eleventh Doctor's exploits, but with a sting in the tail as the viewer learns that all is not well between the Ponds. A good, intriguing piece of scene-setting for the start of the new series.

7.01 – Asylum of the Daleks

Writer: Steven Moffat
Director: Nick Hurran

DEBUT TRANSMISSION DETAILS

BBC One/BBC One HD
Date: 1 September 2012. Scheduled time: 7.20 pm. Actual time: 7.22 pm.

Duration: 48′ 56″

ADDITIONAL CREDITED CAST

Anamaria Marinca (Darla[51]), Naomi Ryan (Cassandra), David Gyasi (Harvey), Nicholas Briggs (Voice of the Daleks), Barnaby Edwards (Dalek 1), Nicholas Pegg (Dalek 2)

PLOT

The Doctor, Amy and Rory are kidnapped by humans converted by nanogenes into unwitting Dalek puppets. They are taken to a spaceship holding the Dalek Parliament, who ask the Doctor to save them from a feared escape by insane inmates of their own Asylum planet. A signal being received from the planet is recognised by the Doctor as music from the opera *Carmen*. It is being transmitted by a young woman named Oswin Oswald, junior entertainment manager on the starship *Alaska*, who says that she crash-landed on the planet a year ago and has been alone there ever since, occupying herself by making soufflés. The Dalek Prime Minister has the Doctor and his companions sent down to the planet via gravity beams, intending that the Time Lord should turn off its normally

---

[51] Full name given in dialogue as 'Darla von Karlsen'.

impenetrable forcefield from within, so that it can then be 'cleansed'. After avoiding some dead members of the *Alaska*'s crew, who have all been converted into Dalek puppets, the Doctor and Amy make their way through the underground levels of the Asylum, where they eventually meet up with Rory. On the way, they narrowly survive a number of encounters with damaged Dalek inmates, thanks in part to remote assistance received from Oswin, who says that she has hacked into the Daleks' systems. However, when the Doctor goes to rescue Oswin, he finds that she herself is actually a Dalek – she was converted soon after she crash-landed, and has since been maintaining her human identity only in a dream. Oswin erases all record of the Doctor from the Daleks' telepathic web and turns off the Asylum's forcefield, enabling the three time travellers to teleport away to the safety of the TARDIS on board the Dalek Parliament's ship, just before it destroys the planet. The Daleks no longer recognise the Doctor, prompting them to ask repeatedly 'Doctor who?' The Doctor drops Amy and Rory back home.

QUOTE, UNQUOTE

- **Rory:** 'So, how much trouble are we in?'
  Doctor: 'How much trouble, Mr Pond? Out of ten? Eleven.'

- **Rory:** 'Amy, you kicked me out.'
  Amy: 'You want kids. You have always wanted kids. Ever since you *were* a kid. And I can't have them.'
  Rory: 'I know.'
  Amy: 'Whatever they did to me at Demons Run, I can't ever give you children. I didn't kick you out. I gave you up.'

- **Oswin/Dalek:** 'Eggs … Eggs-ter-min-ate … Exterminate!'

- **Oswin/Dalek:** 'Run … Run, you clever boy. And remember.'

CONTINUITY POINTS

- The episode's opening scene is set on the devastated surface of the Daleks' home planet Skaro, which features a building shaped like a giant Dalek. Skaro was apparently vaporised at the end of 'Remembrance of the Daleks' (1988), but that could possibly have occurred in the far-distant future; and, according to the novel *War of the Daleks* (BBC Books, 1997), the destroyed planet was in any event not Skaro but Antalin, which the Daleks had set up as a decoy.

- At the start of the story, Amy is working as a photographic model, as first indicated in 'Closing Time' (2011). She and Rory are on the point of getting divorced; it transpires that she has deliberately pushed him away, as she has discovered that, since giving birth to River Song at the time of 'A Good Man Goes to War' (2011), she has become infertile, and she does not want to deprive him of his wish to be a father. By the end of the story, the Doctor has made them realise how much they still love each other, and they have reconciled

- The Dalek Parliament and Dalek Prime Minister were neither seen nor mentioned prior to this episode. The later audio drama 'We Are the Daleks' (Big Finish, 2015) effectively explains their creation, and also the reason for the existence on Skaro of the giant Dalek-shaped building.

- The new paradigm-type Daleks introduced in 'Victory of the Daleks' (2010) are seen in small numbers in the Dalek Parliament, apparently acting in a supervisory or specialist capacity. One white, one blue and several red ones appear – the yellow and orange types are absent – and the casings of the red and blue ones have a more metallic finish than in their debut story. The white one is again identified as the Dalek Supreme. However, the vast majority of the huge number of Daleks in the Parliament are of the earlier, bronze-liveried variety.

- The Dalek Asylum is a planet where the Daleks confine all those of their race who 'go wrong': the battle-scarred and the insane. There are said to be millions of them there. The atmosphere contains a cloud of nanogenes: robotic micro-organisms that convert any creature, living or dead, into one of the Dalek 'puppets' – sleeper agents that, when activated, extrude a Dalek eye-stalk from their forehead and sometimes a Dalek gun-stick from the palm of their hand. Protection from the nanogenes can however be afforded by a wrist-strap device. The Daleks have been seen to use controlled humans as slaves or agents in a number of previous stories, including 'The Dalek Invasion of Earth' (1964), in which they converted people into Robomen, 'The Evil of the Daleks' (1967) and 'Resurrection of the Daleks' (1984).

- The Daleks regard the Doctor as their 'Predator'. The Doctor at one point also refers to himself as 'the Oncoming Storm', another name the Daleks (amongst other races) associate with him, as mentioned in a number of previous stories, including 'The Parting of the Ways' (2005).

- Oswin appears to be bisexual; she implies that she is attracted to Rory, and says that she once fancied a girl called Nina.

- The intensive care section of the Asylum holds Daleks identified by Oswin as survivors of previous battles with the Doctor on the planets Spiridon, Kembel, Aridius, Vulcan and Exxilon. These incidents were seen in, respectively, 'Planet of the Daleks' (1973), 'The Daleks' Master Plan' (1965/66), 'The Chase' (1965), 'The Power of the Daleks' (1966) and 'Death to the Daleks' (1974). As all of the Daleks in the intensive care section are in new-era-style bronze-liveried casings, rather than in the various different classic-era style casings they had in those earlier stories, the mutant creatures within must presumably have been given replacement casings at some point. This would indeed have been necessary if their original casings had been damaged or destroyed – in 'Death to the Daleks', for instance, the Daleks' spaceship was blown up, and it appeared at the time that no Daleks had actually survived that expedition to Exxilon

- A couple of classic-era Daleks are however glimpsed elsewhere in the Asylum, including a Special Weapons Dalek as introduced in 'Remembrance of the Daleks'.

- The Daleks have a telepathic web – referred to by the Doctor as the path-web – which is similar to a hive mind. Oswin erases all record of the Doctor from it.

PRODUCTION NOTES

- This episode and 'The Angels Take Manhattan' were made together as Block Two of Series Seven's production schedule.

- Location recording got under way on 15 March 2012, when the snowy planet surface scenes were taped in the Sierra Nevada National Park in Spain, alongside work being done on 'A Town Called Mercy'. Bute Esplanade in Cardiff was the venue on 5 April for the scene of Amy and Rory waving the Doctor off from outside their house at the very end of the story. The following day, the sequence of Rory being 'acquired' while catching a bus was taped in Mount Stuart Square, Cardiff. The scene of Amy being 'acquired' in her dressing room during a modelling photoshoot was recorded on 7 April at Bristol University's Institute of Advanced Studies. Studio work took place on various dates between 23 March and 1 May. Reflecting the fact that this was a period of transition behind the scenes, it was split between Doctor Who's hitherto regular facilities at Upper Boat on the Treforest Industrial Estate and its new base at BBC Roath Lock, Cardiff Bay.

- A prequel to this episode, written by Steven Moffat and running 2' 34", was made available to view online, initially only in the USA on iTunes and Amazon Instant Video, and later included on The Complete Seventh Series DVD and Blu-ray box set. After a truncated version of the Doctor Who title sequence, minus the show's logo, it opens with the Doctor enjoying cup of tea and a scone in a café when he is confronted by a mysterious hooded figure. The figure tells him that a woman named Darla von Karlsen wants to meet him, and that his help is required. The café then disappears, and the Doctor realises it was just a psychic projection – someone is sending him a dream message. He and the hooded figure are now in another, gloomy interior setting. The Doctor tries to wake up, and finds himself sitting in a deckchair on a beach. However, this is not real either. The hooded figure gives space-time coordinates of the planet where the Doctor will meet Darla, whose daughter is in danger and needs him to rescue her. On waking back inside the TARDIS, the Doctor names the planet as Skaro. This prequel was recorded during the same early-June 2012 shoot arranged for 'Pond Life', with The Plan in Morgan Arcade, Cardiff being used as the café.

- The Doctor Who logo in the opening title sequence was redesigned for Series Seven, and adjusted slightly for each of the early episodes to reflect their respective content. In the case of 'Asylum of the Daleks', the letters making up the series title are covered in Dalek hemispheres.

- The music heard during the sequence of Amy's photoshoot is an instrumental section of the track 'Feel the Love' from Rudimental's album Home (2013). Also heard, as the signal being transmitted by Oswin, is music from Georges Bizet's opera Carmen (1875) – the Doctor claims that he played triangle on the recording, but his contribution got 'buried in the mix'.

- Steven Moffat decided for this episode to relegate the new paradigm Daleks to a background role, as an officer class, with the earlier bronze-liveried variety reinstated to the forefront of the action, as he realised in the light of highly negative viewer reaction to the former that their introduction in 'Victory of the Daleks' had been a mistake. He had previously implied, in a dramatic vignette written for the Doctor Who Experience attraction that opened in London in 2011 and then transferred to Cardiff in 2012, that the new paradigm Daleks' attempt to supersede and eliminate their bronze-liveried predecessors was defeated in a conflict between the two factions.

- In advance publicity for the episode, much was made of the fact that the Asylum would also feature a number of Daleks with classic-era-style casings. In the event, however, only a couple are briefly glimpsed in the transmitted episode.

- The unusually large number of Dalek props used during recording of the episode were obtained from a number of sources, including some from the Doctor Who Experience and some borrowed from private collectors, including one owned by former showrunner Russell T Davies.

- The PA seen at Amy's photoshoot was played uncredited by Zac Fox; his credit for the role was mistakenly included on 'The Angels Take Manhattan' rather than on this episode.

OOPS!

- One shot in the first Dalek Parliament scene is obviously reversed, as the Daleks' sucker arms and gun sticks are on the wrong sides.

- There are a number of shot continuity errors in the episode. These include a flower falling from behind Oswin's ear in one shot but being back in place in the next; an inert Dalek approached by Rory having only one dome light when seen from one camera angle but both from another; and similarly the Doctor having a plaster on his finger in some parts of the action but not in others.

- When Amy, after losing her protective wrist-strap, says that she is scared of being converted into a Dalek puppet, the Doctor tells her to hold on to the emotion, because 'scared isn't Dalek'. However, he has earlier concluded that the very reason why the Daleks want to send him and his companions to the Asylum is that they are scared to go there themselves. Then, later, Oswin discovers that the Daleks hate the Doctor because they fear him.

- In the final scene of the Doctor in the TARDIS console room, the reflection of a camera and a microphone boom can be glimpsed in the floor panels around the console.

- The version of this episode released on DVD and Blu-ray omits a piece of dialogue present on transmission, of a Dalek shouting 'Exterminate, exterminate, exterminate!' as the TARDIS dematerialises from the Dalek Parliament at the end of the story. Copies of the episode made available on iTunes and other online platforms include this dialogue.

CRITICAL REACTION

- 'In recent times the Daleks have been given more depth, and this week really exposed the vulnerability of these creatures encased in metal. The tragedy of Oswin becoming a Dalek without realising it really tapped into this fragility as viewers witnessed a Dalek crying. The sound was childlike and so unfamiliar coming from a creature hell-bent on extermination of other life forms. It is all part of the inversion of how the Daleks are seen, just like "Victory of the Daleks" where one asks the Doctor if he would "care for some tea". It is an important progression in the overall story of the Daleks.' Neela Debnath, Independent website, 1 September 2012.

- 'Finally given the chance to write an episode with the Daleks in, Steven Moffat seems to have had a whale of a time, taking a break from the fear-of-the-normal tropes that have defined most of his scripts. In "Asylum of the Daleks" he delivered his most old-school Doctor Who story to date, a script packed with ace curveballs and zappy dialogue. Director Nick Hurran carried us along with a madcap visual flair and a sense of scale we don't often dare expect.' Dan Martin, Guardian website, 1 September 2012.

- 'Especially as a season-opener, it works very, very well. It doesn't have the scope or ambition of "A Good Man Goes to War" [2011] or "Doomsday" [2006], but neither is it groaning under the weight of a year or more's worth of ferociously complicated plot. The opening, complete with portentous voice-over and atmospherically shadowy figures, tells even the newest viewer everything they need to know about these tinplated gravel-voiced foes and then we're plunged into the story proper, pausing only briefly to scoop up Rory and Amy along the way.' Tom Salinsky, What Culture website, 1 September 2012

ANALYSIS

Having 'Asylum of the Daleks' open with Amy and Rory separated and on the point of divorcing is a shrewd and unexpected twist with which to reintroduce their characters and draw viewers in at the start of the new series; and, importantly, the emotional scenes in which their estrangement is explored, via an outstanding performance from Karen Gillan and strong support from Arthur Darvill, truthfully reflect the shattering impact that a diagnosis of infertility can often have on a couple's relationship. Rory's comment, 'Amy, the basic fact of our relationship is that I love you more than you love me,' puts a tragic slant on what was originally presented, back in the early part of Series Five, as a kind of running joke of him having to compete with the Doctor for his girlfriend's affections; and Amy's heartfelt rebuttal of this notion is what ultimately leads to their reconciliation at the end of the episode. The only negative aspect here is the resurfacing of the rather uncomfortable idea, suggested on a number of previous occasions, that Amy is physically abusive toward Rory, habitually slapping him across the face. Nevertheless, it is always good to see *Doctor Who* touching on such serious real-life issues, and Steven Moffat is to be applauded for his insightful writing of this aspect of the episode.

Less commendable is the fact that there is unfortunately a huge plot hole at the very heart of the main story about the Dalek Asylum. The Dalek Parliament are apparently unable to destroy the planet as it is surrounded by an impenetrable forcefield; yet if they can send the Doctor, Amy and Rory through the forcefield and down to the surface by way of gravity beams, surely they could just as easily send down some small but hugely powerful bombs, or other equally destructive weapons? Adding to the confusion, the Daleks' motivation appears be a concern that, as the forcefield's integrity has been called into question by the earlier crash-landing of the starship *Alaska* (or possibly just its escape pods?), the Asylum's dangerous inmates could be able to break out; yet the Dalek Prime Minister tells the Doctor that the only way he and his companions will be able to escape is if the forcefield is switched off from within – and later it is indeed seen to be the case that they cannot even teleport away while the forcefield is still in place. This suggests that the forcefield is impenetrable after all – or, at least, that although it may let things in, it certainly doesn't let them out – and that the Dalek Parliament have been worrying over nothing! That said, the concept of a confining forcefield that can be switched off only from within is rather ridiculous to start with – effectively giving the inmates easy access to the sole key to their own prison! – and should surely be a rather greater cause of concern to the Dalek Parliament. In short, none of this makes very much sense.

If, however, one can overlook the highly contrived reason for the Doctor and his companions being sent down to the Asylum, then the action that ensues once they get there makes for a very exciting and suspenseful adventure. The scary sequence of the Doctor and Amy being menaced by the reanimated corpses of an *Alaska* escape pod's crew, all of whom have been converted into Dalek puppets, is very well-conceived and executed. So too are the tense and atmospheric scenes of the three time travellers making their way through the dimly-lit underground chambers of the Asylum, as inert and damaged Daleks slowly reactivate around them. Particularly unusual and effective is a dream-like sequence in which Amy, starting to succumb to the effects of the nanogenes in the atmosphere, initially mistakes a number of reviving Daleks for ordinary people, including a young girl pirouetting in a white ballet tutu.

Returning director Nick Hurran, who made such a fantastic *Doctor Who* debut on 'The Girl Who Waited' and 'The God Complex' in Series Six, does an equally fine, stylish job here. Steven Moffat's stated aim to launch Series Seven with a run of episodes resembling mini blockbuster movies is certainly reflected in the visuals throughout 'Asylum of the Daleks'. From the awe-inspiring CGI-achieved shots of hundreds of Daleks gathered in serried ranks in their Parliament, through the snowy mountainside location work done in Spain, to the claustrophobic settings of the Asylum itself, the whole thing has an impressively epic, high-budget look.

The only slightly curious aspect of the episode's realisation is that, after much advance publicity suggesting that the Asylum inmates would include Daleks with various classic-era-style casings – or 'every Dalek ever', as it was put at one point – there are actually only a couple featured in the on-screen action, and then only very briefly. Given that the Daleks in the Asylum's 'intensive care section' are explicitly stated in dialogue to be survivors of previous, classic-era battles with the Doctor, this would surely have been the ideal place to use casings appropriate to the stories in question; but, disappointingly, the opportunity is missed, and the Daleks seen here are all of the 21st Century bronze-liveried variety. That said, it is certainly a blessing that Steven Moffat had the good sense to realise the terrible blunder he made in introducing the dreadful new paradigm Daleks in 'Victory of the Daleks', mercifully ensuring that they are consigned very much to a background supporting role on this occasion.

One particularly noteworthy aspect of 'Asylum of the Daleks' is that it marks Jenna-Louise Coleman's *Doctor Who* debut, here playing Oswin, aka 'Soufflé Girl'. The shock reveal of Oswin's true nature toward the end of the episode is highly effective, and another very clever piece of writing by Steven Moffat. At the time of transmission, there will doubtless have been many casual viewers who had forgotten about or indeed never seen the announcement back in March 2012 that Coleman had been cast as the new *Doctor Who* companion; but, for the show's attentive fans, her sudden appearance right at the start of Series Seven, several months ahead of when she was first expected to be seen, came as a real surprise. Moreover, it set up an intriguing mystery as to how she could possibly go on to become a regular when her character had been turned into a Dalek and then presumably killed with the destruction of the planet at the end of the action. Coleman's performance as Oswin is excellent – or should that be 'eggcellent'? – throughout, and brings a perky breath of fresh air to the show, boding very well for the future.

Having all memory of the Doctor erased from the Daleks' telepathic web, so that his greatest enemies no longer know who he is, is a development very much in keeping with the theme established at the end of Series Six, of the Time Lord withdrawing from universal notoriety and adopting a much lower profile than in the recent past; something that is also touched on at the start of the episode when Darla, appealing to him to save her daughter Hannah, tells him, 'They say you can help,' and he replies, 'Do they? I wish they'd stop.' The closing shots of the Doctor alone in the TARDIS console room, joyfully repeating the Dalek Parliament's parting question 'Doctor who?', recall Dorium Maldovar's highlighting of that same question, and its importance to the Silence, in 'The Wedding of River Song' (2011) – and it is a question that will take on even greater significance as Series Seven draws toward its conclusion ...

All in all, 'Asylum of the Daleks' is a superb opener to this new run of episodes.

7.02 – Dinosaurs on a Spaceship

Writer: Chris Chibnall
Director: Saul Metzstein

DEBUT TRANSMISSION DETAILS

BBC One/BBC One HD
Date: 8 September 2012. Scheduled time: 7.35 pm. Actual time: 7.36 pm.

Duration: 45' 17"

ADDITIONAL CREDITED CAST

Rupert Graves (Riddell), Mark Williams (Brian Williams), David Bradley (Solomon), Riann Steele (Queen Nefertiti), Sunetra Sarker (Indira), Noel Byrne (Robot 1), Richard Garaghty (Robot 2), Richard Hope (Bleytal), Rudi Dharmalingam (Isa Worker), David Mitchell (Robot 1 Voice), Robert Webb (Robot Voice 2)

PLOT

The Doctor is with Queen Nefertiti in Egypt in the year 1334 BC, having just saved her people from an attack by giant alien locusts, when he receives an alert via the psychic paper. With Nefertiti in tow, he travels to the Indian Space Agency (ISA) in the year 2367, where he learns from an officer named Indira that an unidentified spaceship is approaching Earth and failing to respond; if it gets within 10,000 km, missiles will be sent up to destroy it. The Doctor heads to the spaceship to investigate, taking Nefertiti with him and completing a 'gang' of companions by collecting big game hunter John Riddell from the African plains in the year 1902 and Amy and Rory from their home in contemporary England, inadvertently picking up Rory's dad Brian in the process. They discover that the

147

spaceship contains a cargo of live dinosaurs, and that it was originally an ark launched by the Silurians. All the Silurians on board have been slaughtered by a unscrupulous space pirate, Solomon, who sees the dinosaurs simply as a valuable commodity to trade. Solomon is unable to steer the ark, and his legs are badly injured, but the Doctor is able to mend them. When the ISA fire their missiles at the ark, Solomon tries to escape in his own spaceship, taking Nefertiti with him, as he considers her to be of even greater value than the dinosaurs. The Doctor however rescues Nefertiti and alters the signal emitted by Solomon's ship, so that the ISA's missiles are redirected to it and blow it up. Nefertiti decides to join Riddell in 1902, while the Doctor returns Amy and Rory home, and Brian indulges a newfound enthusiasm for tourism.

QUOTE, UNQUOTE

- **Amy:** 'Doctor!'
  Doctor: 'I know! Dinosaurs – on a spaceship!'

- **Brian:** 'What sort of a man doesn't carry a trowel? Put it on your Christmas list!'
  Rory: 'Dad, I'm 31. I don't have a Christmas list anymore.'
  Doctor: 'I do!'

- **Doctor:** 'Brian Pond, you are delicious!'
  Brian: 'I'm not a Pond.'
  Doctor: ''Course you are.'

CONTINUITY POINTS

- The Doctor and Brian have never met before, so Brian may for some reason have missed his son's wedding; certainly he is not seen on screen during the wedding scenes in 'The Big Bang' (2010).[52] Brian also has no prior knowledge of Amy and Rory travelling in the TARDIS; he was under the impression that after their wedding they visited Thailand. The Doctor must however have heard of Brian, as

---

[52] Extra Andy Elvin was cast to play Rory's father in 'The Big Bang' (2010). However, he was neither identified nor credited as such on screen, so he could actually have been another relative, or indeed an unrelated guest.

he knows his name without being told it.

- When the Doctor appears outside Riddell's tent in 1902, Riddell asks him where he has been; apparently he popped out seven months earlier to collect some liquorice, leaving the hunter with 'two very disappointed dancers' on his hands. Clearly the Doctor and Riddell are old acquaintances.

- It has been established in earlier episodes that Amy was born in 1988 or 1989, and that Rory is of a similar age, or possibly slightly younger. This is confirmed in the comic strip story 'The Broken Man' (Panini, 2012), which gives his birth year as 1989.[53] As Rory says here that he is 31 (which is not queried by Brian), this suggests that, from his perspective, 'Dinosaurs on a Spaceship' takes place around the year 2020.[54] This suggests that, for Amy and Rory, some seven or eight years must have passed since the Doctor paid his Christmas visit to them at the end of 'The Doctor, the Widow and the Wardrobe' (2011). The events depicted in 'Pond Life' and 'Asylum of the Daleks' have presumably occurred sometime during that seven or eight year period. Amy says that, prior to the Doctor picking them up at the start of 'Dinosaurs on a Spaceship', they have not seen him for ten months, and that his visits have become increasingly infrequent.

- The Silurians launched the ark as they believed that the Earth was due to suffer a destructive impact – established in 'Doctor Who and the Silurians' (1970) to be from the Moon, which in the event did not strike the planet but instead went into orbit around it. The Silurians on board the ark were looking for another suitable planet on which to settle.

- Solomon is aided by two robots, which he says he picked up cheap. When the Doctor draws attention to their rusty state, Robot 1 says that they have been on the Silurian ship for 'two millennia'. This

---

[53] This disproves the theory that the anomalous issue date of 30/11/90 given on Rory's hospital pass as seen in 'The Eleventh Hour' (2010) was actually his birth date and was simply entered in the wrong place. That was probably therefore just a complete administrative error on the hospital's part.

[54] This is the same year in which the 'older' Amy and Rory are seen from a distance in 'The Hungry Earth' (2010).

suggests that, unless he comes from a very long-lived race, Solomon must have put himself into suspended animation sometime after his arrival there, possibly in the hope that the ship might eventually receive other visitors, including someone who could treat the serious injuries he sustained to his legs after being cornered by three raptors – hence his excitement when he hears Rory use the word 'Doctor'. Before the Doctor mends his legs, he is seen to be hooked up to some type of life-support equipment; it may well be this that has sustained him over such a long period of time.

- Solomon tries to find out how much the Doctor is worth by scanning him with a purple light from an identifying value (IV) system. The Doctor describes this as 'The database of everything across space and time allocated a market value.' Solomon is surprised to discover that the Doctor is not included in the database.

- Solomon's initial aim was to transport the dinosaurs to a commerce colony called the Roxbourne Peninsula.

PRODUCTION NOTES

- This episode and 'A Town Called Mercy' were made together as Block One of Series Seven's production schedule.

- A relatively small amount of location work was carried out this time. The brief scenes inside the home of Amy and Rory were shot at 6 Church Road, Penarth, Cardiff – a neighbouring property to the one that would later be used for 'Pond Life' – on 20 February 2012; the first day of recording on Series Seven. On 22 February, the beach scenes were recorded on Southerndown Beach, Ogmore Vale, Bridgend, which had featured in a number of previous episodes, most notably as Bad Wolf Bay in 'Doomsday' (2006) and 'Journey's End' (2008) and as the surface of the planet Alfava Metraxis in 'The Time of Angels' / 'Flesh and Stone' (2010). Studio recording took place on various dates between 17 February and 23 March at Upper Boat.

- For this episode, the *Doctor Who* logo in the opening titles was given a dinosaur hide texture.

- The dinosaurs featured in the action were realised via a combination of live-action props on set and CGI effects in post-production; and the episode was conceived in the first place partly due to the confidence of the show's regular effects teams – prosthetics suppliers Millennium FX and CGI effects specialists The Mill – in their ability to achieve such elements successfully.

- The sleeping baby Tyrannosaurus Rex that Amy, Riddell and Nefertiti stumble upon in one scene was originally created by Millennium FX for an unrelated exhibit some time earlier; it was pressed into service here when the cost of having CGI raptors in the scene in question was found to be beyond the episode's budget. The CGI raptors that do feature in the episode, in a later sequence where Riddell and Amy fight them off with tranquilliser guns, were not modelled specially for this purpose, but reused from The Mill's work on the ITV show *Primeval* (2007-2011).

- The costumes for Solomon's physically impressive but generally ineffectual robots were originally created for CBBC's science-fiction-themed game show *Mission: 2110* (2010), in which they were called Roboidz. Their reuse in slightly adapted form in 'Dinosaurs on a Spaceship' was another cost-saving measure.

- Nefertiti's appearance was based on a famous ancient bust of the Egyptian queen, attributed to the sculptor Thutmos, which currently resides in Berlin's Neues Museum.

- Solomon's appearance was loosely based on that of celebrity nightclub owner Peter Stringfellow.

OOPS!

- In the shot of the Earth in space, as observed by Brian from the TARDIS doorway, the image of the planet is reversed.

CRITICAL REACTION

- 'This was fun. Big fun. Slight and fluffy and silly, with the occasional

151

creaky bit of plotting (how handy the Doctor accidentally brings Rory's dad along for the ride when the spaceship needs two pilots from the *same gene pool*), but enormously entertaining.' Dave Golder, *SFX* website, 8 September 2012.

- 'With the Doctor for some reason deciding to assemble a "gang" for this episode (à la *Scooby Doo*) we certainly had a different dynamic, but it leant an uneasy mix of the humorous and downright daft. One moment you had the Doctor, Rory and his dad Brian … riding a triceratops to escape [a pair of] camp robots, the next you had a sinister storyline concerning David Bradley's decidedly nasty trader Solomon. This collision was somewhat jarring.' Gavin Fuller, *Telegraph* website, 8 September 2012.

- 'There were more seeds sown for what's beginning to feel like the two main themes underlying this series – Amy and Rory's departure (nods to Amy's mortality and the Doctor's increasingly jarring impact on their everyday lives), and the Doctor's surprisingly judgemental, increasingly grey morality (while he justified it being for the greater good, he could have saved Solomon rather than let him explode). It may not have been perfect, but at least "Dinosaurs on a Spaceship" delivered where it counts, with fun, frivolous Jurassic Larks galore.' Matt Risley, IGN website, 8 September 2012.

ANALYSIS

The mini blockbuster movie approach continues here with an episode very much in the mould of a fun action-adventure romp, with a 'does what it says on the tin' title recalling that of *Snakes on a Plane* (2006). Dinosaurs are a perennial children's favourite, and a staple ingredient of family movie fare, as seen for instance in the highly successful *Jurassic Park* (1993) and its sequels, so they are ideally suited as subject matter for a *Doctor Who* story. Indeed, one suspects they would have featured more often in the show, but for the fact that it is only now that CGI and other effects techniques have progressed to the stage where such creatures can be successfully realised on a relatively modest budget – as demonstrated by the rather unsuccessful attempt to base a story around them some thirty years earlier in 'Invasion of the Dinosaurs' (1974). The wobbly puppets and basic stop-motion models of that third Doctor adventure certainly pale by comparison with the brilliant work contributed by Millennium FX and The Mill to 'Dinosaurs on a Spaceship', which is surely amongst the most impressive effects imagery ever to grace *Doctor Who*. Indeed, so convincing are the dinosaurs that it is quite easy for the viewer to forget that they are effects work at all, and simply to accept them as real. Particularly memorable is the scene where the Doctor, Rory and Brian escape from Solomon's robots by riding off on the back of a Triceratops. Great stuff!

Although the Doctor isn't exactly right when he says he has 'not really had a gang before' – he put one together as recently as in 'A Good Man Goes to War' (2011) – his recruitment of an Egyptian queen and a big game hunter to join him in his latest exploit brings other traditional family movie elements into the mix; and this somewhat bonkers collection of characters adds still further to the fun. That said, however, it does seem rather odd that the Time Lord should count a big game hunter amongst his friends – even Amy at one point expresses distain for 'men who hunt defenceless creatures' – and it doesn't help matters, either, that Rupert Graves' performance as John Riddell, complete with obviously affected 'upper crust' accent, is frankly not very good. A far better move here would have been to bring back John Barrowman as Captain Jack Harkness – who, with the benefit of his immortality, would surely have been an ideal candidate for inclusion in the Doctor's gang.

Riann Steele also sadly fails to make much of an impact in what should have been a strong role as Nefertiti. Writer Chris Chibnall is at least partly to blame for this, though, as he omits to have Nefertiti even so much as comment on the strangeness of the situations in which she finds herself, and at no point does she react convincingly as a person from 1334 BC should. Possibly, as seems to be the case with Riddell, this is not the first time the Doctor has taken her on a trip in the TARDIS, and she has by this point become blasé about the futuristic wonders she witnesses; but if so, this should really have been addressed in dialogue. It is, however, a nice touch on Chibnall's part to have Nefertiti and Riddell hooking up in 1902 at the end of the episode – in the process supplying an explanation for the real-life historical mystery of what became of Nefertiti.

By far the most successful newcomer in 'Dinosaurs on a Spaceship' is Rory's dad Brian, a well-conceived and amusing character brought to life with great charm by the ideally-cast Mark Williams, previously best known for his work as one of the team on the 1990s BBC Two comedy sketch vehicle *The Fast Show* and for playing Ron Weasley's dad Arthur in the *Harry Potter* films, and with one previous *Doctor Who* credit to his name, as

Maxwell Edison in the audio drama 'The Eternal Summer' (Big Finish, 2009). It is a pleasing notion that experiencing this adventure with the Doctor transforms Brian from a man who, in Rory's words, 'hates travelling' and 'only goes to the paper shop and golf', into one who loves touring around the world, sending his son and daughter-in-law postcards from all the various places he has visited, with pictures of himself cut out and stuck onto them! He even sends them one with artwork purporting to show a place called 'Siluria', with dinosaurs pictured next to a police box, possibly suggesting that the Doctor has resettled the creatures on a new planet – although it could also be the case that this is just a humorous mock-up rather than evidence of a genuine trip made by Brian with the Doctor.[55]

While Williams' excellent portrayal of Brian is a good example of an actor well-known for his comedy work successfully filling a *Doctor Who* role, sadly the same cannot be said of the robot voices supplied by David Mitchell and Robert Webb, whose selection to play these parts smacks more of the kind of 'stunt casting' of which 1980s *Doctor Who* producer John Nathan-Turner was sometimes accused – such as when he gave comedian Ken Dodd the role of the Tollmaster in 'Delta and the Bannermen' (1987), or the then popular comedy duo Hale and Pace minor roles in 'Survival' (1989). And whereas that criticism was sometimes unfair when aimed at Nathan-Turner – Hale and Pace, for instance, actually gave perfectly good character performances in their roles as a pair of shopkeepers – here that is sadly not the case. Whoever came up with the idea to have Mitchell and Webb perform their parts as a kind of pastiche of their familiar characters from the popular Channel 4 adult sitcom *Peep Show* (2003-2015), it was a big mistake, putting one in mind of the way that celebrities appearing in Christmas pantomimes often make shoehorned-in allusions to their most well-known roles, complete with a knowing wink to the audience; and here the joke really falls as flat as a pancake – all the more so, one suspects, for those viewers, including many outside the UK, who have never seen *Peep Show,* and who will doubtless have been left mystified.

In a way, it could be said that even this is actually in keeping with the overall feel of the episode, in that it is not uncommon to see popular comedians cropping up in family movies in light-relief cameo roles that,

---

[55] It may or may not be significant that the police box pictured on the postcard is of the design used by the tenth Doctor rather than the eleventh.

more often than not, fail to generate many laughs. Unfortunately, however, most of the other humour in 'Dinosaurs in a Spaceship' is equally unfunny – generally consisting of rather crude and awkwardly contrived sexual innuendo, such as Brian referring to his 'balls' (actually the golf balls he carries in his pocket) and Riddell wielding his 'very large weapon' (a dinosaur tranquilising gun) – suggesting that Chris Chibnall probably does not have a successful career in comedy ahead of him.

On a more positive note, the idea of the Silurian ark is an excellent one, adding an interesting new layer to the Silurian race's backstory even though they are not the main focus of the narrative. The matter-of-fact admission by Solomon that he has systematically massacred all of the thousands of Silurians originally on board the ark is genuinely shocking, and the nasty, avaricious space pirate, well portrayed by the excellent David Bradley, makes for a memorable if somewhat caricatured villain, recalling the more down-to-Earth fictional pirate Long John Silver after the Doctor mends his legs and he starts walking around with the aid of a crutch. That said, however, it is also quite shocking when, at the end of the story, the Doctor dismisses Solomon's pleas and leaves him on board his spaceship to die, when he could quite easily have allowed him onto the ark and thereby spared his life. This is not the first time we have seen a vengeful, angry side to the Time Lord's nature: in 'School Reunion' (2006), the tenth Doctor spoke of having less mercy than in the past; and later, in 'The Family of Blood' (2007), he inflicted surprisingly cruel punishments on the eponymous family members. Here, though, he arguably goes further than ever before, effectively acting as Solomon's executioner.

It seems that not only is the Doctor trying to shake off his former universal notoriety and step back into the shadows – as demonstrated again in this episode by his pleased reaction when Solomon is unable to find any record of him in his comprehensive database-cum-catalogue and exclaims 'You don't exist' – but he is also becoming rather more cold-hearted and ruthless. It will be interesting to see how this new character trait is developed and explored in future episodes. As far as 'Dinosaurs on a Spaceship' is concerned, though, it must be said that the harsh, uncompromising way in which the Doctor dispatches Solomon does sit rather uncomfortably with the more general feeling of this being intended as a fun-filled romp.

Just as the episode's scripting occasionally falters, so too does its on-screen realisation. It is particularly hard to understand the decision to record the scenes in the Silurian ark's engine room on location on a beach. This setting is just completely incongruous, and never for one moment convinces the viewer that the action is taking place within a chamber on board a spaceship. Clearly these scenes would have been far better achieved on a studio set.

Overall, then, 'Dinosaurs on a Spaceship' is something of a mixed bag: an enjoyable, action-packed and generally light-hearted adventure, with some superb dinosaur effects work, a great new character in Brian, an excellent central concept in the Silurian ark and a memorable villain in Solomon, but with an occasional unevenness in tone and a few elements that unfortunately don't quite hit the mark.

7.03 – A Town Called Mercy

Writer: Toby Whithouse
Director: Saul Metzstein

DEBUT TRANSMISSION DETAILS

BBC One/BBC One HD
Date: 15 September 2012. Scheduled time: 7.35 pm. Actual time: 7.36 pm.

Duration: 44' 19"

ADDITIONAL CREDITED CAST

Andrew Brooke (The Gunslinger), Adrian Scarborough (Kahler-Jex), Dominic Kemp (Kahler-Mas), Joanne McQuinn (Sadie), Byrd Wilkins (The Preacher), Garrick Hagon (Abraham), Ben Browder (Isaac), Sean Benedict (Dockery), Rob Cavazos (Walter)

PLOT

The TARDIS deposits the Doctor, Amy and Rory by mistake in the town of Mercy in the American Wild West. The town has been isolated by a formidable cyborg known as the Gunslinger, whose right arm is a deadly energy weapon. The Gunslinger intends to execute an alien named Kahler-Jex, whose spaceship crash-landed nearby and who has since been acting as the local doctor. Jex, however, is being protected by the town marshal, Isaac. The Doctor discovers that, in order to end a long war in which his race were involved, Jex and his team created the Gunslinger and others of its kind by experimenting on unwitting students. The Gunslinger, whose real name is Kahler-Tek, later went rogue and started hunting down and killing its creators, of whom Jex is the last. Disgusted by Jex's war crime, the Doctor is at first inclined to hand him over to the

Gunslinger, but Amy argues against this. Isaac dies after saving Jex from a shot from the Gunslinger's weapon, but not before he has bequeathed his marshal's badge to the Doctor. The Gunslinger then threatens to kill everyone in the town if they do not hand Jex over by noon the next day, but the Doctor devises a plan: he, Rory and some men of the town paint their faces with the same distinguishing mark that is on Jex's, acting as decoys so that Jex can escape back to his spaceship. Jex, however, decides to end the cycle of violence, and commits suicide by activating the spaceship's self-destruct system. The three time travellers depart, leaving the town under the Gunslinger's protection.

QUOTE, UNQUOTE

- **Doctor:** 'Anachronistic electricity, *Keep Out* signs, aggressive stares. Has someone been peeking at my Christmas list?'

- **Doctor:** 'Tea, but the strong stuff: leave the bag in.'

- **Doctor:** 'The Kahler. I love the Kahler. One of the most ingenious races in the galaxy. Seriously. They could build a spaceship out of Tupperware and moss.'

- **Amy:** 'Let him come back, Doctor!'
  Doctor: 'Or what? You won't shoot me, Amy.'
  Amy: 'How do you know? Maybe I've changed. I mean, you've clearly been taking stupid lessons since I saw you last!'

- **Doctor:** 'Don't you see? Violence doesn't end violence, it extends it.'

CONTINUITY POINTS

- The Doctor mentions a previous incident, unseen on screen, in which Rory left his phone charger 'in Henry VIII's *en-suite*'.

- The Doctor was aiming to take Amy and Rory to see the Day of the Dead Festival in Mexico, which is said to be 200 miles to the south of Mercy.

- Isaac mentions that the war – doubtless meaning the American Civil War – ended five years earlier. This accords with the fact that Mercy has a black preacher, which arguably would have been unlikely prior to that. In our universe, the American Civil War ended in 1865, suggesting that the story is set around 1870, although there is plentiful evidence in past episodes that Earth history follows a different course in the *Doctor Who* universe than in ours. The Colt Peacemaker guns seen during the action went on sale in 1873 in our universe.

- The Doctor at one point says, 'I've matured. I'm twelve hundred years old now.' This suggests that about a century has passed for him since his faked death at Lake Silencio, as seen in 'The Impossible Astronaut' (2010) and 'The Wedding of River Song' (2010), when he told Amy that he was 1103. However, he is notoriously inconsistent when it comes to giving his age.

- The Doctor claims that he 'speaks horse', similar to how he claimed to 'speak baby' in 'A Good Man Goes to War' and 'Closing Time' in Series Six. This could be simply a joke, although he does keep up his apparent conversation with his mount, whose name he says is Susan (although it is a male horse), even when no-one else is with him.

- Kahler-Jex's spaceship is protected by Abraxas Security Systems software – motto 'Incinerating intruders for three centuries'. Abraxas was a cyborg creature, somewhat similar in concept to the Gunslinger, introduced in the *Doctor Who* novella *The Cabinet of Light* (Telos Publishing, 2003). *Child of Time* (Telos Publishing, 2007), the last novella in the *Time Hunter* spin-off range, later revealed that it and others like it were created by a sinister time travelling organisation called the Sodality.

- Kahler is also the name of the planet from which the Kahler come.

- The Doctor says to Amy and Rory, 'You know all the monkeys and dogs they sent into space in the '50s and '60s? You will never guess what really happened to them.' He doesn't get to explain, but in the subsequently-released sixth Doctor audio drama 'The Space Race' (Big Finish, 2013), the first dog in space, Laika, returns to Earth to wreak revenge on humanity, having first been augmented by aliens with a missing cosmonaut's larynx and brain, so that it can talk and influence other dogs to obey it.

PRODUCTION NOTES

- This episode and 'Dinosaurs on a Spaceship' were made together as Block One of Series Seven's production schedule.

- 'The Gunslinger' and 'Mercy' were both working titles for the episode.

- A 1' 46" duration video called 'The Making of the Gunslinger', written by Toby Whithouse, directed by Neill Gorton of Millennium FX and produced by Denise Paul, was released on iTunes and later included on *The Complete Seventh Series* DVD and Blu-ray box set. While its title was suggestive of a behind-the-scenes piece, it was actually a prequel to the episode, featuring and narrated by an uncredited Adrian Scarborough as Kahler-Jex and also featuring an uncredited Andrew Brooke as Kahler-Tek, the Gunslinger. Introduced, as usual for a prequel, by a truncated version of the *Doctor Who* title sequence, minus the show's logo, it tells of how 'the golden age of the Kahler' was ushered in by the creation of the Gunslinger cyborgs: unwitting students whose bodies were augmented with military hardware to make them into formidable living weapons.

- All of the location work on this occasion was done in Almeria, Spain, at Fort Apache in the Oasys theme park (also known as 'Little Hollywood') and the neighbouring Fort Bravo (also known as 'Texas Hollywood'). These recreations of American Wild West towns have featured in numerous other film and television productions over the years. The Mercy street scenes outside the marshal's office were taped on 7 March 2012 at Fort Apache, as were the interiors of Kahler-Jex's spaceship. The other Mercy scenes were recorded at Fort Bravo from 8 to 10 and 12 to 14 March. Finally, desert and mountain terrain scenes were shot in a ravine between Fort Apache and Fort Bravo on 15 March. A small amount of studio work was done back at Upper Boat in Cardiff between 19 and 21 March for scenes taking place inside the marshal's office.

- For this episode, the *Doctor Who* logo in the opening titles was given a wooden texture marked with gunshot holes.

- The story is presented as a tale recounted by an unseen narrator whose great-grandmother was a little girl in Mercy at the time the events took place. The narration, which tops and tails the action, was performed uncredited by voice artist Lorelei King. The little girl, who has no dialogue, was played by an uncredited Alba Little.

- Also uncredited, as the voice of the Abraxas Security System, was *Doctor Who*'s regular assistant editor Becky Trotman.

OOPS!

- The Doctor pins Isaac's star badge to his jacket lapel on taking over as marshal, but in one shot it is pinned to his breast pocket instead.

CRITICAL REACTION

- '"A Town Called Mercy" was a proper Western. One glimpse of a cyborg in this environment immediately brought to mind Michael Crichton's 1973 movie *Westworld*. But while that was set in a theme park in the future, this was the real deal. With no eventual reveal that the whole thing was a spaceship, or the result of any perception filters, this was the full-blooded tale of a real town under real siege from a lone gunman – and it came complete with its own noble sheriff, the Doctor on horseback, and, irresistibly, its own *High Noon* moment. Writer Toby Whithouse delivered a complex morality dilemma fizzing with sharp dialogue, Adrian Scarborough's Kahler-Jex brought some British eccentricity, and director Saul Metzstein did an effective job of recreating the look of classics of the genre. If anything, [it] was more effective as a Western than as a *Doctor Who* episode.' Dan Martin, *Guardian* website, 15 September 2012.

- 'For all its good points … "A Town Called Mercy" doesn't quite hit the bullseye for me. It lacks authenticity. I don't believe in it. I don't feel it. The town looks like a set plonked in the middle of a desert. Mercy is literally a one-horse town … I don't believe the Doctor's moral stance; either his wavering or his sudden certitude in dealing with Kahler-Jex. I don't feel anything when the marshal dies or when Jex eventually takes his own life. I adore Westerns and I love *Doctor Who*, but the two worlds have never quite gelled … It looks like a spaghetti Western but must remain peculiarly bloodless in tone. It proceeds at a languorous pace, which is a pleasant contrast to some of the *flash-bang-wallop, did-I-miss-something?* episodes, but does leave me stifling a yawn.' Patrick Mulkern, *Radio Times* website, 15 September 2012.

• 'While the Terminator-meets-Predator killer cyborg offered solid thrills, it was in the Doctor's moral uncertainty that the episode really galvanised. Matt Smith dialled down the wacky to explore the cold, judgemental friction that we've seen simmering away since the Doctor returned in "Asylum of the Daleks". His willingness to cross a line both literal and metaphorical, and throw a mass murderer to the Gatling-gun-happy robo-dogs, prompted a Batman-ish moral dilemma – how many times must his mercy come back to bite him in the (surprisingly chapless) ass before he finally cracked and dished out a murderously final punishment?' Matt Risley, IGN website, 15 September 2012.

ANALYSIS

'A Town Called Mercy' is *Doctor Who*'s first full-on Western since 'The Gunfighters' (1966); and, curiously, it bears a number of similarities to that earlier story. Both open with the Doctor arriving in town with one female companion and one male; both have him getting into danger when he is initially mistaken for another, local doctor; both see him coming under the protection of, and later being deputised by, the town marshal, with a star badge pinned to his lapel; both feature a scene where the townsfolk form an ultimately ineffectual lynch mob; and both have their events related in part by way of voice-over narration (in the form of a ballad in the earlier story). The two even had almost identical working titles: 'The Gunslinger' in the case of 'A Town Called Mercy', and 'The Gunslingers' in the case of 'The Gunfighters'.

In other respects, though, 'A Town Called Mercy' could hardly be more different from its purely historical, wholly studio-bound antecedent. Its central plot puts one far more in mind of the movie *Westworld* (1973), which had its own bald-headed cyborg called the

Gunslinger hunting down a target in a Western setting; and its high production values, complete with extensive sun-drenched location work carried out in Spain, make it a visual treat far removed from anything that *Doctor Who* could have afforded back in the mid-1960s. And whereas 'The Gunfighters' was somewhat humorous in tone, 'A Town Called Mercy' is essentially a quite serious and thought-provoking story – albeit one that still fulfils Steven Moffat's mini blockbuster movie brief for the early part of Series Seven.

The story's seriousness lies in its exploration of the morality both of Kahler-Jex and of the Doctor. Although labelled a war criminal by Rory for the way he created the Gunslingers through experimentation on innocent students, Jex mounts a strong defence of his actions, saying: 'We'd been at war for nine years. A war that had already decimated half of our planet. Our task was to bring peace, and we did. We built an army that routed the enemy and ended the war in less than a week. Do you want me to repent, to beg forgiveness for saving millions of lives? ... War is another world. You cannot apply the politics of peace to what I did. To what any of us did.' There are obvious echoes here of the arguments used by the Allies to justify the dropping of atomic bombs on the Japanese cities of Hiroshima and Nagasaki at the end of the Second World War. Isaac, too, disputes that Jex is a war criminal: 'No, he's the guy that saved the town from cholera, the guy that gave us heat and light.'

Clearly Jex is far from being a one-dimensional villain. 'You think I'm unaffected by what I did?' he asks the Doctor. 'That I don't hear them screaming every time I close my eyes? It would be so much simpler if I was just one thing, wouldn't it? The mad scientist who made that killing machine, or the physician who's dedicated his life to serving this town. The fact that I'm both bewilders you.' The Doctor is unconvinced by this, responding, 'You committed an atrocity and chose this as your punishment. Don't get me wrong; good choice. Civilised hours, lots of adulation, nice weather. But ... justice doesn't work like that. You don't get to decide when and how your debt is paid.' The way it unfolds, though, the story seems to suggest that Jex really is a reformed character. Ultimately deciding to commit suicide rather than flee in his spaceship, he tells the Gunslinger: 'You'll chase me to another planet, and another race will be caught in the crossfire ... I'm ending the war for you, too.' Commendably, there are no black-and-white moral certainties presented here, only shades of grey.

As far as the Doctor himself is concerned, Jex seems to hit a very sore spot when he says: 'Looking at you, Doctor, is like looking into a mirror, almost. There's rage there, like me. Guilt, like me. Solitude. Everything but the nerve to do what needs to be done. Thank the gods my people weren't relying on you to save them.' It is seemingly only after being attacked in this way that the Doctor decides to bundle Jex out of Isaac's office and give him up to the Gunslinger, in the face of Amy's protests. Doubtless Jex's words have brought back painful memories for him of difficult moral choices he has had to make in the past, including at the end of the Time War. Or possibly they have simply pushed him past a breaking point, as suggested when he says to Amy: 'Every time, I negotiate, I try to understand. Well, not today. No. Today, I honour the victims first. His, the Master's, the Daleks', all the people who died because of my mercy!' Eventually, though, the Doctor backs down, after Amy reproaches him: 'You see, this is what happens when you travel alone for too long. Well, listen to me, Doctor. We can't be like him. We have to be better than him.'

This exchange possibly alludes to a political debate accorded many column-inches in the British media at the time of production, about the relative weight given by the criminal justice system to the rights of criminals versus the rights of victims. In *Doctor Who* terms, though, it not only recalls once more the Doctor's comment in writer Toby Whithouse's earlier episode 'School Reunion' (2006) about how much mercy he used to have, but also revisits a theme that can be traced right back to the third ever story, 'Inside the Spaceship' (1964): that of the Doctor needing human companionship to keep him grounded and to moderate his behaviour. In 21st Century *Doctor Who*, this is first addressed directly in 'The Runaway Bride' (2006), when the Doctor, after killing all of the Racnoss Empress's spider children, tells his future companion Donna, 'I don't need anyone,' and Donna replies, 'Yes, you do. Because sometimes, I think you need someone to stop you.' This same idea is returned to in other stories, including the run of specials culminating in 'The Waters of Mars' (2009) and 'The End of Time' (2009/2010), where consciously choosing to travel on his own has clearly contributed toward the Doctor ending up in a very dark state of mind. In the second of the minisodes known as 'Meanwhile in the TARDIS' (2010), he tells Amy that having her with him on his travels enables him to see the universe afresh through her eyes, showing just how important her presence is to him.

Whether by accident or by design, having this issue explicitly highlighted in the episode transmitted immediately after 'Dinosaurs on a

Spaceship' usefully contextualises the Doctor's effective execution of Solomon in the latter. We can now see his hardened attitude and unfamiliar inclination toward ruthlessness as a product of all the time he has spent alone since the end of 'The God Complex' (2011), another Toby Whithouse-scripted episode, when he gifted Amy and Rory their own house and they ceased living in the TARDIS as permanent companions. Indeed, given that he was about 900 years old at the time of 'The God Complex', if one takes at face value his comment in 'A Town Called Mercy' that he is now 1,200, the Doctor may well have spent much of the past 300 years of his life travelling on his own (although we know that he has met up with River Song occasionally, and he may have had other companions – including, perhaps, Queen Nefertiti and John Riddell – in further adventures not seen on screen).

This further demonstrates what a shrewd move it was on Steven Moffat's part to have Amy and Rory become part-time TARDIS travellers, with a separate home life of their own, back in Series Six. By creating a completely different type of Doctor-and-companion dynamic, the only arguable precedent for which was Sarah Jane Smith maintaining her parallel career as a journalist in between making a series of TARDIS trips back in the mid-1970s, it opened up new dramatic territory that is still proving fruitful here in Series Seven – perhaps even more so in 'A Town Called Mercy' than in 'Asylum of the Daleks', where it was exploited in the idea of Amy and Rory having split up in the Doctor's absence, and in 'Dinosaurs on a Spaceship', where it allowed for the introduction of Rory's dad Brian. And with the heavily-trailed departure of Amy and Rory fast approaching, clearly it is something that is going to be of continued significance over the next couple of episodes too.

Whithouse's script for 'A Town Called Mercy' is well up to the high standard set by most of his previous contributions to the show, and manages to pack in a good number of classic Western tropes, including a high noon confrontation between the Doctor and the Gunslinger on the town's main street, where they try to beat each other to the draw – the Doctor drawing his sonic screwdriver instead of a gun! The only aspect that doesn't entirely convince is the Gunslinger's initial unwillingness simply to go into the town and either seize Jex or execute him on the spot. The explanation offered for this is that the powerful cyborg is predisposed, either by programming or by ethics, to try at all costs to avoid inadvertently killing innocents – 'People will get in the way,' he tells the Doctor. However, this is somewhat undermined by two slight oddities: first, that after he does indeed kill the innocent Isaac, he seems to have a clear shot at Jex but still fails to take it; and secondly, that he then threatens to go into the town and kill everyone if Jex is not handed over to him by noon the following day. That said, though, the first of these issues may be as much down to the direction as to the writing of the scene in question; and the second may be overlooked if one simply assumes that the Gunslinger's threat is an empty one – as it is arguably revealed to be when, after entering the town, he does not in fact kill anyone. Certainly he shows his capacity for good at the end when, after realising that Jex, in committing suicide, has perhaps acted more nobly than he himself, he agrees to become the town's peacekeeper. In time-honoured Western fashion, he even gets to exchange the black hat of a villain for the white one of a hero – specifically, the marshal's hat that Isaac previously gave to the Doctor, affording him his first chance since 'The Wedding of River Song' (2011) to wear a 'cool' Stetson.

Occasional glitches aside, Saul Metzstein's direction on 'A Town Called Mercy' outshines that on 'Dinosaurs on a Spaceship', giving a very cinematic look to the proceedings, and it is no surprise to see his name attached to further episodes later in the run. The relatively small guest cast also deliver uniformly strong performances, with Adrian Scarborough bringing suitable levels of complexity to his depiction of Kahler-Jex, Ben Browder (well known to genre fans for his high-profile recurring roles in the US series *Stargate SG-1* and *Farscape*) turning in a sympathetic portrayal of Isaac, and Andrew Brooke lending an imposing physical presence in his part as the Gunslinger, aided by the excellent costume and prosthetic make-up created for the character. The three regulars, too, are as good in their respective roles as one has come to expect by this stage.

Three episodes in, Series Seven has already offered much to enjoy, and also to think about.

7.04 – The Power of Three

Writer: Chris Chibnall
Director: Douglas Mackinnon

DEBUT TRANSMISSION DETAILS

BBC One/BBC One HD
Date: 22 September 2012. Scheduled time: 7.30 pm. Actual time: 7.31 pm.

Duration: 41' 20"

ADDITIONAL CREDITED CAST

Mark Williams (Brian Williams), Jemma Redgrave (Kate Stewart[56]), Steven Berkoff (Shakri), Selva Rasalingam (Ranjit), Alice O'Connell (Laura), Peter Cartwright (Arnold Underwood), David Beck (Orderly 1), Daniel Beck (Orderly 2), David Hartley (UNIT Researcher)

PLOT

Amy recalls a time the Doctor came to stay with her and Rory. It begins one July with the sudden appearance on Earth of huge numbers of identical small black cubes. Troops from UNIT, now headed by Kate Stewart, daughter of Brigadier Lethbridge-Stewart, arrive at the Ponds' house. The Doctor agrees to keep the cubes under observation, but quickly becomes bored and goes off in the TARDIS, leaving Amy, Rory and Brian to do this. In December, some of the cubes at the hospital where Rory works briefly activate, and a patient is kidnapped by two fake orderlies with cube-like protuberances in place of their mouths. By the following June,

---

[56] Full name given in dialogue as 'Kate Lethbridge-Stewart'.

however, the UN has classified the cubes 'provisionally safe'. The Doctor returns and takes Amy and Rory for a night at London's Savoy Hotel on 26 June 1890 as a treat for their wedding anniversary. However, they end up having to deal with a Zygon attack from a buried spaceship. After another trip to the court of Henry VIII, the Doctor gets Amy and Rory home. In July, having been dormant for a year, the cubes suddenly 'wake up'. The activity ceases after 47 minutes, but then a number appears on each cube, counting down from seven. After the countdown reaches zero, everyone near one of the cubes experiences heart failure. Rory and Brian have meanwhile been transported via a wormhole to an orbiting spaceship. The Doctor and Amy follow, having traced the wormhole entrance to the hospital. They are confronted by a projection of a being called a Shakri, and learn that the cubes were intended to wipe out humanity before it could colonise space. The Doctor takes control of the cubes with his sonic screwdriver, using their energy to restart the hearts of all their victims. He and his companions escape back through the wormhole just before the Shakri ship explodes as a result of the energy release.

QUOTE, UNQUOTE

- **Rory:** 'There are soldiers all over my house, and I'm in my pants!'
  Amy: 'My whole life I've dreamed of saying that, and I miss it by being someone else.'

- **Doctor:** 'My! A kiss from a Lethbridge-Stewart. That is new.'

CONTINUITY POINTS

- The 'year of the slow invasion' runs from one July to the next, as indicated by on-screen captions. At the start, Amy tells the Doctor, in reference to the time that has passed since she and Rory left their original home village of Leadworth, 'We think it's been ten years. Not for you or Earth, but for us. Ten years older. Ten years of you, on and off.' It seems likely that this time has been measured either from when the couple first began meeting the Doctor on a semi-regular basis in 'The Eleventh Hour' (2010) or from when they joined him in the TARDIS following their wedding in 'The Big Bang' (2010). Both of those episodes were set in 2010. However, the fact that Amy draws a distinction between the 'ten years' that she and Rory have lived through and the time that has passed 'for … Earth' suggests that the date at the start of the 'slow invasion' may not be simply ten years after 2010, i.e. 2020 – which was probably the 'present' year for the couple in 'Dinosaurs on a Spaceship' (see discussion in the relevant episode entry above). The most likely explanation for this is that the events of 'The Power of Three' begin, for Amy and Rory, a year or so later than those of 'Dinosaurs on a Spaceship'; i.e. possibly in 2021. This would mean that their 'present' year is now later than it would have been if they had never travelled in time at all.

The Doctor could perhaps have arranged this in response to a concern expressed by Amy at the end of 'A Town Called Mercy' that if she and Rory continued making trips in the TARDIS, 'Our friends are going to start noticing that we're ageing faster than them.' If the 'present' year at the start of 'The Power of Three' really is 2021, and if Amy and Rory are correct in thinking they have spent ten years with the Doctor, then they will now have actually aged a year less than their friends on Earth. The fact that the Time Lord sometimes takes them back home to a date later than the one from which he collected them is clearly demonstrated by a scene at the very beginning of the episode, where they return from a TARDIS trip to find they have 59 messages on their answerphone and the milk in their fridge is two months out of date. Rory's comment that 'real life doesn't get much of a look in' compared with 'Doctor life' suggests that there can in fact by long periods of time passing on Earth when he and Amy are absent from their home, off having adventures in the TARDIS. This is confirmed later in the episode when Amy's friend Laura comments, 'You've missed quite a few things, the last year or two,' and Rory's boss Ranjit tells him,

'There are months when we don't see you.'[57]

- Rory has now resumed his former job as a nurse, on a part-time basis, while Amy has apparently abandoned modelling and writes travel articles for magazines.

- Katherine Lethbridge-Stewart, generally called Kate Lethbridge-Stewart, and later just Kate Stewart, first featured in the independent video production 'Downtime' (Reeltime Pictures, 1995), which was set in 1995. The Missing Adventures novel *The Scales of Injustice* (Virgin Publishing, 1996) later established that she was the child of Brigadier Lethbridge-Stewart and his first wife Fiona, who split up in 1970 at the time of 'Doctor Who and the Silurians' (1970), when she was five years old. Hence she was born around 1965; was a toddler at the time of 'The Web of Fear' (1968), which ultimately led to the formation of UNIT; and was aged around 30 at the time of 'Downtime'. By that point she had a son, Gordon, usually called

---

[57] It is unlikely that the total of ten years that Amy and Rory have spent with the Doctor is, on the contrary, significantly longer than the linear time between 2010 and their 'present' year on Earth – which could in theory be an alternative explanation for the distinction that Amy draws between those two things. There are four main reasons for this, in addition to the arguments already set out in support of a later 'present' year. First, Amy phrases her comment to the Doctor, 'Not for you or Earth,' and since we know that a greater amount of time has passed for him than for her and Rory (in fact, the Time Lord is now hundreds of years older than when he first met them), this would seem to suggest that a greater amount of time has passed for Earth too. Secondly, as previously discussed, it appears from 'Dinosaurs on a Spaceship' that the couple's 'present' year cannot be earlier than 2020; and they are also seen to be living in that year in 'The Hungry Earth' (2010) (although this could possibly be due to the TARDIS having taken them there in a trip unseen on screen). Thirdly, it is clear from Amy's comment at the end of 'A Town Called Mercy' that they have not yet aged noticeably faster than their contemporaries on Earth, and that she is keen to avoid that happening, even to the extent of declining the offer of another trip in the TARDIS. Finally, there is also her comment in 'Dinosaurs on a Spaceship' to the effect that the Doctor has been visiting them less and less frequently, and that they have not seen him for ten months prior to that episode, which would seem inconsistent with the idea that their ten years' worth of adventures have been packed in within a significantly shorter period of Earth time.

Gordy, who was nearly five years old. Kate had parted from Gordy's father, Jonathan, two years previously, i.e. around 1993, as established in the novelisation *Downtime* (Virgin Publishing, 1996).[58] In 2003, when she was aged around 38, Kate had an encounter with the Dæmon Mastho, as seen in the independent video production 'Dæmos Rising' (Reeltime Pictures, 2004).[59] It must have been sometime after this that she followed in her father's footsteps by joining UNIT, becoming its head of scientific research and taking charge of all its operations (whether just in the UK or worldwide is unspecified). Assuming that 'The Power of Three' does take place around 2021 (see discussion above), she is aged around 56 by this time.

• Kate arrives with UNIT troops at the Ponds' house after a 'spike in artron energy' is detected there. Artron energy has been established in numerous previous episodes as a type of energy used both by TARDISes and by Time Lords themselves, and associated with travelling through the time vortex. It was first mentioned in 'The Deadly Assassin' (1976).

• According to Kate, the scientific side of UNIT now runs the military, after she 'dragged them along, kicking and screaming' to this position.

• Kate appears never to have met the Doctor prior to 'The Power of Three', and has to scan him with a hand-held device in order to verify his identity by way of his two hearts. (See, however, the entry on 'The Day of the Doctor' below.) The Doctor does not need to ask who Kate is, and so clearly (and unsurprisingly) knows of her, but it is uncertain whether or not he has met her before; if he has, it may well have been when he was in an earlier incarnation and she was just a

---

[58] The *Downtime* novelisation also indicates that Fiona was pregnant six months after the events of 'The Web of Fear'. However, as there is no suggestion in *The Scales of Injustice* or elsewhere that Kate has a younger sibling, possibly Fiona lost that baby or the child died in infancy.

[59] Actress Beverley Cressman, who played Kate in 'Downtime' and 'Dæmos Rising', was born in December 1963. So she was 31 when the former was made, and 39 when the latter was made, just a year or so older than the character.

little girl, who would not necessarily have remembered him.

- During 'the year of the slow invasion', the Doctor whisks Amy and Rory away from a wedding anniversary party at their home, and they make a number of trips in the TARDIS, one of which results in them having to hide in the bedchamber of Henry VIII, whom Amy has accidentally married. It is possible that this is part of the same incident that the Doctor reminded his companions about at the start of 'A Town Called Mercy', where Rory was said to have left his phone charger 'in Henry VIII's *en-suite*'. If so, then this would mean that the events of 'A Town Called Mercy' actually take place during (or perhaps even after) those of 'The Power of Three', and are (unusually) presented to the viewer out of sequence; and Amy's comment at the end of the former episode, 'Our friends are going to start noticing that we're ageing faster than them,' could refer specifically to the friends at the anniversary party. (Brian does in fact notice that, on their return to the party, they are wearing different clothes from when they left.) However, although this is not apparent from the on-screen action, it was reportedly the production team's intention that the bedchamber scene should actually indicate that the Doctor, Amy and Rory had made a return visit to the King's residence to try to retrieve the anachronistic phone charger.

- Amy's accidental marriage to Henry VIII could be said to have made her the Doctor's mother-in-law twice over, since the Time Lord has apparently at different times married both Henry VIII's daughter Elizabeth I, as suggested in 'The End of Time' Part One (2009) (see also 'The Day of the Doctor'), and Amy's own daughter River Song, as seen in 'The Wedding of River Song' (2011).

- The Zygons are mentioned but not seen in this episode. These shape-shifting aliens made their sole previous appearance in the fourth Doctor story 'Terror of the Zygons' (1975).

- The Doctor, Amy and Rory are seen in one scene eating fish fingers and custard – the same concoction that the Doctor enjoyed on his very first meeting with Amy in 'The Eleventh Hour'. The Doctor claims, 'If I had a restaurant, this'd be all I'd serve.' He says that he has run restaurants before, adding 'Who do you think invented the

Yorkshire pudding?'

- The Doctor says to one of the cubes, 'Is that all you can do, hover? I had a metal dog could do that.' This is a reference to his one-time robotic pet K-9.

- Kate is able to send the Doctor a message via his psychic paper. She tells him that she dropped the 'Lethbridge' from her surname because she 'didn't want any favours' in UNIT, although her father guided her 'even to the end', telling her that 'science leads' – something he learned from 'an old friend', clearly meaning the Doctor himself.

- Amy admits to the Doctor that she and Rory might soon decide to stop travelling with him. The Doctor tells her he that has known this for a while, and when she asks, 'Then why do you keep coming back for us?', he replies, 'Because you were the first. The first face this face saw. And you're seared onto my hearts, Amelia Pond. You always will be. I'm running to you, and Rory, before you fade from me.' This is the first time it has been explicitly suggested that the Doctor might – in some cases at least – 'imprint' on and feel a special bond with the first person he sees in each new incarnation. It does however accord with evidence of some previous especially close friendships: for instance, Brigadier Lethbridge-Stewart was the first person that the third Doctor saw; Sarah Jane Smith was the first that the fourth Doctor saw; and Rose Tyler was the first that the tenth Doctor saw.

- The Doctor previously believed the Shakri to be 'a myth to keep the young of Gallifrey in their place'. The Shakri projection says: 'The Shakri exist in all of time, and none. We travel alone, and together. The Seven.' The Doctor adds that the Shakri have been described as 'the pest controllers of the universe'. They serve 'the word of the Tally', which some people call 'Judgement Day, or the Reckoning.'

PRODUCTION NOTES

- This episode was made with 'Pond Life' as Block Three of Series Seven's production schedule. Due to the out-of-sequence recording of this 2012 section of the series, it marked the final work as regulars on the show for both Karen Gillan and Arthur Darvill, although their characters' on-screen departure would not come until the following episode. The scene originally intended to be the last they performed was the one where Amy and Rory enter the TARDIS with the Doctor at the end. This was taped on 12 May 2012, observed by members of the production team past and present, including Steven Moffat and former executive producers Piers Wenger and Beth Willis, and followed by a farewell party. In the event, however, the two actors had to return on 6 June and 28 June to record some pick-up location scenes inside the Ponds' home, and also on the latter date some BBC Roath Lock studio material aboard the Shakri ship, the script for which had been substantially reworked in late rewrites, and Amy's voice-over narration, which was another late addition to the script.

- 'Cubed' was a working title for this episode.

- The story is told partly via a voice-over narration by Karen Gillan as Amy. It opens with her saying, 'Life with the Doctor was like this,' which is followed by a flurry of brief clips taken from various previous episodes featuring Amy and Rory. Another similar montage is seen shortly after.

- The episode features a number of celebrity cameo appearances: scientist Professor Brian Cox discusses the cubes in a television interview; entrepreneur Lord Alan Sugar fires a contestant on *The Apprentice* – the well-known business-related television reality game show over which he presides – for failing in a task involving the cubes; Sugar's regular associates Karren Brady and Nick Hewer are also seen at his side; and BBC newsreaders and journalists Matthew Amroliwala, Sophie Raworth and Emily Maitlis deliver reports about the cubes.

- Five pieces of pop music are heard during the course of the action: 'Titanium' by David Guetta featuring Sia, in a scene where Amy attends her friend Laura's engagement party and agrees to become a bridesmaid; Slade's 'Merry Xmas Everybody' (which has also featured in a number of previous episodes), in a scene at the hospital where Rory works; 'Don't Falter' by Mint Royale featuring Lauren Laverne, played during the first sequence at the party hosted by Amy and Rory to celebrate their anniversary; 'Sense' by the Lightning

Seeds, played during the second anniversary party sequence; and 'The Birdie Song' by the Tweets, played on a loop by one of the cubes.

- Interiors for the scenes at the home of Amy and Rory were shot in two locations in Penarth: Glendale Hotel, which on 30 April 2012 became their lounge; and the previously-featured venue of 7 Church Road, where the remaining material was taped on 30 April, 1, 6 and 7 May and 6 and 28 June. 30 April was also the date on which the brief engagement party scene was taped, at Villa Napoli restaurant on Plymouth Road, Penarth. On 2 and 3 May, recording took place at Caerphilly Castle in Caerphilly both for the UNIT HQ scenes at the Tower of London and for the Henry VIII bedroom scenes. The crew were prevented from recording at the Tower of London itself, owing to activity connected with the London 2012 Olympic Games; a scene of the Doctor and Amy apparently sat outside the Tower on a wall beside the River Thames was achieved using a green screen effect. A private house called Coedarhydyglyn in St Nicholas, Cardiff was used on 4 May for scenes in Brian's study and the sequence at the Savoy Hotel. The same day, and also on 7 June, exteriors of the Ponds' house were taped at the usual Bute Esplanade location. St Cadoc's Hospital in Caerleon, Gwent, was used for the hospital scenes, which were taped on 5 and 12 May. On 9 May, Neath Abby in Neath was the venue for recording of the UNIT laboratory scenes. Aside from the final work at the 7 Church Road location, 28 June also saw pick-up shots being taped of the Doctor examining the cubes in a children's playground, supposedly opposite the Ponds' home, in Belle Vue Park, Albert Road, Penarth. Lastly, the celebrity cameo of Lord Sugar was taped on 29 June on the set of *The Apprentice* in London, the one of Professor Cox was done the following day at the Holiday Inn, Hammersmith, London, and the news reports delivered by real-life journalists completed the episode's outside recording on 8 August in the BBC news studios. A small amount of studio work was done on 10 and 11 May at Upper Boat; and, as mentioned above, the reworked Shakri ship material was taped on 28 June at BBC Roath Lock.

- For this episode, the *Doctor Who* logo in the opening titles was given a pattern resembling the Shakri cubes. The colour grading of the opening title sequence itself was also tweaked to give it a more crimson hue.

- It was writer Chris Chibnall's idea to include Brigadier Lethbridge-Stewart's daughter Kate in this story. Surprisingly, particularly given that he is a long-standing *Doctor Who* fan, it has since been said that he was unaware at the time that she had featured previously in independent video dramas and tie-in novels. However, given that the character in 'The Power of Three' is indistinguishable from the one originally created by Marc Platt in his script for *Downtime*, and is also played by an actress very similar in age and appearance to the one originally cast in that production, this seems an extraordinary coincidence.

- This is the shortest episode of 21st Century *Doctor Who* to date.

OOPS!

- Karen Gillan's radio microphone can be spotted in the back pocket of her jeans in the shot where Amy lifts her legs so that the Doctor can run a vacuum cleaner under them.

- Amy rips open the Doctor's shirt in order to use a defibrillator on him, after his left heart has been stopped by one of the Shakri cubes. In subsequent scenes, however, his shirt is done up again, having apparently lost no buttons nor suffered any other damage.

CRITICAL REACTION

- 'It feels like it's been a long time since we had an episode like this. A big global threat, cameos from BBC newsreaders, a bearded face from a popular reality TV programme. Had the TARDIS taken us back, we wondered, to the Russell T Davies years? Well, yes and no. It captured the feel of slightly older *Doctor Who*, along with the continual build up to events that are very much concerning the current era of the show. Plus, it added in a bit of Time Lord stuff too. Not bad for 42-ish minutes … "The Power of Three" [was] a very, very enjoyable episode of the show, that benefited from a lighter, breezier feel.' Simon Brew, Den of Geek website, 22 September 2012.

- 'The Ponds' penultimate adventure boasts an intriguing premise – we often hear about how companions are the audience surrogate and how the story of the Doctor is told through their eyes, but this is the first episode to really live up to that spiel. As Amy's voiceover suggests, this is the one in which the Doctor becomes a part of his companions' lives, rather than the other way around, and the Time Lord finds domestic life – jobs, a house and other human concerns – confusing and frustrating. Steven Moffat may have claimed in the past that the Doctor and Sherlock Holmes actually have remarkably different personalities, but in many ways "The Power of Three" shows our hero at his most Sherlockian – crushingly bored when not unravelling a mystery.' Morgan Jeffery, Digital Spy website, 22 September 2012.

- 'I feel like there are definite parallels between time travel and drug addiction in *Doctor Who* – like a drug, time travel is fun, it feels naughty, it opens your mind to new and bizarre things, but it wears on your body and your psyche. Regular life doesn't *seem* to hold a candle to drug/time travel-enhanced life, and certainly can't fit into your regular schedule, so you end up neglecting regular life while you chase the dragon. After a while, even if you're still getting something out of your addiction, you're just exhausted by the whole thing. (Note: Drugs are bad.) You cannot invite getting high/the Doctor to your quiet night at home!' Emily V Gordon, TV.com website, 23 September 2012.

ANALYSIS

The central premise of 'The Power of Three', of the Doctor being put in a situation where he has to try to cope with living a normal domestic life on Earth for a time, essentially repeats that of the excellent Series Five episode 'The Lodger' (2010); but if anything it works even better the second time around, partly because it avoids that earlier episode's mistake of sometimes having the Time Lord behave out of character for humorous effect (no head-butting from him here, mercifully), but mostly because the household he descends upon this time is that of his companions Amy and Rory, rather than that of a complete stranger. This once again illustrates the merits, in storytelling terms, of Steven Moffat's decision to give Amy and Rory the highly unusual status of part-time

TARDIS travellers, trying to balance their home life with, as Rory puts it, their 'Doctor life' – something that has by this point become a key theme of the early part of Series Seven, trading on the well-publicised fact that the Ponds will shortly be departing the show. In a satisfyingly well-worked-through character arc spanning the past two-and-a-bit series, the couple have been seen to gradually mature and develop: starting out as childhood friends; becoming girlfriend and boyfriend; growing closer still after Amy fully commits to the relationship at the end of 'Amy's Choice' (2010); getting married in 'The Big Bang'; having a child together, albeit in strange circumstances; and then settling down in a home of their own with – as seen at the start of 'The Power of Three' – domestic chores to attend to and, perhaps in a nod to their ageing, an answerphone message from the local opticians, reporting that a pair of reading glasses are ready for collection. It really is starting to seem a 'long way from Leadworth,' as the Doctor puts it.

There is a particularly moving scene, a kind of night-time interlude half way through the episode, where the Doctor and Amy take a break from the action and sit on a wall by the Thames, having a heart-to-heart talk. Amy tells the Doctor that since he dropped her and Rory back on Earth and gave them their house – as seen at the end of 'The God Complex' (2011) – they have built a life for themselves, and that this and their parallel life travelling with him 'pull at each other', so that 'the travelling is starting to feel like running away'. This is answered by the Doctor with a speech that beautifully encapsulates his own reasons for journeying through time and space: 'I'm not running away. But this is one corner of one country, in one continent, on one planet, that's a corner of a galaxy, that's a corner of a universe, that is forever growing and shrinking and creating and destroying and never remaining the same for a single millisecond. And there is so much, so much to see, Amy. Because it goes so fast. I'm not running away from things, I am running to them, before they flare and fade forever.'

The episode ends with Amy and Rory effectively making a choice between their two lives, as they decide to go off with the Doctor in the TARDIS while Brian stays behind to 'water the plants'. 'Go with him,' Brian tells them. 'Go save every world you can find. Who else has that chance? Life will still be here.' However, he warns the Doctor, 'Just bring them back safe.' This sets things up very nicely for the Ponds' swansong in the next episode.

Overall, 'The Power of Three' strikes a nice balance between the amusing, the poignant and the scary – the scary aspect being the Shakri's plot to wipe out humanity. There is something strangely ominous about the small black cubes, just sitting there waiting for a whole year, obviously intended for some purpose, probably deadly – but what? The answer, when it eventually comes, is – as the Doctor himself says – a clever one: that the Shakri have built in the year's delay to allow time for the human race, with their 'early adopter' nature, to collect the cubes and take them into their homes – similar to the way they welcomed in and adjusted to the presence of the 'ghosts' that later turned out to be Cybermen in 'Army of Ghosts' (2006), or accepted the (deadly, as it turned out) plastic daffodils offered by the Autons in 'Terror of the Autons' (1971). Thus, when the attack comes, by way of a heart-stopping energy pulse determined through a 47-minute period of analysis to be the most effective weapon, the maximum number will be killed. The brief sequence of multiple victims dropping to the ground as their hearts stop is really quite chilling, and the horror of the situation is emphasised when Kate reports that as much as a third of the Earth's whole population could be affected.

The only thing that lets down this aspect of the story to some extent is its resolution. The Shakri, a kind of bogeyman from Gallifreyan myth, is a well-conceived villain with an interesting motivation, brought to life by way of a suitably gruesome make-up design and a strong, menacing performance from the distinguished actor Steven Berkoff, but its threat is ended all too easily by the Doctor, with just a few waves of his sonic screwdriver. It is no great surprise to learn that writer Chris Chibnall's script originally made rather more of this, but was reworked late on in the production process to put a stronger emphasis on the character-focused material involving the Ponds' dilemma over whether or not to continue travelling with the Doctor. While it is understandable why this decision was taken, it is really rather a pity that the Shakri ended up sidelined in this way, and one is left feeling that Berkoff's considerable talents are somewhat wasted in what turns out to be only a minor role.

The other unsatisfactory thing about the story's resolution is the unbelievable way in which the cubes' victims suddenly recover, with no apparent ill effects, after suffering complete heart failure for an extended period – at least twenty minutes, and possibly much longer, if one takes into account the time needed for the Doctor and his friends to travel from UNIT HQ at the Tower of London to the (unspecified) location of the hospital where the wormhole entrance is situated.[60] As is fairly common knowledge, brain death generally occurs after only about five minutes of oxygen deprivation; after twenty minutes, it is likely that few, if any, of the cubes' victims could have survived, and certainly not without experiencing significant brain damage. This very obvious flaw is something that really ought to have been spotted in advance and addressed in the script.

The fact that the hospital where Rory works just happens to be the site of one of the seven Shakri wormhole entrances dotted around the world is itself a rather too convenient coincidence. It is never explained, either, why the two fake orderlies, overseen by a creepy young girl described by the Doctor as an 'outlier droid, monitoring everything', have been abducting patients from the hospital since at least seven months prior to the time the cubes activate – although one can perhaps infer that the abductees have been subjected to analysis as part and parcel of the Shakri's attempt to determine the most effective way of killing human beings. Unfortunately, in another scripting oversight, the only abductee that the Doctor, Amy and Rory seem to have any interest in rescuing from the Shakri spaceship is Brian; the others are all left to their fate when the spaceship explodes at the end. Possibly they are all dead already – they are seen lying immobile on gurneys – but the Doctor makes no move to ascertain this, and one is left with the impression that they have been simply forgotten about.

These minor scripting glitches aside, however, 'The Power of Three' is a fine piece of work by Chris Chibnall, very different in tone and pacing from his earlier contributions to *Doctor Who* (although in a somewhat similar vein to his brilliant character-focused *Torchwood* episode 'Fragments' (2008)), and possibly his strongest yet. It is great to see Rory's dad Brian making a return appearance, and Mark Williams again gives a lovely performance in the role, making the character a highly endearing

---

[60] In 'Closing Time' (2011), Amy and Rory are seen out shopping in a mall in Colchester, Essex. This suggests that the house the Doctor gave them could be somewhere near there. (Clearly Brian lives somewhere close to them, but the location of his house is also unspecified.) The hospital where Rory has his part-time job as a nurse could therefore be one of the central London ones, as these are within manageable commuting distance from Colchester – the train journey from Colchester to London's Liverpool Street station generally takes around fifty minutes to an hour.

one in scenes such as where he diligently records a log of his cube observations. The idea to bring the Brigadier's daughter Kate Stewart into the show as the new head of UNIT was also an excellent one, and assuming it was not simply down to happy coincidence – which seems scarcely believable – the fact that the trouble was taken to maintain continuity with her previous appearances in the spin-off and tie-in media is highly admirable. Jemma Redgrave, one of the latest generation of the famous Redgrave acting dynasty, is very good in the role, although really no better than Beverley Cressman was in 'Downtime' and 'Dæmos Rising', and it is actually rather a pity that Cressman was not given the chance to play Kate again here, perhaps because she was not considered a sufficiently big name in the business.

The return of UNIT is itself very welcome, giving 'The Power of Three' something of the feel of the Earth exile period of the third Doctor's era – a period from which Chibnall previously drew significant inspiration for 'The Hungry Earth' / 'Cold Blood' (2010). One is also put in mind of the Earth invasion stories of Russell T Davies's time as showrunner, when UNIT's HQ beneath the Tower of London was first seen, in 'The Christmas Invasion' (2005), and when celebrity cameos and plot developments relayed via worldwide news broadcasts were commonplace.

With this unusual, quirky and well-realised episode – more mini arthouse movie than mini blockbuster, perhaps, with its strong focus on character – Series Seven continues in very fine form.

7.05 – The Angels Take Manhattan

Writer: Steven Moffat
Director: Nick Hurran

<u>DEBUT TRANSMISSION DETAILS</u>

BBC One/BBC One HD
Date: 29 September 2012. Scheduled time: 7.20 pm. Actual time: 7.20 pm.

Duration: 44' 20"

<u>ADDITIONAL CREDITED CAST</u>

Alex Kingston (River Song), Mike McShane (Grayle[61]), Rob David (Sam Garner), Bentley Kalu (Hood), Ozzie Yue (Foreman), Burnell Tucker (Old Garner), Zac Fox (Photoshoot PA)

<u>PLOT</u>

The Doctor, Amy and Rory are picnicking in Central Park, New York, in 2012. While the Doctor reads aloud to Amy from a pulp detective novel titled *Melody Malone*, Rory goes for coffee, encounters a Weeping Angel in the form of a statue and is transported back to 3 April 1938. There he encounters River Song, who is using the alias Melody Malone, and they are taken by armed men to meet Julius Grayle, a rich collector who has a captive Weeping Angel at his mansion. The Doctor and Amy have since realised that the novel is actually telling their and Rory's own story. By sending a message to River via an inscription on an antique Chinese vase, the Doctor gets a fix on her coordinates and is able to materialise the TARDIS in the mansion – but not without difficulty, as the New York of

---

[61] First name given on screen as 'Julius'.

this era is full of time distortions. Rory has meanwhile fallen foul of some cherub-like 'baby' Angels in Grayle's cellar and been transported to an apartment block called Winter Quay. The Doctor and his friends learn that this has been set up by the Angels as a 'battery farm', where they can repeatedly feed on the time energy of its occupants. Rory is also there as an old man, who dies when they arrive, meaning that he is destined to live out the rest of his life as the Angels' prisoner. The young Rory decides to jump from the roof in order to create a time paradox that will erase Winter Quay from history, and Amy insists on going with him. This plan works, and they return to life in a nearby cemetery. However, a lone surviving Angel sends Rory back in time again, and Amy chooses to follow, despite knowing that the Doctor will never be able to visit them, as their timelines are now fixed and cannot be altered without the added disruption ripping New York apart. River will now have to write the *Melody Malone* novel, recounting what has happened, and send it back to Amy to get it published. Amy adds an afterword to the book, the last page of which the Doctor has not read before, assuring him that she and Rory lived well and were very happy, and asking him to visit her younger self, waiting for him in her garden in Leadworth, to tell her something of her future adventures.

QUOTE, UNQUOTE

- **Amy:** 'Where did you get this book?'
  Doctor: 'It was in my jacket.'
  Amy: 'How did it get there?'
  Doctor: 'How does anything get there? I've given up asking.'

- **Doctor:** 'You said I got too big.'
  River: 'And now no-one's ever heard of you. Didn't you used to be somebody?'
  Doctor: 'Weren't you the woman who killed the Doctor?'
  River: 'Doctor who?'

- **Amy:** 'You think you'll just come back to life?'
  Rory: 'When don't I?'

- **Amy:** 'Raggedy man ... goodbye.'

CONTINUITY POINTS

- The words 'Private Detective in Old Town New York' are printed at the bottom of the front cover of the *Melody Malone* book, but it is unclear if this is a subtitle or simply a tagline. The Doctor tears the last page from the book, saying, 'I always rip out the last page of a book. Then it doesn't have to end. I hate endings.' The chapters of the book are later revealed to be called: 'The Dying Detective', 'The Angels Take Manhattan', 'Missing in New York', 'Taking the Case', 'Night in the Statue Park', 'The Gargoyle', 'The Skinny Guy', 'Julius Grayle', 'Calling the Doctor', 'The Roman in the Cellar', 'Death at Winter Quay' and 'Amelia's Last Farewell'. The seventh chapter, 'The Skinny Guy', is presumably the one in which Melody Malone first encounters Rory in 1938, as this is how she refers to him in the passage of text read out by the Doctor in Central Park. The first six chapters of the book must therefore relate to events prior to the involvement of the Doctor and his companions. Julius Grayle's first name is not given on screen other than in the title of the eighth chapter.

- The Doctor tells Amy that she mustn't 'read ahead' in River's book, saying, 'This isn't any old future, Amy, it's ours. Once we know what's coming, it's fixed.' When she protests, 'Time can be rewritten,' he replies, 'Not once you've read it. Once we know what's coming, it's written in stone.' It appears therefore that if one has foreknowledge of one's own future, one is unable to change it.

- Rory's name is carved on his gravestone as 'Rory Arthur Williams' – the first time his middle name has been revealed. Amy's name is carved as 'Amelia Williams', strangely omitting her previously established middle name, 'Jessica', but confirming that she has started using her husband's surname instead of her maiden name – as also seen when she signs the divorce papers that Rory hands to her at the start of 'Asylum of the Daleks'. The gravestone indicates that Amy died at age 87 and Rory at age 82, so she must have outlived him by some five years following their final relocation to 1930s New York.

- Rory gives a surprised exclamation, 'River, I'm translating,' when he sees the inscription on an antique Chinese vase in Grayle's mansion resolve into the English words 'Rapture of Summer.' She tells him, 'It's a gift of the TARDIS. It hangs around.' It is unclear exactly how this 'gift' works, but it appears that the Doctor himself also has some involvement in bestowing it. In 'The Masque of Mandragora' (1977), the fourth Doctor tells his companion Sarah Jane Smith, 'It's a Time Lord gift I allow you to share,' and in 'The Christmas Invasion' (2005), Rose Tyler is unable to understand the Sycorax language until the tenth Doctor revives from a period of post-regeneration unconsciousness. It appears that the gift can also be withdrawn: when the seventh Doctor's companion Ace quits the TARDIS for a time following a row with him at the end of the New Adventures novel *Love and War* (Virgin Publishing, 1992), it is implied that she loses her ability to understand other languages.

- When the Doctor first attempts to materialise the TARDIS in 1938, the console room becomes filled with fumes, which he clears using the extractor fans, as first featured in 'Let's Kill Hitler' (2011).

- This story takes place relatively late in River's timeline. She is now Professor Song rather than Dr Song, and she tells the Doctor, 'Oh, I was pardoned ages ago …Turns out the person I killed never existed in the first place. Apparently, there's no record of him. It's almost as if someone's gone around deleting himself from every database in the universe.' This refers back to River's imprisonment in the Stormcage Containment Facility for the (faked) killing of the Doctor at the end of 'The Wedding of River Song' (2011), and to the fact that he has since been trying to withdraw from universal attention – as also alluded to in 'Asylum of the Daleks' and 'Dinosaurs on a Spaceship'.

- Grayle's captive Weeping Angel seizes River by the wrist but does not send her back into the past. The Doctor comments, 'I doubt she's strong enough.' This would explain why the weak, reviving Weeping Angels in 'The Time of Angels' / 'Flesh and Stone' (2010) had to simply kill their victims rather than displace them in time. River breaks her wrist to free herself, and the Doctor heals it using some of his regeneration energy. This recalls how she gave up all of her own remaining regeneration energy to save his life in 'The Wedding of River Song'.

- After the time paradox takes effect and the TARDIS ends up back in the cemetery outside New York, River asks the Doctor 'Does the bulb on top need changing?' and he replies, 'I've just changed it.' This refers back to the sequence in the final part of 'Pond Life' where he was seen changing the bulb.

- After the Doctor loses Amy and Rory, River urges him, 'Doctor, don't travel alone'; a sentiment echoed by Amy in her afterword to the *Melody Malone* book. The adverse consequences of the Doctor travelling without human companionship have previously been explored in episodes such as 'The Runaway Bride' (2006) and 'A Town Called Mercy'.

- It is strongly implied at the end of the episode that the Doctor goes back in time to 1996 to talk to young Amelia Pond, waiting for him in her garden in Leadworth on the night following their initial meeting, as previously seen in 'The Eleventh Hour' (2010). This confirms that, even though Amy's childhood must have been changed by her remembering her parents back into existence after the rebooting of the universe in 'The Big Bang' (2010), her initial meeting with the Doctor still took place much as originally seen. It is likely, however, that she did not then continue waiting in her garden and fall asleep on her suitcase, to be taken indoors and put to bed by the Doctor, as also seen in 'The Big Bang'; this was probably erased from her timeline by her remembering her parents back into existence, if not by the Doctor's post-'The Angels Take Manhattan' visit.

PRODUCTION NOTES

- This episode and 'Asylum of the Daleks' were made together as Block Two of Series Seven's production schedule.

- Location work for this episode was split between New York City, USA and more familiar territory in or close to Cardiff, Wales. On 4 April 2012, the School of Physics and Astronomy at Cardiff University was used as the entrance to Winter Quay. Two days later, Custom House in Merchant Place, Bute Street, Cardiff was the venue for taping of the scenes in Grayle's cellar, while the nearby Bay Chambers became the Winter Quay lobby. On 7 April, the

School of Physics and the Institute of Advanced Studies at Bristol University were both used for shots on the Winter Quay stairwells. The New York recording began on 11 April, when the scene of the Doctor, Amy and Rory picnicking in Central Park was completed, along with the sequence of Rory crossing the road with coffee on the nearby corner where Fifth Avenue meets East 60th Street. A sequence of the Doctor and Amy passing through Times Square was begun on 11 April and completed the following day, when their arrival back at the TARDIS in Brooklyn Bridge Park was also recorded. Further locations visited on 12 April were a building on East 43rd Street for exterior shots of Winter Quay; and Battery Maritime Building, Main Street and Grand Central Terminal, all seen during the sequence where Rory and River are forcibly escorted to Grayle's mansion by car. On 13 April, the New York recording was completed with some shots of New York statues, including the General Sherman monument in Grand Army Plaza. Work resumed back in Wales on 16 April, when scenes inside Grayle's mansion were taped in a three-day shoot at a private house called Coedarhydyglyn in St Nicholas, Cardiff (which would also be chosen as a location for 'The Power of Three'). Box Cemetery in Newport was used on 19 April for the cemetery scenes, the New York skyline being added via green screen in post-production. On 21 April, some final exterior shots at Grayle's mansion were recorded on King Edward VII Avenue in Cardiff, and some final interior shots in the Glamorgan Building at Cardiff University. Studio work was carried out between 23 March and 30 April at Upper Boat, and between 21 and 27 April at BBC Roath Lock.

- For this episode, the *Doctor Who* logo in the opening titles was adapted to depict part of the Statue of Liberty's crown. The colour grading of the opening title sequence itself was again tweaked, this time to give it a more grey-green appearance.

- The song 'Englishman in New York' by Sting is heard immediately after the opening titles.

- The prop used for the *Melody Malone* novel was actually a copy of Dashiell Hammett's famous private eye story *The Thin Man* (1934) with a replacement cover. In the first scene in the cemetery, the viewer can briefly see some of the text, which is from Chapter 11 of Hammett's book.

- Grayle's surname is taken from that of a collector of rare jade in Raymond Chandler's second Philip Marlowe novel *Farewell My Lovely* (1940).

- The week after the episode's transmission, BBC Digital published an e-book prequel novella: *The Angel's Kiss*, subtitled *A Melody Malone Mystery*, by Justin Richards. The publicity blurb for this was as follows:

> *On some days, New York is one of the most beautiful places on Earth. This was one of the other days …*

> Melody Malone, owner and sole employee of the Angel Detective Agency, has an unexpected caller. It's movie star Rock Railton, and he thinks someone is out to kill him. When he mentions the 'kiss of the Angel', she takes the case. Angels are Melody's business …
>
> At the press party for Railton's latest movie, studio owner Max Kliener invites Melody to the film set of their next blockbuster. He's obviously spotted her potential, and Melody is flattered when Kliener asks her to become a star. But the cost of fame, she'll soon discover, is greater than anyone could possibly imagine.
>
> Will Melody be able to escape Kliener's dastardly plan – before the Angels take Manhattan?

The Angel's Kiss was also made available later in 2012 as a BBC audiobook read by Alex Kingston, and appeared in print the following year in the BBC Books anthology *Summer Falls and Other Stories*, supposedly compiled by Amy under her married name Amelia Williams after she settled in the 1930s. The accompanying publicity material for the anthology contained the following biographical information: 'Amelia Williams is the editor of the famous Melody Malone series of crime novels, and a bestselling author of several books for children. She lives in New York with her husband Rory and their young son, Anthony. They have a grown-up daughter, Melody, who works as an archaeologist. Melody Malone is the owner and sole employee of the Angel Detective Agency in Manhattan. She is possibly married but lives alone usually, and is older than both her parents.'

- At the very end of the episode, instead of the usual 'Next Time' teaser, two captions are presented, reading 'This Christmas' and 'The Doctor Will Return', intercut with three very brief clips of, respectively, Matt Smith, guest star Richard E Grant and Jenna-Louise Coleman, from the forthcoming Christmas special.

OOPS!

- The photoshoot PA played by Zac Fox, although included in the closing credits of this episode, actually appeared in 'Asylum of the Daleks'.

- The Doctor tears out what is supposedly the last page of the *Melody Malone* book, but the shot shows that it is actually taken from somewhere near the middle.

- The Doctor travels back to the China of 221 BC to leave River a message on a Qing Dynasty vase. However, 221 BC was actually the start of the Qin Dynasty. The Qing Dynasty, when vases of this type were made, began in 1644 AD.

- When Amy and the Doctor arrive at Winter Quay and run into the building, they leave River sitting in their stolen car, shutting the car door behind them. However, when the action cuts to the interior of the building, River is with them in the elevator. (Possibly, unseen by the viewer, she exits the car from the door on the opposite side, and runs into the building a few moments after them.)

- When Amy and Rory jump off the Winter Quay roof and the Doctor looks down at them falling, in one shot River is standing in the background, but in the next she is also at the roof's edge looking down.

- When Amy and Rory first come back to life in the cemetery after creating the time paradox, Rory is still wearing his jacket over his hoodie. A few shots later, however, his jacket has disappeared. (Possibly, unseen, he has for some reason discarded it between shots.)

CRITICAL REACTION

- 'Part of what makes this episode work so well – and it's one of the best of the Moffat era – is the way it does double duty as a twist adventure *and* a highly emotional story of farewells. Everyone who's been paying attention already knows this is the swansong for Karen Gillan and Arthur Darvill, but would anyone have predicted what a wrenching it would be? Maybe it should have been predictable. Throughout the Ponds' era, River has provided a constant reminder that people meant to be together don't always get to stay together. But Amy and Rory's story has been one of people ready to defy this possibility at every turn. Even, as we find out this week, in the face of death.' Keith Phipps, A.V. Club website, 29 September 2012.

- 'It's a pretty ingenious idea, this: the Angels set up a kind of live-in buffet of people who are forced to live out their lives alone in an apartment while the stone bastards feed on their temporal energy. It's very smart, yet very simple. In the past, the Moff has opted for being too clever and complex for the sake of it, but here, he's done it about as straightforward as he can, which I think is to the benefit of the episode and the character relationships at hand. The Angels remain the most consistently scary monster in the history of the show.' Kyle Anderson, Nerdist website, 30 September 2012.

- 'I'm torn. As an episode, "The Angels Take Manhattan" is horribly flawed, riddled with plot holes and numerous unanswered questions. The exit of the Ponds is a cheat – literally "death by plot hole" – and unquestionably senseless. However, the episode also contains moments not just done well, but done *perfectly* – brilliant moments that represent the best *Doctor Who* has to offer.' Clint Hassell, *Doctor Who* TV website, 2 October 2012.

- 'When Amy and Rory jump from the roof, you'd think Rory was invisible, since the Doctor is screaming "Amy! Amy!" Then, when Amy decides to let the Angel take her to Rory, the Doctor does everything in his power to dissuade her. Selfish to the nth degree, right? Not only is he ignoring Rory's welfare, he's ignoring Amy's wishes too: all he cares about is that he gets his own way. Awesome. We hate it when the Doctor's portrayed as some sort of noble do-gooder. Yes, we're sure he's learned from experience over his long lifespans, but think about how selfish, cunning, vain and arrogant the first Doctor is. Some of that's still definitely in there, and a good thing too. Plaster saints are about as interesting to watch as a paint-drying competition.' Uncredited reviewer, Androzani.com website, unspecified date.

ANALYSIS

The last of the mini movie-type episodes making up the 2012 section of Series Seven draws on the style of classic film noir and hardboiled detective fiction – but with a higher-budget look than most film noir, and a timey-wimey plot!

River Song fits into this milieu very well, as a kind of sassy, smart-talking dame, and she looks stunning in her private eye-inspired outfit, complete with fedora, trenchcoat and spectacular cleavage – all of which has apparently prompted the Doctor to exclaim 'Yowzah' even when simply described in her Melody Malone novel! It is great to have this fantastic character back in the show, and Alex Kingston is as superb as ever in the role. The husband-and-wife repartee that River and the Doctor exchange is all highly amusing, and we even get to witness a little more of River's vulnerable side this time, when she breaks her wrist but initially conceals this fact from the Doctor as she does not want to appear frail to him while he himself is 'an ageless god who insists on the face of a 12-year-old' – a rather sad reflection on their relationship, or perhaps even more so on the Doctor, who has earlier said, 'I hate endings.' 'Never let him see the damage; and never, ever let him see you age,' River advises Amy – for whom this is becoming a real issue, as the Doctor has already spotted that she now wears reading glasses (as neatly foreshadowed by the opticians' answerphone message in 'The Power of Three') and has acquired some wrinkles around her eyes.

One rather intriguing aspect of the episode is the clear implication that the character Sam Garner, seen in the pre-opening-titles sequence, may be just an imaginary creation of River's, and the action in which he features simply part of the plot of her novel, told in the usual first-person style of most private eye fiction – just as, for instance, Raymond Chandler wrote his books from the perspective of his Philip Marlowe character. Certainly the author whose fingers we glimpse typing out the story (prior to Amy's afterword) can't be Garner himself, as he quickly comes to grief at Winter Quay; and we also see the author typing two chapter titles from River's novel: '1. The Dying Detective' and later, when the older Rory dies, '11. Death at Winter Quay'. That said, though, it appears from the scene where the Doctor reads aloud from the novel in Central Park that Melody Malone is herself the first-person protagonist of the action. So perhaps the whole thing is even cleverer – and more metatextual – than that, and the unidentified author is actually, in effect, Steven Moffat, making 'The Angels Take Manhattan' a kind of story within a story. In which case, one has to ask, how reliable a narrator is he …?

Aside from River, the other very welcome return in this episode is that of the Weeping Angels. It is good to see them accorded a full reappearance, following a couple of brief cameos in 'The God Complex' (2011) and 'Good as Gold', and particularly pleasing to note the reinstatement of their original *modus operandi* of sending people back into the past in order to feast on the time energy released – something that seemed to get overlooked in 'The Time of Angels' / 'Flesh and Stone' in favour of depicting them simply as vicious killers (although that is retrospectively explained here – see 'Continuity Points' above). That said, however, Steven Moffat makes a few embellishments this time that arguably weaken rather than enhance the basic concept of his celebrated creations. The hardest thing to swallow is that they now seem to have the ability to 'possess' ordinary statues – including the Statue of Liberty, which isn't even made of stone, but is a hollow construction of wood and metal – and make them move about and send people back in time in the same way that they do themselves. The Angels being fictional creatures, there is admittedly no overriding reason why they should not have somehow acquired this ability, or even have had it all along – which would at least make sense, finally, of the closing moments of 'Blink' (2007), when viewers were presented with a seemingly random selection of images of ordinary statues that bore no resemblance to the Angels themselves – but it stretches credibility almost to breaking point.

The sequences involving the Statue of Liberty are problematic for other reasons, too. It is hard to believe that a landmark as prominent and famous as this would not have at least a few pairs of eyes fixed on it at all times – even at night, and in the less heavily-populated era of the 1930s –

and if that is so, and if it obeys the usual rules applying to the Angels, then surely it should be quantum locked and unable to move? Even if it was unobserved to start with, it would be bound to attract attention as soon as it started crashing its way toward Winter Quay. And what exactly *is* that repeated crashing noise heard on the soundtrack both times before the Statue appears? Presumably it is supposed to represent the Statue coming to rest in a new position after each quick-as-a-blink hop that it makes along its route, almost as if it is taking footsteps; but Winter Quay is said to be near Battery Park, which is separated from the Statue's normal island site by a stretch of water, not by land, so this really makes no sense at all. There is another issue here, as well: given that Winter Quay is a 22-storey building, as evidenced by a signboard seen beside the elevator in the lobby, it must be far taller than the Statue, so how is it possible for the Statue to stand at eye level with its roof? The scale is all wrong here: the Statue actually seems to have grown to giant size by the time it reaches the building! Is this simply a case of River exaggerating in her novel ...?

A much better way of getting the same shock value from the Statue's sudden appearance as an Angel but with far greater credibility would have been to make it part of a nightmare experienced by the elderly Sam Garner in his bed at Winter Quay – which would have been completely in keeping with the episode's favoured style, as surreal dream sequences are a quite common feature in film noir. Then, in the later scene where Amy and Rory jump from the roof, they could have been menaced simply by standard Angels, rather than by the Statue – the arrival of which has far less impact the second time around in any case.

Even the ingenious and horrific idea of the Angels having set up a kind of battery farm at Winter Quay, harvesting time energy by sending its trapped and ageing residents back to their rooms whenever they try to escape, raises a few unanswered questions if one gives it any real thought. During the residents' perpetual imprisonment, who attends to their basic needs, such as feeding them, and clothing them in the pyjamas they are seen wearing? Do the Angels somehow employ people to perform these tasks? And why have the Angels not broken all the lightbulbs, blacked out all the windows and kept the interior of the building in total darkness, so that they can move about with absolute freedom? In fact, given that New York is 'the city that never sleeps', where there will always be a lot of people around who could potentially observe them, it seems an odd location for the Angels to have chosen for their battery farm in the first place – despite the Doctor's assertion, 'They've never had a food source like this.'

Fortunately, there are a couple of wholly positive innovations in amongst the more questionable ones. The idea of Grayle keeping one of the Angels chained up, so that it cannot escape even when unobserved, and effectively torturing it to find out 'if it could feel pain', is a chillingly plausible one, and recalls the way his fellow American, Henry van Statten, had a Dalek chained up and tortured in 'Dalek' (2005). The introduction of the cherub-like 'baby' Angels, with their creepy mischievous giggling, is also a fantastic idea, adding a further scary twist to this great monster race.

Visually, 'The Angels Take Manhattan' is an absolute treat. The recreation of 1930s New York is excellent, with settings and costumes that really capture the feel of the period as viewed through the stylistic filter of film noir movies; and the gorgeous New York location recording for the 2012 scenes is the icing on the cake, lending the whole thing a real touch of class. Nick Hurran's handling of the action here is just as impressively cinematic as on 'Asylum of the Daleks', confirming his status as probably the finest director working on *Doctor Who* at this time. There are admittedly a couple of shots that could have been slightly better composed, where Angels appear to be in each other's line of sight without becoming locked into place, and a couple of others that could perhaps have benefitted from a retake, where characters are unfortunately seen to blink while looking at Angels that nevertheless remain immobile; but these very minor flaws are easy to forgive in what is, overall, a scintillating gem of a production.

Sadly, where the story really falters and falls short of the mark is not in its realisation but in its scripting. Aside from the issues already mentioned with regard to certain aspects of the Angels' depiction, there are some other less-than-satisfactory elements. For one thing, it is a hugely convenient coincidence that Rory just happens to be spotted by River immediately after he arrives in 1938 (or, at least, that appears to be the case, as she has no idea how he got there, although the text of her novel seems to suggest that she spotted him in 2012 and followed him for a couple of blocks before he was sent back in time). Then there is the question of how the Doctor could possibly know, when he travels back in time to the China of 221 BC, that the particular vase on which he has the word 'Yowzah' inscribed as a message to River will eventually end up where she can see it as part of the collection in Grayle's mansion, which he has yet to visit. This just doesn't make sense. More critically, though, the most badly handled part of 'The Angels Take Manhattan' is the one to which everything, not just in this episode but in the whole of Series Seven to date, has really been leading up: the writing out of Amy and Rory at its resolution.

The aforementioned sequence where the couple commit suicide by jumping together from the roof of Winter Quay – in Rory's case because this will create a time paradox that wipes the Angels' battery farm from history, and in Amy's case because she cannot bear to live without her husband – is superbly performed and realised, with the couple falling to their deaths in a tight embrace, in a beautiful slow-motion shot. A truly poignant and appropriate end to their story, and one that makes perfect sense. Frustratingly, though, this wonderfully dramatic, emotional, romantic scene turns out to be not the end after all. Instead, Steven Moffat, doubtless baulking at the prospect of having 21st Century companion characters unprecedentedly dying of anything other than old age, lets the couple return to life and then be sent back into the past – presumably to the 1930s again, although that isn't made explicit on screen – by a solitary surviving Angel.

The big problem with this is that the reasons given for the Doctor being unable simply to head off in the TARDIS and rejoin his companions are highly muddled, and don't really make sense. We are told that if he were to try to go back to them, it would 'rip New York apart' due to all the time distortions affecting the city; and also that, by joining Rory in the past, Amy has created 'fixed time', meaning that the Time Lord will never be able to see her again. However, even if one accepts that the final huge time paradox caused by the couple jumping from the roof of Winter Quay has made it impossible for the Doctor to take the TARDIS back to 1930s New York again, or even to use a vortex manipulator as River did to reach that era – 'Less bulky than a TARDIS; a motorbike through traffic,' as she puts it – what is to stop him materialising in a slightly later time period, or a different city, or even a different country, and getting a message to them, asking them to meet him? Clearly it is not impossible for them to be contacted at all, as it is established that River, once she has written her novel, is going to send it to Amy to get it published.

As for the mention of creating 'fixed time', this seems to allude to the fact that the fate of Amy and Rory will be irrevocably determined once River records it in the manuscript of her novel – another of Steven Moffat's trademark predestination paradoxes. 'Once we know what's coming, it's fixed,' the Doctor says at one point earlier in the story. But does that really apply here? Even leaving aside the fact that it doesn't seem to be an inviolable rule – Amy has read in the book that the Doctor is going to break River's wrist, but in the end, River breaks it herself – the Doctor has forbidden the others to 'read ahead' in the book; and until the point when Amy actually gives herself up to the surviving Angel at the end, he seems not to regard it as an insurmountable obstacle that he has spotted that the final chapter is titled 'Amelia's Last Farewell'. We are perhaps given an answer of sorts to this particular puzzle, at least, as River clearly thinks it is the right thing for Amy to join Rory in the past and stop travelling with the Doctor, even though this means she too will never see her parents again – if that were not the case, and given that none of them has yet read the final page of her novel, why could she not simply write a different ending to it, where the Ponds were able against all the odds to be reunited with the Doctor? Or is the – admittedly rather lovely – coda scene, in which the Doctor reads Amy's tear-jerking afterword to the novel, intended to imply that she herself has elected to write a happy ending to her and Rory's story, finally making the choice between 'real life' and 'Doctor life' that they discussed in 'The Power of Three'? River certainly seems to believe that this is the case, as she tells the Doctor, 'Maybe you'll listen to her.'

Responding to a *Doctor Who Magazine* reader's plea for clarification of all this, Steven Moffat later wrote: 'The point is, [the Doctor] can't interfere with their timelines again. Sometimes the time-altering surgery is possible, provided you preserve the outcome (Teselecta-style[62]), but in this case, there were too many paradoxes and timey-wimeys already. One more change, and New York would burn, wherever he met the Ponds. There are only so many changes that time can take, and that's *true*, that is. (That explanation was once in the script – but no non-fans understood why it was necessary. "Of course he can't see her again, that's her grave!" I know, I know – but we're fans, we think differently.)' This, it must be said, is not wholly convincing, and even if it were, one would have to dispute the suggestion that it was reasonable to write down to the general viewing audience by omitting the proper explanation, leaving the story with an ending so confusing that it could not be fully understood without reading the showrunner's later elucidation in a magazine.

If so important a development in the show's mythology as the writing

---

[62] A reference to the plot of 'The Wedding of River Song' (2011).

out of two well-loved companion characters is to be done in such a way that the Doctor is absolutely and unquestionably prevented from ever seeing them again, then the on-screen rationale provided for this really needs to be totally clear and watertight; otherwise, it short-changes the viewers – and certainly the fans, who care most about such things – and leaves open the possibility that it could be unpicked by future writers. That doesn't happen here, and consequently, although it has many admirable aspects and enjoyable elements, 'The Angels Take Manhattan' must sadly be considered, overall, a big disappointment.

On a more positive note, though, Steven Moffat does deserve great kudos for making the very last shot of the episode a reprise of one from 'The Eleventh Hour', of young Amelia Pond sitting on her little suitcase in her garden, looking up as she hears the TARDIS's materialisation noise. Previously, this shot had seemed something of an anomaly, understandable only as part of a dream, as in 'The Eleventh Hour' itself, the Doctor does not actually return to the young Amelia after their initial meeting in 1996, but leaves her sitting there – which is why she later comes to be described as 'the girl who waited'. Now, though, we see that the Doctor does return after all, to tell Amelia something of her future adventures in the TARDIS (a meeting that we can only assume does not change her timeline, causing the destruction of New York, as it would if he revisited her later in her life ...) Whether or not this was something Moffat actually planned right from the outset (and if he did, almost three years in advance, that is even more extraordinary), it is very pleasing to have Amy's story brought full circle in this way, and with a final freeze-frame – recalling the one that marked the end of Sarah Jane Smith's time as a regular TARDIS traveller in 'The Hand of Fear' (1976) – we bid farewell to one of the most popular of *Doctor Who*'s 21st Century regulars.

P.S. (minisode)

Writer: Chris Chibnall

<u>DEBUT TRANSMISSION DETAILS</u>

BBC *Doctor Who* website
Date: 12 October 2012

Duration: 4′ 36″

<u>ADDITIONAL CAST (UNCREDITED)</u>

Mark Williams (Brian Williams)[63]

<u>PLOT</u>

Brian is watering plants at the home of Amy and Rory when a stranger knocks at the door and hands him a letter from his son. Reading the letter, Brian learns that the couple got stuck in New York fifty years before Rory was born, and will not be coming back. Rory explains that the man who delivered the letter is Brian's grandson, Anthony. Brian goes to Anthony, and they hug each other.

<u>QUOTE, UNQUOTE</u>

- **Rory (voice-over):** 'I'm so sorry, Dad. I thought about this for years, and I realised there was one thing I could do. I could write to you. Tell you everything about how we lived. How, despite it all, we were happy. But before I do, I need you to know, you are the best dad any son could've had; and for all of the times I drove you mad, and you

---

[63] Seen only in a live-action reprise from 'The Power of Three'.

P.S

drove me mad, all the times I snapped at you, I'm sorry. I miss everything about you. Especially our awkward hugs.'

CONTINUITY POINTS

- As Rory says that he got stuck in New York at a time fifty years before he was born, and as it has been previously established that he was born around 1989, this confirms that he and Amy were sent back to the late 1930s at the end of 'The Angels Take Manhattan'. Rory was probably around 32 years old at that time, and as the couple's gravestone gave his age at death as 82, this indicates that he probably died around 1988. Similarly, Amy, whose age at death was given as 87, probably died around 1993.

- Rory says that, if he has got it right, the letter will have been delivered a week after he and Amy departed with the Doctor in the TARDIS, as seen at the end of 'The Power of Three'.

- Although Rory says that 'years' passed before he wrote the letter, the actual date of the letter is not given. He adds that Anthony will be able to tell Brian everything, and will have the family albums with him.

- Anthony – who is also mentioned in the publicity blurb for the tie-in novella *Melody Malone: Angel's Kiss* – was adopted by Amy and Rory as a son in 1946. (Amy was infertile, as revealed in 'Asylum of the Daleks'.)

PRODUCTION NOTES

- After writer Chris Chibnall introduced Rory's dad Brian in 'Dinosaurs on a Spaceship', Steven Moffat felt that the character's story deserved to be resolved, but was unable to find a way to fit this into 'The Angels Take Manhattan'. Chibnall consequently offered to write a suitable scene for inclusion as an extra on *The Complete Seventh Series* DVD and Blu-ray box set. This scene was never recorded, however, as actor Mark Williams was unavailable to reprise his role as Brian. It was therefore decided to turn the script into a storyboard-style animation instead. This was released online as 'P.S.', with

199

Arthur Darvill narrating Rory's letter. The live-action final scene of 'The Power of Three', where Amy and Rory depart with the Doctor in the TARDIS, leaving Brian behind, was included by way of a recap, before the title.

- The animation is subtitled 'The scene that was never shot.'

- At the time of writing, 'P.S.' has not had a commercial release.

ANALYSIS

It is rather a pity that Brian was brought into the show only just before Amy and Rory departed, as he was such a good character, and so endearingly portrayed by Mark Williams, that he really deserved to be seen a lot more than he was. It would have been even more of a pity if his story had been left completely unresolved, so it is a very good thing that we at least have 'P.S.', a beautifully-written and very moving addendum. Although the scene works extremely well as an animation, it would have been even better if it could have been realised as a full live-action piece as originally intended. In fact, if Steven Moffat really could not bring himself to have Amy and Rory simply perish after jumping from the roof of Winter Quay at the end of 'The Angels Take Manhattan', a far better way of writing them out than was actually seen in that episode would have been to have had them revive in 1938, rather than in 2012, and live out the remainder of their lives in New York without the grieving Doctor's knowledge, while viewers were tipped off to the truth both through the couple's names appearing on their gravestone and through a scene along the lines of 'P.S.' – which could surely have been very easily recorded at the same time as 'The Power of Three'. Sadly, though, that was not to be.

The Snowmen

Writer: Steven Moffat
Director: Saul Metzstein

DEBUT TRANSMISSION DETAILS[64]

BBC One/BBC One HD
Date: 25 December 2012. Scheduled time: 5.15 pm. Actual time: 5.14 pm.

Duration: 59' 49"

ADDITIONAL CREDITED CAST

Tom Ward (Captain Latimer), Richard E Grant (Dr Simeon), Catrin Stewart (Jenny), Neve McIntosh (Madame Vastra), Dan Starkey (Strax), Joseph Darcey-Alden (Digby), Ellie Darcey-Alden (Francesca), Liz White (Alice), Jim Conway (Uncle Josh), Cameron Strefford (Walter[65]), Annabelle Dowler (Walter's Mother), Ben Addis (Bob Chilcott), Sophie Miller-Sheen (Clara's Friend), Daniel Hyde (Lead Workman), Ian McKellen (Voice of the Great Intelligence), Juliet Cadzow (Voice of the Ice Governess)

PLOT

In England, 1842, a solitary young boy named Walter is playing in the snow when his snowman seems to talk to him. Fifty years on, in his office at the GI Institute, the now adult Dr Simeon puts snow samples into a large transparent globe that speaks in the same voice as the snowman. He then

---

[64] The details given here are for the debut UK transmission. The episode was actually shown first at midday on 24 December 2012 by KST in South Korea, with the dialogue dubbed into Korean.
[65] Dr Simeon as a boy – therefore his surname is 'Simeon'.

has the workmen who collected the samples killed by vicious animated snowmen that appear from nowhere. Elsewhere, the Doctor encounters a Cockney barmaid, Clara, who has also noticed one of the strange snowmen. The Doctor theorises it is made of a type of snow that remembers. Clara follows the Time Lord when he leaves in a hansom cab driven by his Sontaran friend Strax, and later sees him ascend an invisible staircase to a solid cloud, on which sits the TARDIS. The Silurian Madame Vastra and her wife Jenny meanwhile confront Dr Simeon, who warns them this will be 'the last winter of humankind'. Clara has another job, as governess to a Captain Latimer's two children at their home, Darkover House. Her predecessor died after falling into the garden pond, which then froze over. Helped by Vastra and Jenny, Clara brings the Doctor to the house, where an ice replica of the old governess emerges from the pond to menace the family. The Great Intelligence in the globe wants to use the ice governess as a template for multiple duplicates with which to take over the Earth. The Doctor and Clara escape up the staircase to the TARDIS, which is now above Darkover House. However, the ice governess follows and grabs Clara, who falls back to the ground and is badly injured. The Doctor takes the TARDIS to the GI office and deduces that the Intelligence was created by the telepathic alien snow sensing Dr Simeon's thoughts as a young boy. He tries to break the link between them, but the Intelligence has now gained independent existence, and Dr Simeon dies. Back at Darkover House, the tears of Clara and Captain Latimer's children are mimicked by the snow, which consequently melts, ending the crisis. However, Clara then dies. Later, the Doctor sees her full name, Clara Oswin Oswald, on her gravestone, and realises that she was another version of the Dalek-converted Oswin he met on the Dalek Asylum planet. He heads off to solve the mystery of the 'impossible' girl.

QUOTE, UNQUOTE

- **Strax:** 'I suggest a full frontal assault with automated laser monkeys, scalpel mines, and acid!'

- **Vastra:** 'Good evening. I'm a lizard woman from the dawn of time, and this is my wife.'

- **Strax:** 'This dwelling is under attack. Remain calm, human scum!'

- **Clara:** 'There's a man called the Doctor. He lives on a cloud in the sky, and all he does, all day, every day, is to stop all the children in the world ever having bad dreams.'

- **Doctor:** 'It's called the TARDIS. It can travel anywhere in time and space. And it's mine.'
  Clara: 'But it's … Look at it, it's …'
  Doctor: 'Go on, say it. Most people do.'
  [Clara walks round the outside of the TARDIS, then returns to the console room.]
  Clara: 'It's smaller on the outside.'
  Doctor: 'Okay, that is a first.'

- **Clara:** 'Run. Run you clever boy … and remember.'

CONTINUITY POINTS

- Disregarding the advice he received from River and Amy at the end of 'The Angels Take Manhattan', the Doctor has eschewed human companionship since losing the Ponds. He has apparently been living for some time in Victorian London, associating with his friends Vastra, Jenny and Strax but refusing to help them with their investigations. Reflecting his mood, he now wears different, more sombre, Victorian-style clothes, complete with a dark purple frock coat and a battered top hat. However, as Clara engages his interest in the crisis at Darkover House, he emerges from his period of introspection and once again puts on a bow tie.

- Strax was previously presumed to have been killed at the Battle of Demon's Run in 'A Good Man Goes to War' (2011). The Doctor tells Clara, 'He gave his life for a friend of mine once.' When she queries this, he explains, 'Another friend of mine brought him back. I'm not sure all his brains made the return trip!'[66]

- The Doctor is in possession of a creature called a 'memory worm'. He says: 'One touch and you lose about an hour of your memory. Let it

---

[66] The exact circumstances of this will be eventually explained in the minisode 'The Battle of Demon's Run: Two Days Later'.

bite you and you could lose decades.'

- The Doctor has kept Amy Pond's reading glasses, and is seen using them. He has parked the TARDIS high in the air on a cloud of 'super-dense water vapour', accessible via an invisible spiral staircase and, leading down from that to the ground, a retractable ladder. He can change the position of the cloud by exerting a slight influence over the wind, possibly with his sonic screwdriver.

- In her governess job, Clara affects a more refined accent and adopts the alias Miss Montague.

- Dr Simeon clearly believes that Sherlock Holmes is a character created by Arthur Conan Doyle. He tells Vastra, 'You realise Dr Doyle is almost certainly basing his fantastical tales on your own exploits? With a few choice alterations, of course. I doubt the readers of *The Strand* magazine would accept that the Great Detective is, in reality, a woman.' Later, when the Doctor tries to pass himself off as Holmes, donning the cape and deerstalker hat of his popular image, Dr Simeon says, 'I enjoy *The Strand* magazine as much as the next man, but I am perfectly aware that Sherlock Holmes is a fictional character.' In this, however, he is mistaken. It has previously been clearly established that, in the *Doctor Who* universe, Sherlock Holmes is a real person, whose exploits Doyle simply writes about. Most notably, in 1887, Holmes and his associate Dr Watson have an adventure with the seventh Doctor, as recounted in the New Adventures novel *All-Consuming Fire* (Virgin Publishing, 1994), subsequently adapted as an audio drama of the same title (Big Finish, 2015).

- Although the Doctor appears not to realise it, or at least not until he is standing by Clara's graveside at the end of the story, the disembodied entity created through the telepathic alien snow's link with the young Walter Simeon is clearly the same Great Intelligence he previously encountered in 'The Abominable Snowmen' (1967) and 'The Web of Fear' (1968). It takes its name from, or perhaps conversely gives its name to, Dr Simeon's Great Intelligence Institute, aka GI Institute, the address of which is recorded on his business card as 2 Bloomsbury Lane, London N31.

- It is strongly implied that the killer snowmen in this story are what inspired the Great Intelligence to attack the Earth using robot Yeti, aka Abominable Snowmen, in 'The Abominable Snowmen'. Although that story was set in 1935, the Intelligence had laid the groundwork for its attack some two hundred years earlier, when it took possession of the Tibetan lama Padmasambhava, an old friend of the Doctor's. Padmasambhava's mind encountered the Intelligence on the astral plane, which is presumably outside of normal time – explaining how the Intelligence could be there almost two hundred years prior to its creation in Victorian London. The Intelligence appeared to be already aware of the Doctor in 'The Abominable Snowmen', and 'The Snowmen' effectively supplies the reason for this.

- Similarly, it is strongly implied that the Doctor's placing of crystals from the ice governess's body inside a metal tin bearing a 1967 map of the London Underground is what inspired the Great Intelligence to attack via the tube tunnels in 'The Web of Fear'. This is the first time that a specific date has been suggested on screen for the events of 'The Web of Fear', but it is consistent with prior evidence of a mid-1960s setting – specifically, the evidence that these events took place four years prior to those of 'The Invasion' (1968), as explicitly stated by Brigadier Lethbridge-Stewart, and that the latter story, being the first to feature UNIT, was set around the end of the 1960s. (See the discussion of this issue in 'Continuity Points' on 'The Day of the Doctor'.) One character in 'The Web of Fear', Professor Travers, says that it has been 'over forty years' since the incident depicted in 'The Abominable Snowmen', suggesting a later date. However, another character, Julius Silverstein, says that it has been 'thirty years' since Travers brought a deactivated Yeti back from Tibet and gave it to him for his museum, which is again consistent with a mid-1960s date. Since Travers is shown to be a forgetful old man, Silverstein's recollection is likely to be the more reliable.

- The birth date given on Clara's gravestone is 23 November 1866, and the death date is 24 December 1892 – as seen in the story, she dies just as the bells start ringing at midnight to mark the start of Christmas Day. So she has just recently turned 26 at the time of her death.

PRODUCTION NOTES

- This Christmas special and 'The Crimson Horror' were made together as Block Six of Series Seven's production schedule, with their recording significantly overlapping. However, 'The Snowmen' is not normally classed as part of Series Seven proper. It was the first Christmas special to have its debut transmission part-way through the run of a series, rather than between two series.[67]

- The Coal Exchange in Mount Stuart Square, Cardiff, was the first location used for 'The Snowmen'. Recording took place there on 6 and 7 August 2012 for the scenes in Dr Simeon's office at the GI Institute. Fields House in Fields Park Avenue, Allt-Yr-Yn, Newport was used over the next two days for sequences in the Darkover House study and front garden. On 10 August, Cathays Cemetery in Cardiff was used for the graveyard shots. Further Darkover House action was taped on 11, 12, 15, 16 and 17 August at Treberfydd House in Llangasty, Brecon for the back garden and hallway scenes, and on 13, 14 and 21 August at Insole Court, Llandaff, Cardiff for the children's playroom and bedroom scenes. The Cathays Park campus of Cardiff University was the location used on 14 and 28 August for scenes in the GI Institute corridors and back alleys. Corn Street and the adjoining St Nicholas Street in Bristol were used on 20 August for action of the Doctor's cab on the snowy London streets. The following day, Portland Square in Bristol was used as the place above which the TARDIS is initially perched on its cloud. On 24 August, Llandough House in Llandough, Cowbridge was the location for the scene where Clara meets Vastra in her conservatory. Three days later, Treowen Manor in Dingestow, Monmouth was used both for the snow-covered garden of young Walter's house and for the Rose & Crown pub where Clara works as a temporary barmaid. Lastly, 28 August saw recording take place at Merthyr Mawr House in Merthyr Mawr, Bridgend for action in Vastra's living room. Studio recording was carried out at BBC Roath Lock between 10 August and 20 September,

---

[67] Unless you count 'The Feast of Steven', the seventh episode of 'The Daleks' Master Plan', as a Christmas special. This was transmitted on Christmas Day 1965 and had little to do with the events of the episodes either side of it, being a light-hearted run-around.

with some pick-up shots of Victorian London being completed on 23 November.

- The first of two prequels made for 'The Snowmen' was titled 'The Great Detective' and transmitted on 16 November 2012 as part of the BBC's annual *Children in Need* charity telethon. It was topped and tailed by video clips of Matt Smith and Jenna-Louise Coleman, speaking from between two racks of costumes. With a 3' 17" duration, it was written by Steven Moffat and directed by Saul Metzstein, but neither was credited, and unusually there was no brief clip of the *Doctor Who* title sequence at the start. Narrated in a Scottish accent by an uncredited Mark Gatiss, the action features Madame Vastra (described for the first time as 'the Great Detective'), Jenny Flint (whose surname was previously given only in publicity material) and Strax (making his first appearance since his apparent resurrection). It is established that the three are operating in Victorian London as a team of investigators known as 'the Paternoster Row gang', named after the street where Vastra lives. The team's occasional fourth member, the Doctor, emerges from the shadows of a foggy street. He is dressed in his Victorian garb. His friends try to engage his interest with wild tales of potential adventures, but he is uninterested, morosely telling them that he has retired. 'The Great Detective' was later included on *The Complete Seventh Series* DVD and Blu-ray box set.

- The second of the two prequels for 'The Snowmen' was released online by the BBC on 17 December 2012. Titled 'Vastra Investigates' and subtitled 'A Christmas Prequel', it was again written by Steven Moffat – this time credited – and directed by Saul Metzstein – again uncredited – and had a 2' 29" duration. As usual for a prequel, it opens with a brief clip of the *Doctor Who* title sequence, minus the logo. The action begins with Vastra, Jenny and Strax wrapping up another case for their Scotland Yard contact. The inspector – played uncredited by Paul Hickey[68] – is taken aback to learn of Vastra's origins as a survivor of an ancient reptilian race who was accidentally woken by an extension to the London Underground, and even more

---

[68] Hickey's character will later reappear in the Series Eight episode 'Deep Breath' (2014), where his name will be given as Inspector Gregson.

so when she explains that she and Jenny are in love. Vastra and Jenny then depart in a carriage. Jenny notices that it is snowing, which surprises Vastra, as there are no clouds in the sky. This prequel, like the first, was later included on *The Complete Seventh Series* DVD and Blu-ray box set.

- Unusually, 'The Snowmen' also had a prose prequel. Written by Justin Richards, titled *Devil in the Smoke* and subtitled *An Adventure for the Great Detective*, this novella was published as an e-book by BBC Digital on 18 December 2012. It marked the Paternoster Row Gang's debut appearance in tie-in fiction, but while its plot bore some similarities to that of 'The Snowmen', the two were otherwise unconnected. The publicity blurb was as follows:

  Madame Vastra, the fabled Lizard Woman of Paternoster Row, knew death in many shapes and forms. But perhaps one of the most bizarre of these was death by snow …

  On a cold day in December, two young boys, tired of sweeping snow from the workhouse yard, decide to build a snowman – and are confronted with a strange and grisly mystery. In horrified fascination, they watch as their snowman begins to *bleed …*
  The search for answers to this impossible event will plunge Harry into the most hazardous – and exhilarating – adventure of his life. He will encounter a hideous troll. He will dine with a mysterious parlour maid. And he will help the Great Detective, Madame Vastra, save the world from the terrifying Devil in the Smoke.

- In 2013, *Devil in the Smoke* was also released by AudioGo as a Dan Starkey-read audiobook, and published by BBC Books in print form in the anthology *Summer Falls and Other Stories*, supposedly compiled by Amelia Williams.

- On 21 December 2012, the BBC released online a humorous video called 'Songtaran Carols'. This features the final use of the original eleventh Doctor version of the show's title sequence, brief clips of which are seen at the beginning and end. The video has Matt Smith,

Jenna-Louise Coleman, Neve McIntosh, Catrin Stewart and Dan Starkey on the TARDIS console room set, in their respective roles as the Doctor, Clara, Vastra, Jenny and Strax. Strax sings snippets from three well-known Christmas songs – 'Santa Claus is Coming to Town', 'When the Red, Red Robin (Comes Bob, Bob, Bobbin' Along)' and 'Rudolph the Red-Nosed Reindeer' – each with a typically violent Sontaran twist to the lyrics. At the end of the final song, the five actors all break character and burst out laughing. At the time of writing, this has not had a commercial release.

- 'The Snowmen' marks the debut of new regular opening and closing title sequences for the show. These were created by the Peter Anderson Studio – who from the start of Series Seven had succeeded BBC Wales Graphics as regular providers of *Doctor Who*'s graphics – and accompanied by a revised version of Murray Gold's arrangement of the famous Ron Grainer-composed theme music. The opening title sequence features a new logo, and a brief image of the Doctor's face – the first time the latter has been included in one of the 21st Century *Doctor Who* title sequences, although such an image formed part of all but the first of the 20th Century ones.

- This story also features the debut of a new TARDIS console room set – the first to have fallen within the responsibility of the show's current regular designer Michael Pickwoad. Steven Moffat's brief was that this should move away from the quirky, organic look of the previous 21st Century versions, as he wanted viewers to be reminded that the TARDIS is essentially a machine. Hence the new set harks back rather more to the look of the classic-era TARDIS console rooms.

- In a break with normal practice on 21st Century stories featuring the Silurians and the Sontarans, the closing titles of 'The Snowmen' omit to credit the respective creators of those races, Malcolm Hulke and Robert Holmes. Nor is any credit given to Mervyn Haisman and Henry Lincoln as the creators of the Great Intelligence.

- This is the first *Doctor Who* episode to feature a contribution from noted thespian Sir Ian McKellen. McKellen had previously been approached to play the companion to amoral Time Lord chemist the Rani in the two-part *Children in Need* skit 'Dimensions in Time' (1993), but had been unavailable; the character was eventually named Cyrian as an in-joke reference to him.

- Steven Moffat's original intention was that the Victorian-era Clara would not die at the end of 'The Snowmen' but would go on to become the Doctor's regular companion. The two Latimer children, Digby and Francesca, would also have featured in a number of subsequent episodes. In the end, however, he decided instead to create a 21st Century version of Clara to become the companion. The Latimer children were replaced in his plans by another young brother and sister whom the 21st Century Clara would look after as a nanny.

- The closing credits are followed by a 'Coming Soon' trailer of clips from the 2013 section of Series Seven.

OOPS!

- Vastra's lips are green in some shots, but pink in others.

CRITICAL REACTION

- 'Steven Moffat's script hints at potentially interesting parallels between the Doctor, Dr Simeon and Captain Latimer in their shared refusal to deal with those around them, particularly when that isolation is entirely of their own making. The reveal of the Intelligence's true identity as a mirror image of all Dr Simeon's twisted hopes and fears underscores that point, but "The Snowmen" doesn't quite manage to connect Dr Simeon's mistakes with those of the Doctor – Dr Simeon's plight is fascinating on his own terms, but the script could have gone deeper in exploring why people need each other and what happens when they cut themselves off from everything, particularly when that's such a perfectly Christmas sort of theme.' Alasdair Wilkins, A.V. Club website, 25 December 2012.

- 'It was an enjoyable enough romp, I suppose, and I imagine that reference-spotters had a field-day. There were nods not only to *The Snowman* but also to Sherlock [Holmes] – cheekily suggested to have been, in "real life", the lesbian Silurian Madame Vastra. The shadow of Henry James's *The Turn of the Screw* could be detected in the CGI figure of the dead governess, made of ice and snarling "That's the way to do it!" There were shades of Dickens and C S Lewis and maybe even the smoke-fashioned staircase from the *Mary Poppins* film too in the episode's best touch – having the newly refurbished TARDIS float above town on a bed of "super-dense water vapour", reachable only by a vertiginous spiral staircase.' Dominic Cavendish, *Telegraph* website, 25 December 2012.

- 'Where others have been doubting (Rose), reluctant (Martha) and sarcastic (Donna), Clara appears to be a mirror image of the Doctor: fearless, curious and intuitive, a match not only of wits but of shared delight in the power of knowing. That is the perpetual tension that fuels the Doctor. A Time Lord weighted with the wisdom of the ages, believing himself to be the last of his kind, has only his sense of wonder to protect him from the great sorrow born of endless knowledge and experience. Fortunately it is boundless, like his energy, and of all the recent Doctors, Smith best captures the power of wilful youthfulness. Not in appearance, though he is the most boyish of the canon, but in resilience, the springiness that allows a child to find miracles in the mundane, to truly believe that today will be better than yesterday. The world always needs the Doctor, but perhaps never more than on Christmas day.' Mary McNamara, *Los Angeles Times* website, 25 December 2012.

ANALYSIS

The Silurian survivor Madame Vastra, her human maidservant wife Jenny Flint and the Sontaran nurse Strax all made highly memorable debuts in the Series Six story 'A Good Man Goes to War', and it was an astute move on Steven Moffat's part to revive them – literally, in Strax's case – for 'The Snowmen' and have them teamed up at Vastra's house in Paternoster Row in Victorian London. With Vastra's fierce intelligence, Jenny's readiness to spring into action in leather fighting gear, and Strax's brute strength – not to mention his usefulness as comic relief, as amply demonstrated here with much hilarious dialogue based around his bellicose nature and misperceptions of life on Earth – they make up a formidable band of investigators, and could easily sustain their own spin-off series.

Another very welcome return in 'The Snowmen' is that of Jenna-

Louise Coleman as Clara Oswin Oswald. For those viewers who, at the time of 'Asylum of the Daleks', had forgotten or been unaware that she was to become a regular in the show, it is her reappearance here – or, more precisely perhaps, in the brief teaser at the close of 'The Angels Take Manhattan' – that will have produced a jolt of surprise, and led to speculation as to how the Doctor could possibly encounter her again when she seemed to have been turned into a Dalek and then killed in her first episode. That question is only partly answered here, as we learn that the Clara of 'The Snowmen' is actually a different person from the Oswin of the Dalek episode, but has various intriguing similarities to her – not least her appearance and her name! When she too is killed at the end of the story, and we see a brief sequence of another, modern-day Clara passing by her now aged gravestone, declaring 'I don't believe in ghosts,' we are left just as eager as the Doctor to discover the solution to this mystery – which sets things up very nicely for the 2013 section of Series Seven.

As in 'Asylum of the Daleks', Coleman gives a superb, scene-stealing performance here, in what almost constitutes a dual role, with Clara switching from Cockney barmaid to prim-and-proper children's governess during the course of the action – this double life being another pointer, perhaps, to the multi-identity nature of her character. Her chemistry with Matt Smith is excellent, too, which again bodes well for the future.

The scene where Clara first ascends the spiral staircase to the TARDIS, up on its cloud in the sky, is absolutely magical, and a real highlight of the production. So too is her later entrance into the TARDIS – where, for the first time in *Doctor Who*'s history, the camera moves from the exterior, through the police box doors and into the interior in a single continuous shot.[69] The new TARDIS console room set is extremely good, too, and certainly the best so far in 21st Century *Doctor Who*; and the redesigned opening and closing title sequences and revised theme music arrangement are other ongoing elements of the show that get a pleasing make-over here, adding to the feeling that – despite this special coming part-way through a series – the show is effectively entering a new era.

Another very striking and unusual scene is the one where Clara meets

---

[69] Previously, this impressive effect had been achieved only – and rather less smoothly – in the documentary *Doctor Who: Thirty Years in the TARDIS* (BBC One/BBC Two Scotland, 1993).

Vastra for the first time, and the lizard woman challenges her to respond to a series of questions with just single-word answers. This cleverly results in Clara successfully piquing the Doctor's interest by using the word 'pond' – which she intends to refer to the frozen pond in the Darkover House front garden, but which he naturally interprets as a reminder of the recently-departed Amy Pond, whose loss he is still mourning, and whose glasses he has now taken to wearing when he reads.

The suggestion that Arthur Conan Doyle bases his Sherlock Holmes stories on the exploits of Vastra and her Paternoster Row gang is very amusing – and could be seen as an in-joke nod by Steven Moffat to his other hit BBC One series, *Sherlock* – although it is perhaps over-egging things a bit when the Doctor then proceeds to impersonate Holmes, dressing up in deerstalker and cape and fooling about by making a series of improbable – and incorrect – deductions. Another slight misstep in the depiction of the Doctor comes when Moffat has him at one point incongruously refer to Clara as 'some bird' – a dated and distinctly cringe-inducing colloquialism. The Doctor's repeated insulting remarks to Strax about his height, appearance and intelligence also sit rather uncomfortably. On the plus side, it was a good move on Moffat's part to start the story with the Doctor having decided to go into retirement – an idea inspired by a proposal that classic-era script editor Douglas Adams unsuccessfully pitched during his time on the show.[70] This takes one step further the notion of the Time Lord trying to withdraw from universal attention, as touched on in a number of earlier episodes, starting with 'The Wedding of River Song' (2011); and the question 'Doctor who?' is again accorded some significance here, this time being posed by Clara, who eventually tempts the Doctor back into action.

Richard E Grant, whose previous *Doctor Who* credits came when he played an unspecified future incarnation of the Doctor in Steven Moffat's charity spoof 'The Curse of Fatal Death' (1999) and voiced an alternative ninth Doctor in the animated webcast story 'The Scream of the Shalka' (2003), was an interesting choice of actor to guest star in this special. He is suitably sinister in the role of Dr Simeon, but there is no real nuance to his performance, as he delivers all of his dialogue with a kind of supercilious

---

[70] Some sources suggest that Douglas Adams' proposal was actually entitled 'The Doctor Retires', but that is incorrect; 'the Doctor retires' was simply a description of its key idea.

sneer. Probably his best moment comes when Dr Simeon reacts in horror on learning that the deep, booming voice of the Great Intelligence – provided, unpublicised ahead of transmission, by the distinguished Ian McKellen – is actually just a sonically modified imitation of his own higher-pitched tones as a young boy, and that the entity has been created by the telepathic alien snow mimicking his own emotions; or, as the Doctor puts it, 'a parasite feeding on the loneliness of a child and the sickness of an old man'.

The Great Intelligence itself was a fantastic classic-era *Doctor Who* creation positively crying out to be reintroduced in the new-era show, so its inclusion here is another greatly appreciated move by Steven Moffat. Given that it is a disembodied intelligence, there was fortunately no risk of it being given an unsympathetic design make-over, as has happened when some other classic-era monsters have been brought back (although thankfully the inferior action-figure-style battle armour of the 21st Century Sontarans is nowhere to be seen this time, as Strax amusingly sports instead a suitably adapted version of a Victorian butler's attire). That said, however, the killer snowmen that the Intelligence animates as its foot soldiers on this occasion are nowhere near as scary or imposing as the Yeti robots it used previously, which is rather a shame. It would admittedly have made no sense for the Yeti to be seen here – it is clear from 'The Abominable Snowmen' that the Intelligence bases them on the appearance of real Himalayan creatures during its subsequent attack on Tibet – but, given that snowmen can be made in any shape, it would have been good to see them manifesting in a rather more fearsome form. The story's title recalls that of Raymond Briggs' children's book and Christmas family favourite animation *The Snowman*, with its far more sympathetic depiction of snowmen, and the addition of snarling teeth isn't really sufficient to turn these into credible monsters; given that they have no limbs, it isn't even clear how they manage to attack their victims. The telepathic alien snow is also a less-than-memorable threat, given no backstory whatsoever; and the ice governess has to be counted as one of the show's less well-realised CGI creations – which all adds up to the fact that one thing 'The Snowmen' sadly lacks is a truly first-rate menace for the Doctor to thwart.

It has to be said, too, that while it is very welcome to have the Great Intelligence back in the show, there was no call for it to be given an origin story; and certainly not the one presented here. In 'The Abominable Snowmen', it was described in almost mystical terms, as 'intelligence …

formless in space,' encountered on the astral plane during Buddhist meditation by the great lama Padmasambhava. This was expanded upon in the Missing Adventure *Millennial Rites* (Virgin Publishing, 2000), where it was identified as an entity called Yog-Sothoth, one of the H P Lovecraft-inspired Great Old Ones from before the birth of the current universe; and while admittedly that elaboration was also superfluous, it did at least preserve a sense of timelessness and wonder. Although it is just about possible to reconcile all these different accounts if one assumes that, following its creation in 'The Snowmen', the Great Intelligence escapes to the timelessness of the astral plane and becomes known as Yog-Sothoth, there is no question that giving it such a mundane origin as being just a reflection of the introverted nature and 'Victorian values' of one cold-hearted man is rather diminishing, robbing it of much of its previous awe-inspiring quality, and certainly all of its mystery.[71]

The other big problem with 'The Snowmen' is that the resolution of the crisis at the end is decidedly perfunctory, happens independently of anything the Doctor does and, in relying essentially on the power of human tears, has the same mawkishly sentimental quality that marred the previous Christmas special, 'The Doctor, the Widow and the Wardrobe' (2011). It isn't even clear why the snow mimics the tears, since they don't come into contact with it – something previously said to be a prerequisite in the context of the Great Intelligence's plan for the snow to mimic the ice governess.

Sadly, the weakness of the central storyline involving the alien snow and the Great Intelligence means that, despite all the appealing elements and positive qualities mentioned above, 'The Snowmen' ends up being almost less than the sum of its parts, and has to be considered only a qualified success.

---

[71] In the short story 'Legacies' (Candy Jar Books, 2015), part of the *Lethbridge-Stewart* prose spin-off series in which the Great Intelligence also features, a different rationalisation is provided for its various representations over the years. It is described as an imprint of an interdimensional being that exists in many different realities, always ending up as the Great Intelligence and having the same basic attributes, but with different origins.

The Battle of Demon's Run: Two Days Later (Minisode)

Writer: Steven Moffat
Director: Saul Metzstein

DEBUT RELEASE DETAILS

Us iTunes Store/Amazon Instant Video
Date: 25 March 2013

Duration: 2' 52"

CAST (UNCREDITED)

Dan Starkey (Strax), Neve McIntosh (Madame Vastra), Catrin Stewart (Jenny)

PLOT

Strax revives two days after the Battle of Demon's Run to learn from Madame Vastra and Jenny that his wounds, non-fatal after all, have now been healed. Demon's Run is being evacuated, and all of the Doctor's friends being returned to their proper times and places. Vastra and Jenny invite Strax to join them in London, 1888, where they solve crimes and protect the Empire. Although initially reluctant, Strax agrees to go with them.

QUOTE, UNQUOTE

- **Strax:** 'I thank you for your offer, but cannot accept, as you are putrescent alien filth.'

CONTINUITY POINTS

- Strax was previously believed to have suffered a fatal wound in the Battle of Demon's Run, as seen in 'A Good Man Goes to War' (2011).

- As previous established, the 'present' year for Vastra and Jenny when they take part in the Battle of Demon's Run is 1888. This indicates that by the time of 'The Snowmen', set in 1892, Strax is already well established as part of the Paternoster Row gang.

- Vastra says that Jenny has been ostracised by her family because of her 'preferences in companionship'.

- As already seen in 'The Snowmen', Strax has difficulty distinguishing between males and females of other species.

- Although not explicitly stated, it is presumably River Song who takes all of the Doctor's comrades from the Battle of Demon's Run back to their own times and places, using her vortex manipulator – as foreshadowed in 'A Good Man Goes to War'. This must be a lengthy process, hence why Strax, Vastra and Jenny are still at Demon's Run two days after the end of the conflict.

PRODUCTION NOTES

- 'The Battle of Demon's Run: Two Days Later' serves both as a sequel to 'A Good Man Goes to War' and as a prequel to 'The Snowmen' – or, more precisely, to 'The Great Detective', making it a prequel to a prequel! It was initially promoted mistakenly as a prequel to 'The Bells of Saint John', an episode to which it has no connection. It was written by Steven Moffat in anticipation of fans requesting an explanation as to how Strax survived the Battle and came to join Vastra and Jenny as a member of the Paternoster Row gang in Victorian London.

- This minisode received only an online release, and was not broadcast. It was later included on *The Complete Seventh Series* DVD and Blu-ray box set.

ANALYSIS

'The Battle of Demon's Run: Two Days Later' is an enjoyable vignette, with some very amusing dialogue, nicely plugging what would otherwise have been a niggling gap in the show's continuity.

7.06 – The Bells of Saint John

Writer: Steven Moffat
Director: Colm McCarthy

<u>DEBUT TRANSMISSION DETAILS</u>

BBC One/BBC One HD
Date: 30 March 2013. Scheduled time: 6.15 pm. Actual time: 6.14 pm.

Duration: 45' 18"

<u>ADDITIONAL CREDITED CAST</u>

Manpreet Bachu (Nabile), Sean Knopp (Paul), James Greene (The Abbott), Eve de Leon Allen (Angie), Kassius Carey Johnson (Artie), Geff Francis (George), Celia Imrie (Miss Kizlet), Robert Whitelock (Mahler), Dan Li (Alexei), Daniella Eames (Little Girl), Anthony Edridge (Pilot), Fred Pearson (Barista), Jade Anouka (Waitress), Olivia Hill (Newsreader), Matthew Earley (Man With Chips), Isabella Blake-Thomas (Child Reading Comic), Richard E Grant (The Great Intelligence)

<u>PLOT</u>

The Doctor is living at a Cumbrian monastery in 1207 AD when he is surprised to receive a call on the TARDIS's external telephone from a 21st Century version of Clara Oswald, who thinks his number is an internet helpline. He tracks her down to the Maitland family home in London, where she works as a live-in nanny to two children, and arrives just in time to save her from having her mind extracted by a mobile wi-fi base-station in the form of a disguised robot with a revolving head – otherwise known as a Spoonhead. This fate has already befallen many other people worldwide, in an operation overseen from offices on the sixty-fifth floor of the Shard in London by a woman named Miss Kizlet. The victims are selected after they access a free wi-fi network of alien origin. Miss Kizlet and her assistant Mahler try to kill the Doctor and Clara by crashing a wi-fi-controlled passenger plane onto them, but the Doctor materialises the TARDIS on board the plane and prevents this. Miss Kizlet finally succeeds in uploading Clara's mind by tricking her with a Spoonhead in the Doctor's image. However, the Doctor then reprograms the Spoonhead and has it break into Miss Kizlet's office by ascending the near-vertical side of the Shard on an anti-grav motorbike. Miss Kizlet falls victim to the Spoonhead, and in order to save herself, has to order Mahler to download all the minds in the data cloud back into their owners' bodies. As a result, Clara revives. Miss Kizlet is revealed to have been working under the mental domination of the Great Intelligence, which needs human minds to feed on. The Intelligence now withdraws, returning Miss Kizlet and her staff to how they were before it took them over, while UNIT troops arrive to mop up the operation. The Doctor invites Clara to join him on his travels, but she initially declines, telling him to ask her again the following day.

QUOTE, UNQUOTE

- **Doctor:** 'This whole world is swimming in wi-fi. We're living in a wi-fi soup. Suppose something got inside it. Suppose there was something living in the wi-fi, harvesting human minds. Extracting them. Imagine that. Human souls trapped like flies in the world-wide web. Stuck forever, crying out for help.'
  Clara: 'Isn't that basically Twitter?'

- **Doctor:** 'You okay?'
  Clara: 'Sure. Setting up stuff. Need a user name.'
  Doctor: 'Learning fast.'
  Clara: 'Clara Oswald for the win. Oswin!'

- **Miss Kizlet:** 'No-one loves cattle more than Burger King.'

CONTINUITY POINTS

- The Doctor has withdrawn to the solitude of the monastery in 1207 to reflect on and try to work out the meaning of the Victorian Clara's last words, 'Run, you clever boy, and remember.' Demonstrating a previously unknown talent for art, he has painted a portrait of her, with those words added in the bottom right-hand corner.

- Clara has been acting as live-in nanny to a brother and sister named Artie and Angie since their mother died during a week's visit she paid to the family a year earlier. The family's surname is given as Maitland on the household wi-fi network, and the father's name is George. Artie has been reading a hardback book entitled *Summer Falls* by Amelia Williams (aka Amy Pond), and Clara is clearly familiar with its contents, as she tells him that the eleventh chapter is the best, adding, 'You'll cry your eyes out.' The Spoonhead that later attacks Clara disguises itself as the girl pictured in the book's front cover artwork, having obtained the image from Clara's subconscious.

- The 'bells of Saint John' is a term used by the monks at the monastery to describe the ringing of the TARDIS's external telephone in its compartment behind the panel on the left-hand door of the ship's police box shell. This is taken from the St John Ambulance emblem on the adjacent panel on the right-hand door. The Doctor says of the ringing telephone, 'That is not supposed to happen,' although it did occur once previously, in the Steven Moffat-scripted 'The Empty Child' (2005).

- Clara says that she was given the Doctor's phone number by 'the woman in the shop,' who wrote it down for her, telling her that it was 'the best helpline out there'.

- Clara learns from Angie that the password for the Maitland family's internet is 'rycbar123' – the 'rycbar' standing for 'Run, you clever boy, and remember'. It is this that tips the Doctor off to Clara's identity when she mentions it in her phone call to him.

- This Clara Oswald does not have the middle name Oswin.

- The Doctor refers to the TARDIS as his 'mobile phone', telling Clara that this is 'a surprisingly accurate description'.

- When the Doctor is looking after Clara while she is asleep following her first brush with a Spoonhead, he sets down beside her bed a plate of jammie dodger biscuits – established to be a favourite of his in a number of earlier stories such as 'Victory of the Daleks' (2010). He notices that Clara has got a hardback book called *101 Places to See*. There is a pressed tree leaf kept within it, which she later describes as 'Page 1'. She has been writing down and crossing out her age in the front of the book each year since she was 9, although for some unknown reason she has missed ages 16 and 23. The last number written in is 26, suggesting that is Clara's current age.

- Clara's father is alive, as the Doctor mentions having fielded a phone call from him, in which he complained about the government; but no other details are revealed about him.

- The Doctor manages to prevent the wi-fi-controlled plane from crashing on Clara's suburban street, although he says that he does not know how to fly one.

- When Mahler is trying to locate the TARDIS using found footage from tourist cameras etc, he says to his associate Alexi, who thinks he has tracked it to the South Bank, 'Are we sure this time? Earls Court was an embarrassment.' This is a reference to a real police box sited outside London's Earls Court tube station.

- The Doctor has an anti-grav motorbike that he apparently gets out of the TARDIS 'garage'. When Clara asks why they are using this, he says that he doesn't take the TARDIS into battle as it is 'the most powerful ship in the universe and I don't want it falling into the wrong hands'. This implies that, following the Time War, it is the last surviving TARDIS. He later tells a bystander, in reference to the motorbike, 'I rode this in the Anti-grav Olympics, 2074. I came last.' The tenth Doctor offered to take Rose Tyler to the first Anti-gravity Olympics in 'Tooth and Claw' (2006).

- Miss Kizlet states that 'only a tiny number' of the people whose minds are downloaded from the data cloud at the end of the story will survive. It is implied that this is because the others will no longer have bodies for their minds to return to. Presumably the body's autonomic functions continue for some time after the mind is extracted – explaining why Clara revives once her mind is returned – but then eventually cease, causing irreversible death. In many cases, the victim's relatives may well have had their bodies buried or cremated in the interim. The Doctor however says that even those who do not survive will have been released from 'a living hell'.

- When the Great Intelligence withdraws at the end of the story, Miss Kizlet's mind reverts to that of a young child, indicating that that was how old she was when she first fell under its control. As her appearance is that of a woman in her early sixties, it would seem that the Intelligence has been operating through her for some considerable time – possibly more than fifty years.

PRODUCTION NOTES

- This episode was made as Block Eight of Series Seven's production schedule.

- Location recording began at 30 Beatty Avenue, Roath, Cardiff, where scenes at the Maitlands' house were taped between 8 and 12 October 2012. On 11 October, the sequence on board the crashing plane was recorded on a plane owned by eCube Solutions at MOD St Athan in the Vale of Glamorgan. The same date also saw a second unit visit Southerndown Beach in Ogmore Vale, Bridgend – used earlier in Series Seven for the beach scenes in 'Dinosaurs on a Spaceship' – to capture an establishing shot of the clifftop where the monastery is situated – the image of the monastery itself being added in post-production. On 15 October, the Sky Bar of St Paul's Hotel at 10 Godliman Street in the City of London was the venue for taping of the café exterior scenes, where the Doctor goes for coffee while Clara works at her laptop. The same day, further London recording was carried out, when taping of the motorbike sequences got under way on Westminster Bridge, Waterloo Bridge, Horse Guards Road and Admiralty Arch. These sequences were completed the following day, with further material being taped on Westminster Bridge and Waterloo Bridge, and also on The Queen's Walk and St Thomas Street. The crew then returned to Wales, where recording took place on 17 October at Caerphilly Castle, Caerphilly for the monastery interior shots. The same day, an area of ancient woodland at Forest Fawr Country Park, Tongwynlais, Cardiff was used for the entrance to the underground tunnel where the Doctor has stowed the TARDIS in 1207. The café interior scenes were taped on 19 October in a real café at the Senedd Building in Cardiff. In early December, work was carried out at various locations around the world to capture shots for the episode's opening sequence of people using wi-fi devices and collapsing as their minds are extracted. These were St Pancras International Station and the interior of a London-to-Paris Eurostar train on 2 December; the Eiffel Tower in Paris, France later the same day; Conzelman Road in Mill Valley, California, USA on 6 December; Stockton Street and California Street in San Francisco, California, USA, also on 6 December; the Shibuya branch of Starbucks coffee shop and the Shibuya shopping mall in Tokyo, Japan on 7 December; and finally the Senso-ji Buddhist temple in Asakusa, Tokyo, Japan on 8 December. Studio recording was carried out at BBC Roath Lock between 11 and 24 October, with green-screen pick-up shots of Richard E Grant as the Great Intelligence being taped on 21 November. Some final pick-up shots for a sequence at the very start of the episode where the character Nabile falls victim to the Intelligence were done much later, on 18 February 2013, at classic-era *Doctor Who*'s regular studio venue, Television Centre in London.

- A prequel to this episode was placed online by the BBC on 23 March 2013 – two days prior to the release of 'The Battle of Demon's Run: Two Days Later'. Called simply 'The Bells of Saint John: A Prequel', and lasting 2' 37", it opens with the Doctor, wearing his original costume complete with tweed jacket, sitting on a swing in a children's playground. A child comes along and talks to him, and he tells her that he is looking for a girl he has met by chance twice before and lost both times. The child returns to her mother, and it is revealed that she is the very person the Doctor has been seeking: Clara Oswald. The action presumably takes place somewhere in Clara's home town of Blackpool, Lancashire.[72] Production paperwork gives the date as 1999, but this cannot be correct, as Clara would be in her early teens

---

[72] This birthplace is established in later episodes, the first mention of Blackpool coming in 'The Rings of Akhaten'.

by then, and the girl seen here is much younger.[73] The prequel was written by Steven Moffat and features, uncredited, Matt Smith as the Doctor, Sophie Downham as young Clara and Nicola Sian as her mother, Ellie. It was recorded on 26 November 2012 in Roath Park, Cardiff, concurrent with work being done on 'The Name of the Doctor', with John Hayes directing. It was later included on *The Complete Seventh Series* DVD and Blu-ray box set.

- On 4 April 2013, a few days after this episode's transmission, BBC Digital published a tie-in e-book, *Summer Falls* by Amelia Williams, based on the one being read by Artie in 'The Bells of Saint John'. The e-book used the same title font and cover illustration as the in-universe version, and the publicity blurb read as follows:

'When summer falls, the Lord of Winter will arise ...'

In the seaside village of Watchcombe, young Kate is determined to make the most of her last week of summer holiday. But when she discovers a mysterious painting entitled 'The Lord of Winter' in a charity shop, it leads her on an adventure she never could have planned. Kate soon realises the old seascape, painted long ago by an eccentric local artist, is actually a puzzle. And with the help of some bizarre new acquaintances – including a museum curator's magical cat, a miserable neighbour, and a lonely boy – she plans on solving it.

And then, one morning, Kate wakes up to a world changed forever. For the Lord of Winter is coming – and Kate has a very important decision to make.

Summer Falls was also made available on 1 August 2013 as a BBC audiobook read by Clare Corbett, and appeared in print on 24 October 2013 when it was the lead story in a BBC Books anthology with the revised title *Summer Falls and Other Stories*. It was written by James Goss.

---

[73] It will be established in the Series Eight story 'Death in Heaven' that Clara was born on 23 November 1986.

OOPS!

- Just before the Doctor and Clara enter the TARDIS to go and avert the impending plane crash, there is a chair standing next to them that repeatedly switches position between shots; it is behind them when seen from one camera angle, but in front of them when seen from another.

- When the TARDIS materialises on the South Bank, the Doctor passes this off to nearby tourists as a magic trick. He and Clara then collect several coins in his upturned fez, in the manner of street performers. However, when he turns the fez the right way up and places it on a young boy's head, no coins fall out.

- In the same scene on the South Bank, the police box doors change from open to closed between shots. (Possibly the Doctor has set the doors to close automatically after he fetches his anti-grav motorbike from within the ship.)

- During the motorbike riding sequence, the camera can sometimes be seen reflected in the Doctor's shiny crash helmet.

CRITICAL REACTION

- 'Equal parts *The Ring* and *Black Mirror*, and with just a pinch of *Invasion of the Body Snatchers*, "The Bells of Saint John" boasted a strong concept, and nailed the typical Whovian trope of taking something so familiar and commonplace, and twisting it into a nightmarish threat. Sure, the monsters of the week were as terrifying and imposing as their name suggested (we can't see the Spoonheads heading up their own horror franchise anytime soon), but the hook of an omnipresent enemy proved sizeable enough, and tied nicely into the real Big Bad behind it all – Richard E Grant's the Great Intelligence, who it appears is going to be lurking behind numerous machinations to come.' Mark Snow, IGN website, 30 March 2013.

- '[Jenna-Louise] Coleman matches [Matt] Smith's own manic energy, and the episode instantly makes them feel like equals in a way the show often hasn't in its past Doctor and companion pairings. The episode reminds us that the eleventh Doctor is a very old man who just happens to be in a very young man's body, which sets up the great moment when Clara calls the TARDIS a "snog box" – the Doctor's reaction falls somewhere between uncomprehending alien and mortified 11 year old. "The Bells Of Saint John" is a solid enough episode on its own terms, but its major success is in showing why this particular Doctor and this particular Clara are so well matched for each other.' Alasdair Wilkins, A.V. Club website, 30 March 2013.

- 'Moffat's writing is always hurtingly cutting-edge. This one was as if he'd sat in a dark pub for a while with Chris Morris and Charlie Brooker and analysed the Woefulness of Modern Stuff, yet somehow … been given a spoonful of kind honey on his way out. Oh, there were sillinesses. The other baddies were called Spoonheads because the backs of their heads look like … well, you have a guess. The great team of baddies was hiding out somewhere in London, which had been shot with many looming shots of the Shard, in somewhere that was obviously going to be high and rich with self-aggrandising uglyhood.' Euan Ferguson, *Guardian* website, 30 March 2013.

ANALYSIS

At the suggestion of producer Marcus Wilson, 'The Bells of Saint John' was conceived by Steven Moffat as *Doctor Who*'s take on the urban thriller genre. Exciting action scenes such as the one where the Doctor and Clara race to prevent a passenger plane from crashing, and later the one where the Doctor – or rather, as revealed in a clever twist when he removes his crash helmet, his Spoonhead duplicate – rides up the side of the Shard on his anti-grav motorbike, certainly have something of the feel of a James Bond movie, making this the latest in the run of episodes resembling mini blockbusters.

In having the Great Intelligence mount an attack using wi-fi, the showrunner has fallen back on a tried-and-trusted *Doctor Who* trope of taking something familiar to viewers from everyday life and turning it into a deadly danger – previous examples being such varied things as shop-window mannequins and plastic flowers (the Nestene and Auton stories), Bluetooth mobile phone headsets ('Rise of the Cybermen' / 'The Age of Steel' (2006)), diet pills ('Partners in Crime' (2008)) and car sat-navs ('The Sontaran Stratagem' / 'The Poison Sky' (2008)). This is an approach that invariably works well; alien menaces always seem more potent when invading the cosy domestic sphere. This is what third Doctor actor Jon Pertwee often used to describe as the difference between finding a Yeti in the Himalayas and finding one 'sitting on the loo in Tooting Bec' – a particularly apposite analogy in the context of a story featuring the Great Intelligence. The thrill is heightened by virtue of the threat coming from a more incongruous and unexpected source.

That said, the specifics of this particular alien incursion do sometimes seem just a touch too familiar. The independent spin-off drama 'Downtime' (1993) also had the Great Intelligence attacking Earth via the world-wide web – a modern-day 'web of fear' – from a facility with multiple computer terminals, managed by a mentally-ensnared older woman – the Doctor's former companion Victoria Waterfield – and her male henchman, with UNIT involved in the action. The Intelligence's scheme to establish a kind of 'battery farm' of human minds is uncomfortably close in concept to what the Weeping Angels were up to in 'The Angels Take Manhattan', albeit on a grander, planet-wide scale; and its approach of uploading minds after monitoring the victims via their laptop computers is similar, too, to the Wire's attack on the British public via their television sets in 'The Idiot's Lantern' (2006). Miss Kizlet is from the same mould as other powerful, sharp-dressed businesswomen who have turned out to be fronting for alien attackers; particularly Ms Foster in 'Partners in Crime' (2008) and, in *The Sarah Jane Adventures*, Mrs Wormwood in 'Invasion of the Bane' (2007) and 'Enemy of the Bane' (2008). And the Spoonheads, with an ordinary face on one side of their revolving head but a computer interface on the other, strongly recall the information nodes in Steven Moffat's own 'Silence in the Library' / 'Forest of the Dead' (2008). All of these similarities result in the viewer at times feeling a slight sense of *déjà vu*.

One element of the story that is, of course, intentionally familiar is the new companion character Clara Oswald, the 'twice dead' girl who has both mystified and intrigued the Doctor. As the Time Lord himself observes, her job as a children's nanny here mirrors her Victorian counterpart's as a children's governess in 'The Snowmen' – her two charges in both cases being a young sister and brother whose mother has died, leaving their father a single parent. However, unlike that earlier Clara, she has no 'double life' moonlighting as a Cockney barmaid. Despite her amusing speculation that the TARDIS is the Doctor's 'snog box', she also lacks the cheekiness and charm of 'Soufflé Girl' Oswin

Oswald in 'Asylum of the Daleks' – although, in another example of mirroring, she does acquire similar (but possibly temporary) expert computer skills during the course of the action. Even her costume isn't as eye-catching as her predecessors', consisting of simply the kind of everyday clothes one would expect of a young woman in a contemporary middle-class setting. Consequently, of the three different versions of the character we have been presented with to date, she actually seems the least interesting – despite Jenna-Louise Coleman delivering another winning performance in the role. Given that this latest Clara is to be the one who goes on to become a regular in the show, this is rather unfortunate, and means that she is at risk of remaining forever in the shadow of her own alternative selves. In her favour, though, she does display the qualities of bravery, wit and intelligence that the Doctor's companion ideally needs, and also demonstrates an independent streak when she initially spurns his invitation to join him on his travels, telling him to ask her again the next day – suggesting that, like Amy and Rory, she is to be only a part-time TARDIS traveller, maintaining a separate home life on Earth.

This Clara, like her Victorian predecessor, also poses the question, 'Doctor who?' – something that delights the Doctor, who asks her to repeat it, then tells her, 'Do you know, I never realised how much I enjoy hearing that said out loud.' This again emphasises his current desire for anonymity; and indeed, at the start of the story, he has retreated even further into the shadows than in 'The Snowmen', having taken up residence with an order of monks in early 13th Century Cumbria and occupied himself by painting a portrait of the Victorian Clara, to which he has added in one corner her – and Oswin's – last words, 'Run, you clever boy, and remember'. It is when he decides to change out of his monk's habit and smarten himself up for the benefit of modern-day Clara that he makes the choice to discard his familiar tweed jacket in favour of the purple frock coat he was first seen wearing in the Christmas special. This makes him appear more like one of the classic-era Doctors, and also accords better with his generally serious demeanour of late, which is quite far removed from the lively 'mad scientist' persona he displayed at the start of his current incarnation – although an element of that does still resurface from time to time, such as when he tells Clara that he has mended 'a disassembled quadricycle' he found in the garage and then, when she quashes that idea, gleefully exclaims, 'I invented the quadricycle!'

The interplay between the lead characters in these early scenes, when Clara is still understandably suspicious of the eccentric stranger who has just turned up on her doorstep, is especially engaging, and sets things up very nicely for subsequent developments. A particularly effective sequence comes when all the house lights in Clara's street suddenly turn on, while all those elsewhere in London go off, making her and the Doctor a sitting target for the rapidly descending wi-fi-controlled passenger plane – an audaciously inventive piece of scripting. Another pleasing touch is the way Clara manages to keep hold of her coffee mug throughout the whole of the following hectic scramble, where the Doctor whisks her off in the TARDIS to the cabin of the falling plane, they arrive just in time to avert the disaster, then rapidly depart again.

With its prominently-featured central London locations and involvement of UNIT, 'The Bells of Saint John' demonstrates, perhaps even more so than 'The Power of Three', a shift away from the fairytale-like English village settings that typified the contemporary Earth stories of the early part of Steven Moffat's tenure as showrunner, and back toward the more urban locales associated with Russell T Davies's era. Just as 'Army of Ghosts' / 'Doomsday' (2006) featured a secret base situated in a famous London skyscraper – One Canada Square, Canary Wharf – so too does this episode – specifically, the Shard. And just as the ninth Doctor and Rose ran across Westminster Bridge in the very first 21st Century episode, 'Rose' (2005), so the eleventh Doctor and Clara speed across it in an exhilarating motorbike sequence here – adding to the impression created by the new opening and closing titles and the redesigned TARDIS console room set that the advent of Clara marks, in effect, the start of another new era for the show.

Countering any speculation that its reappearance in 'The Snowmen' might turn out to be just a one-off, the return of the Great Intelligence in this very next episode – now manifesting in the image of the special's Dr Simeon – indicates that it features rather more prominently in Steven Moffat's plans; and it will be intriguing to see how this plays out.

Director Colm McCarthy, making his *Doctor Who* debut here, does a fine job of handling the action, which is well-paced throughout and features a strong performance from the excellent Celia Imrie as Miss Kizlet. Even some of the usually unsung minor members of the cast make a memorable contribution – a good example being Matthew Earley, who strikes just the right note as a mentally-controlled chip-eating bystander who reacts with amusing incredulity when the Doctor's anti-grav motorbike heads up the side of the Shard. The montage of shots right at the start of the episode, showing people all around the world collapsing as they fall foul of the threat from the wi-fi, is another well-realised sequence, its almost casual use of overseas location material recorded in France, the USA and Japan demonstrating just how polished a production *Doctor Who* has become these days, managing to achieve an expensive look on what is actually a very modest budget for a BBC drama series. This opening montage is also notable for using the more *Sherlock*-like device of having non-diegetic lines of digital typescript scrolling up the screen, and for introducing another of Steven Moffat's trademark unsettling catchphrases, 'I don't know where I am!', to add to earlier examples such as 'Are you my mummy?' in 'The Empty Child' / 'The Doctor Dances' (2005) and 'Who turned out the lights?' in 'Silence in the Library' / 'Forest of the Dead' – possibly inspired by a similar technique favoured by classic-era writers Bob Baker and Dave Martin, who came up with phrases such as 'Eldrad must live!' in 'The Hand of Fear' (1976) and 'The Quest is the Quest' in 'Underworld' (1978).

All in all, 'The Bells of Saint John' gets the 2013 section of Series Seven off to a great start.

7.07 – The Rings of Akhaten

Writer: Neil Cross
Director: Farren Blackburn

DEBUT TRANSMISSION DETAILS

BBC One/BBC One HD
Date: 6 April 2013. Scheduled time: 6.15 pm. Actual time: 6.15 pm.

Duration: 43' 51"

ADDITIONAL CREDITED CAST

Michael Dixon (Dave[74]), Nicola Sian (Ellie[75]), Emilia Jones (Merry[76]), Chris Anderson (The Chorister), Aidan Cook (The Mummy), Karl Greenwood (Dor'een)

PLOT

The Doctor investigates 21st Century Clara's early life, from the day in 1981 when her parents first met owing to a chance incident where a leaf blew into her father's face and almost caused an accident. However, he finds no answer to the puzzle of her existence. When she asks to be shown 'something awesome', he takes her to the asteroids that make up the rings around the planet Akhaten. On one of these, in a busy marketplace, she befriends a young girl named Merry Gejelh, who as her generation's chosen Queen of Years is the living vessel of her people's history. At a ceremony called the Festival of Offerings,

---

[74] Surname 'Oswald', as indicated by the fact that he is Clara's father.
[75] Maiden surname given as 'Ravenwood'.
[76] Surname given as 'Gejelh' (pronounced 'Gelel').

Merry has to sing a song across space to a fearsome being known as the Old God, who is held in the Pyramid of the Rings on another asteroid nearby. This song, along with items of sentimental value offered up by the ceremony's many attendees of various races, is intended to keep the Old God dormant. When a Chorister at the Pyramid makes a mistake in his answering song, Merry is transported across there in an energy bubble. The Doctor and Clara go after her on a rented space-moped. The Old God wakes, but the Doctor protects Merry from being given over to it, using his sonic screwdriver to hold off three sinister figures called the Vigil. However, he then realises that the true menace is the planet Akhaten itself. Known to the system's inhabitants as Grandfather, it is actually a sentient parasite that craves emotional memories. The Queen of Years is a sacrifice made to it so that it can feed on her living history of her people. The Doctor confronts the creature, telling it to take his memories instead, and it is almost overwhelmed. Clara then offers up the leaf that brought her parents together, which she carries with her in the pages of a book and which represents to her the unfulfilled potential of her mother's prematurely ended life. The huge sentimental value of this finally destroys the creature.

QUOTE, UNQUOTE

- **Doctor:** 'Listen. There is one thing you need to know about travelling with me; well, one thing apart from the blue box and the two hearts. We don't walk away.'

- **Doctor:** 'Take my memories. But I hope you've got a big appetite, because I have lived a long life and I have seen a few things. I walked away from the last Great Time War. I marked the passing of the Time Lords. I saw the birth of the universe, and I watched as time ran out, moment by moment, until nothing remained. No time. No space. Just me. I walked in universes where the laws of physics were devised by the mind of a madman. And I've watched universes freeze and creations burn. I have seen things you wouldn't believe. I have lost things you will never understand. And I know things. Secrets that must never be told. Knowledge that must never be spoken. Knowledge that will make parasite gods blaze.'

CONTINUITY POINTS

- Clara's parents meet when a strong wind blows a tree leaf into her father Dave's face, causing him to stagger onto a road, and her mother Ellie pulls him out of the path of an oncoming car. It is this same leaf that Clara later keeps pressed between the pages of her *101 Places to See* book, as first seen in 'The Bells of Saint John'. We learn here that the book was originally owned by Ellie at age 11, as her name is written on the page before Clara's. Ellie's maiden surname was Ravenwood, and her gravestone states that she was born on 11 September 1960 and died on 5 March 2005. Her cause of death is not revealed, but it is possible that she was killed during the Auton attack seen in 'Rose' (2005), which took place on the same date – also the date when the ninth Doctor first met Rose Tyler.

- Clara wears a red satchel over her shoulder throughout most of this episode, obviously carrying the *101 Places to See* book inside it.

- Akhaten is one of seven planets in the local system, and the system's inhabitants believe that all life in the universe originated there. It is orbited by rings of asteroids, on one of which stands the Pyramid of the Rings of Akhaten, described by the Doctor as a holy site for the Sun Singers of Akhat. The ceremony in which Merry sings takes place on a nearby asteroid – named Tiaanamat in production paperwork, although not on screen – which is also the location of the marketplace where the TARDIS materialises. The Doctor tells Clara that he has been there before, with his grand-daughter – a reference to Susan Foreman, as seen in classic-era *Doctor Who*.

- Clara forms the impression that the TARDIS does not like her. This may be why it does not translate for her the bark-like speech of the alien called Dor'een. However, she is able to understand the other aliens who speak to her on the asteroid. The Doctor says that most of those present come from the local system, and identifies some of them as Pan-Babylonians, a Lugal-Irra-Kush, some Lucanians, a Hooloovoo, a rarely-seen Terraberserker from the Kodion Belt and an Ultramancer.

- According to the Doctor, the Festival of Offerings has been taking place once every thousand years.

- Clara says that as a young girl she used to have a fear of getting lost. Then, when she was aged about 6, she did get lost, one bank holiday Monday on Blackpool beach, but her mum found her, took her home and reassured her. This cured her of her fear.

- In the culture of the asteroids, items of sentimental value are used as currency. When the Doctor and Clara need to rent a space-moped to try to rescue Merry, Clara pays for this with a ring that used to belong to her mother. The Doctor returns this to her at the end of the episode, on behalf of all the people she has saved.

- When the Doctor uses his sonic screwdriver to hold up the Pyramid's very heavy main entrance door, and again when he later deploys it to repel the powerful Vigil, he grimaces and grunts with the effort of doing so. This is arguably the first time it has ever been implied that the device draws energy from the Doctor himself as part of its function – although it does accord with the fact that he often seems able to change its settings without making any physical adjustment, suggesting that he may have a mental link to it.

PRODUCTION NOTES

- This episode was made as Block Nine of Series Seven's production schedule. The draft script was headed 'Alien Planet', although that was really more a descriptor than a working title.

- 'The Rings of Akhaten' was recorded mainly in studio. The relatively small amount of location work began when the pre-opening-titles scene where Clara's parents Dave and Ellie meet was taped on Rupert Brooke Drive, Newport, on 22 October 2012. St Woolos Cemetery, Newport was used the following day for the subsequent scene of Clara standing with her father at her mother's graveside. The crew returned to Rupert Brooke Drive on 27 October to record further material, including an interior sequence in young Clara's bedroom. The final location work was done on 26 November at 30 Beatty Avenue, Roath, Cardiff for a scene at the Maitlands' house, which was recorded in conjunction with material for 'The Crimson Horror' and 'The Name of the Doctor'. Studio recording was carried out at BBC Roath Lock on various dates between 24 October and 30 November.

- The 1981 single 'Ghost Town' by the Specials is heard at the start of the episode, in the scene where Dave and Ellie meet. The year is further established when the Doctor is seen reading the 1981 Summer Special edition of *The Beano* children's comic. On 15 May 2013, D C Thomson & Co, the publishers of *The Beano*, reprinted that edition as part of a *Doctor Who*-themed issue to tie in with the episode.

- On 9 April 2013, three days after this episode's broadcast, the BBC placed online a video called 'Strax Field Report: Doctor at Trafalgar Square', with a 1' 25" duration. The first half of this has Strax in the TARDIS interior, delivering a direct-to-camera report to his home planet Sontar. He states that the Doctor has been sighted in Trafalgar Square in London, and then gives a distinctly garbled summary of the Battle of Trafalgar. The second half consists of a montage of behind-the-scenes clips of a sequence being set up for recording on location in Trafalgar Square for the forthcoming fiftieth anniversary special. Eight additional 'Strax Field Report' videos would be released during the course of 2013, all of them taking the format of Strax addressing his home planet from within the TARDIS; these others, though, would include no behind-the-scenes clips. None of the 'Strax Field Report' videos was titled on screen, and none of them has received a commercial release.

OOPS!

- When the Doctor and Clara exit the TARDIS after it materialises in the marketplace, the Doctor leaves the door ajar. However, when Clara returns later, she finds it closed. (Possibly the Doctor has gone back unseen and closed the door in the interim, as he disappears from the action temporarily; or possibly the ship has deliberately shut Clara out, as she observes, 'I don't think it likes me.')

- In the marketplace, the Doctor says that the sonic screwdriver is the only item of sentimental value that he has on him, and that he does not want to give it up, as it is useful. However, in a slightly earlier scene, he is seen wearing Amy Pond's reading glasses, which clearly are also of great sentimental value to him.

- Clara's leaf is inconsistent in shape and size between scenes, and also between this episode and 'The Bells of Saint John', betraying the fact that a number of different prop leaves were used during recording.

CRITICAL REACTION

- 'The episode was written by *Luther* creator Neil Cross, and I must say, he's a terrific writer for going so far outside of what he normally does, or at least what I know him for. *Luther*'s a gritty cop drama about serial killers and corruption and redemption, and this episode is, at its heart, about a little girl who is scared to sing in public. It's something to which we can all relate. It also allows us to get to know Clara – *this* Clara – better than we already thought we did, in her curiosity and then wish to help the small Queen of Years, who is made to memorise the sum total of the history of her people, if only to be sacrificed to an ancient god. I adore Jenna-Louise Coleman. She is the absolute perfect companion, and she and Matt Smith, who is also just phenomenal every single week, get on so spectacularly that I'm glad we have another six weeks with them.' Kyle Anderson, Nerdist website, 6 April 2013.

- 'There's a ... sequence, which lasts a good few minutes, in which the entire main cast (albeit that that's all of three people) are basically separated and acting by themselves to a green-screen. It looks fantastic, but unfortunately it plays rather skewed. With a mute and almost inanimate Big Bad (there was plenty of scope for the Minor Bad to rescue the situation, if only it had been cast as a speaking part! But it *is* a nice twist, if not an entirely original one, when [what first seemed to be] the Big Bad turns out to be the Minor Bad, and it transpires that there's another Big Bad literally on the horizon that has been hiding in plain sight the whole time), it's as if Smith (and to a lesser extent Coleman) is giving out and not receiving, and it isn't just the lack of interaction that causes the sequence to underwhelm; the notion that the Doctor is talking to a giant globe millions of miles away, and that this globe is not just hearing him but understanding him too, is probably a suspension of disbelief too far. You can throw in all the explanation you like; it simply doesn't play convincingly.' J R Southall, *Starburst* website, 6 April 2013.

- '[The writer] gets a little too flowery toward the end of this episode, laying it on a bit thick as the Doctor gushes about the cosmic origins of every unique and special being in the universe, while Clara becomes uncharacteristically verbose as she turns her mother's missing future into a weapon that can repel even a ravenous [planet]. And, while it's nice to see science fiction dabbling in matters musical, the alien hymns on display here are disappointingly Earth-like in their soppy pop-ballad styling and cloyingly literal lyrics. Matt Smith and Jenna-Louise Coleman sell the schmaltz though, and between the abundance of fantastic creature make-ups and the surprisingly heavy themes, it's easy to forgive the basic fact that the episode is really nothing more than a series of conversations.' Dan Whitehead, Birth Movies Death website, 6 April 2013.

ANALYSIS

'The Rings of Akhaten' begins very promisingly indeed. The opening sequence, where the Doctor observes Clara's parents Dave and Ellie meet, fall in love and start to raise their child, only for Ellie to die at the young age of 44, somewhat recalls how he first encountered Amy as a little girl – although his shadowing of the family here does make him seem a bit like a stalker! The only real issue is that, in the scene at Ellie's graveside, actor Michael Dixon has been insufficiently aged to convince that Dave is some 24 years older than when he first met Ellie in 1981; in fact, he looks only a few years older than Clara herself – more like an older brother than her father – despite Jenna-Louise Coleman's hair having been restyled to give the impression that she is in her late teens, and this leaves the viewer briefly confused as to what is actually being depicted. Further make-up effort was really needed here. Nevertheless, this opening material does serve to sketch in the new companion's backstory in a very economical and effective way.

The TARDIS's initial arrival at the Rings of Akhaten gives Clara the 'awesome' sight she was seeking, courtesy of a very good CGI sequence of the planet and its orbiting asteroids – the first of many impressive images in what is a visually outstanding episode. Equally pleasing are the scenes set in the bustling marketplace on Tiaanamat, where the Doctor and Clara encounter beings of various alien races. The costumes and masks for these came mostly from stock held by the show's regular prosthetics suppliers Millennium FX, whose director Neill Gorton had long wanted to be involved in creating something akin to the iconic Mos Eisley cantina scene from *Star Wars* (1977), which likewise featured numerous different types of alien creatures. Writer Neil Cross would doubtless have recalled that scene too, although he might have had in mind as well the Animoid Row bazaar in the Ridley Scott-directed *Blade Runner* (1982), as his script quotes from that movie in a couple of lines of dialogue – including the Doctor's comment 'Home again, home again, jiggity jig' when he takes Clara back to the Maitlands' house at the end – and places similar emphasis on the significance of memories – a theme also explored in much of showrunner Steven Moffat's *Doctor Who* writing.

Egypt was clearly another source of inspiration for Cross, as is evident in the name Akhaten, which is very close to that of the Ancient Egyptian sun god Akhenaten, and in the fact that the Old God, referred to by the Doctor at one point as the Mummy, is imprisoned in a Pyramid. Furthermore, the marketplace of Tiaanamat resembles the souks of Egyptian cities such as Cairo; and even the Specials' 'Ghost Town', heard on the soundtrack at the very start of the episode, opens with an Egyptian-sounding flute section, although this could be just a coincidence.

In showing how Clara has to cope with the culture shock of adjusting to a completely alien environment, the marketplace scenes also recall some previous companions' maiden TARDIS trips, particularly Rose's in 'The End of the World' (2005) and, perhaps to a lesser extent, Amy's in 'The Beast Below' (2010). Clara certainly proves herself well up to the challenge as, quickly overcoming any apprehension she might have felt, she befriends the frightened young girl Merry and helps her to hide from her pursuers, including the three sinister figures referred to as the Vigil, before reassuring her that she will succeed in the task she has been assigned. The idea of a young girl from each generation on Tiaanamat being chosen as the new Queen of Years, responsible for becoming a living record of her people's history, is an intriguing one, and sets things up very nicely for the rest of the story.

Up until about 18 minutes into the episode, there has really been very little to fault, and it has all been thoroughly enjoyable. Sadly, however, from this point on, things starts to unravel a bit, owing to shortcomings in both the scripting and to some degree the direction. The problems begin when the action moves into the great semicircular amphitheatre where the Festival of Offerings is held. Unlike the marketplace, which seemed to be enclosed and came across as a believably real place, the amphitheatre is seen to be open to space, and the viewer immediately starts to question how the asteroid could possibly sustain a breathable atmosphere. The earlier scene where the Doctor and Clara walked out onto a much smaller asteroid on first arriving in the TARDIS just about avoided this issue, it having been well established in past episodes that the ship's surrounding forcefield can protect its occupants from the ravages of space even when they venture just outside the open police box doors. Here, though, there is no such get-out; and the implausibilities mount when Merry starts to sing and it is revealed that her voice can somehow be heard in the Pyramid on the neighbouring asteroid, having apparently carried across a great distance of space that one would normally expect to be a vacuum incapable of transmitting sound waves. Then the Doctor and Clara ride from one asteroid to the other on a space-moped, without giving the slightest thought to the possibility that they might need to put on spacesuits. Finally, at the episode's climax, the two travellers even manage to communicate with the sentient planet Akhaten, aka Grandfather, across a still wider gulf of space.

Admittedly *Doctor Who* has always taken certain liberties with scientific principles in its depiction of alien environments. Almost every place the TARDIS has ever visited has seemed to have a breathable atmosphere and Earth-like gravity, and this extraordinary state of affairs is rarely even commented upon by the Doctor and his companions – although sometimes, particularly when the action is set on a spaceship, there might be a brief mention of life-support systems, artificial gravity or the like. This is a convention that the show's writers have had to adopt in order to be able to tell exciting dramatic stories without getting too bogged down in technicalities that might also make their scripts difficult to realise on screen. But for 'The Rings of Akhaten' to show people flying through space without the benefit of protective clothing or breathing apparatus, and to have voices carrying over extraordinary distances through what should be a vacuum, simply stretches credibility too far, and makes it impossible for the viewer to suspend disbelief.

Of course, one can come up with rationalisations. For instance, perhaps the space-moped has a forcefield like the TARDIS's, shielding the Doctor and Clara and supplying them with air to breathe. Or perhaps Grandfather has by some means created an artificial atmosphere extending throughout its rings, and also artificial gravity to assist its worshippers. Admittedly this would beg the question how Tiaanamat's inhabitants could possibly survive after Grandfather is destroyed – but perhaps they could simply relocate to one of the other planets in the system, given that interplanetary travel seems commonplace there. The point is, though, that the script itself makes no attempt to provide any such rationalisations, and consequently the scenario seems utterly unconvincing. Even if the Doctor knows from his experience of such things that travelling between asteroids on the space-moped poses no danger, surely one would expect a bright young woman like Clara, on her very first adventure away from Earth, to query why they do not need spacesuits? One of the principal functions of the *Doctor Who* companion character has traditionally been to ask the sort of questions that the viewer at home might ask, allowing the Doctor to provide a plausible-seeming explanation, even if that explanation often involves a good deal of technobabble; but that simply doesn't happen here.

This is not to suggest that the audience ought to be spoonfed information and left with nothing to work out for themselves, but at least the basic elements of the story ought to be made clear enough that they can be readily understood, and unfortunately that just isn't the case with 'The Rings of Akhaten'. In fact, so muddled is the exposition that – certainly judging from online reviews and comments – many viewers seem to have been left with the mistaken impression that Akhaten is a sentient sun rather than, as the writer intended, a sentient planet – one of seven worlds orbiting that system's star. But who can really blame them, given that the name Akhaten is clearly based on that of an Ancient Egyptian sun god, and that the Doctor at one point refers to the Pyramid as 'a holy site for the Sun Singers of Akhat'?

It doesn't help matters that Farren Blackburn's direction sometimes fails to give a clear impression of where the two asteroids, and the characters on them, are located in relation to each other. For instance, a brief shot of the two asteroids in space just isn't sufficient to establish that the scene introducing the Choristers takes place inside the Pyramid, particularly given that it is immediately followed by one in the amphitheatre on Tiaanamat, where Merry steps up onto a podium to prepare to sing. It is only toward the end of the episode, too, that it is clearly indicated that the Pyramid's interior chamber is actually at its apex; before that, the viewer is left to guess exactly where it is situated within the edifice. In another moment of confusion, the Doctor at one point makes to enter the Pyramid via its closed main door, but when the shot switches to the interior chamber, he is seen coming in instead through the alternative 'secret door' – which, for reasons best known to the building's presumably deranged architect, is positioned only a few feet away. Then, while the Time Lord is delivering his impassioned – and very well acted – speech imploring Grandfather to take his memories, Clara makes a space-moped trip from the Pyramid to the amphitheatre seemingly in the blink of an eye, and shortly afterwards repeats the trick coming back the other way, almost as if the two places are right next to each other rather than on separate asteroids. In short, the basic visual grammar of these sequences is distinctly awry.

There are other puzzling aspects of the story, too. For example, what exactly is the set-up between the Old God and Grandfather? The Doctor says, 'I thought the Old God was Grandfather, but it wasn't. It was just Grandfather's alarm clock.' This appears to be confirmed when, after the Old God is woken, a beam of light shoots out from the Pyramid, rousing Grandfather in turn. But how did the Old God come to be imprisoned in the Pyramid in the first place? And why does Clara ask the Doctor, 'Who's the Old God? Is there an Old God?', when she has already seen the Old God in the Pyramid, and what she should really be querying is surely the existence of a separate Grandfather. This certainly doesn't help the viewer to follow events.

Another key aspect of the story that isn't properly explained is the role that the Queen of Years plays in the Festival of Offerings. The Doctor appears to indicate that the idea of the 'long song' keeping the Old God dormant is essentially a sham, and that Merry is really intended as a sacrifice to Grandfather. He tells her, 'No, we didn't wake him. And you didn't wake him, either. He's waking because it's his time to wake, and feed. On you, apparently. On your stories … The soul's made of stories, not atoms … He threatens to wake, they offer him a pure soul. The soul of the Queen of Years.' If this is correct, then the same must presumably have been true of Merry's predecessors as well. Certainly Merry seems to think so, as she says of the Vigil, 'If the Queen of Years is unwilling to be feasted upon … it's their job to feed her to Grandfather.' But if she knows this, then why does she start out apparently still believing that it is important for her to perform the song correctly?

Since the Doctor also states that the Festival takes place only 'every thousand years or so, when the Rings align', this would seem to suggest either that Merry's race are exceptionally long-lived, or else that not every

Queen is unlucky enough to have to take part in a Festival. Nevertheless, if it is indeed fairly routine for the Queen to be sacrificed, then this would explain why the Doctor and Clara are the only ones to show any great concern when Merry is whisked away from the Festival in an energy bubble – Merry's own evident distress presumably being attributable to fear rather than surprise. Then again, if the song is really just an irrelevance, why does the Chorister at the Pyramid react with alarm when he appears to make a mistake in his contribution to it – although Merry later thinks that it was she who was at fault – and why is it his mistake that seems to cause the Old God to start to stir? Is this meant to imply that a mistake is bound to be made at every Festival? Despite the Chorister appearing to believe otherwise, it certainly seems inconceivable that this is the first time the 'long song' has ever hit a snag, given that the Doctor says of it, 'It's been going for millions of years, Chorister handing over to Chorister, generation after generation after generation.' Is the Chorister simply ignorant of the true situation? The scripting is so opaque and contradictory here that it is really anyone's guess.

The idea of a song being able to pacify a godlike entity is perhaps a little farfetched to start with – although this is not the first time that incidental music composer Murray Gold's pseudo-operatic stylings have been shown to be capable of soothing an alien being, as the same thing happened with Abigail Pettigrew and the flying shark in 'A Christmas Carol' (2010). It must be just a fortunate coincidence that the Old God, like the shark, appreciates that particular type of music … At times, it must be said, the song seems not so much long as interminable.

Even the idea of Grandfather feeding on the Queen of Years' memorised history of her people is rather fudged, as Clara manages to destroy the creature by offering up her leaf, which represents something quite different: all the infinite possibilities of her mother's prematurely curtailed life. The notion of Grandfather posing a threat to the Queen of Years, and indeed to the whole star system and beyond, is also undermined by the fact that the Doctor and Clara are completely unharmed by their encounter with it, suggesting that it isn't actually extracting the memories from its victims, but simply sharing them. Possibly it is only the fact that Grandfather is destroyed that saves the two time travellers; but, again, this isn't made clear.

Despite having many positive aspects – its impressive visuals; its pleasingly convincing alien marketplace setting; its well-designed and suitably scary monsters in the form of the Vigil and the Old God; and its strong performances from Matt Smith, Jenna-Louise Coleman and young Emilia Jones as Merry – 'The Rings of Akhaten' is ultimately an episode of two halves: the first half (roughly speaking) is superb, but sadly the second is seriously flawed, leaving the viewer with a sense of disappointment that, like Clara's mother, it has failed to realise its full potential.

7.08 – Cold War

Writer: Mark Gatiss
Director: Douglas Mackinnon

DEBUT TRANSMISSION DETAILS

BBC One/BBC One HD
Date: 13 April 2013. Scheduled time: 6.00 pm. Actual time: 6.03 pm.

Duration: 41′ 29″

ADDITIONAL CREDITED CAST

Liam Cunningham (Captain Zhukov), David Warner (Professor Grisenko), Tobias Menzies (Lieutenant Stepashin), Josh O'Connor (Piotr), James Norton (Onegin), Charlie Anson (Belevich), Spencer Wilding (Skaldak), Nicholas Briggs (Voice of Skaldak)

Ice Warriors created by Brian Hayles

PLOT

The TARDIS arrives on the bridge of the Russian submarine *Firebird* near the North Pole in 1983, a time of great Cold War tension. A fearsome reptilian creature, found buried in the polar ice by scientist Professor Grisenko, has been thawed out on board and is now running amok. The submarine is sinking fast, but the Doctor manages to persuade its commander, Captain Zhukov, to direct it laterally, so that its descent is halted by a rocky ledge at a depth of 700 metres. However, the two time travellers are then stranded on board when the TARDIS suddenly leaves without them. The Doctor identifies the creature as an Ice Warrior: it is Grand Marshal Skaldak, a Martian hero, who has been trapped in the ice for some 5,000 years. Skaldak sends out a distress signal, but when there is no response, he assumes the rest of his people are now dead. Having been attacked by the Russian crew, he temporarily discards his outer armour so that he can move around freely and learn more about his enemies. He then determines to wipe out humanity by firing some of the submarine's nuclear missiles, triggering a devastating global conflict. The Doctor and Clara are trying to persuade him to show mercy when the submarine is drawn up to the surface by an energy beam and he is teleported away to a spaceship hovering overhead, his signal having been finally answered. Skaldak could still fire the missiles remotely, but does not do so, and the Martian spaceship departs. The Doctor admits to Clara that the TARDIS left them behind because he had reset the HADS – the Hostile Action Displacement System. It is now at the South Pole, and he wonders if Captain Zhukov might give them a lift …

QUOTE, UNQUOTE

- **Professor Grisenko:** 'We were drilling for oil in the ice. I thought I'd found a mammoth.'
  Doctor: 'It's not a mammoth.'

- **Skaldak:** 'My world is dead, but now there will be a second Red Planet. Red with the blood of humanity!'

- **Skaldak:** 'Well Doctor, which of us shall blink first?'

CONTINUITY POINTS

- The TARDIS's materialisation on board the submarine is a diversion from the Doctor's intended destination of Las Vegas.

- When the Doctor is searched, the objects in his pockets include a Barbie doll, a ball of string and a toffee apple.

- Grand Marshal Skaldak is described by the Doctor as 'Sovereign of the Tharsisian caste. Vanquisher of the Phobos Heresy. The greatest hero the proud Martian race has ever produced.' Later, he adds, 'It was said his enemies honoured him so much, they'd carve his name into their own flesh before they died.' Skaldak himself says: 'I was

Fleet Commander of the Nix Tharsis. My daughter stood by me. It was her first taste of action. We sang the songs of the Old Times. The Songs of the Red Snow.'

- A Grand Marshal previously featured in 'The Seeds of Death' (1969), but only its head and shoulders were seen, on a video screen. It wore a more open mask than Skaldak, similar to that of the Ice Lord officer class introduced in the same story, but with sequin-like adornments.

- The Doctor explains the Ice Warriors' background: 'Martian reptile known as the Ice Warrior. When Mars turned cold, they had to adapt. They're bio-mechanoid. Cyborgs. Built themselves survival armour so they could exist in the freezing cold of their home world, but a sudden increase in temperature and the armour goes haywire.' This is the first time that the Martians' nature as bio-mechanoids has been explicitly confirmed on screen, although in 'The Ice Warriors' (1967), the Doctor notes that the lead Warrior's helmet has an electronic connection.

- The Doctor explains to Clara that the TARDIS's translation matrix allows her to speak and understand Russian.

- The ancient Martian code is said to be, 'Harm one of us and you harm us all.'

- The Doctor says that he has never seen an Ice Warrior out of its armour before. While this is true, he has seen Ice Lords, who do not wear the same bulky armour, and also, in the *Radio Times* eighth Doctor comic strip story 'Ascendance' (1996), a female Martian without armour. The Doctor later tells Clara, 'For an Ice Warrior to leave its armour is the gravest dishonour.'

- The Ice Warriors, like the Time Lords, use sonic technology, as seen in previous stories with their sonic guns and cannons. The Doctor describes this as 'the song of the Ice Warrior.'

- The Doctor describes the operation of the HADS as: 'If the TARDIS comes under attack, gunfire, time winds, the sea, it relocates.' He says that he rarely uses it. The HADS was first mentioned in 'The Krotons' (1968/69).

PRODUCTION NOTES

- This episode was made as Block Five of Series Seven's production schedule.

- 'Cold War' was recorded almost entirely at BBC Roath Lock, between 13 and 29 June 2012. Only two pieces of outside work were carried out. The first, for scenes in the submarine's engine room, took place on 25 June at Llanwern Steelworks in Newport. The second, for the sequence on top of the submarine's conning tower, was done on 30 June, much closer to home, at Port Teigr on the area of ground between BBC Roath Lock and the *Doctor Who Experience* venue. Model work was carried out later by the freelance Model Unit at Halliford Film Studios, Shepperton, Middlesex between 4 and 6 September.

- This is the first television story to involve the Ice Warriors since 'The Monster of Peladon' (1974). They had previously featured in 'The Ice Warriors', 'The Seeds of Death' and 'The Curse of Peladon' (1972); and made brief cameo appearances in 'The War Games' (1969) and 'The Mind of Evil' (1971).

- Professor Grisenko is heard signing along to Ultravox's 1981 song 'Vienna' on his Walkman cassette player. He also at one point listens to Duran Duran's 1982 hit 'Hungry Like the Wolf', and later encourages Clara to sing this song to keep her spirits up; advice that she eventually takes.

- The design of the model submarine used for the production was based on the Project 667BD Murena-M class Russian vessel, also known by its NATO reporting name of Delta II.

OOPS!

- When the crewmember named Piotr applies a blowtorch to the block of ice in which Skaldak is frozen, the Ice Warrior starts to move almost straightaway, even though only the surface of the block is being melted by the flame, and then breaks out as if there has been just a hollow shell of ice around him rather than a solid mass. (Possibly simply being in the relatively warm environment of the submarine has somehow caused the inside of the block to melt already?)

- Just before the TARDIS dematerialises from the submarine due to the activation of the HADS, there is a shot where the right-hand police box door has been mistakenly left wide open.

CRITICAL REACTION

- 'The bulk of the episode ... proved to be a decent one in all, once again choosing to establish the year in which it was set – 1983, we're seemingly treading slowly through Clara's life – through music ... Still, the wrap up, once more, was a bit disappointing. It feels as though there's a continual over-reliance on a good speech and some sonic screwdriver waving at the moment to conclude *Who* stories. [That] may be a little [unfair] to Mark Gatiss's script. Yet it didn't, when everything was finalised, feel wholly satisfying. Granted, there was plenty to enjoy beforehand, but endings are tricky things, and that's where "Cold War" arguably struggled the most.' Simon Brew, Den of Geek website, 13 April 2013.

- 'Grand Marshal Skaldak is the show's most memorable villain in a while, thanks to his stern, occasionally psychopathic approach to problem solving, and an environment that helps make the bulky, heavy creature design imposing rather than laughably naff. Which is thanks in no small part to writer Mark Gatiss, who's crafted a script laced with enough physical and atmospheric tension to match the historical backdrop. Every encounter with Skaldak could go either way – and tellingly, it's only when one side attacks out of fear that everything starts to get bloodily, messily out of hand.' Mark Snow, IGN website, 13 April 2015.

- 'Mark Gatiss's script is taut, with detail where it's needed, but otherwise allowing no flab across its shortish 41-min running time. It's well matched by director Douglas Mackinnon's tight shots, askew angles, vivid palette and often gloomy lighting. The sequence where Clara tumbles underwater, loses and regains consciousness, is breathtakingly composed. The nods to *Alien* and the sense of dread as the crew are picked off one by one are brave for the timeslot. Surely everyone watching fears for Professor Grisenko as he sits pontificating in that hatchway – an obvious target. But no. The Martian goes for Clara first, then the Prof.' Patrick Mulkern, *Radio Times* website, 13 April 2013.

ANALYSIS

Old-school *Doctor Who* fans often used to talk in terms of there being a 'big five' monster races in the show's classic era: meaning the Daleks, the Cybermen, the Yeti, the Ice Warriors and the Sontarans. The Daleks, the Cybermen and the Sontarans have all, of course, featured extensively in the 21st Century revival; and although the Yeti have yet to appear, their controlling Great Intelligence has now re-emerged as Series Seven's recurring foe. The Ice Warriors, though, seemed for a long time to have been left (ironically) out in the cold, even as the show's writers were coming up with new stories for other classic-era races of lesser standing, such as the Autons, the Silurians and even the Macra. In short, the Ice Warriors were long overdue for a rematch with the Doctor; and, thankfully, that unsatisfactory state of affairs has now been remedied in 'Cold War', reintroducing Brian Hayles' marvellous creations after an absence of some 38 years.

Writer Mark Gatiss has said in interviews that he thought there was still a lot of untapped story potential left in the Martians; and he was absolutely right. Perhaps most notably, in their previous televised appearances it had never been established whether or not they could emerge from their reptilian outer shells. In fact, there was to start with a degree of ambiguity as to whether these shells were sets of armour or, on the contrary, just a natural part of their anatomy. Hayles himself originally envisaged the Martians as having a Viking-like appearance, and consequently his scripts for their debut story, 'The Ice Warriors', made no mention of them being reptilian. Their leader, Varga, was said to have on a 'hood-like and ominous' metal space helmet with 'an electronic ear piece, almost a sculptural design' and 'what looks like a strip of glass, photo-electric cell facets'. There were also said to be pulsing lights on his forehead and chest. The clear implication was that the Ice Warriors were humanoid aliens wearing space armour. When costume designer Martin Baugh came to visualise them, however, there was a concern to avoid them looking too similar to the Cybermen, so he drew inspiration instead from a crocodile's shell. In a later interview, he said, 'The armour wasn't meant to be something they put on in the morning: it was intended as an integral part of them, like a turtle's shell.' The Ice Warrior costumes created for that debut story had slight differences in appearance, too, again suggesting natural variation rather than manufactured uniformity – although, against this, some of them had a decidedly unnatural-looking sonic gun incorporated into the right arm of their shell. In subsequent stories, at any rate, it was Hayles' take on the Martians that began to hold sway. 'The Seeds of Death' introduced a sleeker, more humanoid officer class, which in 'The Curse of Peladon' and 'The Monster of Peladon' came to be known as an Ice Lord, and it seemed that this must be what the creatures looked like when not wearing their bulky armour – albeit that the head was still largely concealed by a helmet.

In 'Cold War', we finally get confirmation that an Ice Warrior can indeed venture outside of its armour. We never get to see the full body, just a vague shape scuttling past the camera, but we do at last find out what the head looks like, and also the hands. The hands each have three long, thin fingers with black nails at the end, and it has to be said that these are not at all well realised, looking like the kind of rubber monster gloves one might find as part of a Halloween fancy dress outfit. The head, on the other hand, is an impressive CGI creation that is suitably scary and also completely consistent with what has been implied before by glimpses caught through the helmet's eye and mouth apertures. Also, whether by coincidence or by design, it is pleasingly similar in appearance to the head of the female Martian named Luass depicted in the 1996 *Radio Times* comic strip story 'Ascendance', written by Gary Russell and drawn by Lee Sullivan.

What the rest of the body looks like can only be guessed at; but judging from the shape of the hands, and the fact that Skaldak leaves his armour specifically so that he can move about with greater ease through the cramped confines of the Russian submarine, one would have to suppose that it is quite spindly. The revelation that the armour can walk about without an occupant, being activated by remote control, actually makes it seem more like a vehicle than a protective shell, almost akin to the way a Dalek's casing serves to transport the frail creature within. Although this does not tally with the appearance of the Ice Lords featured in earlier stories, it may perhaps be that the Martian race has subdivided at some point, with the officer class retaining strong bodies but the warrior class for some reason atrophying and having to resort to wearing armour. The Doctor says that Skaldak is 'Sovereign of the Tharsisian Caste,' so possibly each Martian caste is comprised of a separate subspecies. The only time the head of an Ice Lord, as opposed to an Ice Warrior, has ever been exposed in *Doctor Who* fiction is in the New Adventures novel *Legacy* (Virgin Publishing, 1994), again written by Gary Russell, when, as part of a ruse, the seventh Doctor's companion Bernice Summerfield deliberately unmasks one named Savaar, and even gives him a passionate kiss. However, as this occurs in print rather than on screen, and no description is given, it is impossible to say if Savaar's facial features resemble Skaldak's in 'Cold War'.

It was *Legacy* that first introduced the concept of the Martians having a caste system, and the novel seems to have influenced the writing of 'Cold War' in other ways too, from minor elements such as the repetition of a joke about the Ice Warriors wearing 'shell suits' and confirmation of the existence of powerful females within their ranks, to more major ones such as the emphasis placed on their adherence to a code of honour. The idea that the Martians are an honourable race has long had currency within *Doctor Who* fandom, but their four classic-era television stories really offer very little in the way of evidence to back this up. In 'The Seeds of Death', for instance, they act more like a band of interplanetary thugs; and, unlike the natives of the planet Peladon, they make no mention of honour in 'The Curse of Peladon' or 'The Monster of Peladon' either. It could perhaps be argued that it is a trait intrinsic to warriors; but really it is only in the tie-in fiction, and *Legacy* in particular, that the idea of the Ice Warriors being honour-bound creatures is properly established. This is just the latest of many cases where aspects of the groundbreaking New Adventures novels have filtered into 21st Century *Doctor Who*.

Another, perhaps more obvious influence on 'Cold War' is, unsurprisingly, the work of Brian Hayles, and in particular 'The Ice Warriors'. Aside from the fact that Mark Gatiss finally brings to the screen Hayles' original idea of the Ice Warrior's armour having electronic attachments and – as seen when Skaldak sends out his distress signal – a pulsing light in its chest, he essentially recreates one of the scenes in that first story where Varga and his crew are melted out of solid blocks of ice. Similarly, when Clara goes to talk to Skaldak while the Doctor listens in over a video link, this mirrors a sequence in 'The Ice Warriors' where

Victoria, the Doctor's then companion, is placed in exactly the same position. And the dialogue about Professor Grisenko initially thinking he had discovered a prehistoric mammoth in the ice cleverly references Hayles' original inspiration for his story, which was reading a mid-1960s newspaper report about just such a discovery – although in 'The Ice Warriors' itself, it is a mastodon that the scientists mistakenly believe they have found. Hayles may also have recalled the similar storyline of an alien creature being dug out of the Arctic ice in the movie *The Thing from Another World* (1951), based on the John W Campbell novella *Who Goes There?* (1938); and both that and its remake *The Thing* (1982) inevitably come to mind when watching 'Cold War'.

Having the action take place on board a submarine was a great move on Gatiss's part, as the enclosed, claustrophobic setting really helps to ramp up the tension. A certain amount of dramatic licence is taken here, as in fact a Russian submarine of the early 1980s would have had an even more cramped interior, and would have been incapable of launching nuclear missiles on battery power from 700 metres below the surface, meaning that the threat Skaldak poses to the world is not a realistic one; but this is excusable, given production constraints within a television studio and the need to tell an exciting story. Certainly the action successfully captures the feel of being trapped in a terrifyingly dangerous situation deep beneath the polar ice, with water seeping in and a constant fear of the vessel's hull rupturing, and the crew members being picked off one by one by a relentless alien attacker in much the same way as those of the *Nostromo* are stalked by the creature in *Alien* (1979). This also recalls the base-under-siege scenarios characteristic of the second Doctor's era, of which 'The Ice Warriors' and 'The Seeds of Death' were two prime examples; and a further call-back to that era comes with the Doctor's explanation to Clara about the HADS device first mentioned in 'The Krotons', the distinctly limited usefulness of which is amusingly exposed here when the TARDIS leaves the two time travellers behind in a position of dire peril.

To have the story set during a period of heightened Cold War tension was another astute choice on Gatiss's part. Apart from recalling similarly-themed movies such as *Ice Station Zebra* (1968), based on the Alistair Maclean novel of the same title, and the 1984-set *The Hunt for Red October* (1990), this allows for the Mutually Assured Destruction philosophy underlying the global nuclear stand-off of that time to be neatly paralleled in the climactic confrontation where the Doctor threatens to blow up the submarine if Skaldak launches its missiles. It is interesting to speculate how this situation would have resolved itself had Skaldak's Martian comrades not come to his rescue at the crucial moment.

Another likely influence here is the fifth Doctor story 'Warriors of the Deep' (1984), in which a group of Silurians and Sea Devils storm an underwater human base during another Cold War in the year 2084 and, like Skaldak, threaten to precipitate the destruction of humanity by launching its nuclear missiles. The seventh Doctor story 'Battlefield' (1989) also features a similar storyline. In addition, 'Cold War' resembles the ninth Doctor episode 'Dalek' (2005), in that it reintroduces a classic-era monster race through a single individual, who is initially kept chained up by the humans. Skaldak is by no means a one-dimensional character, either, as demonstrated by the fact that he is ultimately swayed by the arguments of the Doctor and Clara in favour of showing mercy and compassion, foreshadowing his race becoming members of the peaceful Galactic Federation as seen in 'The Curse of Peladon'.

In design terms, the new version of the Ice Warrior armour is excellent, being a very striking and respectful updating of the 1960s original, and possibly the most successful example yet of a classic-era monster being restyled for the new-era show – certainly superior to what was done with the Sontarans and the Silurians (and the less said about the new paradigm Daleks, the better). It is admittedly rather a shame that a decision was taken not to reproduce the distinctive Lego-style claws of the originals, but that is just a minor niggle, and hardly detracts from the overall outstanding quality of the redesign.

The only thing that really lets down the on-screen presentation of Skaldak is the fact that his voice is quite different from the hissing rasp established for the Ice Warriors in their earlier stories, with much (though thankfully not quite all) of the sibilance replaced by a strange kind of gurgling noise. This is a great pity, as the voice was one of the most celebrated and memorable features of the original creations, and could be heard being imitated in school playgrounds up and down the UK in the late 1960s and early 1970s. In fact, the change is all the harder to understand when one learns that many of the cast and crew on set during the making of 'Cold War' were also amusing themselves by doing imitations of the classic-era voice. Mark Gatiss even jokingly suggested that the episode ought to be called '*Dasssss Boot*'; a play on the title of the German submarine movie *Das Boot* (1981). It does make one wonder what the point is of bringing back old monsters if some of the iconic features that made them so popular in the first place are going to be needlessly discarded. Director Douglas Mackinnon does have form in this regard, though, as it was he who also took the equally misconceived decision to change the Sontarans' voices when they made their 21st Century debut in 'The Sontaran Stratagem' / 'The Poison Sky' (2008).

Another lapse in direction comes in the scene at the end of the episode where the main characters emerge onto the conning tower of the submarine while the Ice Warriors' spaceship hovers overhead. Even if the Doctor might be blasé about the sight of such a spaceship – although blasé isn't really the eleventh Doctor's style – Clara and Captain Zhokov should surely be captivated by it, and almost unable to tear their eyes away. In fact, though, Mackinnon has them giving it barely a glance as the Doctor and Clara natter on about the HADS – although at least Professor Grisenko, standing a little behind them, seems to take a bit more interest. Apart from the Doctor, they even descend back into the submarine before the spaceship departs, almost as if they have got bored – although the fact that they are in freezing Arctic conditions and not wearing coats might perhaps account for this hasty retreat! Overall, though, Mackinnon does a good job, delivering some tense drama and plenty of scares in the well-realised scenes on board the stricken submarine.

'Cold War' is, all in all, a superb episode, and leaves the viewer eager for further Ice Warrior appearances in future – preferably in stories where there is more than just one of them. Indeed, they still hold so much interest that they could easily support a more extended run of episodes – a 'Mars trilogy' perhaps? One can only hope that there is not another gap of 38 years before they make their next return to the show!

7.09 – Hide

Writer: Neil Cross
Director: Jamie Payne

DEBUT TRANSMISSION DETAILS

BBC One/BBC One HD
Date: 20 April 2013. Scheduled time: 6.45 pm. Actual time: 6.44 pm.

Duration: 44' 51"

ADDITIONAL CREDITED CAST

Dougray Scott (Alec Palmer), Jessica Raine (Emma Grayling), Kemi-Bo Jacobs (Hila), Aidan Cook (The Crooked Man)

PLOT

The Doctor and Clara arrive just after 11 pm on 25 November 1974 at the isolated Caliburn House, where scientist Professor Alec Palmer and psychic Emma Grayling are investigating reported sightings of a ghostly figure, who always seems to be in the same stance. Returning with Clara to the TARDIS, the Doctor makes a series of trips to the same site at different points throughout Earth's history, each time taking a photograph of the figure. In this way, he determines that it is actually moving, but at a very slow rate relative to normal time. It is in fact Hila Tacorian, a time travel pioneer from the future, who has become trapped in a collapsing pocket universe co-located with the house, being pursued by a terrifying crooked creature. By linking Emma up to a device called a psycho-chronograph, which amplifies her psychic abilities, the Doctor is able to pass through a wormhole into the pocket universe and rescue Hila. He himself is then trapped, but Clara saves him using the TARDIS. Once back at Caliburn

House, the Doctor realises that Hila was not the only 'ghost': there is another of the crooked creatures in the house. Again calling on Emma's psychic assistance, he takes the TARDIS once more into the pocket universe to fetch the creature there and reunite it with its fellow, explaining that this is not a ghost story, but a love story.

QUOTE, UNQUOTE

- **Alec:** 'Relax, Emma. He's Military Intelligence. So, what is all this in aid of?'
  Doctor: 'Health and safety. Yeah. The Ministry got wind of what's going on down here. Sent me to check that everything's in order.'
  Alec: 'They don't have the right.'
  Doctor: 'Don't worry, guv'nor, I'll be out of your hair in five minutes. Oh! Oh, look. Oh, lovely. The ACR 99821. Oh, bliss. Nice action on the toggle switches. You know, I do love a toggle switch. Actually, I like the word toggle. Nice noun. Excellent verb.'

- **Clara:** 'Say we actually find her. What do we say?'
  Doctor: 'We ask her how she came to be whatever she is.'
  Clara: 'Why?'
  Doctor: 'Because I don't know, and ignorance is … what's the opposite of bliss?'
  Clara: 'Carlisle.'
  Doctor: 'Yes. Yes, Carlisle. Ignorance is Carlisle.'

- **Doctor:** 'You want me to be afraid? Then well done. I am the Doctor, and I am afraid.'

CONTINUITY POINTS

- The Doctor says that empathics are 'the most compassionate people you will ever meet … And the loneliest. I mean, exposing themselves to all those hidden feelings; all that guilt, pain and sorrow …'

- When Clara says that the TARDIS doesn't like her, the Doctor reassures her, 'The TARDIS is like a cat. A bit slow to trust, but you'll get there in the end.'

- The Doctor tells Clara that he once had a hatstand in the TARDIS, although he seems a little confused on the point. A hatstand was one of the items regularly seen in the TARDIS console room in the 1980s stories.

- Hila Tacorian has been trapped in the pocket universe for only a little over three minutes, from her perspective, before the Doctor arrives to rescue her, although hundreds of years have passed in normal time. The Doctor says that she is the great, great, great, great, great granddaughter of Alec and Emma, i.e. seven generations removed from them, so it seems probable that she comes from the 22nd Century. This is consistent with his earlier comment that she is from 'hundreds of years' in their future.

- The Doctor describes the pocket universe as, 'A distorted echo of our own. They happen sometimes but never last for long.' He says non-psychic technology will not work there.

- The psycho-chronograph device that the Doctor rigs up to enable Emma to open the wormhole to the pocket universe incorporates both 'a blue crystal from Metebelis III' – a larger example of which was seen previously in 'The Green Death' (1973) and 'Planet of the Spiders' (1974) – and 'a subset of the Eye of Harmony' – the Eye of Harmony being the TARDIS's power source (see also the entry on 'Journey to the Centre of the TARDIS').

- The Doctor describes the wormhole as, 'A reality well! A door to the echo universe.' It is occasional sightings of this, manifesting as a spinning black disc, that have caused the Caliburn House ghost to be referred to locally as 'the Witch of the Well'.

- When the Doctor is trapped in the pocket universe, the TARDIS's cloister bell rings in warning.

- The TARDIS activates its voice visual interface, a function first seen in 'Let's Kill Hitler' (2011), in order to communicate with Clara via a holographic avatar of herself. It tells her, 'I'm programmed to select the image of a person you esteem. Of several billion such images in my data banks, this one best meets the criterion.' Clara is not impressed!

- At the end of the episode, the Doctor attributes the strength of Emma's psychic link with Hila to the fact that they are related. Presumably Caliburn House, which Alec owns, will be passed down through the family, explaining why Hila's pioneering time travel attempt is carried out there in her own future year.

PRODUCTION NOTES

- This episode was made as Block Four of Series Seven's production schedule.

- A number of different locations were used to represent Caliburn House. The first was Manor House, Plas Llanmihangel, Cowbridge, South Glamorgan, where recording of the dining room scenes took place on 22 and 23 May 2012. The second was a house called Tyntesfield in Wraxhall, Bristol, where the crew shot further interior sequences on 24, 25 and 28 May. Gethin Woodland Park in Merthyr Tydfil was the location on 29 May for the scenes set in the pocket universe. Caliburn House exteriors were then recorded at Margam Country Park in Margam, Port Talbot on 30 and 31 May, and further interiors, including the music room scenes with the wormhole, at Hensol Castle in Miskin, Pontyclun, Mid Glamorgan from 1 to 4 June. A small amount of studio work was carried out at BBC Roath Lock, including for the TARDIS interior scenes, on 19 June, 22 September and 18 October, with a pick up shot being done on 27 November.

- This episode had the working titles 'Phantoms of the Hex' and 'The Hider in the House'. The Doctor's unexplained reference to 'the hex' at one point toward the end of the episode is a hangover from an earlier script draft under the former of these titles.

OOPS!

- Matt Smith mispronounces the word 'Metebelis' both times it occurs in the dialogue, putting the emphasis on the second syllable rather than the third. (This was spotted in time for it to be corrected before transmission, but the episode had already been sent for Blu-ray and DVD mastering by then, so it was decided to stick with the incorrect original, to avoid creating a discrepancy between the transmitted version and the commercially-released version. It seems surprising, though, that the mistake was not caught earlier, such as at the initial cast read-through. In fictional terms, possibly it can be put down to a quirk of the TARDIS's translation function.)

- There are a number of noticeable shot continuity errors in the episode. For instance, in an early sequence where the Doctor takes a swig from a bottle of milk, the bottle switches from his right hand to his left hand between shots; and, most obviously, part-way through a sequence in the pocket universe where the Doctor has removed his bow tie, there are two close-ups where he is still wearing it.

CRITICAL REACTION

- 'The monsters were pleasingly unsettling, with hints of *The Ring*, *The Thing* and more all surfacing in a mélange of messy, creepy weirdness. Admittedly, the impact was lost somewhat by episode's end, but at least "Hide" revelled in the enjoyable peekaboo scares of being stalked by something forever just out of sight … Equally, the left-field genre detour didn't completely convince, and felt jarringly underwhelming considering the spooky set-up, but at least it tried something unique – and the brain-scratching quandary of how to save the FVOD (Forgettable Victim of the Day) resulted in something that probably tickled most fanboy's geekbone. Let's just say this is probably the only time in my life I'll get to write "bungee jumping into a dying universe".' Mark Snow, IGN website, 20 April 2013.

- '"Hide" was a beautiful episode in every category and gave a very sci-fi reason for a very Gothic phenomenon. It employed elements of *The Haunting*, *The Evil Dead* and the excellent time travel series *Sapphire & Steel*, and gave us an episode that was poignant and exciting. There really is nothing like the high you get from watching a good story told well.' Kyle Anderson, Nerdist website, 20 April 2013.

- 'We haven't had an episode quite so scary since the extremely creepy Silence graced our screens. Not only did "Hide" ratchet the terror up to 11, it brought home the fact that when *Who* is good … boy, is it really, *really* good … This season (and I'm including the first half that aired last year) has been rather lighter and more straightforward than [Steven] Moffat's previous two, and while the change in tone is a bit of a relief from the sometime clever-clever complexity, there is a feeling of something, *something* missing. For the most part, spectacle has replaced substance and the storylines have gotten simpler. In *Doctor Who* terms, a simpler story often means much more running about. There's not much running about [in "Hide"], and it's all the better for it. Mr Moffat, with all due respect – can we have more of this please?' Jon Cooper, *Mirror* website, 20 April 2013.

ANALYSIS

Although it reached the screen two weeks later, 'Hide' was actually written and recorded several months before writer Neil Cross's other Series Seven contribution, 'The Rings of Akhaten', making this his *Doctor Who* debut. Unfortunately, it isn't a terribly auspicious one. Although very different in theme and setting from that other episode, it is in some respects quite similar to it, in that it has a lot of good things going for it, but sadly falls apart when it comes to the exposition and explanations. In fact, it is even more flawed in that regard, ultimately rendering it largely nonsensical.

On the plus side, it was a great idea on Cross's part to draw inspiration from Nigel Kneale's brilliant television play *The Stone Tape* (BBC Two, 1972), presenting a scenario in which a team of people – or, in this instance, just two, one of whom was originally supposed to be Kneale's famous creation Professor Quatermass, until rights problems ruled that out – use technological means to try to discover the true nature of a centuries-old ghost in a creepy old manor house on the moors – the ghost in this case being referred to locally as 'the Witch of the Well'. This type of story is something that *Doctor Who* has rarely done before – although 'Image of the Fendahl' (1977) was clearly also influenced by *The Stone Tape*, and by Kneale's work more generally, and there was an eighth Doctor audio adventure called 'The Witch from the Well' (Big Finish, 2011) – and one of the best things about 'Hide' is its wonderfully spooky atmosphere. In fact, it is rather a pity that *Doctor Who*'s scheduling at this point meant that the episode had to go out in the spring, as a Halloween slot would have been ideal for it. The sequence where the Doctor and

Clara explore the rooms and hallways of the dilapidated old house, with only the flickering light from a candelabra to guide their way, is extremely effective. The only slight misstep comes when, in an incident where Clara feels a ghostly hand holding hers and there is a flash of lightning and a roll of thunder outside, the Doctor appears to be just as scared as his companion – which is really out of character for him, as he should be too brave, and too sceptical of the supernatural, to be that easily spooked. But perhaps we should just assume that he is only mirroring Clara's reaction here, perhaps to make her feel better about the fact that she is afraid.

Another aspect of the story that works very well is the rather sweet, shy romance between Alec Palmer and Emma Grayling, who are initially too reserved to declare their true feelings for each other, but are eventually brought together by the Doctor. Both characters are very well acted, by Dougray Scott and Jessica Raine respectively, but Alec is the more interesting of the two, as his background is revealed in greater detail. According to the Doctor, he served in the Second World War as Major Alec Palmer, a member of the Special Operations Executive – also known as the Baker Street Irregulars (after the location of their London headquarters) and the Ministry of Ungentlemanly Warfare – 'specialising in espionage, sabotage and reconnaissance behind enemy lines'. This suggests that the Professor is probably in his mid-fifties – although Scott himself was only 46 at the time of production. 'You're a talented watercolourist,' the Doctor adds, 'professor of psychology and ghost hunter.' It is indicated that he was awarded the Victoria Cross for his wartime bravery, including disrupting U-Boat operations across the North Sea and sabotaging railway lines across Europe, although he tries to avoid talking about his experiences by claiming that he was a prisoner of war. It is also said that he has previously had his work stolen by the Government, then been 'fobbed off with a pat on the back and a letter from the Queen'. Emma, by contrast, is given no backstory at all, beyond the fact that she is an 'empathic psychic'; meaning, as she explains, 'Sometimes I sense feelings, the way a telepather can sense thoughts.' Given that Emma's abilities are really crucial to the whole story, it is a pity that we don't learn more about her, and about how she came to work with Alec as his assistant.

There are, though, some interesting character notes for the Doctor and Clara in this episode. The Doctor clearly still sees Clara very much as a puzzle. 'You are the only mystery worth solving,' he tells her at one point;

and although ostensibly he is talking about humanity in general, he could just as easily be referring to her in particular. Toward the end of the story, it is revealed that his real reason for visiting Caliburn House was not to find out about the ghost, but to talk to Emma and see if she could sense anything special about Clara. The fact that he already knows all about Alec and Emma on his arrival suggests that he has actually researched their lives in advance – possibly, as he claims, from the SOE's files. He also recognises Hila Tacorian when he sees her, and while in this case his foreknowledge could well be due simply to the fact that her failed time travel attempt will be a well-known historical event in the future, the impression the viewer is left with is that he is pursuing a carefully planned scheme of the type more usually associated with his seventh incarnation. It is almost as if the puzzle of Clara is starting to obsess him; which is certainly a novel departure from the traditional Doctor-and-companion dynamic.

As for Clara herself, this episode sees her continuing to come to terms with her new life of adventuring in time and space. Emma's assessment of her is that she is 'Very pretty, very clever, more scared than she lets on.' Nevertheless, she seems, overall, rather less scared here than she did in 'Cold War', and although this could be partly because her situation is actually less perilous this time, it could also be because she is starting to get used to facing danger. What really shakes her in 'Hide' is her realisation of how the Doctor's time travelling affects his perspective on humanity. This comes after a series of TARDIS trips have afforded them snapshots – literally – of the whole of Earth's history. In a terrific passage of dialogue, neatly illustrating the gulf between their respective viewpoints, Clara struggles with the fact that they have 'just watched the entire life-cycle of Earth, birth to death,' while the Doctor, for his part, can't begin to understand why she has a problem with this. 'To you, I haven't been born yet,' she tells him, 'and to you I've been dead a hundred billion years. Is my body out there somewhere, in the ground?' 'Yes, I suppose it is,' he confirms – and perhaps he has in mind here also the Victorian-era Clara at whose graveside he stood at the end of 'The Snowmen'. 'But here we are, talking,' Clara points out. 'So I am a ghost. To you, I'm a ghost. We're all ghosts to you. We must be nothing.' It is at this point that the Doctor makes his remark about humanity being 'the only mystery worth solving'; but clearly it is going to be a while yet before Clara becomes fully comfortable with all the implications of time travel.

In fact, it seems that Clara is still trying to decide exactly how she feels about the Doctor. This emerges most clearly in a very nice scene where she questions Emma as to whether or not she and Alec are in a relationship. 'What about you and the Doctor?' Emma asks. 'Oh, I don't think so,' Clara replies, in what is hardly an unequivocal denial; and she is clearly taken aback when Emma warns her, 'Don't trust him. There's a sliver of ice in his heart.' This recalls an exchange in 'Cold War' where Captain Zhukov recognises in the Doctor a fellow soldier, and it serves to remind the viewer that there is a coldly pragmatic streak to the Time Lord's nature, as demonstrated most clearly by the genocidal action he took to end the Time War.

'Hide' also revisits the intriguing idea first posited in 'The Rings of Akhaten' that the TARDIS has for some reason taken a dislike to Clara. Here we see it effectively insulting her via a hologram of herself, then initially refusing to grant her access so that she can go and rescue the Doctor from the pocket universe, before eventually relenting and piloting her there itself. This not only deepens the mystery surrounding her character, but arguably implies a greater degree of self-will on the ship's part than has ever been suggested before.

As with 'The Rings of Akhaten', until quite a long way into the action it seems that 'Hide' is going to be a thoroughly enjoyable episode. It is only at about the thirty-minute mark, when the Doctor passes through the wormhole, that things start to go awry. Prior to this, it has been carefully established that time in the pocket universe moves at a much slower rate than in the Doctor's own universe; hence why it appears to those in Caliburn House that Hila Tacorian's ghostly figure is not moving, although in fact it is. As soon as the Doctor arrives in the pocket universe, though, this seems to be completely forgotten about, and the plot advances in parallel on both sides of the wormhole. It could be the case that, when Emma opens the wormhole, this somehow synchronises the passage of time between the two universes; but, if so, it would have been nice to have this explained in the episode itself, if only by way of some typical Time Lord technobabble. The fact that the Doctor's psycho-chronograph is linked up to a number of clocks, which all go haywire when the device is activated, isn't nearly enough to clarify what is going on. Admittedly the Doctor does say, on first encountering Hila, 'Collapsing universe. You and me, dead, two minutes,' suggesting that the passage of time might indeed have suddenly accelerated on that side of the wormhole; and this is in line with a comment he made earlier, to the effect that the pocket universe would decay 'back into the quantum foam' within about three minutes if he were to take the TARDIS there. However, compounding the confusion, he ends up spending at least five minutes in the pocket universe, and it seems completely unchanged at the end of that!

Then there is the fact that the TARDIS tells Clara, via the hologram it creates in her image, that if it were to enter the pocket universe, the entropy there would very quickly drain its energy: 'In four seconds, I'd be stranded. In ten, I'd be dead.' This accords with the Doctor's earlier explanation as to why he could not use his ship to rescue Hila. In the event, though, the TARDIS does go into the pocket universe, apparently for longer than ten seconds, and certainly for longer than four, and is patently not stranded. In fact, it even manages to repeat the manoeuvre at the end of the episode, to allow the Doctor to fetch the creature referred to in the closing credits as the Crooked Man. And still the pocket universe shows no sign of collapsing! Possibly the Doctor miscalculated how long the pocket universe would last, and possibly the TARDIS was deceiving Clara as to how long it could survive there; but if so, again, there is no explanation given in the episode itself, and the viewer is left with the distinct impression that the story just hasn't been fully thought through.

The TARDIS's journey into the pocket universe is problematic in another respect too. Earlier in the action, it has been clearly shown that the device the Doctor has rigged up to enable Emma to open the wormhole is drawing power from the ship via some cables connected to a panel on the back wall of its police box exterior. When it dematerialises, however, this again seems to be totally forgotten about. How can Emma continue to maintain the wormhole, and the cables continue to glow with power (as seen in a couple of brief shots), when the connection to the ship must have been abruptly severed? Possibly the TARDIS's power was needed only to kick-start the process, and Emma was then able sustain it on her own; but, if so, this certainly isn't evident from the on-screen action. Given that it isn't really necessary in plot terms for the TARDIS to go into the pocket universe at all, since the Doctor could just as easily be rescued using the rope and harness affair that has already been used to bring Hila back to Caliburn House, it is tempting to wonder if this was actually a late addition to the script, conceived simply in order to give Clara something to do at the climax. If so, it could surely have been much better integrated.

There are other aspects of the story that aren't properly explained either. For instance, how can Hila's shouted words 'Help me' be heard at one point in Caliburn House, and why do they then appear in icy lettering on the wall, only to fade away again shortly afterwards? Is this some kind of strange side-effect of Emma's psychic sensing of Hila's emotions? Surely Hila can't be responsible for writing the words herself, given how many thousands of years of normal time would have to pass in order for them to be seen? And where do the Crooked Man and its mate actually originate from? Goodness knows.

The basic problem here is that the decision to have two different 'ghosts' haunting Caliburn House – not just Hila, but the Crooked Man as well – has overloaded the plot, making it impossible for either strand to be properly developed and resolved. Once Hila is rescued from the pocket universe, she makes very little further contribution to the story. She is given hardly any dialogue, we learn next to nothing about her or her time travel experiment, and we do not even find out what becomes of her at the end – the Doctor says he can't return her home, as her disappearance is a fixed point in time, but then she simply vanishes from the action. Nor do we find out what becomes of the Crooked Man and its mate, beyond the Doctor saying that he can take them to a safe place far away from the pocket universe. Since nothing that has happened in the story really justifies his belief that they are a kind of lovesick couple, yearning for each other from opposite sides of the wormhole, this just comes across as a recklessly optimistic assumption on his part. In view of the Crooked Man's outwardly threatening behaviour in the pocket universe, they could just as easily want to team up to wreak havoc on Earth, or prey on humanity as a new food source. It is admittedly a nice idea that their love story essentially mirrors that of Alec and Emma, but this simply isn't given enough plot room to breathe, and the whole thing is wrapped up in an incredible rush.

More positively, 'Hide' also marks the *Doctor Who* debut of director Jamie Payne, and he does an absolutely outstanding job on it. The strong performances he gets from the main cast and the effectiveness of the spooky 'haunted house' set-up have already been noted, but there are many other praiseworthy aspects. Most striking of all are the superb scenes where the Doctor ventures into the pocket universe. The mist-shrouded woodland location work for this is very eerie and unnerving; an effect enhanced by muted colour grading in post-production giving it a sickly, pale-green look. The Time Lord's unaccustomed fear in these scenes is palpable, and in this case entirely appropriate, not least because the Crooked Man's design and presentation – via a movement effect that has it scuttling forward in small, staccato increments – makes it a very scary monster indeed.

There are other impressive directorial touches throughout the episode too, such as a great two-shot where the Doctor and Alec face each other with their features illuminated only by the light from the candelabra held between them, and there is no question that 'Hide' is a very fine-looking episode. Sadly, though, this can't fully compensate for the problems with the script, and what we are left with in the end is, essentially, a fine-looking muddle.

7.10 – Journey to the Centre Of the Tardis

Writer: Steve Thompson
Director: Mat King

DEBUT TRANSMISSION DETAILS

BBC One/BBC One HD
Date: 27 April 2013. Scheduled time: 6.30 pm. Actual time: 6.30 pm.

Duration: 44′ 49″

ADDITIONAL CREDITED CAST

Ashley Walters (Gregor van Baalen), Mark Oliver (Bram van Baalen), Jahvel Hall (Tricky), Sarah Louise Madison (Time Zombie), Ruari Mears (Time Zombie), Paul Kasey (Time Zombie).

PLOT

A space salvage vessel operated by the van Baalen brothers Gregor and Bram and their android associate Tricky seizes the TARDIS using a dangerous magno-grab device, badly damaging it in the collision. The Doctor is ejected from his ship, and enlists the three salvage men's unwilling help to go back in and search for Clara. When Gregor tries to steal part of the TARDIS's architectural reconfiguration system, the ship retaliates by turning its corridors into an inescapable maze. The Doctor is eventually reunited with Clara, while Tricky learns that he is not in fact an android: Gregor and Bram, really his elder brothers, just fooled him into believing that he was, after an accident caused him to lose his memory and need some artificial implants. The Doctor, Clara and the three salvage men are pursued through the TARDIS interior by terrifying Time Zombie creatures with charred bodies and glowing eyes. These are eventually revealed to be their own future selves, having suffered the harmful effects of exposure to the ship's power source, the Eye of Harmony. Time is becoming jumbled up within the ship, due to the engine at its centre having exploded in the collision with the salvage vessel. The Doctor, however, is able to reach through a time rift to a point prior to the collision and pass to his earlier self the magno-grab's remote control unit, which he took from the van Baalens at the outset. His earlier self is then able to use this to switch the magno-grab off before it does any real damage, erasing the crisis from the timeline.

QUOTE, UNQUOTE

- **Doctor:** 'Smart bunch, Time Lords. No dress sense, dreadful hats, but smart.'

- **Doctor:** 'What are you, eh? A trick, a trap?'
  Clara: 'I don't know what you're talking about!'
  Doctor: 'You really don't, do you.'
  Clara: 'I think I'm more scared of you right now than anything else in that TARDIS.'
  Doctor: 'You're just Clara, aren't you.'

- **Clara:** 'You call yourself "Doctor". Why do you do that? You have a name. I've seen it. In one corner of that tiny –'
  Doctor: 'If I rewrite today, you won't remember. You won't go looking for my name.'
  Clara: 'We'll still have secrets.'
  Doctor: 'It's better that way.

- **Doctor:** 'I need to know if you feel safe. I need to know, you're not afraid.'
  Clara: 'Of?'
  Doctor: 'The future. Running away with a spaceman in a box, anything could happen to you.'
  Clara: 'That's what I'm counting on. Push the button.'

CONTINUITY POINTS

- Encouraging Clara to try piloting the TARDIS herself, the Doctor tells her 'Take the wheel,' before immediately correcting himself. This obliquely refers to a scene in writer Steve Thompson's earlier episode 'The Curse of the Black Spot' (2011) where the Doctor disputed the pirate Captain Avery's suggestion that the ship's atom accelerator could be referred to as its wheel. He then says he will make it easy for Clara to operate the controls by shutting them down to 'basic mode'. In doing so, he inadvertently leaves the ship open to being seized by the van Baalen brothers' magno-grab device. This works by projecting what looks like a kind of tractor beam, described by the Doctor as a 'magnetic hobble-field' – which must be extremely powerful, judging from the damage done to the TARDIS. The Doctor says of the magno-grab: 'Outlawed in most galaxies, this little beastie can disable whole vessels unless you have shield oscillators … which I turned off so that Clara could fly. Damn it.'

- The van Baalens find they are unable to break through the doors of the police box using either a large hammer or a cutting tool, and Bram incorrectly assumes it is made of metal.

- After the TARDIS is damaged, its cloister bell rings in warning.

- The Doctor convinces the van Baalens that he has set the TARDIS to self-destruct at the end of a countdown, but later admits that no such system exists.

- When Gregor queries the fact that the TARDIS interior is level, while the police box exterior is lying on its side, the Doctor explains: 'The TARDIS is special. She has her own gravity.' This accords with what has been established in previous stories, although clearly the internal gravity can sometimes be affected by what is occurring outside – such as when, in this episode, the ship is buffeted by the magno-grab.

- To clear the console room of noxious fumes, apparently caused by a fuel leak, the Doctor uses its extractor fans, as he did also in 'The Angels Take Manhattan'.

- The Doctor says that the TARDIS interior is 'infinite'. The rooms seen in this episode include: a storeroom containing, amongst many other things, the Doctor's cot, as featured in 'A Good Man Goes to War' (2011), and what appears to be one of the police box models made as a young girl by Amy Pond; an observatory; a swimming pool; and an extensive library, where Clara finds a large book called *The History of the Time War*, from which it appears that she learns the Doctor's real name (although this is erased from her memory at the end of the story), and the *Encyclopedia Gallifreya*, in which information is stored in liquid form in a series of small bottles.

- Gregor's hand-held scanner tells him that the TARDIS contains: 'Dynomorphic generators, conceptual geometer, beam synthesiser, orthogonal engine filters.' The dynomorphic generator was first mentioned in 'Time-Flight' (1982), the conceptual geometer in 'The Horns of Nimon' (1979/80), and the interstitial beam synthesiser in 'The Curse of Peladon' (1972).

- Gregor's scanner later tells him that the TARDIS's architectural reconfiguration system could give him 'everything' he ever wants, its value being 'incalculable'. When he queries this, it clarifies: 'More valuable than the total sum of any currency. Living metal. Bespoke engineering. Whatever machine you require, this system will build it.' When Gregor tries to steal part of the system, the Doctor tells him: 'If you walk out of here with that circuit, the TARDIS will try to stop you … Ever seen a spaceship get ugly? … She won't relinquish it. Her basic genetic material.' The truth of this is subsequently proved when the TARDIS turns its corridors into a labyrinth, effectively trapping everyone inside it.

- Probably due to the TARDIS's systems being partly disabled, Bram is easily able to remove a panel from the central control console, in contrast to the difficulty Rose Tyler experienced in doing something similar in 'The Parting of the Ways' (2005).

- A number of different duplicates of the console room are seen. The Doctor explains that these are 'echoes': 'The console room is the safest place on the ship. It can replicate itself any number of times.'

- The Doctor at one point displays on a TARDIS console screen a graphic with a large central circle captioned 'Engine Status: Overload', and around it smaller circles captioned 'Eye of Harmony', 'Arch-Recon' (obviously short for architectural reconfiguration), 'Console Room', 'Library' and 'Observatory' – all referring to rooms seen during the course of the action. He then explains that the engine room is at the centre of the TARDIS, and that if the damage to the engine is not fixed, the consequences will be catastrophic.

- The Doctor subsequently tells Clara, 'There's a rupture in time somewhere on board the ship. A small tear in the fabric of the continuum. It must have happened when the TARDIS was pulled in by the salvage vessel. The TARDIS is leaking.' When Clara queries *what* it is leaking, he adds, 'The past. You and me. Everything we've done, everything we've said. Recent history. It's not real. It's a memory.'

- The Doctor also reveals that 'the fuel's spilled out' from the TARDIS's primary fuel cells, exposing 'the rods'. These metal rods subsequently start to break apart and pierce through the corridor walls. It is unclear what function they normally play in the TARDIS's operation.

- The TARDIS's power source, the Eye of Harmony, is described by the Doctor as: 'Exploding star in the act of becoming a black hole. Time Lord engineering. You rip the star from its orbit, suspend it in a permanent state of decay.' This accords with what has been seen previously. 'The Deadly Assassin' (1976) showed that the original Eye of Harmony, the main power source for all TARDISes, was in the Capitol on the Time Lords' home planet Gallifrey. However, later stories, including the 1996 TV movie and the Past Doctor Adventures novel *The Quantum Archangel* (Virgin Publishing, 2001), expanded on this by indicating that all TARDISes constructed after a certain point, including the Doctor's, contain a mathematically-modelled duplicate or fraction of the original. Since the link to the original was presumably severed at the end of the Time War, the Doctor now needs to refuel his ship periodically with time rift energy, as seen in 'Boom Town' (2005).

- The Doctor tells Clara, Gregor and Tricky that they can survive for only a minute or two in the Eye of Harmony chamber, and then their cells will liquefy and their skin will start to burn. It is this process that ultimately creates the Time Zombie creatures. However, it seems that the Doctor has underestimated the bearable exposure time, as he and Clara spend quite a bit longer than two minutes in the chamber without suffering any apparent ill effects.

• When the Doctor and Clara try to enter the engine room, described by the Doctor as the 'heart of the TARDIS', they are at first confronted with a seemingly impassable ravine. However, the Doctor eventually realises that this is a 'snarl'; 'The TARDIS is snarling at us, trying to frighten us off. We need to jump.' When they do jump, they find themselves in the engine room: a white void with pieces of broken metal suspended all around them. The Doctor says: 'The engine, it's already exploded. It must have been the collision with the salvage ship … She wrapped her hands around the force. Froze it … Temporary fix. Eventually this whole place will erupt.'

• The Doctor says that he has piloted the TARDIS 'for 900 years'. If one is to believe the indications given in earlier episodes that he is around 1200 years old, this would indicate that he began piloting the TARDIS when he was about 300 years old. However, he is notoriously inconsistent when talking about his age and other related matters, so it is doubtful how much reliance can be placed on this.

PRODUCTION NOTES

• This episode was made as Block Seven of Series Seven's production schedule.

• Recording took place almost entirely in studio at BBC Roath Lock, on various dates between 4 September and 27 November 2012. There were only two days' location work done for the episode: the first on 4 September in a warehouse on a Central Utilities Building site at Celtic Way, Newport, for scenes on the deck of the salvage vessel; the second on 28 November in Argoed Isha quarry near Llansannor in the Vale of Glamorgan for the sequence where the TARDIS creates the false ravine.

- The opening title sequence was adjusted slightly for this episode to add a slight judder to the image of the TARDIS when it first appears, reflecting the fact that in the action immediately prior to this it is under attack by the magno-grab.

- The Cult's 1989 single 'Fire Woman' is heard in the sequence where the TARDIS is pulled on board the salvage vessel, and again in the one at the end where the Doctor seeks out that same point in time in order to enable his earlier self to turn off the magno-grab. The music is not simply part of the soundtrack but is actually intended to be playing on board the salvage vessel, as the Doctor says, 'I need to find the music.'

- The scene where Bram tries to dismantle the TARDIS control console features brief audio clips from various earlier stories, including '100,000 BC' (1963), 'Colony in Space' (1971), 'The Robots of Death' (1977), 'Rose' (2005), 'Smith and Jones' (2007), 'The Beast Below' (2010) and 'The Doctor's Wife' (2011).

- This is the first televised *Doctor Who* episode to include the word 'TARDIS' in its title. The title was inspired by that of the famous Jules Verne novel *Voyage au Centre de la Terre* (1864), translated into English as *Journey to the Centre of the Earth* (1871).

OOPS!

- The Doctor uses his sonic screwdriver to etch the words 'Big Friendly Button' into the magno-grab remote control unit, as a message to his earlier self. However, in the scene where the unit rolls across the console room floor just prior to the opening title sequence, it can be seen that there is actually no lettering on the prop.

CRITICAL REACTION

- 'This episode often feels like a TARDIS-bound companion piece to last week's "Hide", both in its depiction of time travel and in its insight into the Doctor. As Professor Palmer observed last week, experience makes liars of us all, and the Doctor's untruths in this episode are often motivated not by any particular malice but [by] the terrible knowledge he feels he must protect. Steve Thompson's script doesn't make this explicit, but it appears the Doctor deduces the nature of the monster straightaway, as he spends the rest of the episode desperately trying to convince Clara that some questions are better left unanswered. His lie about the TARDIS self-destruct is a more straightforward deception, the sort of thing the audience, if not the van Baalen brothers, should see through immediately, but it works because Matt Smith commits entirely to this darker version of the Doctor.' Alasdair Wilkins, A.V. Club website, 27 April 2013.

- 'The "joke" Gregor and Bram play on Tricky creates so many problems, I don't even know where to begin … Are we to believe that Tricky never questioned his continuing need to eat, breathe or use the bathroom? Has he not cut himself shaving and realised that he does, in fact, feel pain? Further, why does Tricky continue to recite his "No fear, no hate, no pain" mantra – even using it as logic for Gregor to cut his arm off – *while grimacing in pain from being pinned to a wall*? (And why does it take the Doctor to tell Gregor to cut through the metal rod instead of Tricky's arm?)' Clint Hassell, *Doctor Who* TV website, 27 April 2013.

- 'From the opening mid-space "attack", to mentions of cyborgs, time travel and all the fantastical possibilities of what a TARDIS unleashed could offer, [Steve] Thompson infused the tale with a vim and vigour that revelled in the series' magical, wonderment-filled roots. And it was in the titular exploration that the episode truly sang, with a Roald Dahl, Willy Wonkian joy in uncovering hidden rooms and secrets. There were geeky glimpses aplenty, but seeing the gargantuan library, swimming pool, fuel-core and hippy-bonkers [architectural reconfiguration] room (aka the budget *Avatar* tree) certainly scratched the initial itch. And with some distinctly *Sunshine*-y influences felt throughout, "Journey" had – at times – a sci-fi style that managed to match the substance.' Mark Snow, IGN website, 27 April 2013.

- 'Depicting the TARDIS interior was never going to be a picnic, because we've all got ideas of it in our heads, and budget-busting ideas they are too … but, nevertheless, we can't help feeling that they could have tried just a little more earnestly than this … If we hadn't read about what his intention was here, we would have wondered if [Steven] Moffat was playing some kind of meta-ironic corridor-related joke on us. Even things that look a bit more spectacular are ruined by their context. That globey tree thing, for example, seems so utterly random, and we have to put up with the vision of the Doctor begging Gregor not to vandalise it. (Not to mention the stupidity of Gregor assuming that yanking off one random piece of it would do him any good. And when Gregor ignores him, the Doctor just trots along with him, weakly trying to reason with him. Dude's damaging the TARDIS, Doctor! Do something!) As for the Eye of Harmony, well, it looks pretty, but having just told us how dangerous it is being in its vicinity, the Doctor's lengthy lecture on how it all works is just ridiculous.' Uncredited reviewer, Androzani.com website, unspecified date.

ANALYSIS

After a strong start, Series Seven has by this point begun to falter a bit, with 'The Angels Take Manhattan', 'The Rings of Akhaten' and 'Hide' all having significant plot issues, suggesting that their scripts could have benefited from going through another draft or two before being put into production. Unfortunately, with 'Journey to the Centre of the TARDIS', we come to the weakest episode yet.

The problems begin straightaway when, after introducing the set-up with the three salvage men via some very clunky dialogue ('You're a lucky boy, Tricky. You're an android. You don't get bored'), writer Steve Thompson proceeds to have the TARDIS become badly damaged in the most deeply contrived of ways. Wanting Clara to 'make up' with his ship, the Doctor tries to get her to pilot it herself (despite the later revelation that, at this point, he still doesn't fully trust her), and in order to make this easier for her (apparently because she is a girl!), he disables some of its systems, including nonsensically its defensive 'shield oscillators' – which action, in a huge coincidence, just happens to leave it susceptible to being seized by the illicit magno-grab device being operated by the salvage men. Then, in a baffling *non sequitur*, we see that the police box has been dumped almost on its side in a bay within the salvage vessel, with noxious fumes somehow seeping out from the interior, while the Doctor has been inexplicably ejected altogether and is now lying half-buried under a nearby pile of scrap. Notwithstanding that the salvage men then fail in their attempts to break open the doors, this just makes the TARDIS seem ridiculously vulnerable – more like the unremarkable escape pod that Tricky initially mistakes it for than an incredibly advanced product of Time Lord technology – and, to add insult to injury, we later learn that its minor collision with the salvage vessel has actually caused its engine to suffer a catastrophic explosion!

The action continues to unfold in bizarre fashion as the Doctor is suddenly back on his feet again, having somehow managed to extricate himself from the pile of scrap by means unseen, and then for no apparent reason decides it is vital he has the three salvage men's help to rescue Clara from her merely assumed situation of peril inside the TARDIS. Thankfully, it later becomes apparent that his astonishing offer to hand his ship over to the men in lieu of a fee is just a ruse, as is his subsequent starting of a (fake) self-destruct countdown to give them a further incentive to assist him; but the fact that he even allows them inside his TARDIS – where, as he should surely have predicted, they quickly prove far more of a hindrance than a help – seems completely out of character. One can only assume that his concern for Clara's safety has seriously clouded his judgement at this point.

It was showrunner Steven Moffat's idea to ask Steve Thompson to come up with a story set almost entirely inside the TARDIS, partly because he had been extremely disappointed by the way the ship's interior had been depicted in the classic-era story 'The Invasion of Time' (1978) and wanted, in effect, to exorcise that bad memory by presenting something far more impressive. However, while Moffat's feelings about 'The Invasion of Time' were certainly shared by many other fans at the time of that story's transmission, arguably this was due in large part to the fact that they were simply unused to the idea of the TARDIS's internal architecture being just as mutable as its external appearance (or, at least, as its external appearance ought to be, if the chameleon circuit was working properly). Having expected the ship's interior to be made up exclusively of the type of gleaming white, roundel-bedecked corridors and rooms they had seen previously – the sole exception being the wood-panelled secondary control room introduced in 'The Masque of Mandragora' (1976) – they were greatly disconcerted to be presented with brick-walled passages, industrial-looking stairwells and dilapidated areas with curtained-off bays that seemed as if they could be part of, say, a disused mental hospital – which was actually one of the locations used for the filming. Only a bathroom in the form of a swimming pool with a futuristic wall design was less negatively received. With the benefit of hindsight, though, it is now apparent that 'The Invasion of Time' was actually an admirably groundbreaking story in that regard – albeit by virtue of production necessity rather than positive intent.

While the idea of the TARDIS's internal spaces encompassing a variety of different environments was taken little further in the classic-era stories – the main exceptions being the cloister room introduced in 'Logopolis' (1981) and the Gothic-themed chambers seen in the 1996 TV movie – it was greatly expanded upon in the later tie-in media, and especially in the original novels and audio dramas. Here, readers and listeners were even introduced to parts of the ship that seemed more like outdoor areas, including in the novel *Vampire Science* (BBC Books, 1997) the wonderful notion of one where thousands of colourful butterflies float over a sunny hillside, and in the audio drama 'No Place Like Home' (Big Finish, 2003) a full cricket pitch, fields and gardens, and a rainforest section.

Due in part to these established precedents, fans are these days far more comfortable with the idea of the TARDIS having a variable internal appearance, as reflected in the new-era show itself with mentions of it having different 'desktop themes'; a term first used in the minisode 'Time Crash' (2007). Now, the innovative approach taken in 'The Invasion of Time' no longer seems so radical or hard to swallow. Were it not for the creative ingenuity of the behind-the-scenes team involved in that story's production, it is questionable if their 21st Century successors would have been so bold in their own TARDIS redesigns, such as with the incorporation into the eleventh Doctor's original console of such seemingly incongruous everyday items as an old typewriter, a bicycle lamp and a desk bell.

In short, the reasoning behind Steven Moffat's decision to commission a largely TARDIS-bound episode was essentially flawed. Indeed, 'Journey to the Centre of the TARDIS' is itself clearly influenced by 'The Invasion of Time', featuring rooms with a variety of different designs – including the swimming-pool bathroom, and even a storeroom with a brick-walled entrance arch – and introducing the architectural reconfiguration system that makes all this possible. The latter device, with glowing white egg-like orbs hanging from the fronds of a huge structure resembling a weeping willow tree, is a very striking and memorable creation, but unfortunately rather too obviously similar in appearance to the Tree of Souls that featured prominently in the movie *Avatar* (2009). This seeming lack of inspiration on the part of the show's regular production designer Michael Pickwoad is unfortunately reflected in other aspects of his TARDIS interior too – the first time since he took over from Edward Thomas in 2010 that his work has fallen noticeably below its usual outstanding level. For some reason, he has chosen to dispense with the wonderful hexagonal TARDIS corridors he created for 'The Doctor's Wife' (2011) in favour of a far less interesting design of metallic angled arches that would be more suited to a run-of-the-mill science-fiction spaceship – rather reminiscent, in fact, of the corridors of *Star Trek: The Next Generation*'s *Enterprise*. These are even less appropriate to the TARDIS than the brick-walled corridors of 'The Invasion of Time', which at least had the merit of being in keeping with the quirky eccentricity and early-20th Century look of the police box exterior. Possibly Pickwoad felt that, having redesigned the console room for 'The Snowmen', he had to come up with a new, matching form of corridor as well; but, whatever the reasoning, it was a big mistake.

There are even incongruous spaceship-style sliding metal doors placed at intervals along the corridors, operated by way of circular hand-sensors on the walls – though doubtless this was a misjudged script requirement rather than a poor design decision. Also disappointing is the fact that all the corridors seem to be on the same level; no stairways, ramps or elevators are seen (aside from the usual stairs in the console room, and a ladder that Bram discovers below the console itself), and little attempt is made to suggest the characters moving vertically through the ship, even when they are supposed to be heading toward its centre. Newly-introduced rooms such as the TARDIS library look impressive when depicted in CGI shots – the frozen-in-time white void of the engine room being the best-realised aspect of all – but much less so when represented by studio sets, suggesting that, on what was clearly a low-budget episode altogether, the design allocation was probably somewhat stretched here, to the point where it was straining to meet the demands of the script.

Ironically, the net effect of all these factors is that, despite the more modern techniques available to the production crew, the TARDIS interior actually ends up being rather less successfully depicted in 'Journey to the Centre of the TARDIS' than it was in 'The Invasion of Time' – the exact opposite of what Steven Moffat and Steve Thompson were aiming for! Certainly it falls far short of what was achieved with the somewhat similar storyline in 'The Doctor's Wife', which remains unmatched in this regard in 21st Century *Doctor Who*.

A problem of a different sort arises when the Doctor strangely starts talking about the TARDIS having 'fuel cells' and says, effectively confirming an earlier assumption by the salvage men, 'the fuel's spilled out, so the rods will be exposed', as if the ship is powered by some kind of combustion engine or perhaps a nuclear reactor – again, more like an ordinary spaceship that a Time Lord vessel. This is directly contradicted just a few minutes later, when it is correctly shown that the power source is actually the Eye of Harmony, containing a star suspended in a state of continuous collapse into a black hole. However, the real reason for Steve Thompson's shoehorning in of the reference to 'rods' that will 'start to warp' and 'maybe even break apart' quickly becomes apparent, as a series of ordinary metal rods suddenly start to pierce through the corridor walls at various angles, one of them eventually pinioning the luckless Tricky by his shoulder. This again is a highly contrived piece of plotting that completely fails to convince.

As the story staggers on, one misstep at a time, we then get the utterly ludicrous sequence where Tricky learns that he has been somehow, er, tricked by Gregor and Bram into believing that he is an android, when really he is their younger brother. This has been likened by some reviewers to the much-derided development in the classic-era story 'The Android Invasion' (1975) where ex-astronaut Guy Crayford suddenly discovers that he has a perfectly good eye beneath the eyepatch he has been duped into wearing. In fact, though, it is worse than that, because Crayford's previous failure to realise he is uninjured actually has the sound explanation that he has been brainwashed by his alien Kraal masters; and the scene of him removing the eyepatch and discovering the truth is symbolic of him finally throwing off his mental conditioning due to the Doctor's intervention. In 'Journey to the Centre of the TARDIS', by contrast, there is no plausible reason for Tricky's prior inability to tell that, apart from bionic eye and synthetic voice-box implants, he is an ordinary man of flesh and blood, presumably performing all the normal bodily functions.

To add to the absurdity, there are a number of scenes where Tricky is depicted as if he really were an android. For instance, he claims on more than one occasion to be able to sense the TARDIS's distress. Possibly he is just deluding himself, or possibly he has some previously unsuspected empathic ability that enables him to relate to the ship's feelings. However, there can be no such explanation for the fact that, after he is freed from the metal rod, he seems to shed no blood whatsoever, and even his uniform appears undamaged. The only sign that he was ever injured is that he holds his hand to the area where the wound ought to be, and winces a bit! Perhaps the metal rod did not go right through him, but only trapped him; but, if so, that makes rather a nonsense of the subsequent debate about whether or not Gregor should cut his arm off in order to free him.

Then we come to the story's resolution. Most science fiction fans harbour a particular dislike of endings that make use of a metaphorical 'reset button' – a plot device that restores everything to exactly how it was when the action first began, rendering the whole thing essentially pointless – and 'Journey to the Centre of the TARDIS' actually goes one step further than that by featuring a *literal* reset button in the form of the van Baalan brothers' magno-grab remote control unit. It is hard to shake the feeling that Steve Thompson has included this intentionally as a kind of teasing in-joke at the fans' expense. That said, though, the saving grace here is that the reset button does not in fact completely undo everything that has happened in the episode. It is made clear at the end that, in a change from how things originally panned out, Tricky is soon going to be spared his brothers' continued deception. It is also heavily implied that – due no doubt to his special relationship with time – the Doctor can still remember everything that has happened, including an intense conversation he has had with Clara in which he has challenged her to admit if she is 'a trick, a trap' and finally accepted that she knows nothing about the two *alter egos* he has previously encountered.

Fortunately, there are a few other plus points to the episode. It is interesting to see the TARDIS interior, usually a place of refuge and safety, transformed into one of threat and danger. Director Mat King – another newcomer to *Doctor Who* – does a reasonable job with the script and sets he is given to work with, bringing an unsettling sense of claustrophobia to the corridor scenes; and although it isn't really clear why exposure to the Eye of Harmony should transform the ship's occupants into Time Zombies, these make for suitably scary monsters. It is an ingenious idea that, when Gregor tries to steal one of the glowing orbs from the architectural reconfiguration system, the TARDIS protects itself by sealing off doors and turning its interior into an inescapable maze. Another good move is the inclusion of 'echo' console rooms, making good use of the available standing set by presenting it in a disconcertingly different way. Clara is again given some good material in this episode, not to mention a particularly eye-catching costume, as she continues to develop and adjust to life on board the TARDIS; and both she and the Doctor are, as usual, very well portrayed by the show's regulars. By contrast, however, the three van Baalan brothers, who make up the entirety of the unusually small main guest cast, are all rather poorly acted, compounding the episode's problems.

Most of those problems, though, come down to the script; and given that Steve Thompson was also responsible for Series Six's weakest episode, 'The Curse of the Black Spot', it has to be said that, whatever his other strengths as a writer, he has yet to show his suitedness to *Doctor Who*.

7.11 – The Crimson Horror

Writer: Mark Gatiss
Director: Saul Metzstein

DEBUT TRANSMISSION DETAILS

BBC One/BBC One HD
Date: 4 May 2013. Scheduled time: 6.30 pm. Actual time: 6.29 pm.

Duration: 44' 45"

ADDITIONAL CREDITED CAST

Dame Diana Rigg (Mrs Gillyflower[77]), Rachael Stirling (Ada[78]), Catrin Stewart (Jenny), Neve McIntosh (Madame Vastra), Dan Starkey (Strax), Eve de Leon Allen (Angie), Kassius Carey Johnson (Artie), Brendan Patricks (Edmund[79] & Mr Thursday), Graham Turner (Amos), Olivia Vinall (Effie[80]), Michelle Tate (Abigail), Jack Oliver Hudson (Urchin Boy[81]).

PLOT

In Yorkshire, 1893, noted chemist and mechanical engineer Mrs Gillyflower is founding a puritanical community called Sweetville, based around a factory claimed to be making matches. However, a number of dead bodies

---

[77] First name given on screen as 'Winifred'.
[78] Surname 'Gillyflower'; she is Mrs Gillyflower's daughter.
[79] Surname presumably 'Thursday', as he is Mr Thursday's brother. As both are portrayed by the same actor, they may be twins.
[80] Surname presumably 'Thursday', as she is Edmund's wife.
[81] Name given on screen as 'Thomas Thomas'.

have been found in a nearby canal, stained bright red – a phenomenon termed locally 'the Crimson Horror'. A Mr Thursday, whose brother Edmund is one of the victims, seeks help from the Paternoster Row gang; and, after he shows them some photographs of Edmund's body, in which they discover an image of the Doctor's face imprinted on the dead man's eye, they head north to investigate. Jenny infiltrates the factory and encounters the Doctor, who has been held captive there by Mrs Gillyflower's blind daughter Ada after surviving the Crimson Horror, possibly due to his non-human physiology. He explains that he and Clara fell into a trap while investigating the factory themselves. Mrs Gillyflower is putting the Sweetville recruits into suspended animation; sometimes this process goes wrong, causing the Crimson Horror, and the bodies are dumped into the canal. With Jenny's help, the Doctor finds Clara and revives her from suspended animation. They learn that Mrs Gillyflower's mysterious 'silent partner' Mr Sweet is a red, leech-like creature that has survived from prehistoric times and has now attached itself to her chest, in a supposedly symbiotic relationship. Venom from Mr Sweet has been used in diluted form to effect the suspended animation process, but now Mrs Gillyflower plans to launch a quantity of pure venom into the atmosphere using a rocket, her aim being to wipe out all of humanity apart from her Sweetville recruits, who will later wake to repopulate the Earth. Vastra and Jenny remove the venom from the rocket before it is fired, and Strax shoots Mrs Gillyflower dead. Ada then kills Mr Sweet with her cane. On her return to the 21st Century, Clara is alarmed to learn that Artie and Angie have found some old photographs of her and the Doctor on the internet, and guessed that they are time travellers.

QUOTE, UNQUOTE

- **Strax:** 'Jenny? If this weak and fleshy boy is to represent us, I strongly recommend the issuing of scissor grenades, limbo vapour and triple-blast brain-splitters.'
  Vastra: 'What for?'
  Strax: 'Just generally. Remember, we are going to … the North.'

- **Clara:** 'What's going on?'
  Doctor: 'Haven't you heard, love? There's trouble at t'mill!'

- **Doctor:** 'Mrs Gillyflower, you have no idea what you're dealing with!

In the wrong hands, that venom could wipe out all life on this planet!'
Mrs Gillyflower: 'Do you know what these are? The wrong hands!'

- **Mrs Gillyflower:** 'Forgive me, my child. Forgive me.'
  Ada: 'Never.'
  Mrs Gillyflower: 'That's ... my ... girl ...'

CONTINUITY POINTS

- When the Doctor tells Clara, 'I once spent a hell of a long time trying to get a gobby Australian to Heathrow Airport,' this is a reference to Tegan Jovanka, a companion of his fourth and fifth incarnations. His subsequent reassurance, 'Brave heart, Clara,' is an adaptation of something his fifth incarnation often said to Tegan.

- The Paternoster Row gang are mystified as to how Clara is still alive, as they mistakenly assume that she is the same girl they met, and saw killed, in the events of 'The Snowmen', set a year earlier in 1892. The Doctor is at a loss to explain.

- Vastra recognises the red leech venom, and says that she previously saw its symptoms 'about 65 million years' ago. However, in 'The Hungry Earth' (2010), the Doctor implied that the Silurians went into hibernation some 300 million years prior to the 21st Century. This suggests that there may be a previously unsuspected chapter in Silurian history, in which at least some of them actually revived at some point after their initial hibernation and resumed their rule of the Earth (as was their original plan), until they or their descendants were forced to retreat back into their shelters some 65 million years ago – most probably to avoid the same fate as the dinosaurs, which died out at that time after a space-freighter crashed into the planet, as seen in 'Earthshock' (1982). Vastra would seem to have been one of that much later group, which may possibly explain why she and others like her differ in appearance from the earlier Silurians seen in 'Doctor Who and the Silurians' (1970) and 'Warriors of the Deep' (1984). She adds, 'My people once ruled this world ... But we did not rule it alone. Just as humanity fights a daily battle against nature, so did we. And our greatest plague, the most virulent enemy, was the repulsive red leech ... A tiny parasite. It infected our drinking water. And once in our systems, it secreted a fatal poison.'

- The old photographs of Clara and the Doctor that Angie and Artie have found on the internet show them aboard the Russian submarine *Firebird* in 1983 in 'Cold War' (a posed shot of them with Captain Zhukov, Professor Grisenko and two junior submariners, presumably taken after the end of the on-screen action) and in Caliburn House in 'Hide' (a more candid shot with Alec Palmer and Emma Grayling; as Palmer has his camera in his hands in the photograph, it would seem that he must have taken this himself by angling the lens at the group's reflection in a mirror). Angie and Artie have also found an image of Clara's namesake from 'The Snowmen' (a posed formal portrait), which they have understandably mistaken for her.

PRODUCTION NOTES

- This episode and 'The Snowmen' were made together as Block Six of Series Seven's production schedule, with their recording significantly overlapping.

- Location work for 'The Crimson Horror' got under way on 2 July 2012 in Bute Town, Caerphilly, for the scenes at Sweetville's entrance gates. The following day saw the crew moving to the Holy Trinity Presbyterian Church, Trinity Street, Barry, for the sequence of Mrs Gillyflower's recruitment meeting. Also recorded that day, in the Dock Office at Barry Docks, was the scene of Jenny and the other new recruits queuing to sign up for Sweetville. 6 July saw the crew visit London House, Bullring, Llantrisant, to tape material outside Madame Vastra's Yorkshire residence and some street scenes. On 26 July, Tonyrefail School in Gilfach Road, Tonyrefail was used for scenes in the Sweetville office and in the local mortuary. Brigantine Place in Cardiff was the venue on 2 August for recording of parts of the flashback sequence of the Doctor and Clara and the discovery of a body in the local canal. 24 August saw the scene of Mr Thursday visiting Vastra in the orchid house of her London home being taped at Llandough Castle in Llandough, the Vale of Glamorgan. Three days later, Treowen Manor in Dinglestow, Monmouth was used for an interior scene at Vastra's Yorkshire residence. Barry Pump House on Hood Road, Barry was the location on 25 October for a night-time scene of Strax and Thomas outside the Sweetville factory. The sequence of the Paternoster Row gang in their carriage heading north was taped outside the Coal Exchange in Mount Stuart Square, Cardiff on 16 November. Then, concluding the location work, the scene of Clara returning to the Maitland family home at the end of the episode was recorded at the usual venue of 30 Beatty Avenue, Roath on 26 November, along with material for 'The Rings of Akhaten' and 'The Name of the Doctor'. Studio recording took place at BBC Roath Lock on various dates between 4 July and 16 November.

- This was the one hundredth *Doctor Who* episode to be transmitted since the 21st Century run began in 2005.

- Steven Moffat had originally intended to write this Doctor-lite episode himself, but when scheduling conflicts prevented this, he offered the task to his old friend and fellow *Sherlock* creator and executive producer Mark Gatiss. Gatiss wrote the parts of Mrs Gillyflower and Ada especially for Dame Diana Rigg and her daughter Rachael Stirling, affording them their first joint screen appearance. Rigg was also able to use her genuine Doncaster accent for the first time in one of her screen roles.

- Mark Gatiss drew part of his inspiration for 'The Crimson Horror' from a mention of 'the repulsive story of the red leech' at the start of Sir Arthur Conan Doyle's short story 'The Adventure of the Golden Pince-Nez', published in the collection *The Return of Sherlock Holmes* (George Newnes, 1905). He based Sweetville on Saltaire in West Yorkshire, which was founded in 1851 as a model (i.e. ideal) village by wool industrialist Titus Salt, who had a daughter called Ada. The name Sweetville, however, is a variation on that of another model village, Bourneville on the outskirts of Birmingham, this one founded in 1898 by George Cadbury. Mr Thursday's name was drawn from an alias used in G K Chesterton's metaphysical thriller novel *The Man Who Was Thursday: A Nightmare* (J W Arrowsmith, 1908).

OOPS!

- The attendees at the meeting where Mrs Gillyflower attempts to drum up new Sweetville recruits join in communal singing of the poem 'Jerusalem', the music for which was not composed until 1916, well after the story's 1893 setting. Similarly, when Mrs Gillyflower sings a short section of the hymn 'To Be a Pilgrim' later in the action, it is an anachronistic 1906 version. (This must be one of the many ways in which Earth history in the *Doctor Who* universe differs from that in ours.)

CRITICAL REACTION

- 'You can't accuse Mark Gatiss of lacking ambition. Victorian philanthropy, apocalypticism, optography, penny dreadfuls and a neat twist on the madwoman in the attic theory were all merrily thrown into the bubbling brew of Gatiss's story, the hundredth episode of *Doctor Who* since it returned in 2005. And what a centenary episode this turned out to be. In the hands of a lesser writer than Gatiss, "The Crimson Horror" could have buckled under the weight of its own ambition. But this crammed in idea after idea while still maintaining a terrific, breezy pace and delivering a fantastically satisfying story.' Ben Lawrence, *Telegraph* website, 4 May 2013.

- 'This episode didn't really further any larger storylines, save for my suspicion that the Doctor and Clara are in love, but it was a fully-fleshed-out story in a fully-formed, imaginative world, which didn't feel rushed or too easily solved in the last five minutes. And that, to me, makes a great standalone *Doctor Who* episode. Perhaps the follow-up to "The Crimson Horror" will [involve] Vastra, Jenny, and Strax investigating Clara, since the Doctor seems content with her story as is; he's no longer obsessed with "figuring her out".' Emily V Gordon, TV.com website, 5 May 2013.

- 'Especially impressive is [Mark] Gatiss's inclusion of William Blake's poem, "And Did Those Feet in Ancient Time" in Gillyflower's homily … The poem, now most familiar as the hymn "Jerusalem", recounts a fabled visit by a young Jesus to England, where he briefly establishes heaven … in contrast to the "dark Satanic mills" of the industrial revolution. Both this heaven on Earth, and the title of the hymn, are referenced later by Ada, when she comments that "there will be room for us in the new Jerusalem". By utilising historically-relevant religious rhetoric as motive, Gatiss strengthens both Gillyflower's

character, and his script's setting.' Clint Hassell, *Doctor Who* TV
website, 7 May 2013.

- 'Perhaps more than any other episode [Mark Gatiss has] written, this
is the most full-on Gatissian. (Have I just coined a new term?) This is
a man steeped in Victorian literature, horror movies, black comedy…
and here he's piped it into *Doctor Who*, adding more than a dash of
The Avengers. I mean, yes, former *The Avengers* icon Diana Rigg is the
guest star, obviously. But "The Crimson Horror" also captures the
lurid tone of those mid-'60s episodes, where Steed and Mrs Peel
(Rigg) would take on a camp and dastardly baddy, played by a well-
known actor …, who'd often have a peculiar pet and a ludicrous
scheme for world domination/destruction. What strikes me as
unusual, for today's *Doctor Who*, is how thoroughly vile a villainess
Winifred Gillyflower is allowed to be. She has no redeeming
qualities, no vestige of human kindness; she's wicked to the core. She
may sound a little like Mary Whitehouse, hectoring the gullible from
her pulpit on "the moral decay and the coming apocalypse", but in
planning Sweetville, her "shining city on the hill" that will save only
the finest human specimens for her "golden dawn", Gillyflower is a
proto-Nazi in charge of a full-scale eugenics programme.' Patrick
Mulkern, *Radio Times* website, 4 May 2013.

ANALYSIS

Mark Gatiss's previous five *Doctor Who* television scripts have ranged
from the very good – 'The Unquiet Dead' (2005) and this series' 'Cold
War' – to the really rather poor – 'Victory of the Daleks' (2010) – but 'The
Crimson Horror', his sixth, is unquestionably his strongest yet. Indeed,
this episode is one of Series Seven's high points, and stands amongst the
best of *Doctor Who*'s entire 21st Century run.

Gatiss is well known to have a particular passion for Victorian-era
gothic fiction, including the Sherlock Holmes stories and the lurid 'penny
dreadful' tales mentioned at one point in the episode's dialogue, and he
hails from Sedgefield in County Durham, just north of Yorkshire; so the
setting of 'The Crimson Horror' in Victorian-era Yorkshire really plays to
his strengths (just as did the 1860 setting of 'The Unquiet Dead' back in
Series One). Indeed, it might almost be said that this was an episode he
was born to write.

Doctor Who has always done Victorian settings particularly well, previous examples having featured in 'The Evil of the Daleks' (1967) and 'The Talons of Weng-Chiang' (1977), and 'The Crimson Horror' is a worthy successor to those earlier classics. In fact, Gatiss's richly evocative dialogue in this episode at times recalls that of the celebrated writer of 'The Talons of Weng-Chiang', the late, great Robert Holmes. For instance, a certain Yorkshire town comes in for a deliciously amusing roasting from Mrs Gillyflower as she addresses her meeting of potential Sweetville recruits: 'Bradford, that Babylon for the Moderns, with its crystal light and its glitter. All aswarm with the wretched ruins of humanity. Men and women crushed by the devil's juggernaut! And moral turpitude can destroy the most delicate of lives. Believe me, I know. I know.' Another choice example comes when, on learning that her blindness was caused not by her drunken father as she has always been led to believe, but by Mrs Gillyflower experimenting on her with the leech venom, Ada rounds on her mother with a scathing condemnation: 'You hag! You perfidious hag! You virago! You harpy! All these years, I have helped you, served you. Looked out for you. Does it count for nothing? Nothing at all?'

Basing the story around one of the 'model villages' set up in the late 1800s by religiously-motivated philanthropic industrialists such as Titus Salt (Saltaire) and the Lever Brothers (Port Sunlight) was a good move on Gatiss's part, and the script is full of authentic-seeming period touches, such as Mrs Gillyflower's temperance-style recruitment meeting and the post-industrial revolution, 'dark, Satanic mill'-type factory at the heart of Sweetville – which actually turns out to be manufacturing nothing at all, its fake machine noises being broadcast through rows of loudspeaker horns of a typically ostentatious Victorian design. Ada passing trays of food to the imprisoned Doctor through a hatch at the bottom of his cell door is reminiscent of housekeeper Mrs Pritchard feeding the captive Control creature through a similar hatch in 'Ghost Light' (1989), another excellent classic-era *Doctor Who* story with a Victorian setting; and the mortuary scenes somewhat recall those of 'The Talons of Weng-Chiang' – although this episode's coarse mortuary attendant Amos is far removed from the latter's genteel pathologist character Professor George Litefoot. His gleefully morbid reactions to the victims of the Crimson Horror – 'Hell fire! That's put me right off me mash. Another one!' – are actually more akin to those of the ghoulish old woman who in 'The Talons of Weng-Chiang' finds a bloated corpse floating, not in a canal, but in the Thames – 'On my oath, you wouldn't want that served with onions.

Never seen anything like it in all my puff. Oh, make an 'orse sick, that would.'

Although, for production scheduling reasons, the Doctor and Clara play only a limited part in proceedings this time, Gatiss has made a positive virtue of that necessity. His idea of having the Doctor recount their earlier investigations by way of a condensed flashback, presented in the form of a sepia-tinted vintage film (although not a silent black-and-white one, as would have been the case at the time), is absolutely inspired, and succeeds in making their involvement seem rather greater than it actually is. The fact that the two leads are somewhat in the background also, of course, allows the Paternoster Row gang to come to the fore. Gatiss is the first writer aside from their creator Steven Moffat to have been given an opportunity to use these three wonderful characters in a story, and he makes a great job of it, capturing their distinctive traits perfectly. If anyone had any doubts that they could easily support a spin-off show of their own, then 'The Crimson Horror' should surely have dispelled them. They make for a splendidly eccentric team of investigators, their unconventional relationships and unusual appearances intersecting with polite Victorian society in a way that affords much scope for incident and amusement – as demonstrated for instance when Mr Thursday promptly faints on first seeing the reptilian features usually kept hidden behind Madame Vastra's veil, and again on first being confronted with Strax's Sontaran countenance.

As in 'The Snowmen', Strax is the focus of much of the episode's humour, his typically bellicose suggestions for weapons deployment being patiently rebuffed by Vastra. His delight is palpable when, at one point, he finally gets to cast off his black cape disguise and enter the fray in his Sontaran armour, firing his weapon at a group of assailants and shouting his race's battle cry of 'Sontar-ha!' 'Strax! You're overexcited,' chides Vastra. 'Have you been eating Miss Jenny's sherbet fancies again?' 'No ...' replies Strax, unconvincingly. Another amusing scene comes when the horse pulling their carriage fails to take the Sontaran where he wants to go. 'Do you have any final words, before your summary execution?' he asks the animal, raising his weapon as if to shoot it. 'Fourth one this week, and I'm not even hungry!' Fortunately, before he can carry out his threat, he is given street directions by a young urchin named Thomas Thomas – a witty allusion to the well-known TomTom sat-nav system.

Jenny, meanwhile, is pleasingly allowed a particularly large slice of the action on this occasion. She is the one chosen to attend Mrs Gillyflower's meeting and infiltrate the Sweetville factory, and later she gets to rescue the Doctor and show off her unarmed combat skills in a sequence where she peels off her outer clothes to reveal the leather fighting suit first seen in 'The Snowmen' – a possible nod to guest star Dame Diana Rigg, whose iconic role as Emma Peel in the fantastical '60s spy show *The Avengers* often involved her engaging in similar fights in similar tight-fitting outfits.

The only false note in the entire story comes when the Doctor, elated at being cured of the incapacitating Crimson Horror, grabs Jenny, bends her over backwards and kisses her on the lips. Given that this is completely uninvited and unwanted by Jenny – as must be obvious to him, since he knows she is a lesbian, and married, and she responds by slapping his face – it is easy to understand why some fan commentators have criticised it as being tantamount to a sexual assault. It might be argued in mitigation that the Doctor is simply caught up in the moment and that his motivation is in no way sexual; but then again, this is called into question by a later piece of business where he reacts guiltily on realising that he has raised his sonic screwdriver into a symbolically erect position at the sight of Jenny disrobing to reveal her fighting suit. At any rate, while to describe it as a sexual assault is probably overstating things, the kiss is certainly an unwelcome inclusion that a judicious script editor ought to have excised.

In terms of its realisation, though, the episode is virtually flawless. Director Saul Metzstein has done a fantastic job of bringing the action to the screen, and Rigg and fellow guest star Rachael Stirling both deliver terrific performances in their respective parts, which are very well written by Gatiss. If anything, Stirling actually outshines her famous mother, as her role as the blind Ada, a tragic figure embittered by her years of exploitation, is the more demanding of the two, and one that she pulls off entirely convincingly. Mr Sweet is a delightfully disgusting little creation, and the Crimson Horror itself is decidedly gruesome, making its victims appear as if their bodies have been horribly scalded by the huge vats of diluted venom into which they have been dunked. Matt Smith's performance in the scenes where the Doctor is still afflicted by his own exposure to this process is actually very unsettling, the painful rigidity of his movements putting one in mind of the stiff-legged, zombie-like gait of Frankenstein's Monster, or even of rigor mortis; further testament to the brilliance of the actor's portrayal of the Time Lord. The BBC's design departments, including those responsible for costume and make-up, have always been renowned for their expertise in recreating particular historical periods, and 'The Crimson Horror' is no exception to the rule, with all aspects of its Victorian setting being meticulously depicted.

It is entirely fitting that the one hundredth episode of 21st Century *Doctor Who* should showcase so admirably the superb scripting, tremendous acting and outstanding production quality it can achieve at its very best.

7.12 – Nightmare in Silver

Writer: Neil Gaiman
Director: Stephen Woolfenden

DEBUT TRANSMISSION DETAILS

BBC One/BBC One HD
Date: 11 May 2013. Scheduled time: 7.00 pm. Actual time: 7.01 pm.

Duration: 44' 39"

ADDITIONAL CREDITED CAST

Eve de Leon Allen (Angie), Kassius Carey Johnson (Artie), Jason Watkins (Webley), Warwick Davis (Porridge[82]), Tamzin Outhwaite (Captain[83]), Eloise Joseph (Beauty), Will Merrick (Brains), Calvin Dean (Ha-Ha), Zahra Ahmadi (Missy), Aidan Cook (Cyberman), Nicholas Briggs (Voice of the Cybermen)

The Cybermen created by Kit Pedler & Gerry Davis

PLOT

The Doctor is persuaded by Clara to take Angie and Artie to a huge outer-space amusement park called Hedgewick's World, for which he has a golden ticket. However, by the time of their arrival, the park is closed down. They meet a man named Webley, who owns a hall of waxworks

---

[82] Real name given in dialogue as 'Emperor Ludens Nimrod Kendrick, called Longstaff the Forty-First, the Defender of Humanity, Imperator of Known Space'.
[83] Name given in dialogue as 'Alice Ferrin'.

and three deactivated Cybermen, one of which is a chess-playing puppet operated from beneath by a man named Porridge. On spotting some insect-like silver creatures nearby, the Doctor leaves the two children behind and takes Clara off to investigate. However, the insect-like creatures then reactivate the Cybermen, and part-convert Webley into a Cyberman himself. The children are seized and placed into a walking coma state. Also present on the planet is a platoon of inept troops sent there as a punishment. Having used his psychic paper to convince them he has authority from the currently-missing Emperor, the Doctor puts Clara in charge while he leaves to try to rescue the children. On entering a huge Cyber-tomb, he is attacked by the insect-like Cybermites, following which the Cyberiad – the Cybermen's collective consciousness – tries to turn him into a new Cyber-Planner. While the Doctor battles for control of his own mind, engaging his new Cyber-Planner aspect in a chess match, Clara and the troops try to hold back the constantly upgrading Cybermen, three million of which now revive from the tomb. The Doctor eventually gains the children's release, then expels the Cyber-Planner from his mind using the golden ticket – gold being anathema to the Cybermen. Porridge, admitting that he is really the Emperor, activates the troops' planet-imploding bomb in order to wipe out the Cybermen, while he and the others – except for the still-controlled Webley – are teleported to safety aboard the imperial flagship in space.

QUOTE, UNQUOTE

- **Clara:** 'I trust the Doctor.'
  Captain: 'You think he knows what he's doing?'
  Clara: 'I'm not sure I'd go that far.'

- **Clara:** 'Do you think I'm pretty?'
  Doctor: 'No, you're too short and bossy and your nose is all funny.'
  Clara: 'Good enough!'

- **Doctor:** 'Nice ship. Bit big. Not blue enough.'

CONTINUITY POINTS

- The Doctor describes Hedgewick's World as 'the biggest and best amusement park there will ever be,' and Porridge confirms, in response to a question from Clara, that it is indeed the biggest in the (known) universe.

• Webley's World of Wonders contains waxwork replicas of, amongst others, a Shansheeth (first seen in *The Sarah Jane Adventures*: 'Death of the Doctor' (2010)), a Uvodni (*The Sarah Jane Adventures*: 'Warriors of Kudlak' (2007)), a Blowfish (*Torchwood*: 'Kiss Kiss, Bang Bang' (2008)), a ventriloquist's dummy ('The God Complex' (2011)) and an Ultramancer, a Pan-Babylonian and a Lugal-Irra-Kush ('The Rings of Akhaten').

• Webley describes his chess-playing Cyberman exhibit as 'the 699th wonder of the universe'. The '700 wonders of the universe' were originally referred to by the third Doctor in 'Death to the Daleks' (1974), and when the Exxilon city was destroyed at the end of that story, he said, 'Now the universe is down to 699 wonders.'

• The Cybermen are said to have been defeated, and supposedly destroyed, 1,000 years prior to the unspecified date when 'Nightmare in Silver' takes place. Porridge tells Clara that Hedgewick 'bought the planet cheap' after it had been 'trashed in the Cyber-Wars'. The Cyber-Wars have been mentioned in a number of previous stories, including 'Revenge of the Cybermen' (1975); 'Earthshock' (1982); the novel *The Dimension Riders* (Virgin Publishing, 1993); the novel *Theatre of War* (Virgin Publishing, 1994); and the audio drama 'Last of the Cybermen' (Big Finish, 2015). They appear to have begun in the 23rd Century – the date mentioned in *Theatre of War* – and ended in the 26th Century – the date given in 'Last of the Cybermen'. This suggests that 'Nightmare in Silver' is set around the 36th Century. Some time prior to 2526, the year in which the events of 'Earthshock' take place, the forces opposing the Cybermen scored a significant victory owing to the invention of the glitter-gun, a weapon firing gold sourced from the planet Voga, as recounted in 'Revenge of the Cybermen'. Porridge, however, states, 'We couldn't win. Sometimes we fought to a draw, but then they'd upgrade themselves, fix their weaknesses and destroy us. It's hard to fight an enemy that uses your armies as spare parts.' Eventually, though, the Cybermen were defeated by blowing up the Tiberian spiral galaxy: 'A million star systems. A hundred million worlds. A billion trillion people.' Although not explicitly stated, it is implied that the

Tiberian spiral galaxy was where all the Cybermen were believed to be located at that time. The troops now have standing orders that if they find a Cyberman, and can't destroy it immediately, they are to implode the planet they are on, as this is the only sure-fire way of killing it.

- Given that the gap in space left by the destruction of the Tiberian spiral galaxy 1,000 years earlier can be seen from Hedgewick's World, it must be less than 1,000 light-years away – quite close in astronomical terms. This would explain how the Cybermen were able to mount a secret operation transporting damaged units to the planet for repair, using a specially-constructed Valkyrie ship, as recounted by the Cyber-controlled Webley.

- The Cyberiad, mentioned for the first time in this episode, is the Cybermen's collective neural network, or hive mind. Cyber-Planners are controlling intelligences, as previously seen in 'The Wheel in Space' (1968) and 'The Invasion' (1968).

- The Doctor points out that as the Cybermen convert only humans, a Time Lord is no use to them – as first mentioned in 'Closing Time' (2011). However, the part-converted Webley tells him, 'Well, that was true a long time ago. But we've upgraded ourselves. Current Cyber-units use almost any living components.'

- The Doctor is able to block the Cyber-Planner from discovering some of the information in his mind, including that about Clara – although he lets slip that he regards her as 'the Impossible Girl'. However, he does grant access to his memories of Time Lord regeneration – at which point, images are seen of each of the previous ten Doctors. He says he could regenerate again in order to destroy the Cyberiad's connection to him, but that he does not want to do so, because 'who knows what we'll get next?'

- The Cyber-Planner notes that there is no record of the Doctor anywhere in the data-banks of the Cyberiad, and discovers that he has been eliminating himself from history. This accords with what has been seen in previous stories, starting with 'The Wedding of River Song' (2011).

- The Doctor tells the Cyber-Planner, 'I know things you don't. For example, did you know, very early versions of the Cyber operating system could be seriously scrambled by exposure to things like gold or cleaning fluid? And what's interesting is, you're still running some of that code.' The mention of cleaning fluid relates to a sequence in 'The Moonbase' (1967) where the Doctor's companions successfully attacked a group of Cybermen using a 'cocktail' of various different solvents. Gold, as indicated above, was first established as being capable of destroying Cybermen in 'Revenge of the Cybermen'. There, the Doctor said that coating their breathing apparatus with gold dust effectively suffocated them. It later stories such as 'Silver Nemesis' (1988), however, it became apparent that the metal was much more generally damaging to the creatures, repelling them almost akin to the way that garlic wards off vampires.

- The Doctor says, 'The Time Lords invented chess. It's our game.'

- Porridge says that, as Emperor, he rules a thousand galaxies. He asks Clara to marry him, to ease his loneliness, but she declines.

PRODUCTION NOTES

- This episode was recorded on its own as Block Ten of Series Seven's production schedule.

- Working titles for the episode at various stages during its development were 'The Last of the Cybermen', 'Silver Ghosts', 'A Nightmare in Silver' and 'The Last Cyberman'.

- The main location work for 'Nightmare in Silver' was carried out at two castles representing Natty Longshoe's Comical Castle. The first was Castell Coch in Cardiff, where recording took place from 7 to 9 November 2012; the second was Caerphilly Castle in Caerphilly, where sequences involving the Doctor's chess match were taped on 14 and 15 November. Between those two, on 10 November, the scenes in the state room of the imperial flagship were recorded at the City Hall in Cathay's Park, Cardiff; and on 13 November, the sequences in the barracks were shot at Newbridge Memorial Hall in High Street, Newbridge. MoD St Athan in Barry was used on 16 November for recording of the scenes inside the Doctor's mind and the Cyberiad, and of some further Natty Longshoe's Comical Castle interiors. Lastly, work originally due to be carried out at Uskmouth Power Station in Newport on 21 November for the Hedgewick's World power station had to be rescheduled due to bad weather, eventually being completed on 26 November. Studio recording took place at BBC Roath Lock on various dates between 10 November and 1 December.

- The first four scenes of the shooting script were dropped shortly before recording, both because the script was over-length and because they would have entailed a difficult-to-schedule night shoot with child actors Eve de Leon Allen and Kassius Carey Johnson. These scenes would have taken place after dark, partly in a graveyard near the house where Clara, Angie and Artie live, and partly in the TARDIS. They would have shown Clara persuading a reluctant Doctor to take the children on a journey with them, by pointing out that he is so much older than her that she herself is effectively a child to him. Artie would then have suggested a number of 'educational' historical destinations, all of which the Doctor would have baulked at, having faced dangers there in previous television stories (e.g. the Aztec civilisation – 'The Aztecs' (1964) – and Pompeii before the eruption of Vesuvius – 'The Fires of Pompeii' (2008)). The Doctor would eventually have agreed to take them to Hedgewick's World as a compromise. It would also have been established here that he did not want to leave the children in the TARDIS on their own, in case they touched some of the controls and caused mayhem; hence his later suggestion that they sleep in Webley's World of Wonders, believing this to pose a lesser risk.

- Even with the trimming of the script, the first edit of the episode still ran some ten minutes too long, necessitating numerous small edits to bring it down to the required running time.

- Hedgewick's World was originally to have been called Lampwick's World, until it was discovered that the latter was the name of a real company, selling lamps.

- Unlike his previous episode, 'The Doctor's Wife' (2011), Neil Gaiman scripted 'Nightmare in Silver' without any significant input from showrunner Steven Moffat. He was ultimately disappointed by its on-screen realisation.

- The idea of the chess-playing Cyberman was drawn from the Turk, a real-life chess-playing automaton constructed in the late 18th Century, which likewise had a human operator hidden in its base. The Turk previously inspired an audio drama featuring the Cybermen, 'The Silver Turk' (Big Finish, 2011), and influenced Steven Moffat in the creation of the Clockwork Droids in 'The Girl in the Fireplace' (2006). Before that, it was mentioned in the Eighth Doctor Adventures novel *The Adventuress of Henrietta Street* (BBC Books, 2001).

OOPS!

- The castle is referred to as 'Natty Longshoe's Comical Castle' in the dialogue, but captioned simply 'Natty Longshoe's Castle' when seen on visitor maps of Hedgewick's World.

- It is said that the planet will be imploded by the troops' bomb, but when the bomb is activated at the climax of the action, it actually appears to explode.

CRITICAL REACTION

- 'The Cyber-Planner ... isn't a new idea. It was established in 1968 and back then looked like an assemblage of junk that had been found lying around the visual effects workshop. It was also marginally more effective, and certainly more sinister, than its representation here: dodgy swirling backgrounds for the meeting of Time Lord and Cyber minds, and prosthetics glued to Matt Smith's face. And here we reach the principal failing of the drama: the many scenes where the Cyber-Planner-possessed Doctor flips between personas. Despite Matt Smith's gallant efforts, they're a mess. The dialogue should have been tightened. Less frenetic camerawork might have given the scenes focus, elicited a concentrated performance. Instead, the star of the show is left to flounder, to look like a big kid play-acting at being goody then baddy. It's exposing – and uncomfortable to watch, for the wrong reason.' Patrick

Mulkern, *Radio Times* website, 11 May 2013.

- 'It was all very clever and whipped along at a quick-fire pace – so rapid in fact that if you blinked you would have missed poor old Tamzin Outhwaite's guest appearance. But I loved the way that this episode actually looked like proper sci-fi, with ghostly grey vistas of the abandoned theme park looming under dark skies; I also admired the script, which was full of humour and sharp lines including a wonderful, musing payoff from the Doctor to Clara: "A mystery wrapped in an enigma squeezed into a skirt that's just a little bit too tight."' Sarah Crompton, *Telegraph* website, 11 May 2013.

- 'This could have been a gripping, exciting tale that … rejuvenated the Cybermen. But it's not … The plot, such as it is, can be broken down into two strands: Clara … leads a faceless army of grunts against an apparently unstoppable force of Cybermen, while the Doctor gets possessed by minuscule Cybermites, leading to a game of chess and some strange gesticulating and gurning. That's about the size of it. Apart from one notable exception, all of the supporting characters get zilch to do. The redesigned Cybermen are about as scary as a jar of lollipops. And worst of all, any drama is extinguished by the presence of the supremely irritating Maitland kids.' John Bensalhia, Shadowlocked website, 7 June 2013.

ANALYSIS

There are a lot of interesting ideas and appealing elements in Neil Gaiman's script for 'Nightmare in Silver', but unfortunately they never quite come together to make a coherent whole.

Take, for instance, Hedgewick's World. A huge outer-space amusement park is a well-chosen setting for a *Doctor Who* story, and arriving after the place has closed down is a typical kind of mistake for the Doctor to make. However, the timeline given for events prior to this point doesn't really make much sense. The Cyber-controlled Webley says, 'The Cyber-Planners built a Valkyrie' – presumably a type of Cyber-ship – 'to save critically damaged units and bring them here and, one by one, repair them.' The Doctor then surmises, and Webley does not disagree, 'The people who vanished from the amusement park – they were spare parts, for repairs.' According to Porridge, though, Hedgewick did not actually buy the planet until after it had already been 'trashed in the Cyber-Wars'. This would seem to imply two possible alternatives for the sequence of events – neither of them very credible. Either Hedgewick bought the devastated planet and ill-advisedly opened his amusement park there while the battle was still raging nearby, and on seeing this the Cybermen decided to establish a secret base on the same site in order to take advantage of the situation; or Hedgewick bought the devastated planet after the Cybermen had already established their secret base there, and probably after the battle had already ended, and it was simply a fortuitous coincidence, from their point of view, that he then built his amusement park in the same place, attracting lots of potential 'spare parts'. Either way, it is hard to understand how the workers responsible for the park's construction, maintenance and security can have failed to spot, and warn the authorities, that a huge Cyber-base was also being built in the vicinity, or (in the second scenario) was already present.

The Cyber-base is at one point referred to as a 'tomb', and its design also recalls somewhat the one seen in 'The Tomb of the Cybermen' (1967) – which is a nice tip of the hat to that acclaimed classic-era story. Here, though, what the entombed Cybermen are waiting for is not simply any new arrivals of sufficient intelligence to be converted into additional members of their race, but specifically children, who are needed 'to build a new Cyber-Planner', because 'a child's brain, with its infinite potential' is perfect for this purpose – an idea recalling how the Daleks linked a young girl's brain to their battle computer for a similar reason in another classic-era story, 'Remembrance of the Daleks' (1988). Again, though, this doesn't really add up. If the Cybermen's tomb was already present on the planet before the amusement park was built (the second scenario outlined above), there would have been lots of children flocking to the attraction as soon as it opened. And if the Cybermen established their tomb after the amusement park was already in operation (the first scenario), similarly there would have been plenty of children present amongst the visitors. One can only suppose that people must have stopped coming to Hedgewick's World almost immediately after the Cybermen started abducting visitors to use as spare parts, so that they had no opportunity to take any suitable children. That admittedly does not seem entirely implausible – the sudden, unexplained disappearance of numerous visitors would have been bound to generate a lot of negative publicity and dissuade others from coming, and certainly from bringing their children – but this begs another salient question: why did the disappearance of all those people not prompt a thorough investigation, leading to the discovery of the Cybermen's presence at that stage?

Possibly the mystery of the vanishing visitors is what accounts for troops having been dispatched to the planet. The deployment of a single inept 'punishment platoon' seems hardly an adequate response, though, and there is nothing in the episode's dialogue to establish what their mission actually is, beyond the Captain's statement that they have been sent there so that they 'can't get into trouble' – so the bizarrely incongruous presence of a military barracks in the middle of an amusement park is left as another puzzling aspect of the story for viewers to scratch their heads over.

Also unexplained is the huge coincidence of Porridge – aka Emperor Ludens Nimrod Kendrick, called Longstaff the Forty-First, the Defender of Humanity, Imperator of Known Space – being present on the planet, apparently hanging about beneath Webley's chess-playing Cyberman exhibit so that he will be ready to operate it on the off-chance that any visitors happen to drop in – which presumably they never have, prior to the arrival of the TARDIS travellers, given that the park had already closed down even before Webley got there. Clearly Porridge is desperately trying to escape the weight of his imperial responsibilities, but how and why has he ended up in Hedgewick's World, and in Webley's World of Wonders in particular? Did he arrive on the planet with Webley, or bump into him after they were both already there? And, come to that, why did Webley bother setting up his show in the first place, if Hedgewick's World was already out of action? It's all a mystery.

So many things in this story seem to happen not because there is any well-motivated reason for them to do so, but simply because they are needed to meet particular plot requirements. Notable examples include the Cybermites not part-converting Artie and Angie like they do Webley and the Doctor, but simply putting them into a 'walking coma' state with their brains in 'standby mode'; all of the areas of Hedgewick's World that the characters need to use turning out still to have operational power, even though the park is disused and the rest of it appears wrecked; and the Cyber-Planner implausibly shutting down its entire force of three million Cybermen so that it can devote more processing power to solving the chess conundrum the Doctor sets it.

Perhaps the most disappointing aspect of 'Nightmare in Silver', though, is its depiction of the Cybermen. Prior to transmission, Neil Gaiman stated that one of his aims was to 'make the Cybermen scary again'. Even leaving aside the false implication that the 21st Century Cybermen were not already scary, when given suitable material, there was no way he was going to achieve that aim with this story, in view of the approach he chose to take with it. The Cybermen have always been at their most scary when portrayed as a lurking menace, infiltrating through stealth and emerging from the shadows to threaten their victims with conversion into others of their kind; and rather less scary when depicted as oversized tin soldiers marching about in robotic unison while others do the talking on their behalf – albeit that the latter mode of presentation can still lead to some excellent stories; 'The Invasion', the first in which it was adopted, being a good example. Accordingly, the Cybermen's scariest scenes in 'Nightmare in Silver' are the ones where they first begin to revive amongst the creepy waxworks in the darkened hall of Webley's World of Wonders, and later stalk the patrolling troops through the amusement park's grimy power station and service area; but the fear factor decreases significantly as soon as the full army of three million emerge from their tomb and start parading about *en masse* to the accompaniment of the now-standard Cyber-stomp sound-effect – which, to his credit, Gaiman was keen to lose – with the controlled Doctor acting as their mouthpiece.

Gaiman has spoken in interviews about having enjoyed watching the '60s Cyberman stories as a child, and the influence of those early classics can certainly be seen at times in 'Nightmare in Silver'. Aside from the aforementioned inclusion of a tomb from which the revived Cybermen emerge, the survival of a single Cybermite at the end of the story recalls how a single Cybermat escaped destruction at the end of 'The Tomb of the Cybermen'; the TARDIS's arrival on the Spacey Zoomer ride's mock-up of the Moon's surface, which prompts Angie to remark, 'This is like a Moonbase or something,' is an obvious nod to 'The Moonbase', which is also referenced more subtly in the fact that Hedgewick's World likewise boasts a 'weather controller', and in the way the metallic circuitry that appears on the faces of the part-converted Webley and the Doctor resembles the tracery of black lines that spread across the faces of the Cybermen's neurotropic virus victims in that earlier story; and the inclusion of a controlling Cyber-Planner is a call-back to 'The Wheel in Space' and 'The Invasion', in which that concept first featured. The Cyberman stories of the '70s and '80s are meanwhile the source of the idea that gold is anathema to their race. These are all very pleasing examples of well-remembered elements of past adventures being referenced and reused in order to enhance a current one. Something else that Gaiman gets spot on is the idea of the Cybermen being a race struggling to survive against the threat of extinction – indeed, the troops' Captain starts out mistakenly believing that they are already extinct, just as the base commander Hobson did in 'The Moonbase'.

Where things start to go wrong is with the new developments that Gaiman throws into the mix: chiefly, the notion of the Cybermen having a kind of collective consciousness, the Cyberiad, and that of them being able to overcome threats by almost instantly upgrading themselves, in ways that are then automatically shared with all other members of their race. The main problem is that, while these are indeed novelties as far as the Cybermen are concerned, and are not bad ideas *per se*, they are well-known features of *Star Trek: The Next Generation*'s Borg. The Cybermites, although an inventive and scary extrapolation from the Cybermats, also recall the nanoprobes that the Borg use to convert people; the faces of the part-converted Webley and the Doctor physically resemble those of the Borg; and the Doctor's inner struggle with the Cyber-Planner for control of his own mind echoes the turmoil suffered by Captain Jean-Luc Picard (Patrick Stewart) on his assimilation to become Locutus of the Borg in one of *Star Trek: The Next Generation*'s most celebrated storylines. It has often been suggested that the Borg were themselves partly inspired by the Cybermen, so if imitation is indeed the sincerest form of flattery, then it could be said that this is simply a case of *Doctor Who* returning the compliment. However, the consequence is that, for anyone familiar with the American series, these supposed innovations actually come across as being highly derivative.

The specific upgrades that Gaiman has elected to show are also somewhat problematic. In one early scene, a Cyberman suddenly starts to move at super-high speed in order to snatch Angie away from the troops' barracks – a sequence realised using a rather impressive type of visual effect popularised by *The Matrix* movie franchise and generally referred to as 'bullet time'. But this begs the question, if the Cybermen can now move that fast, why do they not do it more often, or indeed always? We see several other situations during the course of the action where it would surely be of use to them, but they fail to take advantage of it. A little later on, they demonstrate another new trick: the ability to detach their hand, or even their head, in order to mount a surprise attack. Again, they do this only once in each case (although one of them does also rotate its head through 180 degrees at one point), when they could surely exploit the tactic more often; but, that aside, the really unfortunate thing about this particular newfound ability is that it places unwelcome emphasis on perhaps the least potent aspect of the 21st Century Cybermen – specifically, the fact that they no longer have, as their classic-era predecessors did, largely flesh-and-blood bodies augmented by and encased within artificial parts (except in emergency situations, as first seen in *Torchwood*: 'Cyberwoman' (2006)), but instead are almost entirely robotic, save for their modified organic brains. While, admittedly, the prospect of having one's brain removed, modified and placed inside a robotic shell is hardly attractive, this lacks the full body-horror appeal of the creatures' original conception. It also, in this instance, sits rather awkwardly with the suggestion that the amusement park's visitors have been taken for use as spare parts.

To be fair to Neil Gaiman, though, not all of the shortcomings in the Cybermen's depiction in 'Nightmare in Silver' are down to the script. Sadly, it has to be said that the latest updating of their costumes is not at all successful. Gaiman requested that these new versions be given blank faces akin to those in 'The Moonbase' and 'The Tomb of the Cybermen', and while the end result technically fulfils that brief, it is far from impressive. Whereas the masks used in those mid-'60s stories had a ghastly, skull-like quality, the ones introduced in 'Nightmare in Silver' are basically egg-shaped, giving the Cybermen a moon-faced, almost endearing look. The bodies, too, are poorly designed, being (colour aside) so similar in appearance to the powered suits of armour featured in the *Iron Man* comic books and movies that they seem almost to be inviting a lawsuit, reinforcing the unfortunate impression that this is a highly derivative reimagining. The relatively crude Cyber-suits of the mid-'60s stories were actually far more effective, because they looked like exactly the sort of things that might have been knocked together in grimy machine-shops by a race desperately short of raw materials and struggling to survive. Those created for 'Nightmare in Silver' are altogether too slick and shiny to represent a battle-ravaged army of creatures on the brink of extinction. A far better and more imaginative idea, and one more in keeping with the contemporary zeitgeist, might have been for them to have been given a steampunk look, suggesting that they had made opportunistic use of spare parts not only from the amusement park's visitors, but also from its fairground arcades, rollercoaster rides and other attractions, even though this might have brought them visually even closer to the Borg.

While on the subject of the episode's on-screen realisation, another problem is that the studio sets for the Spacey Zoomer ride and Webley's World of Wonders have a rather cheap and tawdry look to them, suggesting that, as on 'Journey to the Centre of the TARDIS', the show's usually excellent designer Michael Pickwoad was possibly hamstrung by an inadequate budget here. There doesn't seem to be anything particularly comical or even interesting about the location-recorded setting of Natty Longshoe's Comical Castle, either. Even taking into account the fact that the amusement park is supposed to be falling into disrepair, the overall impression given is more of a space-age Butlins than a space-age Disneyland; although, as the Doctor claims entrance to the park with a golden ticket – which, rather improbably, turns out to be made of real gold – and Webley has a Willy Wonka-esque costume, it seems that at least some of those involved in the episode's creation were probably aiming more for the feel of Roald Dahl's *Charlie and the Chocolate Factory* (Joseph Schindelman, 1964), the 2005 movie version of which was directed by sometime Neil Gaiman collaborator Tim Burton.

It doesn't help matters that the viewer is given little sense of where all the different areas of Hedgewick's World are in relation to each other, and no sense at all of where the Cyber-tomb is in relation to any of them – an issue with Stephen Woolfenden's direction rather than with the design work. Indeed, Woolfenden's handling of this, his only *Doctor Who* episode to date, is altogether disappointing. The action has a disjointed feel to it, and it isn't always clear what is supposed to be happening. For instance, in one scene after the Doctor and Clara leave the two children to sleep in Webley's World of Wonders, Cybermites are seen swarming all over Angie's mobile phone, but this then seems to be completely forgotten about until almost the end of the episode, when the girl is given a new, TARDIS-supplied phone by the Doctor – although how he knows that she no longer has the old one is another mystery. Apparently the intention here was to show the Cybermites disabling the phone in order to ensure that Hedgewick's World remained cut off from all outside contact – an idea reflected in the subsequent revelation that the troops' communicators are also broken – but it requires a considerable leap of deduction on the viewer's part to work this out. Similarly opaque is a later sequence where, following an argument with Clara and Porridge in the upper gallery of Natty Longshoe's Comical Castle, the Captain is killed by a blast of energy just as she is about to activate the planet-imploding bomb, after which we get a cut-away shot to a Cyberman with a gun on the ground far below. Seemingly the idea here was to imply that the Cybermite that had previously been shown spying on the Captain, Clara and Porridge had conveyed the situation to the Cyberiad, allowing the Cyberman to pinpoint and shoot the Captain from a distance – but this is by no means evident, and to make matters worse, the Cyberman's positioning suggests that the shot would have had to have been fired at an impossible angle in order to hit its target; which may perhaps explain why it is not actually depicted on screen.

Possibly some of these shortcomings are accounted for by the fact that the material Woolfenden recorded had to be significantly trimmed in the edit in order to bring the episode down to the required running time; but, of course, the viewer can judge only on the basis of what actually appears in the final version. This is by no means the end of the episode's problems, either. Although Jason Watkins gives a good performance as Webley, and Warwick Davis an excellent one in the well-written role of Porridge, aka the Emperor – rare highlights in the production – Tamzin Outhwaite is sadly miscast as the troops' Captain, named in the dialogue, though not in the closing credits, as Alice Ferrin. Even allowing for the fact that her unit is supposed to be an inept punishment platoon, she conspicuously lacks the physical presence and toughness needed to convince the viewer that she would ever have been accepted for military service in the first place, let alone have risen to the rank of an officer – and a rebellious one at that, as she says she was assigned to the platoon for disobeying orders. The actors portraying the other troops also fail to make much of an impression, being similarly unsuited to their parts. The two Maitland children, Angie and Artie, are played quite competently by Eve de Leon Allen and Kassius Carey Johnson respectively, but their characters are somewhat irritating, being essentially stereotypical middle-class know-it-all kids with hearts of gold, and their presence detracts from the drama more often than it enhances it.

Even Matt Smith, for all his formidable acting skills and inventiveness, struggles a bit in this episode, as he doesn't quite manage to pull off the scenes where he is required to make a series of instant back-and-forth transitions between Doctor and Cyber-Planner personalities. This was, though, a challenge that any actor would have found it extremely difficult if not impossible to meet, given the way the scenes in question are written and directed. Just to add to his difficulties, there is even a sequence where Smith is called upon to do impressions of his two predecessors, Christopher Eccleston and David Tennant! A different approach should have been taken here, with the rapid-switch dialogue either significantly cut down – which would have had the added benefit of easing the episode's running-time problems – or else reworked and incorporated into the far more successful scenes set in the virtual landscapes of the Doctor's mind and the Cyberiad, where Smith gets a chance to play the two personalities separately, and does a much better job of delineating between them. Mind you, however these scenes had been done, it would still have been rather odd to hear the Cyber-Planner taunting the Doctor for being so emotional when, at odds with the Cybermen's supposed nature, it seems even more emotional itself!

As for Clara, her characterisation here is curiously inconsistent with what has gone before. Previously she has come across as an ordinary young woman who, although certainly resourceful, is still adjusting to a life of making occasional trips in space and time, and still understandably scared by the various perils she encounters. This time, though, she scarcely bats an eyelid when suddenly put in charge of the platoon of troops, and proceeds to order them about with complete self-assurance. She calmly asserts her newly-bestowed authority over the Captain, and even takes it upon herself to fire the troops' anti-Cyberman gun, using it with fearless proficiency, as if this is the sort of thing she does every day. The only thing she doesn't get to do is attack one of the Cybermen with the gold badge of command that the Doctor transfers from the Captain's uniform to her jacket – an action that turns out to have less significance than might perhaps have been predicted. One can only speculate that, between 'Journey to the Centre of the TARDIS' and 'The Crimson Horror' (from which 'Nightmare in Silver' appears to follow straight on), she must have had a number of other adventures unseen on screen, allowing her to become much more at ease with facing danger – and, incidentally, offering plenty of scope for future tie-in writers to fill in the gaps! This would make sense of the suggestion toward the end of the episode that the Doctor and Clara have now fallen into a routine whereby he comes to pick her up every Wednesday – his and the TARDIS's usual whims permitting!

One thing the script does do rather well is explore further the question of what exactly the Doctor's feelings are toward Clara. When the Cyber-Planner gets access to the Time Lord's mind, it becomes privy to his innermost thoughts, and appears to detect that, where his companion is concerned, these go beyond the purely platonic. In a sequence where Clara tries to determine whether or not the Doctor currently has the mental upper hand by challenging him to tell her something only he knows, he says, 'Clara … I suppose … I'm the only one who knows how I feel about you right now. How funny you are – so funny … and pretty. And the truth is, I'm starting to like you in a way that is more than just –' As he leans forward, making as if to kiss her, this is enough to convince Clara that it is not in fact the Doctor speaking but the Cyber-Planner, prompting her to slap him across the face to bring him back to his senses, explaining, 'Because even if that *was* true – which it is obviously not – I know you well enough to know that you would rather die than say it.' But is the Cyber-Planner really just putting words into the Doctor's mouth, or is it, as Clara seems to fear, revealing true desires that he himself would rather not admit to? The Doctor's subsequent denial that he considers Clara pretty could be simply a case of him covering his tracks.

An intriguing coda to this comes later on when, after Clara has returned home and left him alone in the TARDIS, the Doctor reflects that she is, 'A mystery wrapped in an enigma squeezed into a skirt that's just a little bit too … tight.' Some fan commentators, perhaps overly sensitive to any hints of sexism following the minor controversy regarding the Doctor's kissing of Jenny in 'The Crimson Horror', decried this as an inappropriately salacious remark for him to make. However, given the look of surprise that suddenly crosses his face almost immediately after he has spoken the sentence, a possible alternative interpretation is that it is evidence of the Cyber-Planner having a lingering influence on his mind – a kind of mental equivalent of the lone Cybermite surviving in space after the destruction of the planet, giving notice that the menace of the Cybermen is not entirely eradicated. At any rate, whether or not the Doctor really does find Clara attractive is a question that only subsequent episodes will be able to answer.

In summary, then, 'Nightmare in Silver' is an episode that has a lot going for it, and certainly offers plenty of food for thought and discussion; and Neil Gaiman is to be applauded for what he has tried to achieve with the updating of the Cybermen. Sadly, though, it has some significant flaws in most key aspects of its production, including its writing, design and direction, so that ultimately it falls well short of achieving its full potential and has to be judged a major disappointment.

7.13 – The Name of the Doctor

Writer: Steven Moffat
Director: Saul Metzstein

DEBUT TRANSMISSION DETAILS

BBC One/BBC One HD
Date: 18 May 2013. Scheduled time: 7.00 pm. Actual time: 6.59 pm.

Duration: 44' 26"

ADDITIONAL CREDITED CAST

Alex Kingston (River Song), Richard E Grant (Dr Simeon), Neve McIntosh (Vastra), Catrin Stewart (Jenny), Dan Starkey (Strax), Eve de Leon Allen (Angie), Kassius Carey Johnson (Artie), Nasi Voutsas (Andro), David Avery (Fabian), Michael Jenn (Clarence[84]), Rab Affleck (Archie), Samuel Irvine (Messenger Boy), Sophie Downham (Young Clara), Paul Kasey (Whisper Man), John Hurt (The Doctor)

Silurians created by Malcolm Hulke
Sontarans created by Robert Holmes

PLOT

Having been given by a convict, Clarence deMarco, the space-time co-ordinates of the planet Trenzalore, supposedly the location of the Doctor's greatest secret, Madame Vastra convenes a psychic 'conference call' with Jenny, Strax (who is in Glasgow, having a fight with a friend named Archie), Clara (in the Maitland family home) and River Song (in data-

---

[84] Surname given in dialogue as 'DeMarco'.

ghost form, following her death in the Library). Their minds are still in the psychic dreamscape when they are attacked by fearsome Whispermen, avatars of the Great Intelligence, which manifests in the form of Dr Simeon. Jenny is killed, and the Intelligence instructs Clara to warn the Doctor that his friends are lost unless he goes to Trenzalore. On waking, Clara tells the Doctor what has happened, and he takes her to Trenzalore in the resisting TARDIS, explaining that it is the location of his own grave. On arrival, they see in the distance a future TARDIS, its police box exterior having grown to giant size as it too is dying. With the aid of the ghostly River, they manage to gain access to its interior, wherein lies the Doctor's sealed tomb. The Paternoster Row gang have also been brought there by the Intelligence, and Strax has managed to restart Jenny's heart, reviving her. The Intelligence threatens to kill all of the Doctor's friends unless he opens his tomb by speaking his name. When he refuses, River does so instead, though the others do not hear her. At the centre of the tomb are the Doctor's remains: not a body, but intertwined energy strands representing his timestream. The Intelligence dissipates itself into the strands, intending to rewrite every part of the Doctor's history as an act of revenge, turning all of his past victories into defeats. Clara, having finally realised why she is 'the Impossible Girl', goes after it, so that she can nullify its actions. The Doctor bids farewell to River, then enters his own timestream, determined to rescue Clara. There, on a battlefield, they encounter his greatest secret: a previously unknown former incarnation, who forswore the name 'Doctor'.

<u>QUOTE, UNQUOTE</u>

- **Doctor:** '"The Doctor has a secret he will take to the grave. It is discovered." He wasn't talking about my secret. No, no, no, that's not what's been found. He was talking about my … grave. Trenzalore is where I'm buried.'

- **Strax:** 'Unhand me, ridiculous reptile!'

- **Doctor:** 'You are always here, to me. And I always listen, and I can always see you.'
  River: 'Then why didn't you speak to me?'
  Doctor: 'I thought it would hurt too much.'
  River: 'I believe I could have coped.'

Doctor: 'No. I thought it would hurt me. And I was right.'

- **Doctor:** 'Look, my name, my real name – that is not the point. The name I chose is "the Doctor". The name you choose, it's like a promise you make. He's the one who broke the promise.'

- **War Doctor**[85]**:** 'What I did, I did without choice.'
  Doctor: 'I know.'
  War Doctor: 'In the name of peace and sanity.'
  Doctor: 'But not in the name of the Doctor.'

CONTINUITY POINTS

- The first Doctor and his grand-daughter Susan are seen stealing their faulty TARDIS from the repair shop on Gallifrey. A caption dates this simply to 'A Very Long Time Ago …' The Doctor is already wearing the Edwardian-style attire familiar from his televised adventures. This suggests that either some early Gallifreyan clothing resembled that style, or that the Doctor already had a fascination with Earth and its culture even prior to departing his home planet.

- Clara tells Angie and Artie that she got her soufflé recipe from her mother, who was 'a great woman'.

- The address of the Maitland family home where Clara works as a live-in nanny is 30 Oak Street, Chiswick, as seen on the envelope that Vastra sends in 1893, to be delivered by hand on 10 April 2013. In the letter inside, Vastra explains that the Doctor gave her Clara's contact details for use in case of emergency. This suggests that, since 'The Crimson Horror', there must have been at least one further meeting between Vastra and the Doctor, unseen on screen.

- When Clara joins her and Jenny in the dreamscape of the psychic conference call, Vastra says, 'Time travel has always been possible in dreams.'

---

[85] The incarnation portrayed by John Hurt is not identified as 'the War Doctor' until 'The Night of the Doctor', but is described as such here for the avoidance of confusion.

- This is the first episode to feature River Song in data-ghost form from after the time she died in the Library in 'Forest of the Dead' (2008). The Paternoster Row gang are aware of her situation, and have clearly had other psychic encounters with her in the past. When Vastra asks her, of the Doctor, 'He's still never contacted you?', River replies, 'He doesn't like endings' – repeating something she said previously in 'The Angels Take Manhattan'. At the end of the episode, the Doctor reveals that he has always in fact been aware of her ghostly presence and able to hear her, but has not talked to her as he would have found it too painful. He tells her, 'There is a time to live and a time to sleep. You are an echo, River. Like Clara. Like all of us, in the end. My fault, I know, but you should've faded by now.' She responds, 'It's hard to leave, when you haven't said goodbye.' He asks how he can do this, and she tells him, 'There's only one way I would accept. If you ever loved me, say it like you're going to come back.' He complies with this, telling her, 'See you around, Professor River Song.' When River subsequently fades away, this would seem, on the face of it, to mark the end of her presence accompanying the Doctor as an 'echo'. However, there is a sting in the tail, as she leaves him with a conundrum: 'I was mentally linked with Clara. If she's really dead, then how can I still be here?' The meaning of this is uncertain. It could be simply confirmation that Clara isn't really dead – as proves to be the case when the Doctor subsequently goes to rescue her from his timestream – or, as seems more likely, it could be a suggestion that River's data-ghost continues to have some kind of independent existence outside of the Library's computer.

- Trenzalore was first mentioned in 'The Wedding of River Song' (2011). There, Dorium Maldovar told the Doctor the legend: 'On the fields of Trenzalore, at the Fall of the Eleventh, when no living creature can speak falsely, or fail to answer, a question will be asked. A question that must never, ever be answered.' He went on to explain that the question was that of the Doctor's name: 'Doctor who?' In 'The Name of the Doctor', it is revealed that the Doctor's name, when spoken, opens his sealed tomb, although whether or not this is why the question 'must never, ever be answered' is left uncertain.

- River confirms that she knows the Doctor's name, as first revealed in 'Forest of the Dead'.

- The Doctor says that he always suspected what Trenzalore was, but didn't want to find out for himself. He tells Clara: 'When you are a time traveller, there is one place you must never go. One place in all of space and time you must never, ever find yourself.' He goes on to explain that Trenzalore is the location of his grave. When Clara asks him how it is possible for him to have a grave, he says, 'Because we all do, somewhere out there in the future, waiting for us. The trouble with time travel, you can actually end up visiting.' This essentially reprises a conversation they had in 'Hide'.

- To extract the coordinates of Trenzalore from Clara's memory, the Doctor connects her to the TARDIS's telepathic circuits, which were first mentioned at the end of 'Frontier in Space' (1973).

- The Doctor says of the Paternoster Row gang, 'They cared for me during the dark times – never questioned me, never judged me, they were just … kind. I owe them. I have a duty.' The 'dark times' is a reference to the period he spent living in isolation in Victorian London after losing Amy and Rory, as seen in 'The Great Detective' and 'The Snowmen'.

- On arriving on Trenzalore, the Doctor says, 'I'm a time traveller. I've probably time-travelled more than anyone else … Meaning … my grave is potentially the most dangerous place in the universe.' He adds that the point where the TARDIS has crash-landed is 'a battlefield graveyard, my final battle'. When he and Clara see the huge future TARDIS in the distance, he explains, 'When a TARDIS is dying, sometimes the dimension dams start breaking down. They used to call it a size leak. All the bigger-on-the-inside starts leaking to the outside. It grows.'

- Referring to the battle on Trenzalore, the Great Intelligence says: 'It was a minor skirmish by the Doctor's blood-soaked standards. Not exactly the Time War, but enough to finish him. In the end, it was too much for the old man.' When Vastra protests that the Doctor has never been 'blood-soaked', he adds, 'Tell that to the leader of the Sycorax. Or Solomon the trader. Or the Cybermen, or the Daleks. The Doctor lives his life in darker hues, day upon day, and he will have other names before the end. The Storm. The Beast. The Valeyard.' The leader of the Sycorax was killed by the Doctor at the end of 'The Christmas Invasion' (2005), and Solomon at the end of 'Dinosaurs on a Spaceship'. The Valeyard featured in 'The Trial of a Time Lord' (1986), and was said to be an amalgamation of the darker aspects of the Doctor's nature, somewhere between his twelfth and final incarnations. In the audio story 'The Trial of the Valeyard' (Big Finish, 2013), the Valeyard claims that he was inadvertently created by the Doctor himself, during experiments to try to break the usual 12 regeneration limit imposed on the Time Lords by their founder Rassilon; however, this account is of questionable veracity. The audio story 'The Brink of Death' (Big Finish, 2015) indicates that the Valeyard was actually created by the Time Lords using black ops technology, possibly to serve as a weapon.

- When Clara is in the future TARDIS, she starts to recall the events of 'Journey to the Centre of the TARDIS', including her discussion with the Doctor where he told her about having previously met two other versions of her, both of whom died. The Doctor says, 'The TARDIS is a ruin, the telepathic circuits are awakening memories you shouldn't even have.'

- The Whispermen are insubstantial humanoid representations of the Great Intelligence. They kill by reaching into their victims' chests and stopping their hearts. They take on the features of Dr Simeon when necessary for the Great Intelligence to communicate verbally.

- The Intelligence implies that the Doctor's name is one word.

- When River appears outside the Doctor's tomb, Dr Simeon's eyes seem to follow her, suggesting that the Great Intelligence is aware of her ghostly presence.

- When the characters enter the Doctor's tomb, the TARDIS's cloister bell starts to ring, but the sound is muffled and discordant, reflecting the fact that the ship is dying. The tomb has a similar appearance to the TARDIS's current console room, but is overgrown with vines, and where the console would normally stand is a vertical column of spinning, intertwined energy strands, which the Doctor describes as follows: 'Time travel is ... damage. It's like a tear in the fabric of reality. That is the scar tissue of my journey through the universe. My path through time and space, from Gallifrey to Trenzalore … My own personal time tunnel, all the days, even the ones that I, er … even the ones that I haven't lived yet.' The Great Intelligence says, 'The Doctor's life is an open wound, and an open wound can be entered.' It then proceeds to do this, intending to rewrite the Doctor's history. It recognises that it will be killed in the process, and says: 'It matters not, Doctor. You thwarted me at every turn. Now, you will give me peace, as I take my revenge on every second of your life!' As the Doctor's life starts to be rewritten, Vastra sees that local star systems are starting to disappear. She tells Jenny, 'The Doctor's timeline has been corrupted. His every victory reversed. Think how many lives that man's saved, how many worlds.' However, Clara then enters the Doctor's timestream and restores his history to its original state. As she goes, she tells the Doctor, 'Run, you clever boy, and remember me' – a slightly extended version of the 'Run, you clever boy, and remember' line previously spoken by Oswin in 'Asylum of the Daleks' and Victorian-era Clara in 'The Snowmen', presumably reflecting the fact that she is the original template for all the other versions of herself, and therefore the one that must be remembered.

- Clara says, of her various encounters with the Doctor throughout his timestream, 'Sometimes it's like I've lived a thousand lives in a thousand places. I'm born, I live, I die. And always, there's the Doctor. Always, I'm running to save the Doctor. Again, and again, and again. And he hardly ever hears me. But I've always been there.' The fact that Oswin in 'Asylum of the Daleks' and the Victorian-era Clara in 'The Snowmen' did not already know who the Doctor was when they helped to save him, whereas the other multiple Claras clearly do, may perhaps be due to the fact that, when she jumps into his timestream, 21st Century Clara has prior awareness of those two particular versions of herself, and of the fact that they were a mystery to the Doctor, making them fixed aspects of their shared history.

- When Clara encounters the first Doctor in the act of stealing the TARDIS on Gallifrey, she dissuades him from taking his original choice, telling him, 'Don't steal that one, steal this one. The navigation system's knackered, but you'll have much more fun.' Judging from what is established in 'The Doctor's Wife' (2011), she is probably influenced in this by the TARDIS itself.

- The TARDISes in the repair shop on Gallifrey are seen in their natural, undisguised state, as featureless silver-grey cylinders with a sliding door at the front. These somewhat resemble the Master's undisguised TARDIS as seen in 'The Claws of Axos' (1971), although that was box-shaped rather than cylindrical – a difference probably accounted for by the fact that it is a more advanced model than the Doctor's. The SIDRATs seen in 'The War Games' (1969) were also box-shaped, but these were created by the War Chief based on the TARDIS design, and so could differ in 'natural form'.

- Before entering his own timestream, the Doctor tells the Paternoster Row gang, 'Now … if I don't come back – and I might not – go to the TARDIS. The fast return protocols should be on, she'll take you home, then shut herself down.' The fast return switch was first mentioned in 'Inside the Spaceship' (1964).

- When the Doctor goes to rescue Clara, he tells her, 'I'm everywhere. You're inside my timestream. Everything around you is me.' Clara says that she can see all of his different faces, and he explains, 'Those are my ghosts. My past. Every good day, every bad day.' Just before they encounter his previously unknown secret incarnation, he admits that his timestream is collapsing in on itself, due to him having entered it. However, he refuses to leave until he has saved Clara.

PRODUCTION NOTES

- This episode was made on its own as Block Eleven of Series Seven's production schedule.

- The relatively small amount of location recording carried out for 'The Name of the Doctor' began on 16 November 2012 at the Coal Exchange in Mount Stuart Square, Cardiff, where the sequence of Strax having his fight in Glasgow was taped. The scenes at the Maitland family home were recorded on 26 November, along with material for 'The Rings of Akhaten' and 'The Crimson Horror'. On 28 November, Merthyr Mawr House in Merthyr Mawr, Bridgend was used for scenes in Madame Vastra's house. Lastly, on the same date, Cardiff Castle in Castle Street, Cardiff was the location for the Victorian prison sequence and the scenes set in the catacomb beneath the Doctor's tomb. Studio recording took place at BBC Roath Lock on various dates between 19 November and 1 December, with some pick-up shots of the battlefield and the reveal of the War Doctor being completed on 26 March and 5 April 2013, as part of the work done for 'The Day of the Doctor'.

- A caption reading 'Introducing John Hurt as the Doctor' is superimposed over the last shot of the on-screen action.

- There is no 'Next Time' teaser at the end of this episode; instead, the closing credits begin with the caption 'To Be Continued ... November 23rd'. On some subsequent commercial releases of the episode in certain territories, this was abbreviated to just 'To Be Continued'.

- On 11 May 2013, the BBC broadcast on its Red Button service, and also made available online, a 3' 32" video entitled 'She Said, He Said: A Prequel', written by Steven Moffat. Despite the title describing this as a 'Prequel', it could perhaps be more properly seen as a sequel or coda to 'The Name of the Doctor'. Set in an unspecified chamber containing elements from a number of recent episodes, such as a killer snowman from 'The Snowmen', the Doctor's painting of Clara from 'The Bells of Saint John' and the chess-playing Cyberman from 'Nightmare in Silver', plus sundry other items, including what appears to be a sculpture of the ninth Doctor's head, it has something of the feel of a dream sequence. It is divided into two parts, featuring first Clara and then the Doctor delivering a monologue while the other remains silent and immobile. Both of them speak of how they finally learned the other's secrets, 'the day we went to Trenzalore'. This video was later included on *The Complete Seventh Series* DVD and Blu-ray box set.

- *The Complete Seventh Series* DVD and Blu-ray box set also features a second prequel to 'The Name of the Doctor'. Entitled 'Clarence and the Whispermen', and again written by Steven Moffat, this has a 2' 11" duration. Set in Vastra's time, 1893, it shows Clarence deMarco in his prison cell being tormented by three Whispermen. They mention the Doctor, imprint the Trenzalore co-ordinates on his memory and instruct him to convey their meaning and purpose to 'the reptile detective'. When he asks them what kind of men they are, they reply: 'We are not men. We are the Intelligence. All of time and space is known to us.' They tell him that he will receive a pardon, sparing him from his expected hanging the next day, and that he will have a good, long life, 'Except, you will always have such trouble sleeping.'

- Two further 'Strax Field Report' videos were placed online by the BBC to tie in with this episode. The first, on 16 May 2013, was also called 'The Name of the Doctor', ran for 49", and had Strax informing his home planet that he has learned from a psychic medium about a forthcoming battle that will have something to do with the Doctor's greatest secret. The second, on 18 May, was titled 'A Glorious Day', ran for 43", and entailed Strax reporting to Sontar that 'a glorious day of brutality, mercilessness and property damage' is approaching, as the Doctor and 'the Impossible Boy' he travels with are threated by a campaign to destroy his present, past and future.

- The shots of the first Doctor encountering Clara as he and his grand-daughter Susan prepare to steal the TARDIS on Gallifrey utilise colourised clips from 'The Aztecs' (1964), coupled with dialogue from 'The Web Planet' (1965). Clips of later Doctors encountered by the multiple Claras inside the Doctor's timestream – seen first in the pre-opening titles sequence and then reprised later in the episode – are sourced from 'The Invasion of Time' (1978), 'Arc of Infinity' (1983), 'The Five Doctors' (1983), 'Dragonfire' (1987) and 'The Snowmen'. Doubles are also used at certain points to represent the first, second, fourth, fifth, sixth, eighth, ninth and tenth Doctors. The pre-opening titles sequence also features clips from 'The Rings of Akhaten' of Clara's parents meeting, and of her young life. Brief clips from 'Journey to the Centre of the TARDIS' are seen in the sequence where Clara starts to remember the events of that episode.

- When the Doctor directs the sonic screwdriver at the energy strands representing his timestream, audio clips are heard of iconic lines of dialogue from '100,000 BC' (1963), 'The Moonbase' (1967), 'The Time Monster' (1972), 'Genesis of the Daleks' (1975), 'The Caves of

Androzani' (1984), 'The Trial of a Time Lord', 'The Parting of the Ways' (2005), 'Voyage of the Damned' (2007) and 'The Pandorica Opens' (2010).

- The sequence where the Great Intelligence starts to rewrite the Doctor's timestream incorporates additional clips from 'The Aztecs' and 'The Web of Fear' (1968).

- When Vastra and Jenny begin the psychic conference call, part of the 'Spring' section of Vivaldi's composition *The Four Seasons* (1725) is heard on the soundtrack.

- Steven Moffat inserted the reference to Solomon the trader into this script in response to disquiet expressed by some fans that the Doctor's effective execution of that character at the end of 'Dinosaurs on a Spaceship' was an uncharacteristically ruthless action for him to take.

OOPS!

- The telegram that Vastra sends to Strax is received by him in Glasgow, but is addressed to 'Oldmeldrum', which is a village in Aberdeenshire, over 150 miles away. (Possibly, in this instance, the name is not that of the village, but of the establishment that Strax is visiting?)

- Vastra's letter to Clara mistakenly gives the intended year of delivery as 'Twenty Thousand & Thirteen' rather than 'Two Thousand & Thirteen'.

CRITICAL REACTION

- '"The Name of the Doctor" has ingredients that "the casual viewer" can enjoy – great monsters, some genuinely scary scenes, zippy dialogue and fantastic performances from the cast, particularly our two leads. But despite Steven Moffat's protestations, this finale is unashamedly a fanfest, and it might run the risk of alienating any viewer who doesn't know their Tom Baker from their Colin. Still, in this fiftieth anniversary year, just this once, I think it's okay for

Doctor Who to get its geek on.' Morgan Jeffery, Digital Spy website, 18 May 2013.

• 'Arguably this story started last autumn with "Asylum of the Daleks" (arguably, because you could say it started in winter 1963) and it'll (probably) end this autumn with the fiftieth anniversary. So, "The Name Of The Doctor" is just a lot of middle. A stepping stone. A mere cog in a massive continuity machine. To be honest, who cares? Who cares when the cog is so gorgeously crafted it transcends mere function and dazzles in its own right? It may make no sense outside of the machine, but that doesn't make it any less striking. Viewers without a degree in *Who*-ology might miss out on some of the more esoteric references, and certain plot beats might not make a lot of sense to them, but they're still going to love the broad strokes. Those of us who can spot a line from "Castrovalva" or a sound bite from the first Doctor or a reference to the Doctor's penultimate incarnation, well … we're simply being rewarded that little bit more.' Dave Golder, *SFX* website, 18 May 2013.

• 'This has been a patchy series, to put it kindly, but thankfully it has finished on a high. The last two episodes – the Victorian romp, then the return of the Cybermen – have been a return to form. This climactic episode was even better. It was momentous, moving and thrilling, yet somehow still found time to be very funny in flashes (mainly thanks to the highly quotable Strax). The only downsides? A tad too much clunking exposition, the odd spot of creaky CGI and some unconvincing metaphors about soufflés and leaves. However, the biggest catch of all is that it's now a six-month wait for November's fiftieth anniversary special. Still, that should be just enough time to digest this breathless, brilliant finale.' Michael Hogan, *Telegraph* website, 18 May 2013.

ANALYSIS

'The Name of the Doctor' is in some respects a clever repackaging of an assortment of memorable elements from previous 21st Century *Doctor Who* stories, all in subtly reworked form. The Doctor's friends participating in a psychic 'conference call' recalls their predecessors having a sub-wave network discussion in 'The Stolen Earth' (2008); the prospect of the Doctor's past victories being erased from history by the Great Intelligence is a larger-scale take on the central storyline of 'Turn Left' (2009); the stars gradually winking out in Trenzalore's night sky resembles the universe collapsing as it is swallowed up by the cracks in time in 'The Big Bang' (2010); Clara throwing herself into the Doctor's timeline to aid him throughout his lives is reminiscent of Rose Tyler seeding herself throughout time and space in Bad Wolf form in 'The Parting of the Ways' (2005); and Clara creating the past events that result in her travelling with the Doctor in the first place is a predestination paradox of the type featured in numerous previous episodes, particularly those written by Steven Moffat, starting with 'Blink' (2008).

Looking further back to classic-era *Doctor Who*, the idea of multiple versions of Clara being scattered through time echoes the fate met by Scaroth, last of the Jagaroth, in 'City of Death' (1979); and the Doctor being aghast at finding the site of his own grave is something that first occurred in 'Revelation of the Daleks' (1985) – although on that occasion it turned out to be a trick played on him by the Daleks' creator Davros. If one considers also the BBC's eighth Doctor novels of the late 1990s, the focus on the Doctor's tomb recalls the significance attached to his coffin in *Alien Bodies* (BBC Books, 1997) by Lawrence Miles (another example of Steven Moffat apparently drawing inspiration from the work of probably his most vitriolic critic from the world of officially-sanctioned *Doctor Who* fiction) while the depiction of his timestream as strands of intertwined bio-data repeats an idea from *Unnatural History* (BBC Books, 1999) by Kate Orman and Jonathan Blum.

Interviewed for *Doctor Who: The Brilliant Book 2012* (BBC Books, 2011), Moffat said, 'It's almost impossible not to disappoint the [show's] absolute diehard enthusiasts – people like me – who examine every line, every moment, and think about it between episodes. I'm not writing for them. I cannot. I'm writing for the other 100% of the audience.' However, while he was no doubt sincere in that sentiment, 'The Name of the Doctor' is really the type of *Doctor Who* that only a diehard fan could fully appreciate; and the type that only a diehard fan could write. Only someone steeped in *Doctor Who* lore could come up with ideas such as the Doctor having a previously unknown additional incarnation; or a companion who surreptitiously assists all of the Doctor's past selves, even influencing his choice of TARDIS when he first quits his home planet; or whole star systems disappearing as the Doctor's timestream is rewritten by an old adversary in an act of revenge. It simply wouldn't occur to a more casual viewer to think that the Doctor's many victories over alien aggressors must have made him integral to the whole history of the universe.

Despite the Doctor's determination to retreat into the shadows at the end of 'The Wedding of River Song' (2011) – which he has clearly acted upon since, as touched on in a number of subsequent episodes, and confirmed in 'Nightmare in Silver' when the Cyber-Planner notes, 'You've been eliminating yourself from history' – it seems that he is actually still at the heart of everything. 'The Name of the Doctor' is almost entirely about the Doctor: his name, his tomb, his timestream, his greatest secret. Indeed, the viewer is by this point starting to realise that the whole of Steven Moffat's first three series in charge of the show have had an overarching plot revolving around the momentous consequences that will follow for the universe if the Doctor simply speaks his own name on Trenzalore, and the attempts of various of his adversaries either to prevent this from happening or, conversely, to bring it about. The show has become, both literally and figuratively, all about answering the question, 'Doctor who?'

Whether or not this is a welcome development is really down to the individual viewer's personal taste; but clearly *Doctor Who* has to move with the times if it is to survive and flourish. It is hard to imagine any drama serial in the early 21st Century maintaining a strong popular following without engaging its audience's interest and emotional investment in its central characters. According the Doctor this degree of prominence does, admittedly, have a downside, in that it makes the universe seem a much smaller place than it should be. In an infinity of space and an eternity of time, shouldn't even the Doctor's amazing feats still be relatively insignificant? But this is an aspect of realism that *Doctor Who* abandoned a long time ago. After all, in an infinite, eternal universe, all of which is in theory accessible via the TARDIS, there is no logical reason why the Doctor should keep coming to 20th and 21st Century Britain. There have been various attempts at rationalisation of this over the years, such as the Doctor trying to return his human companions to their own time and place, the Time Lords exiling him to 20th Century Earth, and the Earth being his favourite planet, or even his mother's home planet; but of course the real reason is simply that this is where the show is made and watched! Which is precisely why, to the casual viewer, there seems nothing odd about it at all. Indeed, during the early part of Russell T Davies's time as showrunner, he made a conscious decision to set all of his stories on, or at least within sight of, Earth; and while this caused disgruntlement amongst some long-time fans, it undeniably helped to win the show acceptance amongst new viewers. It is only really during the Steven Moffat era that the Doctor has again started to wander more widely in time and space.

The one aspect of 'The Name of the Doctor' that does temporarily shift the focus a little away from the Doctor is its resolution of the ongoing Series Seven storyline about the show's other central character, Clara, being 'the Impossible Girl'. The mystery of her prior *alter egos* turns out to have a very ingenious solution, and the way the multiple Claras' integration into the Doctor's timestream is depicted on screen, via the incorporation of shots of Jenna-Louise Coleman, wearing a succession of era-appropriate outfits, into clips from numerous classic-era stories, is really rather brilliant – especially considering the less-than-ideal technical quality of some of the source materials. Combining newly-shot images with old footage is, admittedly, not a wholly original idea – the most notable precedents being the insertion of the title characters of the films *Zelig* (1983) and *Forrest Gump* (1994) into various historical sequences, and the creation of an entire episode of *Star Trek: Deep Space Nine*, 'Trials and Tribble-ations', by combing footage from an original *Star Trek* series episode, 'The Trouble with Tribbles', with newly-shot material – but this is the first time it has been attempted in *Doctor Who*, and the results are excellent, bringing together new-era and classic-era elements of the show's history in a way that satisfyingly reinforces the impression that they comprise a unified whole. The pre-opening titles sequence, where these composite clips are first seen, is perhaps the most breathtaking the show has ever presented, and gets the episode off to a flying start. It is especially wonderful, in *Doctor Who*'s fiftieth anniversary year, to be able finally to see for ourselves how the Doctor and his grand-daughter Susan first embarked upon their travels in the TARDIS, by way of some *bona fide* footage of the show's original star, the late, great William Hartnell.

In the space of just a few episodes, Clara has become arguably the Doctor's most important companion ever, in view of the way in which, we now know, she has given him unseen assistance from the sidelines in all of his previous adventures. One imagines that, with his fan sensibilities, Steven Moffat will have found it amusing to reflect that he has now effectively created a restrospective explanation for any number of plot holes in past stories, such as the long-puzzled-over mystery of whose hand it is that is seen unlocking the door of the storeroom in which the Doctor is held prisoner in the second episode of 'Image of the Fendahl' (1977): clearly it is Clara's!

If Moffat had chosen to write Clara out at this point, 'The Name of the Doctor' would have stood as a perfectly fitting conclusion for her character, and she would still have left a very significant mark on *Doctor Who* history. Indeed, one passage of her dialogue comes across very much like a farewell speech: 'I don't know where I am. I don't know where I'm going, or where I've been. I was the born to save the Doctor, but the Doctor is safe now. I'm the Impossible Girl, and my story is done.' Clearly, though, the showrunner thought there was still sufficient mileage left in the character to justify having the Doctor rescue her from his timestream at the end. This raises the prospect of her being given, in effect, a new lease of life in subsequent episodes; and it will be interesting to see where this takes her, now that the 'Impossible Girl' arc has been concluded.

There is, in fact, a sense of Moffat endeavouring to wrap up a number of ongoing storylines in this season finale in order to clear the decks, as it were, for more major dramatic developments in the forthcoming fiftieth anniversary special. Just as it could have made a suitable exit story for Clara, it could equally well have been an apt swansong for the fabulous River Song, superbly played, as ever, by Alex Kingston. To have River manifesting in data-ghost form from after her death in 'Forest of the Dead' was a great idea on Moffat's part, giving a very unexpected further twist to her ever-tangled relationship with the Doctor. It is debatable what the Doctor means when he tells her, 'You are always here, to me. And I always listen, and I can always see you.' Most probably he is speaking figuratively – suggesting that River is always with him in spirit, if not in person – as it seems highly unlikely that her data-ghost has actually been an unacknowledged companion by his side ever since 'Forest of the Dead'. Indeed, River herself says at one point that the only reason for her continued presence on Trenzalore is that she and Clara remain mentally linked: 'It's the conference call. I kept the line open.' The Doctor certainly appears to believe that this is the case; otherwise, he would not be stumped by River's parting question, 'I was mentally linked with Clara. If she's really dead, then how can I still be here?' On the other hand, though, when River asks, in response to the Doctor's comment about her always being with him, 'Then why didn't you speak to me?', this suggests a more literal interpretation, as does his reply that he would have found it too painful, and his subsequent description of her as 'an echo' that 'should've faded by now'. One possible way of reconciling these two apparently contradictory implications is that the Doctor means he can always see River's ghostly form whenever she joins in one of Vastra's séance-like psychic conference calls – as the one featured in this episode is clearly not the first. At any rate, whatever the explanation, there is no question that this farewell exchange between the Doctor and River is sensitively written, beautifully acted and deeply poignant. There is even room for a little well-judged humour as, after kissing River, the Doctor says, 'Since nobody else in this room can see you, God knows how that looked,' and there is then an amusing shot of the Paternoster Row gang watching on in rather embarrassed puzzlement!

Also concluded in this episode is the running storyline begun in 'The Snowmen', or perhaps more precisely in 'The Abominable Snowmen' (1967), of the Doctor's perennial battle with the Great Intelligence – which appears to be destroyed once and for all at the end of the action, in its ultimately abortive attempt to poison the Time Lord's history. Clara's repetition of the phrase 'I don't know where I am!' when she enters the Doctor's timestream serves as a neat reminder to the viewer of how she and all of the Intelligence's other victims used that same expression on being uploaded to the data cloud in 'The Bells of Saint John', and also recalls how Oswin repeatedly asked 'Where am I?' on becoming aware of her true Dalek nature in 'Asylum of the Daleks'. This helps to reinforce the idea of Series Seven's events coming full circle and being resolved. The implicit likening of the Doctor's timestream to a data cloud also gives an interesting new perspective on that concept.

All things considered, if 'The Name of the Doctor' really does turn out to be the Intelligence's final appearance in *Doctor Who*, then it can at least be said to have gone out with a bang. Returning as Dr Simeon – or, more accurately, the Intelligence's facsimile of him – Richard E Grant gives, if anything, an even less subtle performance than in 'The Snowmen', but serves well enough as the physical representation of a malevolent disembodied entity. The Whispermen, meanwhile, make for very effective new *Doctor Who* monsters. Their blank white faces and snarling mouths somewhat recall those of the killer snowmen as which the Intelligence previously manifested in 'The Snowmen' (and also, incidentally, those of the Trickster in *The Sarah Jane Adventures*), but they are far scarier than that, their gaunt humanoid forms and Victorian-undertaker-style attire giving them a distinctly nightmarish quality. While some long-time fans might still bemoan the fact that the Yeti have not been revived in 21st Century *Doctor Who*, it is a nice touch that they are at least acknowledged in this episode, by way of the inclusion of a fleeting clip of them from 'The Web of Fear' in the sequence where the Intelligence starts to attack the Doctor's timestream. It has to be admitted, too, that it is questionable how credibly these particular classic-era creatures, originated in a time of relatively indistinct, black-and-white television pictures that perhaps made them appear more fearsome than they really were, could be realised in the unforgiving glare of today's full-colour, high-definition broadcasts. In any case, the Whispermen certainly make for excellent substitutes.

The Paternoster Row gang being on hand to witness the Intelligence's demise adds appropriately to the sense of closure, given that they were also present at its creation in 'The Snowmen'. Having now featured in three of the last nine episodes, and also in a number of minisodes and online extras over the same period, this fantastic trio could almost be said by this point to have attained the status of semi-regulars. Certainly they are the most successful recurring characters to have been introduced to the show during Matt Smith's time as the Doctor, and their presence always enlivens any episode in which they appear. The superbly-constructed sequence here where, during their psychic conference call, Jenny appears to have been murdered by the Whispermen, much to Madame Vastra's evident distress, is genuinely shocking; and the ease with which Strax is subsequently able to restart her heart, using what is, in effect, nothing more than a compact defibrillator, cleverly highlights the Victorian-era lizard-woman's unfamiliarity with technology that is entirely unexceptional to the Sontaran, and indeed to the 21st Century viewer.

In terms of its on-screen realisation, 'The Name of the Doctor' is another polished and stylish piece of work by director Saul Metzstein, confirming him to be an excellent addition to the ranks of the show's regular behind-the-scenes contributors. The production is again virtually flawless, with all of the story's widely varied settings – Victorian-era London and Glasgow, 21st Century Chiswick, the psychic dreamscape, the battlefield graveyard of Trenzalore, the Doctor's tomb and the Doctor's timestream – being equally well depicted.

All in all, 'The Name of the Doctor' makes for an outstanding conclusion to Series Seven. And the icing on the cake comes right at the end, with the stunning revelation of the Doctor's previously unknown John Hurt incarnation. While the crashing up of the large accompanying caption 'Introducing John Hurt as the Doctor' is, it must be said, a case of unnecessary overkill, not to mention confusingly at odds with the immediately preceding dialogue establishing that he did not in fact act in 'the name of the Doctor', this highly dramatic sequence sets things up superbly for the landmark fiftieth anniversary special – although, with an epic storyline spanning the Doctor's entire history and all of his incarnations, 'The Name of the Doctor' is a strong enough episode to stand as an early anniversary special in itself.

The Inforarium (Minisode)

Writer: Steven Moffat
Director: Marcus Wilson[86]

DEBUT RELEASE DATE

24 September 2013 on the North American editions of *The Complete Seventh Series* DVD and Blu-ray box set.

Duration: 1' 55"

ADDITIONAL CAST (UNCREDITED)

Laurence Saunders (Master Librarian)

PLOT

The Doctor appears in recorded hologram form inside the Inforarium – 'the greatest source of illicit information in recorded history' – as its Master Librarian worriedly detects a data breach. The Doctor says that he has been deleting every piece of information about himself from every database in the universe, and that while the Inforarium's security systems prevent him from doing so in this instance, he can ensure that all of its data about him is memory-proofed, meaning that it will be forgotten seconds after it is learned. The Master Librarian denies that this is possible, but as the Doctor's hologram fades away, he worriedly detects a data breach – and the whole sequence of events starts over again.

---

[86] Uncredited.

QUOTE, UNQUOTE

- **Master Librarian:** 'You're what?'
  Doctor: 'A recorded message.'
  Master Librarian: 'Then how can you be replying to me?'
  Doctor: 'Very predictable.'

CONTINUITY POINTS

- The Inforarium has been selling its illicit information to the Daleks, the Cybermen and the Sontarans, which is 'just naughty'.

- The Master Librarian states that the Inforarium's data is secure because it is quantum stored and exists at 12 levels of reality.

- The Doctor explains that memory-proofing is a trick he learned from the Silence – creatures that can be remembered only as long as they are observed, as established in Series Six.

- In terms of broadcast/release date, 'The Inforarium' marks the final appearance of the eleventh Doctor's original costume, complete with tweed jacket. However, in terms of the series' chronology, this minisode probably precedes 'The Bells of Saint John: A Prequel', in which that costume also features – the only time the Doctor is seen wearing it at a point definitely subsequent to the departure of Amy and Rory.

PRODUCTION NOTES

- This minisode was not broadcast or released online. It was included only as an extra on *The Complete Seventh Series* DVD and Blu-ray box set.

ANALYSIS

This minisode plugs a gap in the ongoing Series Seven narrative by depicting on screen something that is only spoken about in the transmitted episodes: the Doctor's 'mission' to erase himself from all universal databases.

Clara and the Tardis (Minisode)

Writer: Steven Moffat
Director: Jamie Stone[87]

DEBUT RELEASE DATE

24 September 2013 on the North American editions of *The Complete Seventh Series* DVD and Blu-ray box set.

Duration: 2' 07"

PLOT

Clara enters the TARDIS console room, demanding to know what the ship has done with her bedroom. She speculates that its antipathy toward her might be due to fact that she is the first girl the Doctor has 'brought home', but it disproves this by displaying on one of its screens a series of images of previous female companions. A second Clara then comes into the console room, explaining that she is from the following night. She is still seeking her bedroom. Soon, they are joined by multiple additional Claras, all wanting to know where their bedroom is.

QUOTE, UNQUOTE

- **Clara:** 'Where is it? I know what just happened. I went to the bathroom – thank you for the hologram leopard, by the way; an unexpected pleasure – and my bedroom was completely missing! Just tell me where you put it.'

---

[87] Uncredited.

CONTINUITY POINTS

- As Clara is by this point a sufficiently well-established TARDIS traveller to have her own bedroom, but is still encountering some hostility from the ship, this minisode is probably set around the same time as 'Hide'.

- The past companions whose images appear on the TARDIS screen are Ace (Sophie Aldred), Martha Jones (Freema Agyeman), Nyssa (Sarah Sutton), Peri Brown (Nicola Bryant), the first Romana (Mary Tamm), the second Romana (Lalla Ward), Rose Tyler (Billie Piper), Sarah Jane Smith (Elisabeth Sladen) and Amy Pond (Karen Gillan).

PRODUCTION NOTES

- This minisode was not broadcast or released online. It was included only as an extra on *The Complete Seventh Series* DVD and Blu-ray box set.

- This is the only *Doctor Who* story (outside of tie-in media) ever to feature just a single character (discounting the TARDIS itself).

ANALYSIS

The TARDIS's initial antipathy toward Clara, as seen in 'The Rings of Akhaten' and 'Hide', is never explicitly explained during the course of Series Seven, but is implicitly accounted for by the ship perceiving her nature as 'the Impossible Girl' and baulking at her presence. In other words, it is an early indication of the same impulse that later causes the ship to resist materialising on Trenzalore in 'The Name of the Doctor', leading the Doctor to explain, 'I'm about to cross my own timeline in the biggest way possible – the TARDIS doesn't like it.'

As slight as the plot of 'Clara and the TARDIS' is, it must be said that it does in some respects engender a certain sense of *déjà vu*. When the TARDIS shows Clara a series of images of the Doctor's past female companions, this essentially repeats a sequence involving Amy in the second of the two 'Meanwhile in the TARDIS' minisodes from 2010; and when a pair of Claras say 'We've got to share a bed' and exchange a significant look, this hints at intriguing sexual possibilities in the same way as the presence of a pair of Amys did – both to Rory and to Amy herself – in the 'Time' minisode from 2011. However, the scene works well enough on it own merits, and brings an amusing new slant to the 'multiple Claras' theme running through Series Seven; possibly a sign of the TARDIS anticipating or even hinting at how Clara will be split into countless iterations of herself when she enters the Doctor's timestream.

Rain Gods (Minisode)

Writer: Neil Gaiman[88]
Director: Stephen Woolfenden[89]

<u>RELEASE DATE</u>

24 September 2013 on the North American editions of *The Complete Seventh Series* DVD and Blu-ray box set.

Duration: 1' 39"

<u>ADDITIONAL CAST (UNCREDITED)</u>

Alex Kingston (River Song)

<u>PLOT</u>

The Doctor and River Song are being herded by two spear-wielding guards across the surface of the Planet of the Rain Gods, having arrived there accidentally when they really intended to go out to a restaurant. River hopes that the Doctor has a plan to save them from being sacrificed to the Rain Gods, but the only thing he can suggest is that they try to distract the guards and then run away. Luckily, it suddenly starts pouring with rain, and the two guards are both stunned by lightning, allowing the Doctor and River to escape back to the TARDIS.

<u>QUOTE, UNQUOTE</u>

- **River:** 'That was your plan?'

---

[88] Incorrectly credited to Steven Moffat on screen.
[89] Uncredited.

Doctor: 'Well it worked, didn't it?'
River: 'Basically, you hoped for lightning. That was it?'
Doctor: 'And here we are.'
River: 'We should be burning at the stake right now. It's lucky for you you're pretty.'
Doctor: 'You were in no danger. I knew something would come up.'
River: 'No you didn't!'
Doctor: 'I did! I promise I did!'

CONTINUITY POINTS

- For the Doctor, this minisode almost certainly occurs sometime after 'The Snowmen', as he is wearing his purple Victorian frock coat. For River, it almost certainly takes place at some point during her imprisonment in the Stormcage Containment Facility; underneath her scarf and leather jacket, she has on the same grey dress seen previously in the closing scenes of 'A Good Man Goes to War' (2011).

PRODUCTION NOTES

- This minisode was not broadcast or released online. It was included only as an extra on *The Complete Seventh Series* DVD and Blu-ray box set.

- The script for this minisode was adapted by writer Neil Gaiman from material that he originally wrote for the pre-opening titles sequence of his Series Six episode 'The Doctor's Wife' (2011). That earlier version featured Amy and Rory rather than River, and had to be dropped for budgetary reasons, although it was subsequently adapted into comic-strip form for *Doctor Who: The Brilliant Book 2012* (BBC Books, 2011).

- Gaiman later indicated that he was not unduly put out about the error that saw Steven Moffat incorrectly receive the on-screen credit for 'Rain Gods'. He viewed this as an unintentional *quid pro quo* for the fact that the packaging of the North American editions of *The Complete Seventh Series* DVD and Blu-ray box set mistakenly listed him as the writer of Moffat's episode 'The Name of the Doctor'.

ANALYSIS

Along with the 'First Night' and 'Last Night' minisodes included on *The Complete Sixth Series* DVD and Blu-ray box set, 'Rain Gods' gives a brief opportunity to see on screen – rather than just hear spoken about – the type of escapades that ensue when the Doctor slips away from his companions, temporarily liberates River from the Stormcage Containment Facility and takes her off on a romantic interlude. The chemistry between Matt Smith and Alex Kingston is as great as ever, and the audience is left wishing for more – it would have been fantastic to see them paired up in this way for some complete episodes, rather than just a few minisodes.

The Night of the Doctor (Minisode)

Writer: Steven Moffat
Director: John Hayes

DEBUT TRANSMISSION DETAILS

BBC iPlayer
Date: 14 November 2013.

Duration: 6′ 49″

ADDITIONAL CREDITED CAST

Emma Campbell-Jones (Cass), Clare Higgins (Ohila)

PLOT

A young woman named Cass is trying to send a distress signal from a crashing spaceship, having already teleported off her fellow crew members. The eighth Doctor arrives on board in the TARDIS and offers to rescue her, but she refuses on learning that he is a Time Lord, disgustedly telling him to get back to his battlefield. The ship crashes on the planet Karn, and the Doctor and Cass are both killed. However, the Sisterhood of Karn temporarily revive the Doctor, and offer him a chance to regenerate using their Elixir of Eternal Life, which will allow him to choose his next incarnation's characteristics. The Sisterhood's leader Ohila insists that he cannot ignore the Time War forever, and he eventually agrees to become a warrior. He drinks from the goblet Ohila gives him, and regenerates into the young War Doctor.

QUOTE, UNQUOTE

- **Doctor:** 'I'm a Doctor. But probably not the one you're expecting.'

- **Doctor:** 'I'm not part of the war. I swear to you, I never was.'
  Cass: 'You're a Time Lord.'
  Doctor: 'Yes, I'm a Time Lord, but I'm one of the nice ones.'
  Cass: 'Get away from me!'
  Doctor: 'Well, look on the bright side. I'm not a Dalek.'
  Cass: 'Who can tell the difference anymore?'

- **Doctor:** 'It's not my war. I will have no part of it.'
  Ohila: 'You can't ignore it forever.'
  Doctor: 'I help where I can. I will not fight.'
  Ohila: 'Because you are the good man, as you call yourself?'
  Doctor: 'I call myself the Doctor.'
  Ohila: 'It's the same thing in your mind.'
  Doctor: 'I'd like to think so.'

CONTINUITY POINTS

- The planet Karn, its Sisterhood and their Elixir of Life first featured in 'The Brain of Morbius' (1976). The New Adventures novel *Time's Crucible: Cat's Cradle* (Virgin Books, 1990) established that the Sisterhood are descended from the Pythias who once ruled ancient Gallifrey. The eighth Doctor's life was previously saved by them when he visited Karn at a later point in its own history in the two-part audio drama 'Sisters of the Flame' / 'The Vengeance of Morbius' (Big Finish, 2008).

- As established in 'The Brain of Morbius', the Sisterhood's Elixir is used by the Time Lords on occasion, such as 'when … there's some difficulty in regenerating a body'. Ohila tells the Doctor, 'Our Elixir can trigger your regeneration, bring you back. Time Lord science is elevated here on Karn. The change doesn't have to be random. Fat or thin, young or old, man or woman?' The Time Lords previously gave the second Doctor a degree of choice over the appearance of his next incarnation when they sentenced him to exile on Earth with a new body in 'The War Games' (1969).

- Ohila also tells the Doctor, 'The war between the Daleks and the Time Lords threatens all reality. You are the only hope left.'

- Before regenerating, the Doctor recalls his friends and companions, including five of those from the Big Finish audio dramas: Charley, C'rizz, Lucie, Tamsin and Molly.

- The eighth Doctor's last words are 'Physician, heal thyself,' a well-known phrase originating from Luke 4:23 in the King James version of the Bible, and the War Doctor's first are 'Doctor no more.'

PRODUCTION NOTES

- This minisode was initially made available on the BBC iPlayer and the BBC YouTube channel on 14 November 2013 – coincidentally, Paul McGann's birthday. Two days later, it was also added to the BBC Red Button service. The release had originally been planned for several days later, but it was brought forward as the BBC feared that the secret of McGann's surprise reappearance as the Doctor was about to leak to the public. The minisode was subsequently given its debut commercial release as an extra on 'The Day of the Doctor' DVD and Blu-ray discs.

- The minisode was recorded wholly at BBC Roath Lock, on 7 and 8 May 2013.

- The young War Doctor is represented by an image taken from John Hurt's appearance in the BBC's classic series *I, Claudius* (1976).

ANALYSIS

Although less than seven minutes long, 'The Night of the Doctor' rates as one of the most remarkable stories in *Doctor Who*'s long history. Devised in order to show how John Hurt's War Doctor came into being, clarify the position he occupies in the Doctor's personal timeline and explain why he does not use the name 'Doctor', it meets all of those objectives and then some. The result is a fantastic piece of drama that successfully achieves the difficult balancing act of using established *Doctor Who* continuity in a way that long-time fans of the show will find thrilling, but less committed viewers will also be able to understand and appreciate. The script is word-perfect, and it is no great surprise to learn that Steven Moffat has since spoken of it as being his own personal favourite of all those he has written for the show. John Hayes' direction is faultless, too, and the supporting performances by Emma Campbell-Jones as Cass and Clare Higgins as Ohila are both excellent. But the absolute star of the show is the seemingly ageless Paul McGann, making a surprise return as the eighth Doctor – something that many fans had been clamouring to see ever since his one and only previous on-screen appearance in the 1996 TV movie. His wonderful performance here is utterly compelling, demonstrating once again what a crying shame it is that he has never had a full television run as the Doctor to go alongside his many superb contributions to Big Finish's ranges of *Doctor Who* audio dramas. One can only sincerely hope that this will not prove to be the last time we get to see him in the show itself; but if it does, he could scarcely have bowed out on a higher note.

The Day of the Doctor

Writer: Steven Moffat
Director: Nick Hurran

DEBUT TRANSMISSION DETAILS

BBC One/BBC One HD
Date: 23 November 2013. Scheduled time: 7.50 pm. Actual time: 7.50 pm.

Duration: 76′ 38″

ADDITIONAL CREDITED CAST

Christopher Eccleston, Paul Mcgann, Sylvester Mccoy, Colin Baker, Peter Davison, Tom Baker, Patrick Troughton, William Hartnell (The Doctor), Tristan Beint (Tom), Jemma Redgrave (Kate Stewart[90]), Ingrid Oliver (Osgood), Chris Finch (Time Lord Soldier), Peter de Jersey (Androgar), Ken Bones (The General), Philip Buck (Arcadia Father), Sophie Morgan-Price (Time Lord), Joanna Page (Elizabeth I), Orlando James (Lord Bentham), Jonjo O'Neill (Mcgillop), Tom Keller (Atkins), Aidan Cook (Zygon), Nicholas Briggs (Voice of the Daleks & Zygons), Barnaby Edwards (Dalek 1), Nicholas Pegg (Dalek 2), John Guilor (Voice-Over Artist)

Daleks created by Terry Nation
Zygons created by Robert Banks Stewart
The Cybermen created by Kit Pedler & Gerry Davis

---

[90] Full name 'Kate Lethbridge-Stewart'.

PLOT

Clara is teaching in a new job at Coal Hill School in Shoreditch when she is summoned to meet the Doctor. She travels by motorbike to the TARDIS, which is then grabbed by a UNIT helicopter and, with the Doctor left dangling from its base, airlifted to Trafalgar Square. There the Doctor and Clara are met by UNIT's Kate Stewart and taken into the National Gallery, where in a secret Under-Gallery some mysterious figures have broken out of a 3D Gallifreyan painting, which actually holds a frozen moment of time. Meanwhile, on Gallifrey, the War Doctor decides that the devastating last great Time War between his people and the Daleks can continue 'No more'. He steals the Moment, an immensely powerful sentient weapon, from the Omega Arsenal and takes it to a barn-like building where he prepares to use it to destroy both sides in the conflict. However, manifesting in the Bad Wolf form of Rose Tyler, the Moment sends both the eleventh Doctor and the War Doctor to join the tenth Doctor in England, 1562, where he has just become engaged to Queen Elizabeth I in a mistaken attempt to expose her as a shape-shifting Zygon – which, it turns out, was actually disguised as his horse. The three Doctors are imprisoned by the Queen in the Tower of London, where they are joined by Clara, who has travelled back in time using Captain Jack Harkness's vortex manipulator, obtained from UNIT's Black Archive below the 21st Century Tower of London. They learn that the Zygons intend to invade the 21st Century by concealing themselves as figures in the Gallifreyan painting until the time is right to emerge. After the tenth Doctor has kept his promise to marry the Queen, the three Doctors and Clara use another Gallifreyan painting, entitled either *Gallifrey Falls* or *No More*, to follow the Zygons. They emerge in the Black Archive, where the Zygons have duplicated Kate and her colleagues and are trying to gain control of the dangerous alien artefacts stored there. Kate is prepared to destroy the whole of London with a nuclear warhead to prevent this from happening, but the Doctors activate the building's inbuilt memory filters so that the UNIT team and their Zygon duplicates no longer know which of the two they are, and are thus forced to negotiate with each other. The Moment then transports the War Doctor back to the barn on Gallifrey, and has the tenth and eleventh Doctors join him there. The three are about to join forces to activate the Moment when the eleventh Doctor announces that, having had 400 years to think about it, he has come up with a different plan. Enlisting the aid of all of their other incarnations in their respective TARDISes, the Doctors attempt to make Gallifrey disappear by placing it in a parallel pocket universe, akin to freezing it in one of the 3D paintings. The Daleks that have been firing on the planet then inadvertently destroy themselves. The eleventh Doctor bids farewell to the War Doctor and the tenth Doctor in the Under-Gallery, but is then joined by the Curator, an elderly man resembling the fourth Doctor, who tells him that the Gallifreyan painting is actually called *Gallifrey Falls No More* – confirming that the Doctors succeeded in their plan to save the planet.

QUOTE, UNQUOTE

- **War Doctor:** 'Ow!'
  The Moment: 'What's wrong?'
  War Doctor: 'The interface is hot.'
  The Moment: 'Well, I do my best.'
  War Doctor: 'There's a power source inside … You're the interface?'
  The Moment: 'They must have told you the Moment had a conscience. Hello! Oh, look at you. Stuck between a girl and a box. Story of your life, eh, Doctor?'

- **Queen Elizabeth:** 'These Zygon creatures never even considered that it was me who survived rather than their own commander. The arrogance that typifies their kind.'
  Clara: 'Zygons?'
  Queen Elizabeth: 'Men.'
  Clara: 'And you actually killed one of them?'
  Queen Elizabeth: 'I may have the body of a weak and feeble woman, but at the time, so did the Zygon.'

- **War Doctor:** 'You're about to murder millions of people.'
  Kate: 'To save billions. How many times have you made that calculation?'
  Eleventh Doctor: 'Once. Turned me into the man I am now. I'm not even sure who that is anymore.'
  Tenth Doctor: 'You tell yourself it's justified, but it's a lie. Because what I did that day was wrong. Just wrong.'
  Eleventh Doctor: 'And because I got it wrong, I'm going to make you get it right.'

- Clara: 'The Doctor … my Doctor … he's always talking about the day

he did it. The day he wiped out the Time Lords to stop the war.'
War Doctor: 'One would.'
Clara: 'You wouldn't. Because you haven't done it yet. It's still in your future.'
War Doctor: 'You're very sure of yourself.'
Clara: 'He regrets it. I see it in his eyes every day. He'd do anything to change it.'
War Doctor: 'Including saving all these people. How many worlds has his regret saved, do you think? Look over there. Humans and Zygons working together in peace. How did you know?'
Clara: 'Your eyes. You're so much younger.'
War Doctor: 'Then, all things considered, it's time I grew up. I've seen all I needed. The moment has come.'

CONTINUITY POINTS

- The Coal Hill School signboard indicates that the Chairman of the Board of Governors is 'I Chesterton' and the Headmaster is 'W Coburn'. The former of these is Ian Chesterton, companion to the first Doctor, who was once a science master at the school. The latter is possibly Wendy Coburn, who was a Coal Hill School classmate of the Doctor's grand-daughter Susan in the spring of 1963, as recounted in the novella *Time and Relative* (Telos Publishing, 2001) – although, if so, it is surprising she is not described as 'Headmistress' or 'Head Teacher'. (The surname 'Coburn' pays homage to Anthony Coburn, the writer of the first televised *Doctor Who* story, '100,000 BC' (1963).) Coal Hill School was first established as being in Coal Hill Road, Shoreditch, in 'Remembrance of the Daleks' (1988) – although fans had previously speculated that Shoreditch was its location, based in part on the area of London seen in an aerial view on the TARDIS scanner screen as it departs from I M Foreman's nearby scrapyard at the end of the very first episode, 'An Unearthly Child' (1963). The school emblem seen on the signboard in 'The Day of the Doctor' is virtually identical to the one seen on the equivalent signboard in 'Remembrance of the Daleks', consisting of a white shield bearing a red cross, with a dragon to either side of it.

- Clara appears to be teaching her class at Coal Hill School until around 5.15 pm, almost two hours later than most London secondary schools finish. This suggests that the school day may be longer in the *Doctor Who* universe than in ours, or that Clara's pupils were being kept later than usual for some reason, or that the clock on which the time is seen is broken. When the TARDIS is airlifted to Trafalgar Square, after Clara has travelled to it by motorbike, it is still daylight, so if it is later than 5.15 pm, it must be summertime.

- The 21st Century sequences are not dated on screen, although from Clara's perspective they clearly occur later than the 10 April 2013 scenes in 'The Name of the Doctor'. It generally takes four years to become a teacher – a three-year degree course plus a one-year teacher training course – but as Clara is in her late twenties by 2013, she could well have achieved that qualification when she was younger, before she started working as a nanny – so the fact that she is now in a new teaching job gives no clue as to exactly how much time has passed. Given that she looks hardly any older than in 'The Name of the Doctor', the likelihood is that, for her, 'The Day of the Doctor' takes place around the summer of 2013, or possibly the following year. If so, Kate Stewart is around 48 years old at this point[91], and the events of 'The Power of Three', set around 2021, still lie some eight years in her future. This implies that, although 'The Day of the Doctor' is not the eleventh Doctor's first meeting with Kate, it is her first meeting with him. Some support for this can perhaps be found in the formal way she greets him, apologising for having effectively hijacked him in the TARDIS: 'Doctor, as Chief Scientific Officer, may I extend the official apologies of UNIT.' The corollary of this is that in 'The Power of Three', when she gives the impression of not having encountered the Doctor before, she is being misleading. The most likely explanation for this is that she realises he is at an earlier point in his timeline than when she has met him previously, and pretends she does not know him so as (like River Song) to avoid giving away 'spoilers' about his future. 'The Day of the Doctor' establishes that she has researched the Doctor's history and even effectively vetted some of his companions, so the fact that in 'The Power of Three' he is with Amy and Rory, and is wearing his original outfit complete with tweed jacket, would reveal to her that

---

[91] The same age as actress Jemma Redgrave when 'The Day of the Doctor' was recorded.

he has yet to experience the events of the attempted Zygon invasion, which she has already lived through. This might be why, on first seeing him in 'The Power of Three', she immediately comments on his 'dress sense'.

- Clara, like the Doctor, can now close the TARDIS doors with a snap of her fingers.

- As seen in previous stories, starting with 'The Christmas Invasion' (2005), UNIT's London base is beneath the Tower of London.

- When the Doctor calls Kate Stewart's personal mobile phone, the ringtone is the TARDIS materialisation noise. Presumably the Doctor obtained her number when he met her, eight years or so in her future, in 'The Power of Three'.

- UNIT regularly use the illusions performed by celebrity magician Derren Brown as a cover story for their activities.

- *Gallifrey Falls No More* holds a frozen slice of time from the fall of Gallifrey's second city, Arcadia. Regarding the painting, the eleventh Doctor says: 'I've had many faces, many lives. I don't admit to all of them. There's one life I've tried very hard to forget. He was the Doctor who fought in the Time War, and that was the day he did it. The day I did it. The day he killed them all. The last day of the Time War. The war to end all wars, between my people and the Daleks. And in that battle there was a man with more blood on his hands than any other, a man who would commit a crime that would silence the universe. And that man was me.' The fact that Clara has to ask about the War Doctor indicates that she does not fully recall what occurred when she entered the Doctor's timestream at the end of 'The Name of the Doctor'. Later, the eleventh Doctor says of his predecessors, 'You've met them before. Don't you remember?', and she replies, 'A bit.'

- The General and Androgar are members of the Gallifrey High Command, also referred to by the first Doctor as the War Council of Gallifrey. When they are first seen entering the War Room, from where they clearly co-ordinate all Time Lord military action,

Androgar notes, 'The High Council is in emergency session. They have plans of their own.' This refers to events depicted in 'The End of Time' Part Two (2010), the Gallifrey sequences of which are contemporaneous with those of 'The Day of the Doctor'. In that earlier episode, the Time Lord President, Rassilon, asks, 'What news of the Doctor?' A Time Lord replies, 'Disappeared, my Lord President,' and a Time Lady adds, 'But we know his intention. He still possesses the Moment. And he'll use it, to destroy Daleks and Time Lords alike.' In 'The Day of the Doctor', it is revealed that the Doctor obtains the Moment from the Omega Arsenal of forbidden weapons, in the sealed Time Vaults. Like Rassilon, Omega was one of the founders of Time Lord society, as revealed in 'The Three Doctors' (1972/73).

- The General describes the Moment as, 'The galaxy eater. The final work of the ancients of Gallifrey. A weapon so powerful, the operating system became sentient. According to legend, it developed a conscience.' The Moment's interface manifests as the Bad Wolf version of Rose Tyler especially for the Doctor's benefit, drawing her face and form from his future. This may perhaps help to explain why the ninth Doctor is immediately drawn to Rose when he later meets her.

- The Moment says that the Doctor's punishment for destroying Gallifrey, and killing all of its children in the process, is that he will survive the event. She offers to show him what he will become, telling him 'I'm opening windows on your future. A tangle in time through the days to come, to the man today will make of you.'

- The tenth Doctor says that he is 904 years old. From his perspective, the events of 'The Day of the Doctor' probably take place shortly before those of 'The End of Time' Part One (2009), as at the start of that episode he implies that he has recently married Queen Elizabeth I. He has presumably formed an intimate relationship with the Queen by the time we see them enjoying their picnic together in 1562, as he also implies in 'The End of Time' Part One that she is no longer 'the Virgin Queen', and this is essentially confirmed in 'The Beast Below' (2010), and also alluded to here when he says, 'The Virgin Queen? So much for history.' They have certainly been together long enough for them to have had a joint oil portrait painted of them, as seen covering the entrance to the Under-Gallery in the 21st Century. The fact that he runs out on her immediately after their wedding ceremony would explain why she is so angry with him when she sees him 37 years later at the end of 'The Shakespeare Code' (2007).

- It is unclear how Queen Elizabeth comes to have the painting *Gallifrey Falls No More*, and how she comes to write the letter that she leaves to be received by the Doctor in the 21st Century, reading: 'My dearest love, I hope the painting known as *Gallifrey Falls* will serve as proof that it is your Elizabeth who writes to you now. You will recall that you pledged yourself to the safety of my kingdom. In this capacity, I have appointed you as curator of the Under-Gallery, where deadly danger to England is locked away. Should any disturbance occur within its walls, it is my wish that you be summoned.' The Doctors recognise *Gallifrey Fall No More* (although they do not realise that is its full title), but are puzzled as to how it has ended up in the Under-Gallery. The implication seems to be that this has all been arranged by their later (or possibly alternative) incarnation referred to as the Curator, who says of the painting, 'I acquired it in remarkable circumstances.'

- Kate says of the Under-Gallery, 'This is where Elizabeth I kept all art deemed too dangerous for public consumption.'

- Kate phones her colleague Malcolm – probably UNIT scientific advisor Malcolm Taylor, as seen in 'Planet of the Dead' (2009) – and tells him, 'I need you to send me one of my father's incident files, code-named Cromer. '70s or '80s, depending on the dating protocol.' The file in question presumably relates to the events of 'The Three Doctors', when Kate's father Brigadier Lethbridge-Stewart initially believed that UNIT headquarters had been transported to the coastal town of Cromer in Norfolk, although in fact it had passed through a black hole to the antimatter domain of Omega. When Clara subsequently says, 'I think there's three of [the Doctors] now,' Kate replies, 'There's a precedent for that.' The "70s or '80s' comment is an in-joke reference alluding to a long-standing controversy within *Doctor Who* fandom as to whether the UNIT stories of the third

Doctor's era are set in the 1970s or the 1980s. As discussed in detail in previous books in this series, the reason for this controversy is hard to fathom, as the overwhelming weight of on-screen evidence clearly supports a 1970s dating – not least the fact that 'Mawdryn Undead' (1983) explicitly establishes that Brigadier Lethbridge-Stewart is retired from UNIT by 1977. One of the very few pieces of evidence advanced in support of their case by those fans who favour a 1980s dating – that Sarah Jane Smith says in 'Pyramids of Mars' (1975) that she comes from 1980 – actually points to a 1970s dating, as this occurs several years later in her timeline than her initial meeting with the third Doctor in 'The Time Warrior' (1973/74), which must therefore be set several years prior to 1980.

- Staff at UNIT's Black Archive beneath the Tower of London have their memories wiped at the end of each shift, as a security measure. There are automated memory filters built into the walls and ceiling. The place is sealed by lock and key, rather than by electronic means, as a measure to try to keep the Doctor out, as he would not approve of the collection of dangerous alien artefacts held there. Kate (or rather, as it later transpires, her Zygon duplicate) tells Clara, 'The whole Tower is TARDIS-proofed.' It is unclear exactly how this has been achieved, although the eleventh Doctor later attributes it to 'Alien technology plus human stupidity.' Zygon-Kate adds that Clara herself has a 'top-level security rating' from her last visit – which Clara does not remember, owing to a memory wipe – and that UNIT screen all of the Doctor's known associates, to prevent information about him and the TARDIS from 'falling into the wrong hands'.

- In the event of alien incursion, a nuclear warhead positioned twenty feet beneath the Black Archive can be used to self-destruct the place in five minutes. The warhead is keyed to Kate's voice-print.

- The Black Archive contains a noticeboard to which are pinned photographs of many of the Doctor's past companions, including his grand-daughter Susan, Ian Chesterton, Barbara Wright, Sara Kingdom (pictured with UNIT's Captain Mike Yates), Polly, Ben Jackson, Victoria Waterfield, Zoe Heriot, Nyssa, Kamelion, Rose Tyler (pictured with UNIT's Captain Magambo) and Martha Jones. It is unclear in exactly what circumstances each of these photographs was taken.

- Captain Jack Harkness is said to have bequeathed his vortex manipulator to the UNIT Archive 'on the occasion of his death – well, one of them'. This is an allusion to the fact that Captain Jack is immortal, as established in 'The Parting of the Ways' (2005).

- The tenth Doctor says that there were 2.47 billion children on Gallifrey when the Time War was ended.

- When Osgood is duplicated by a Zygon, the only thing not copied is the inhaler she uses to treat her asthma.

- After they have been duplicated by the Zygons, Osgood finds Kate still alive but draped in Zygon-like tendrils. 'Those creatures, they turn themselves into copies,' she says. 'And they need to keep the original alive; refresh the image, so to speak.' This fact was first established in 'Terror of the Zygons', where it was stated that the body-print needed to be renewed 'every few hours', and the human originals had to remain connected to the Zygons' equipment in order for this to happen.

- Having discovered the Zygons' plans, Queen Elizabeth says, 'The Zygons lost their own world. It burnt in the first days of the Time War. A new home is required.'

- It is unclear if the Zygons featured in 'The Day of the Doctor' and those seen in 'Terror of the Zygons' are all part of the same group, or if they came to Earth separately. Those in 'Terror of the Zygons' reveal that their spaceship crash-landed in Loch Ness 'centuries' before that story's mid-1970s setting, so it certainly possible that over the course of those centuries some of them spread out across Great Britain, or even more widely across the world. On the other hand, those in 'The Day of the Doctor' do appear to possess more advanced duplication techniques, and in 1562 they already know what has become of their world – named in the Eighth Doctor Adventures novel *The Bodysnatchers* (BBC Books, 1997) as Zygor – whereas those in 'Terror of the Zygons' have only 'recently' learned that it 'was destroyed in a stellar explosion'. The spaceship seen in 'Terror of the Zygons' is certainly not the only Zygon craft to have reached Earth, as is evident from *The Bodysnatchers* and various other tie-in stories, such as the audio drama 'The Barnacled Baby' (BBV Productions, 2001) and the tenth Doctor novel *Sting of the Zygons* (BBC Books, 2007).

- On seeing a Zygon enter one of the 3D paintings, the War Doctor explains, 'It's not a picture, it's a stasis cube. Time Lord art. Frozen instants in time, bigger on the inside, but could be deployed as –' The tenth Doctor then completes the sentence, saying, '– suspended animation! Oh, that's very good. The Zygons all pop inside the pictures, wait a few centuries till the planet's a bit more interesting, and then out they come.' It is unclear how the stasis cubes happen to be in Elizabethan England. Possibly the tenth Doctor gave them to Queen Elizabeth as a present, or possibly the Zygons acquired them from the Time Lords before their planet was destroyed in the Time War.

- Kate tells her Zygon duplicate, 'Somewhere in your memory is a man called Brigadier Alistair Gordon Lethbridge-Stewart. I am his daughter.' Given that a Zygon from 1562 could have no personal knowledge of events involving the Brigadier in the mid-1970s, she is presumably referring here to the memory it has acquired from her. 'Terror of the Zygons' established that the Zygons do take on not only the physical form of those they duplicate, but also at least some aspects of their memory, and 'The Day of the Doctor' explicitly confirms this when Osgood's Zygon duplicate taunts her, 'Ooo, you've got some perfectly horrible memories in here, haven't you? So jealous of your pretty sister. I don't blame you. I wish I'd copied her.' In the independent video drama 'Zygon: When Being You Just Isn't Enough' (BBV Productions, 2008), it is indicated that a Zygon duplicate has a telepathic link with the mind of its human original.

- The Black Archive contains the Space-Time Telegraph that the fourth Doctor gave as a gift to Brigadier Lethbridge-Stewart, as established in 'Revenge of the Cybermen' (1975). The eleventh Doctor describes this as a 'hotline straight to the TARDIS'.

- On their arrival in the barn-like building on Gallifrey, the tenth Doctor tells the eleventh Doctor and Clara, 'These events are time-locked. We shouldn't even be here.' This is in line with what has been established in previous episodes, such as 'The Stolen Earth' (2008).

- The Doctors adapt one of the stasis cubes used in the creation of the 3D Time Lord art to try to achieve a situation where Gallifrey is, as the tenth Doctor puts it, 'Frozen in an instant of time, safe and hidden away.' The War Doctor elaborates that the planet will be, 'Held in a parallel pocket universe.' This is presumably akin to the pocket universe seen in 'Hide'. The twelfth Doctor joins all of his predecessors in their collaboration to execute this plan, although it is unclear if they are aware of his involvement.

- The War Doctor realises that he won't remember that he tried to save Gallifrey rather than destroy it. The eleventh Doctor confirms this: 'The timestreams are out of sync. You can't retain it, no.'

- The eleventh Doctor tells the tenth, 'I saw Trenzalore. Where we're buried. We die in battle among millions ... That's how the story ends. Nothing we can do about it. Trenzalore is where you're going.' The tenth Doctor's parting words are, 'I don't want to go' – the same as his last words in 'The End of Time' Part Two.

- The Curator says that Gallifrey is 'lost ... perhaps', and tells the eleventh Doctor that he has a lot to do, prompting him to ask, 'Is that what I'm supposed to do now? Go looking for Gallifrey?' The Curator replies, 'Well, it's entirely up to you. Your choice, eh? I can only tell you what I would do if. I were you ... Ah, if I were you! Oh, perhaps I was you, of course. Or perhaps, you are me ... Or perhaps it doesn't matter either way. Who knows, eh? Who knows?'

- The special ends with what appears to be a dream sequence, as the eleventh Doctor emerges from the TARDIS to stand on a cloud with all of the previous Doctors (including the War Doctor), while speaking the following monologue: 'Clara sometimes asks me if I dream. "Of course I dream," I tell her. "Everybody dreams." "But what do you dream about," she'll ask. "The same thing everybody dreams about," I tell her. "I dream about where I'm going." She always laughs at that. "But you're not going anywhere. You're just wandering about." That's not true. Not any more. I have a new destination. My journey is the same as yours, the same as anyone's. It's taken me so many years, so many lifetimes, but at last I know where I'm going. Where I've always been going. Home. The long way round.'

PRODUCTION NOTES

- 'The Day of the Doctor' was made as a one-off special, and was the first *Doctor Who* story ever to be recorded and transmitted in stereoscopic 3D. (The 1993 *Children in Need* skit 'Dimensions in Time' had made use of a different, more rudimentary 3D system developed by American inventor Terry D Beard. Relying on the so-called Pulfrich effect, this worked only so long as the camera showed lateral motion, and required the viewer to wear spectacles with one darkened lens and one transparent one.)

- From this story onwards, Jenna-Louise Coleman chose to be credited simply as Jenna Coleman.

- Location work got under way on 2 April 2013 in the grounds of the Ivy Tower in Tonna, Neath, for the sequence of the tenth Doctor and Queen Elizabeth I having their picnic interrupted by a Zygon. Two days later, Gelligaer Common in Fochriiw, Merthyr was the venue for taping of the scene where Clara enters the TARDIS on her motorbike – Jenna Coleman being doubled for this by a stunt rider – and for that of the police box then being picked up by the UNIT helicopter. MOD St Athan in St Athan, Barry was used on 6 April for some green-screen effects work. On 8 April, shots involving Coleman, along with Jemma Redgrave as Kate Stewart and Ingrid Oliver as Osgood, were recorded in London by Tower Bridge and outside the Tower of London. The following day, the brief London shoot for the special was completed with the sequence of the TARDIS being deposited in Trafalgar Square, near the entrance to the National Gallery. Returning to Wales, the crew spent the next three days at MOD Caerwent in Monmouthshire for taping of the Elizabethan-era woodland scenes where the three Doctors first come together. On 15 April, the National Museum of Wales in Cardiff was used to represent the National Gallery for some further exteriors of the building and a few interiors. Scenes in the War Doctor's and the tenth Doctor's TARDIS console rooms were taped on 16 April using set elements from the standing exhibits at the *Doctor Who Experience* attraction, within walking distance of BBC Roath Lock. Chepstow Castle in Chepstow, Monmouthshire was used on 17 April for scenes taking place at the Elizabethan-era Tower of London, including the tenth Doctor's wedding to Queen Elizabeth I. The Coal Hill School exteriors were taped on 2 May on Cwmdare Street in Cardiff, with Jenna Coleman again doubled by a stunt rider for the sequence where Clara sets off on her motorbike and passes through a tunnel, represented by Butetown Tunnel on the A4232 road. On the same day, the Coal Hill School interiors were recorded at Gladstone Primary School in Whitchurch Road, Cathays, Cardiff. Lastly, from 3 to 5 May, Mamhilad Park Industrial Estate in Pontypool was used for scenes of the fall of Arcadia. Studio recording took place at BBC Roath Lock on various dates between 28 March and 2 May, with a pick-up shot of Peter Capaldi's Doctor being taped later, on 3 October.

- Two further humorous 'Strax Field Report' videos were released online to promote 'The Day of the Doctor'. The first, on 7 November 2013, was entitled 'The Zygons', ran for 58" and had Strax reporting to Sontar about the Zygons' ambitions to take over the Earth using their shape-shifting powers. The second, on 17 November, was called 'Queen Elizabeth', had a 47" duration and saw Strax relaying intelligence about a forthcoming meeting between the Doctor and the Queen.

- A prequel to 'The Day of the Doctor' was released on the BBC iPlayer on 21 November 2013. Entitled 'The Last Day', this had a 3' 42" duration, was written by Steven Moffat, directed by Jamie Stone and produced by Denise Paul. It was recorded at BBC Roath Lock on 9 May 2013 and featured three uncredited cast members: Chris Finch (Time Lord Soldier), Barry Aird (Edogar) and Alan Gill (New Recruit). The action opens with a Time Lord army new recruit – Gill's character – being fitted with a head-cam, being briefed by an officer – Aird's character, unnamed on screen – and then taking up duty as part of the Arcadia defence force. He and a colleague – Finch's character, also seen in 'The Day of the Doctor' itself – are monitoring the skies when first one Dalek and then a whole host of them breach the supposedly impenetrable array of 400 sky-trenches and fly in to attack. A Dalek exterminates the new recruit. This prequel was subsequently given its debut commercial release as an extra on 'The Day of the Doctor' DVD and Blu-ray discs.

- Matt Smith and Jenna Coleman recorded a 38" radio advert for the special, which was played on various BBC radio stations in the run-up to transmission.

- When transmitted at 7.50 pm on 23 November 2013, 'The Day of the Doctor' was simulcast in 94 countries and given 3D cinema screenings in over 1,500 theatres worldwide. The simulcast was an unprecedented achievement subsequently recognised in the famous *Guinness World Records* book. A certificate to this effect was presented to Steven Moffat on 24 November at the official *Doctor Who* Celebration event in London by the book's editor in chief, Craig Glenday, who was quoted as saying: 'Who else but the time-twisting Doctor could appear in 94 countries at once? This outstanding achievement is testament to the fact that the longest-running sci-fi TV show in history is not just a well-loved UK institution but a truly global success adored by millions of people.' In the UK, the special's cinema screenings generated takings of £1.7 million at the box office, giving it third place in the week's chart, behind only the Hollywood blockbusters *The Hunger Games: Catching Fire* (£12.2 million) and *Gravity* (£2.4 million). The US box office takings totalled $4.8 million.

- Most of the worldwide cinema screenings were preceded by two short videos – which, like the cinema version of the anniversary special itself, were subtitled in appropriate languages in non-English-speaking territories. The first, running 4' 03", has Strax briefing the audience on proper cinema viewing etiquette, including turning their 'communications devices' to silent, maintaining 'a minimum volume during the consumption of fluids and nutrition packs', and avoiding the criminal use of 'recording equipment'. On learning, to his horror, that the movie is not about the campaigns fought by his predecessors Linx, Staal and Storr, but about the

Doctor, Strax hurriedly informs his assembled clone batch that this is a drill to test their resolve. The second video, of 3' 17" duration, features the tenth and eleventh Doctors, with a brief appearance by the War Doctor standing with his back to them at the end, and essentially serves the purpose of getting the audience to put on and become familiar with their 3D viewing spectacles. These videos were subsequently released as extras on the *50th Anniversary Collector's Edition* DVD and Blu-ray box set.

- In some territories, transmission of 'The Day of the Doctor' was preceded by a video entitled 'A Message from Strax'. Lasting 18", this has the Sontaran interrupting the audience's social media use and instructing them, 'Stop Tweeting and watch the movie, you pitiful human scum'. This has not received a commercial release.

- On the day of transmission, the BBC placed online and on its YouTube account a deleted scene from 'The Day of the Doctor'. With a running time of 18", this shows the three Doctors in 1562, being led in chains to the gates of the Tower of London, where they are to be imprisoned. The tenth Doctor disputes the eleventh's assertion that his shoes 'bring the cool', while the War Doctor bemoans the fact that his successors have not stopped talking 'since Richmond'. This scene has not been released commercially.

- Steven Moffat originally wrote 'The Day of the Doctor' to feature the ninth, tenth and eleventh Doctors, but had to replace the ninth with the newly-conceived War Doctor when, after some consideration, Christopher Eccleston declined to return to the part. If Billie Piper had not been available to appear as the Bad Wolf version of Rose Tyler, Moffat's intention was that the Moment would manifest as a younger female child.

- The series' original opening title sequence is used here (in modified and shortened form) for the first time since 'The Moonbase' (1967). This is the first instance in the show's history of an episode using a previously-retired title sequence.

- When Clara leaves Coal Hill School at the start of the story, a clock is seen showing the time as 5.16 – the time when *Doctor Who* began on

23 November 1963. Later, the access code to Captain Jack's vortex manipulator is given as 1716231163 – another reference to that time and date.

- When Clara says to the three Doctors, 'You told me the name you chose was a promise. What was the promise?', the tenth Doctor replies, 'Never cruel or cowardly,' and the War Doctor adds, 'Never give up, never give in.' These phrases were first used in a much-quoted description of the Doctor's character given by Terrance Dicks in the revised second edition of the book *The Making of Doctor Who* (Target Books, 1976).

- The scene where all of the Doctors unite to save Gallifrey incorporates clips from 'The Daleks' (1963/64), 'The Tomb of the Cybermen' (1967), 'Colony in Space' (1971), 'Image of the Fendahl' (1977), 'Frontios' (1984), 'Attack of the Cybermen' (1985), 'Battlefield' (1989), the 1996 TV movie, 'Rose' (2005) and 'The Parting of the Ways' (2005). Audio clips are also used from some of these stories, and from others, including 'Fury from the Deep' (1968) and 'The Five Doctors' (1983).

- 'The Day of the Doctor' features a unique closing title sequence, incorporating images of the faces of all twelve principal actors to have played the Doctor up to this point, including John Hurt.

- Murray Gold composed considerably more original incidental music for this special than was ultimately used, as the production team preferred to reuse music from other 21st Century episodes – such as a passage from 'Aliens of London' / 'World War Three' (2005), heard during the sequence where the Doctor hangs from the base of the TARDIS as it is deposited in Trafalgar Square. Much of the unused music was subsequently included on the Silva Screen double CD release *Original Television Soundtrack: 'The Day of the Doctor' / 'The Time of the Doctor'* (2014).

- The idea of an alternative, elderly version of the fourth Doctor first featured in the script for the ultimately abandoned thirtieth anniversary story 'Lost in the Dark Dimension' in 1993.

OOPS!

- Given that, if Kate Stewart triggers the nuclear warhead beneath the Tower of London, she will be effectively committing suicide, the tenth Doctor's warning 'This is not a decision you will ever be able to live with!' makes little sense. (One can only assume that he is preoccupied with thoughts of how he himself has been impacted by his analogous decision to end the Time War by activating the Moment.)

- When the Doctors inform the Gallifrey High Command that they are going to 'freeze' the planet, Matt Smith's script can be seen lying on the TARDIS console just behind him.

- There are various shot continuity errors in the production. For instance, after the tenth Doctor is kissed by Queen Elizabeth at their wedding ceremony, his collar is up in the first two shots but down in the next; and when, in the closing scenes at the National Gallery, the tenth Doctor asks what the painting of Gallifrey is called, the door to his TARDIS is seen to be open in the background, whereas in shots either side of this it is closed. Also, all CGI shots of the TARDIS exterior feature the eleventh Doctor's version of the police box, complete with St John's Ambulance badge on the right-hand door, even when depicting the earlier Doctors' ships.

CRITICAL REACTION

- 'There were superb performances all round. Current incumbent Matt Smith did his much-loved wacky schtick, while perennial favourite David Tennant brought back all the quips and mannerisms that made us love his Doctor so much. Added into the mix is the legendary John Hurt, whose new take on one of the true stalwarts of television brings class, intelligence and a whole new A-list dimension to the world of *Doctor Who* – a world that surely feels a bit more blessed after today.' Jon Cooper, *Mirror* website, 23 November 2013.

- 'By the end I had so many questions. Is his real name "Never Cruel or Cowardly"? I was hoping for "Graham". Are the Gallifreyan children all right? What does it mean if you fail at doing the right thing as long as you didn't succeed in doing the wrong? "Did you understand that?" I ask the 10-year-old. "Yes. He destroyed Gallifrey. Then he undestroyed it. It was brilliant." Three-year-old: "I think it was happy." From the seven-year-old: single thumb up (note: not double).' Viv Groskop, *Guardian* website, 23 November 2013.

- 'Here, through an alliance of three generations of the Doctor, [the decision to destroy Gallifrey] was reversed. Like the notorious episode of *Dallas* where the previous series turned out to be a dream, this was basically Moffat rewriting *Doctor Who* history, TV history. It seemed a bit rich considering all the emotional mileage the programme has milked out of the Doctor's angst in the past, and somewhat ironic given that rewriting history … is the one thing the Doctor is always telling his companions he can't do. You can't help wonder if Moffat will regret it. Being responsible for a holocaust surely gave the Doctor an added depth and edge. The devastation he inflicted was his burden. Without it, there is a danger he will simply be an eccentric, albeit one who can journey through space and time.' Jim Shelley, *Mail* website, 23 November, 2013.

- 'John Hurt was a fantastic counterpoint to the physicality of Tennant and Smith. With one withering look, he was able to silence his younger selves. "Am I having a mid-life crisis?" he asked with all the bewilderment of a man who, ironically for an alien, had just been confronted with his own mortality. As for the assistants, Jenna Coleman's Clara was touching and Billie Piper was transfixing as the "Bad Wolf" Rose. Less impressive was Joanna Page's Elizabeth I. Perhaps because we have been spoiled by Cate Blanchett's, Helen Mirren's and Glenda Jackson's meaty, cerebral performances, Page's interpretation (complete with slight Welsh accent) felt sketchy and there was no palpable chemistry between her and Tennant. "You're just a bad copy," the Doctor told the Virgin Queen, and the viewer had to agree.' Ben Lawrence, *Telegraph* website, 2 December 2013.

ANALYSIS

Sadly, 'The Day of the Doctor' has a great big hole at its heart, and that hole is Christopher Eccleston-shaped. Given that the story was originally conceived as a kind of modern-era take on the classic-era adventure 'The Three Doctors', with the ninth and tenth Doctors teaming up with the eleventh for a celebratory Time Lord epic, Eccleston's unfortunate refusal to take part – which really did him no credit at all – left showrunner Steven Moffat with the same kind of headache that 1980s producer John Nathan-Turner faced when fourth Doctor actor Tom Baker likewise made a late decision not to appear in the twentieth anniversary equivalent, 'The Five Doctors'. (It seems these multi-Doctor anniversary stories are always destined to be one key cast member short: 'The Three Doctors' itself had to be rewritten to give first Doctor actor William Hartnell a greatly diminished role due to his poor health – although he did at least appear.) Short of going back to the drawing board and devising a completely different tale – which was presumably ruled out by time constraints, even if he had been inclined to do so – any work-around that Moffat came up with was bound to be something of a compromise. That said, there was an obvious approach surely staring him in the face, which for some reason he regrettably failed to take: that is, to give the third lead role in the story to Paul McGann's eighth Doctor, of whom the fans had been crying out to see more ever since his wonderful debut appearance in the 1996 TV movie failed to lead on to the hoped-for full series.

It had never been firmly established in preceding stories whether McGann's Doctor or Eccleston's was the one who had ended the last great Time War, so Moffat could very easily have substituted the former for the latter in his script with little other rewriting required. In fact, there were hints in 'Rose' that Eccleston's Doctor was newly regenerated when he first appeared, making it even more plausible that McGann's was the one responsible. And what better way to have demonstrated that the anniversary special was celebrating the whole of *Doctor Who's* glorious fifty-year run than to have had the two latest modern-era Doctors partnered with one of their old-school predecessors? Sadly, it was not to be, and McGann was consigned instead to an all-too-brief return in 'The Night of the Doctor' – the outstanding results of which simply served to confirm what a brilliant, and still sorely underused, Doctor he is.

Having said all this, the idea that Moffat eventually settled upon – of there being a previously-unknown incarnation of the Doctor between the established eighth and ninth – was both ingenious and bold. Ingenious because, in all of the speculation that fans had indulged in over the years about the Doctor's involvement in the events of the Time War, and specifically its ending, this was a possibility that no-one had ever seriously considered before; and bold because it represented quite a radical shake-up of the show's accepted mythology, and one that the audience might have found it hard to take.

Previous stories had given few clues as to what really happened in the Time War, so this was unquestionably legitimate dramatic territory for Moffat to explore – notwithstanding the views previously expressed both by him and by his predecessor Russell T Davies to the effect that the specifics of the conflict were best left to the viewer's imagination. There is also an argument, put forward persuasively by Moffat in subsequent interviews, that it made more sense for the (supposed) double genocide of the Time Lords and the Daleks to have been committed by a newly-conceived War Doctor, specifically primed to be a warrior, than by the McGann incarnation, who seems altogether too gentle in nature to have been responsible for such an atrocity. On the other hand, though, given that 'The Day of the Doctor' is ultimately about the War Doctor's redemption, would it not have been even more affecting to have had an embittered, war-hardened eighth Doctor placed in that position? It does seem rather odd that a story explicitly designed to celebrate *Doctor Who*'s remarkable history should effectively tear up and rewrite a significant part of that history.

Fortunately, by having the new incarnation eschew the use of the name 'Doctor', Moffat did at least cleverly avoid throwing out the numbering of the established Doctors – which would have created no end of problems in merchandising terms, not to mention confusion for fans and others trying to discuss and write about the show. Thankfully, the Matt Smith incarnation can still be referred to as 'the eleventh Doctor' – a term explicitly used by Clara herself in 'The Name of the Doctor' – without any great risk of misunderstanding. The introduction of the War Doctor also had the incidental benefit of opening up the potential for a whole host of exciting new tie-in stories to be written about this previously unsuspected chapter in the Time Lord's history. The real masterstroke, though, was the choice of highly distinguished actor John Hurt to fill the role. It generally takes the viewing public a little time to get used to and accept a new Doctor, so whoever was chosen for this part was going to face an uphill struggle to engage their immediate interest in the plight of an incarnation they had never seen or even heard of before (save for the enigmatic cameo at the end of 'The Name of the Doctor' and, for those who had watched it, the fleeting post-regeneration appearance in 'The Night of the Doctor'). Few actors could have made as instant an impact as Hurt, who turns in a superb performance as an older, battle-weary version of the Time Lord. He is particularly impressive in his compelling scenes opposite the always excellent Billie Piper – a very worthy addition to the special's cast, sensibly given a role that allows her to portray a kind of alternative version of Rose Tyler without further disturbing that iconic character's legacy – and, all things considered, he just about manages to pull off this difficult task.

It is really pushing things a step too far, though, when Moffat introduces, at the end of the story, yet another previously unseen and unknown incarnation of the Doctor, played by Tom Baker. It is left somewhat ambiguous whether this Curator is an elderly version of the fourth Doctor, perhaps from some different timestream or parallel universe, or whether he is a future incarnation who simply happens to look like an elderly version of the fourth Doctor. The latter is the explanation most strongly hinted at; but, in the end, any attempt at rationalisation is arguably superfluous – or, as the Curator himself puts it, 'Perhaps it doesn't matter either way.' What we really have here is not the current Doctor meeting another incarnation, past or future, but the current Doctor meeting Tom Baker. It could be said to be the most blatant fourth-wall-breaking moment since the first Doctor turned to camera and wished viewers at home a Happy Christmas at the end of the 1965 episode 'The Feast of Steven'. There is not even a hint of Doctorish eccentricity about the clothes Baker is wearing – they could easily be simply what the actor happened to have on when he arrived at the studio.

It is as if, having wisely chosen not to overcrowd the drama by writing in parts for a whole host of the show's surviving classic-era regulars – most of whom, with the passage of time, now understandably look nothing like they did in their heyday – Steven Moffat suddenly realised how unpopular an exclusive modern-era focus would be with many diehard fans and lost his nerve at the last minute. The only level on which Baker's appearance works is that of pure nostalgia – and, to be fair, for some fans that seems to have been more than sufficient justification for it. However, in terms of the show's mythology, it really doesn't make much sense. Is it at all likely that the Doctor might at some point in the future actually 'retire' and content himself with being curator of the National Gallery's secret Under-Gallery? Or is the TARDIS-like patterning seen on the wall in these closing scenes of the story intended to suggest that the Under-Gallery is not really part of the National Gallery at all, but the interior of the Curator's ship? In his own words, 'Who knows?'

The other unfortunate aspect of Tom Baker's inclusion is that it comes across as a snub to the other surviving classic-era Doctors, Peter Davison, Colin Baker and Sylvester McCoy, who had to content themselves with appearing instead in the amusing spoof *The Five(ish) Doctors Reboot*. This impression is perhaps unintentionally reinforced when the Curator speaks of the Doctor revisiting only 'the old favourites' amongst his former faces.

It would, in this author's opinion, have been far better if Tom Baker's appearance had been omitted altogether and the classic-era Doctors' active involvement had been confined to the sequence where – via the use of vintage clips, and a little new dialogue for the first Doctor courtesy of impressionist John Guilor – they help to implement the plan to save Gallifrey.[92] However, even this latter element doesn't work as well as it might. While it is just about possible to accept that, with the aid of the Moment, the Hurt, Tennant and Smith Doctors could enlist the help of their former selves – and even their future, Peter Capaldi incarnation, as seen in a brief but dramatic shot of his eyes – to play a part in events that they will subsequently forget, this overlooks the fact that the first and second Doctors were never able to steer the TARDIS accurately (and some of their successors struggled to do so too), let alone direct it to perform the kind of complex manoeuvres suggested here. Again, this is a case of not so much celebrating the show's history as rewriting it. The sequence is also slightly marred by the fact that the clips of the seventh Doctor featured in it are taken not only from his own era but also from his appearance in the 1996 TV movie, where he looks quite a bit older and has a different costume – producing an awkward inconsistency.

This is all a great pity, as the basic idea of centring a story around the end of the Time War was a very good one. It has always seemed hard to reconcile the appallingly drastic measure the Doctor apparently took then – the total destruction of both the Daleks and his own people the Time Lords – with his established character. In confronting his enemies, he has often maintained that the end never justifies the means, so just how terrible must the Time War have been in order to compel him to go

---

[92] The classic-era Doctors did, after all, have their own celebratory team-up adventure in Big Finish's audio release 'The Light at the End' (2013) (although unfortunately that turned out to be, in this author's estimation, a rare misfire in the usually excellent audio range).

completely against his own long-espoused principles? Fans have often wondered how he could have brought himself to carry out an act that would inevitably have killed any of his own family members who still lived on Gallifrey, not to mention old friends such as his one-time companion Leela, but 'The Day of the Doctor' poses an even more poignant question: what about all the Gallifreyan children?

The key to the story can arguably be found in its very first line of dialogue, when Jenna Coleman as Clara, now in a teaching job, delivers a quote from Marcus Aurelius: 'Waste no more time arguing about what a good man should be. Be one.' This cleverly foreshadows the moral dilemma that the War Doctor and his successors will ultimately face – in which the words 'no more' will take on considerable significance – while also referring back to the discussion in the Series Six episode 'A Good Man Goes to War' (2011) about whether or not the Doctor qualifies as 'a good man'. Moffat's choice of Aurelius to quote from is an interesting one in itself. Emperor of Rome from 161 to 180 AD, he was renowned as both a soldier and a thinker. Many of his beliefs bear a striking similarity to key principles of Buddhism – a philosophy that has had a strong influence on *Doctor Who* over the years – and his treatise *Meditations* (170-180 AD), from which the quote in question is taken, essentially describes how to find and preserve equanimity in the midst of conflict by drawing inspiration from nature. The aptness of this in the context of Moffat's story is readily apparent.

It is in its raising of issues such as this, and in its examination of the Doctor's motivations and morality, that 'The Day of the Doctor' is at its most successful. It would have been all too easy for Moffat to have presented a more straightforward Doctor-versus-monsters battle in this anniversary special, but while there is certainly no shortage of spectacle on offer, the showrunner has to his credit crafted a surprisingly thought-provoking and cerebral tale. This serves as a fitting testament to the kind of intelligent, multi-layered storytelling of which *Doctor Who* has always been capable.

There are, though, a few curious aspects to the script. One of the most jarring of these comes when the Moment labels David Tennant's Doctor as 'The man who regrets' the action he took to end the Time War, and Matt Smith's as 'The man who forgets.' The former description doesn't really do justice to the fine characterisation of Tennant's Doctor during Russell T Davies' time as showrunner, which continued the study of the theme of 'survivor guilt' begun with Christopher Eccleston's incarnation;

and the latter simply doesn't make any sense, given that Clara at one point says, 'The Doctor, my Doctor, he's always talking about the day he did it; the day he wiped out the Time Lords to stop the War.'

Mention of Clara brings to mind the fact that while 'The Day of the Doctor' has an absolutely fantastic beginning – opening in perfect fashion with a version of the original 1963 title sequence and theme music, then a shot of a sign pointing to I M Foreman's junkyard at 76 Totter's Lane and a scene set in Coal Hill School; both key settings of *Doctor Who's* very first episode, 'An Unearthly Child' – it completely fails to address what happened after the cliff-hanger ending of 'The Name of the Doctor', where Matt Smith's Doctor and Clara were left seemingly trapped in the Doctor's own timestream. The viewer is presumably supposed to infer that they escaped, rejoined the Paternoster Row gang on Trenzalore and then returned to Earth together in the TARDIS; but it would have been nice to have had this at least alluded to in a line or two of dialogue.

Another awkwardness is that, whereas in 'The End of Time' (2009/2010) the Doctor stated that during the course of the Time War the Time Lords became more dangerous than any of his other enemies (a point reinforced by Cass's comment in 'The Night of the Doctor' about them having become indistinguishable from the Daleks), in 'The Day of the Doctor' the three Doctors ultimately deem their race worthy of being saved, albeit consigned to a kind of limbo, whereas the Daleks are still allowed to wipe themselves out – in a credibility-straining variation on that old joke where two villains shoot at the hero from opposite directions and end up killing each other when the hero ducks. The very concept of a Time War also implies that the conflict is being waged across time, not in one particular time zone, so even the suggestion of it having a 'last day' is somewhat odd, to say the least. The whole thing seems to be treated in a rather more simplistic way here than it has been previously, particularly during Russell T Davies' tenure.

It was from BBC Books' highly-regarded Eighth Doctor Adventures range of the late 1990s and early 2000s that Davies originally drew the notion of the Doctor becoming embroiled in a Time War, so it is perhaps fitting that a number of elements of 'The Day of the Doctor' appear to have been inspired by aspects of the final novel in the Time War arc, the Peter Anghelides and Stephen Cole-penned *The Ancestor Cell* (2000). Specifically, *The Ancestor Cell* describes a plan for Gallifrey to be shifted into a separate, bottle universe in order to avoid the Time War; sees forbidden Time Lord super-weapons being sourced from a sealed underground vault; and involves three different versions of the Doctor, one of whom no longer uses that name, coming together in a conclusion where one of them destroys both Gallifrey and its enemies by pressing down on a big brass trigger lever – the equivalent of this in 'The Day of the Doctor' obviously being the literal 'big red button' symbolising the choice the Doctor faces as to whether or not to activate the Moment. The difference is that, in *The Ancestor Cell*, the Doctor's actions have the affect of averting the Time War before it even begins, rather than ending it when it reaches its 'last day'.

The actual design of the big red button, resembling a jewel in a lotus, incidentally appears to be another subtle allusion to Buddhist teaching, and perhaps also a reference back to the third Doctor's swansong, 'Planet of the Spiders' (1974), in which the Jewel in the Lotus mantra, 'Om mani padme hum', figured prominently. It also somewhat recalls the 'big friendly button' with which the Doctor reset events in 'Journey to the Centre of the TARDIS'.

One of the most eagerly anticipated aspects of 'The Day of the Doctor' was undoubtedly David Tennant's return as the much-loved tenth Doctor. The sequence where he enjoys a picnic with Queen Elizabeth I, only to detect the presence of a shape-shifting Zygon, disguised initially as his horse and then as the Queen herself, is great fun – despite not quite managing to convince that they are basking in the sun, when clearly the recording actually took place in freezing cold weather. However, when the Matt Smith and John Hurt Doctors join the Tennant one in Elizabethan England, the scenes of the three of them interacting with each other unfortunately don't work as well as might have been expected. The main problem is that the Tennant and Smith Doctors are essentially quite similar – being comparable in age, height, build, speech pattern and general 'geekiness' – and indeed the script seems intent on highlighting this fact, for instance by having them both put on their 'brainy specs' at the same time and both wield their sonic screwdrivers in identical fashion. This means that when Moffat attempts to have them engage in amusing verbal sparring in the same way as their predecessors did during similar team-ups – such as when the first Doctor memorably derided the third and second as 'a dandy and a clown' in 'The Three Doctors' – it just falls flat, and the humour seems distinctly forced. Their macho posturing over the relative sizes of their respective sonic screwdriver is lame, and there simply isn't enough contrast between the two of them to make their rather tame 'matchstick man' and 'chinny' jibes stick. (And just what exactly are 'sandshoes'?)

This isn't a problem with the Hurt incarnation, of course; but in this case, a different issue presents itself. It is always a dangerous move in any production to have one of the lead characters actually draw attention to the show's own shortcomings, but that is essentially what happens here when the War Doctor gives voice to certain reservations that many fans have long had about the depiction of the modern-era Doctors. 'Am I having a mid-life crisis?' he wonders, as his successors wave their sonic screwdrivers phallically in his direction. 'Why are you pointing your screwdrivers like that? They're scientific instruments, not water pistols!' The eleventh Doctor's use of the juvenile-sounding phrase 'timey-wimey' is greeted with predictable disdain; and Queen Elizabeth's kissing of the tenth Doctor at their wedding ceremony prompts the bemused question, 'Is there a lot of this in the future?' In short, the War Doctor shines a spotlight on some of the most commonly criticised and clichéd aspects of his successors' characterisation. It is almost as if he has been reading the fan forums!

Where the interaction between the three Doctors does succeed is in the way it produces the story's denouement in the climactic sequence in the barn on Gallifrey. There is a similarity here with the situation presented in 'A Christmas Carol' (2010). Just as that Christmas special has the elderly Kazran Sardick feeling compelled to change his ways on witnessing his younger self's frightened reaction to what he has become, so in this instance the eleventh Doctor is prompted to come up with a new, more humane way to end the Time War as a result of the War Doctor seeing how he and the tenth Doctor have turned out. The justification for this is very cleverly established in the earlier, initially superfluous-seeming scene in the dungeon of the Tower of London, where the Moment points out to the War Doctor that if he starts running a subroutine on his sonic screwdriver, it will still be running four hundred years later – in terms of his own timeline – on the eleventh Doctor's equivalent device, because, 'It's the same screwdriver. Same software, different case.' This neatly illustrates how, by showing the War Doctor what he will become, the Moment starts him thinking about how he can devise a better outcome to the Time War, which eventually bears fruit three incarnations down the line. Or, as the eleventh Doctor puts it, 'Gentlemen, I have had four hundred years to think about this. I've changed my mind.' The same trick is then pulled for a third time when all thirteen Doctors work together, or rather in succession, to perform the complex calculations needed to freeze Gallifrey in a parallel pocket universe. The only slight drawback here is that, in order to avoid undoing everything that has gone before this in 21st Century *Doctor Who* and effectively restarting the modern-era show from scratch – which would doubtless have been too bold a move even for him – Moffat has really had little choice but to fudge things somewhat at the end of the story, so that (leaving aside the Curator) only the eleventh Doctor is aware that he did not in fact destroy Gallifrey along with (most of) the Daleks. His predecessors all lose their memories of these events and are left in ignorance of what really happened – so that, from their perspective, nothing has changed, and there has been no rewriting of their history. To the rest of the universe, too, it still appears as if Gallifrey has been destroyed – or so we are led to believe at this point ...

Now that he has found a way to avoid wiping out his own people, and thereby been redeemed, logically it would seem that the eleventh Doctor should start to develop the maturity that the War Doctor found lacking in his successors, as indicated when he asked them, 'Do you have to talk like children? What is it that makes you so ashamed of being a grown up?' – the answer being, of course, that their shame derives from their memories of what he did in the Time War. Or perhaps the theme of him needing to 'grow up' is instead foreshadowing his next regeneration ...?

On the subject of regeneration, it is very pleasing that Steven Moffat was able to include a scene toward the end of the story where the War Doctor returns to his TARDIS – a fantastic set, fittingly combining the classic-era white, roundel-patterned walls with aspects of the first modern-era console room – and transforms into the ninth Doctor, completing the final link in the chain of the Doctor's timeline. 'The Night of the Doctor' and 'The Day of the Doctor' now serve, in essence, as bookends to the War Doctor incarnation. It is just a pity that the regeneration effect was not continued a little longer, to show Christopher Eccleston's face more clearly. The explanation Moffat has subsequently given for this – that it would have been 'unprofessional and disrespectful', in view of Eccleston's decision not to take part in the production – doesn't really make much sense, given that other clips of the actor are used elsewhere in the special. Perhaps the rumours that circulated shortly after transmission were correct, and the sequence was actually shortened in post-production because it was judged unconvincing – although that too is rather hard to believe, given that fan video artists with far lesser resources subsequently uploaded to YouTube their own perfectly effective extended versions (along with, admittedly, a few less-than-effective ones!) incorporating a full reveal of Eccleston's features.

One very positive aspect of 'The Day of the Doctor' is its reintroduction of the Zygons, following on from the brief reference made to them in 'The Power of Three'. Having had only one previous appearance in the television show, way back in the fourth Doctor story 'Terror of the Zygons', they might perhaps have been considered a surprising choice for inclusion in the fiftieth anniversary special, but their popularity with fans has always far exceeded what one would normally expect of a one-off monster – owing in part to their superb original costume design, devised by subsequent multi-Oscar winner James Acheson – and they have featured many more times in tie-in media stories. The new prosthetic suits created for their on-screen reappearance here are very impressive, being pleasingly similar and respectful to the original design but also more flexible and mobile, making them appropriately scary creatures. The idea of them trying to invade the 21st Century by way of a 3D Gallifreyan painting – a very apt inclusion in *Doctor Who*'s first 3D production – is well-conceived, too, and provides a good pretext for UNIT's involvement in the story.

UNIT has been such an important part of the show's history since its creation in 1969 that it would have seemed distinctly odd had it not figured in some way in this anniversary special; and the return of the excellent Jemma Redgrave as Kate Stewart is very welcome indeed, as is the introduction of the wonderful new character Osgood, brilliantly played by Ingrid Oliver. With her hero-worshipping of the Doctor, even down to wearing a replica of his fourth incarnation's trademark scarf, Osgood can be seen as an affectionate tribute by Steven Moffat to *Doctor Who*'s legion of devoted, cosplaying fans all around the world, and it is no surprise that they quickly took her to their hearts.

The idea of UNIT having Black Archive facilities containing potentially dangerous alien artefacts first cropped up in *The Sarah Jane Adventures* story 'Enemy of the Bane' (2008), and it makes perfect sense that the Zygons should use their shape-shifting abilities to try to gain access to the one at UNIT HQ beneath the Tower of London. Especially effective are the scenes where Kate, Osgood and fellow UNIT operative McGillop – nicely portrayed by Belfast-born actor Jonjo O'Neill – come face to face with their Zygon duplicates, and then all of them have their memories altered by the Doctors so that they no longer know if they are human or Zygon and are forced to try to negotiate a settlement – although the two Osgoods do manage to work out which of them is which, but silently agree to say nothing. The situation here is clearly intended to parallel that on Gallifrey, with two essentially indistinguishable sides squaring up to each other, and both risking annihilation via the deployment of a 'doomsday weapon' – in this case, a nuclear warhead positioned twenty feet below the Black Archive. Frustratingly, though, we never get to see the outcome of the negotiation, and this aspect of the plot is simply left hanging. While it is no great stretch to realise that it is setting up a scenario that will probably be returned to and resolved in a later episode, it would surely have been better for a one-off anniversary special to have told a more self-contained story. One is left at the end with the dissatisfied feeling the programme-makers simply ran out of time and decided to focus on wrapping up the Time War aspect of the plot at the expense of presenting a proper conclusion to the UNIT-versus-Zygons aspect.

In production terms, 'The Day of the Doctor' has a cinematic, high-budget look to it, suggesting that the BBC probably spent a little more this time than is usual for *Doctor Who* – no doubt in recognition of the special occasion and the ambitious plans for worldwide simulcast transmissions and cinema screenings. The Time War action sequences, featuring some outstanding model shots by the Model Unit and excellent CGI work by Milk, the successor company to former regular contributors The Mill, are all highly impressive, and it is great to see the Daleks featuring strongly here, causing mayhem as ever – to have had the Doctor's greatest foes omitted from the fiftieth anniversary special would have been unthinkable. The early stunt sequence where the TARDIS is airlifted to Trafalgar Square by helicopter, with the Doctor left dangling from the base, is both spectacular and amusing; the Gallifrey scenes, featuring some redesigned Time Lord costumes, are very well-realised; and really the whole 76-minute special is a visual treat. Nick Hurran, one of the absolute best directors to have worked on *Doctor Who* in recent years, was an excellent choice to handle things behind the cameras, and if the end result is a touch less stylish than his previous contributions to the show, then this can perhaps be excused by the fact that he was somewhat constrained by the exacting requirements of shooting in 3D for this unique assignment.

So, what are we left with at the end of 'The Day of the Doctor'? A kind of partial, have-your-cake-and-eat-it reboot of 21st Century *Doctor Who* in which the Doctor does not destroy Gallifrey after all, but fails to realise this until almost the end of his Matt Smith incarnation. A previously-unknown Time War incarnation of the Doctor interposed between the Paul McGann and Christopher Eccleston versions. Another previously-unknown, probably future, incarnation who looks like an elderly version of the fourth. And a potential new direction for the show, in which the Doctor contemplates embarking on a quest to find Gallifrey. It remains to be seen to what extent that latter aspect will be pursued, but the idea does seem somewhat at odds with the Doctor's traditional wanderlust nature. Admittedly there has always been a degree of ambiguity apparent in his feelings toward his home world. Right back in 'An Unearthly Child', he said of himself and his grand-daughter, 'Susan and I are cut off from our own planet without friends or protection. But one day we shall get back. Yes, one day, one day.' Then, at the end of 'The Massacre of St Bartholomew's Eve' (1966), he agonised to himself, 'Perhaps I should go home, back to my own planet. But I can't. I can't.' In later years, on the other hand, he never seemed too keen on visiting Gallifrey, even when he had the opportunity to do so; and that was before the Time Lords were corrupted and changed 'right to the core' (as he put it in 'The End of Time') by their participation in the Time War. In fact, the ending of 'The Day of the Doctor' could almost be seen as a polar opposite of that of the twentieth anniversary special, 'The Five Doctors', when the fifth Doctor was asked to remain on Gallifrey as the Time Lord President but chose instead to go on the run again in the TARDIS. 'After all,' he noted, 'that's how it all started.'

'The Day of the Doctor' is a hugely ambitious production, packed with great characters, interesting ideas and exciting incident, but is somewhat hamstrung by Christopher Eccleston's non-participation, attempts to do too much, and in the end turns out to be a rather less satisfying celebration of *Doctor Who*'s fifty-year run than the superb 'The Name of the Doctor'. In short, as birthday cakes go, this is a distinctly overegged one.

The Time of the Doctor

Writer: Steven Moffat
Director: Jamie Payne

<u>DEBUT TRANSMISSION DETAILS</u>

BBC One/BBC One HD
Date: 25 December 2013. Scheduled time: 7.30 pm. Actual time: 7.30 pm.

Duration: 61' 05"

<u>ADDITIONAL CREDITED CAST</u>

Orla Brady (Tasha Lem), James Buller (Dad), Elizabeth Rider (Linda), Sheila Reid (Gran), Mark Anthony Brighton (Colonel Albero), Rob Jarvis (Abramal), Tessa Peake-Jones (Marta), Jack Hollington (Barnable), Sonita Henry (Colonel Meme), Kayvan Novak (Voice of Handles), Tom Gibbons (Young Man), Ken Bones (Voice), Aidan Cook (Cyberman), Nicholas Briggs (Voice of the Daleks & Cybermen), Barnaby Edwards (Dalek 1), Nicholas Pegg (Dalek 2), Ross Mullan (Silent), Dan Starkey (Sontaran), Sarah Madison (Weeping Angel), Peter Capaldi (The Doctor)

Daleks created by Terry Nation
Cybermen created by Kit Pedler & Gerry Davis
Sontarans created by Robert Holmes

<u>PLOT</u>

A mysterious signal, being broadcast through all space and time, draws the Doctor and many of his adversaries – including the Daleks and the Cybermen – to investigate its planet of origin. A protective shield has been placed around the planet by the Church of the Papal Mainframe, who were first on the scene, but their Mother Superious, Tasha Lem, is an old friend of the Doctor's, and she teleports him down to the surface along with Clara, who was seeking his help with a Christmas dinner she was cooking for her family. The two friends make their way to a town called Christmas, where the Doctor discovers one of the cracks in time first encountered at the start of his current incarnation. The signal is coming through the crack from the other side. Handles, a severed Cyberman head that the Doctor has been using as a robotic companion, identifies it as Gallifreyan, and eventually translates it as the question 'Doctor who?' The Doctor realises that if he were to answer, the Time Lords would take this to mean that it was safe for them to return to the universe. He cannot do so, though, as the aliens besieging the planet – which Tasha Lem identifies as Trenzalore – would immediately attack, and the Time War would begin anew. The Doctor has no choice but to remain in Christmas, defending it from the alien forces trying to break through the Church's shield, while he tricks Clara into returning to Earth in the TARDIS. Tasha Lem eventually brings Clara back to Trenzalore, hundreds of years in its future, as the Doctor is dying of old age and is no longer able to regenerate. Speaking through the crack in time, Clara implores the Time Lords to help him, and they do so by sending him a whole new regeneration cycle. As he starts to regenerate, the Doctor fires out streams of energy to destroy all the aliens attacking the planet. He then returns to the TARDIS, where Clara sees him transform into a new man.

QUOTE, UNQUOTE

- Clara: 'Emergency! You're my boyfriend!'
  Doctor: 'Ding dong! Okay, brilliant. I may be a bit … rusty in some areas, but I will glance at a manual.'
  Clara: 'No, no, you're not actually my boyfriend.'
  Doctor: 'Oh, that was quick. It's a rollercoaster, this phone call.'
  Clara: 'But I need a boyfriend really quickly.'
  Doctor: 'Well, I hope you're nicer to the next one!'

- Doctor: 'We all change … when you think about it. We're all different people all through our lives. And that's okay, that's good. You've got to keep moving. So long as you remember all the people that you used to be. I will not forget one line of this. Not one day. I swear. I will always remember when the Doctor was me.'

- New Doctor: 'Kidneys! I've got new kidneys. I don't like the colour.'
  Clara: 'Of your kidneys?' [TARDIS starts lurching violently.]
  'What's happening?'
  New Doctor: 'We're probably crashing. Oh!'
  Clara: 'Into what?'
  New Doctor: 'Stay calm. Just one question. Do you happen to know
  how to fly this thing?'

CONTINUITY POINTS

- At the start of the story, the Doctor identifies some of the alien
  spaceships 'parked' above Trenzalore as belonging to 'Daleks,
  Sontarans, Terileptils, Slitheen.' Other spaceships are also seen,
  including of the type usually used by the Judoon. Of all these races,
  the only one not to have appeared in 21st Century Doctor Who so
  far is the Terileptils; they featured in the classic-era story 'The
  Visitation' (1982). When a new ship arrives in orbit, the Doctor fails
  to realise that it belongs to the Cybermen – until he materialises the
  TARDIS on board and is attacked by the creatures! A little later,
  when Clara asks him to identify a large, cube-shaped ship, he tells
  her: 'Papal Mainframe. It's like a great big flying church. The first
  ship to arrive. They are the ones who shielded the planet. They can
  get us down there.' The Church and its military Clerics first
  appeared in 'The Time of Angels' (2010) – set in the 51st Century –
  and also featured prominently in 'A Good Man Goes to War' (2011)
  – set in the 52nd Century. Given that, from their perspective, the
  Church's arrival at Trenzalore in 'The Time of the Doctor' precedes
  the events of Series Six (see below), this must also occur no later
  than the 52nd Century, and possibly several centuries earlier.

- From Clara's point of view, 'The Time of the Doctor' appears to take
  place not long after 'The Day of the Doctor'. (However, in a deleted
  scene – see 'Production Notes' below – she tells the Doctor that she
  has missed him, indicating that it is not immediately after.) It is
  probably therefore either Christmas Day 2013 or Christmas Day
  2014 when she phones the Doctor to ask for his help. She is
  preparing Christmas dinner for her father, his mother (i.e. her

grandmother) and a woman named Linda. Although not explicitly stated, it would appear that Linda is Clara's stepmother. Assuming that her father is of a similar age to her birth mother – his first wife, Ellie – who was established in 'The Rings of Akhaten' to have been born in 1960, he would be in his early to mid-fifties by this point, which is consistent with his appearance. The high-rise flat in which the family gathering takes place would seem to be Clara's. She presumably moved there after leaving her job as nanny to the Maitland children and starting work at Coal Hill School. It must therefore be within reasonably easy commuting distance of Shoreditch in London, although its exact location is unspecified.

- The Doctor tells Clara that the 'organics are all gone' from the severed Cyberman head he has dubbed 'Handles', but that there is 'still a full set of data banks'. He adds that he found it at 'the Maldovar market'. The Maldovarium, presided over by Dorium Maldovar, was first seen in 'The Pandorica Opens' (2010).

- When Handles first identifies the mysterious signal as coming from Gallifrey, the Doctor protests, 'Gallifrey is gone.' Clare, however, says, 'Unless you saved it. You thought you might have.' The Doctor replies, 'Even if it survived, it's gone from this universe.' This essentially restates the position as it was left at the end of 'The Day of the Doctor'.

- The Doctor describes the Church of the Papal Mainframe as the 'security hub of the known universe … keeping you safe in this world and the next'. Visitors to the Church are expected to be naked, although it is acceptable to use devices that project a holographic impression of clothes – an approach adopted by the Doctor and Clara. Tasha Lem says that everyone in the Church is 'trained to see straight through holograms'.

- The TARDIS can home in on its key, enabling the Doctor to summon his ship from the Church of the Papal Mainframe to the surface of Trenzalore.

- Trenzalore is subject to a truth field, which is said to be strongest near the clock tower. The Doctor and Clara are both affected by it when they first arrive. Although they intend to conceal their true identities from the locals, the Doctor immediately says, 'I'm the Doctor. I'm a Time Lord from the planet Gallifrey. I stole a time machine and ran away, and I've been flouting the principal law of my own people ever since.' Clara, before she is interrupted, blurts out, 'I'm an English teacher from planet Earth, and I've run off with a man from space because I really fancy–' When asked her name, she gives a revealing indication of how she sees herself, adding, 'Bubbly personality masking bossy control freak.' The Doctor later deduces that the Time Lords have sent the truth field through the crack in time along with their coded message, 'Doctor who?', in order to ensure an honest answer is given. This accords with Dorium Maldovar's statement in 'The Wedding of River Song' (2011): 'On the fields of Trenzalore, at the fall of the eleventh, when no living creature can speak falsely or fail to answer, a question will be asked. A question that must never, ever be answered.' Once he has been on Trenzalore for some time, however, it appears that the Doctor learns how to overcome the truth field, as he later makes several deceptive statements. Even at the beginning, he considers it 'quaint'.

- The Doctor describes the crack in time as, 'A split in the skin of reality ... A tiny sliver of 26 June 2010. The day the universe blew up.' This refers to the events of 'The Big Bang' (2010), when the universe was destroyed by the TARDIS exploding and was then rebooted by the Doctor. The Doctor realises that the Time Lords have identified this point on Trenzalore as a weak spot through which they can potentially break back into the universe.

- It is revealed here, by way of a brief flashback, that what the Doctor saw in the room containing his fear in 'The God Complex' (2011) was one of the cracks in time.

- The Doctor enables Handles to decode the Time Lords' message using the Seal of the High Council of Gallifrey, which contains an algorithm imprinted in its atomic structure. He tells Clara that he obtained the device when he, 'Nicked it off the Master in the Death Zone' – a reference to events seen in 'The Five Doctors' (1983). Once Handles reveals that the message is 'Doctor who?', the voice heard continuously repeating this question is that of the General in charge of the Time Lord War Council, as seen in 'The Day of the Doctor'.

- When the Doctor decides to remain in Christmas and become its Sheriff, Tasha Lem announces to the Church of the Papal Mainframe: 'Attention. Attention all Chapels and Choirs of the Papal Mainframe. The siege of Trenzalore is now begun. There will now be an unscheduled faith change. From this moment on, I dedicate this Church to one cause: silence. The Doctor will not speak his name, and war will not begin. Silence will fall!' This sets up the situation previously established in Series Six, when Madame Kovarian and the creatures known as the Silents attempted to have the Doctor killed by River Song. Toward the end of the siege – the length of which is unspecified, but is considerably in excess of three centuries – Tasha tells the Doctor: 'The Kovarian Chapter broke away. They travelled back along your timeline and tried to prevent you ever reaching Trenzalore ... They blew up your time capsule, created the very cracks in the universe through which the Time Lords are now calling.' The Doctor replies: 'The destiny trap. You can't change history if you're part of it.' Tasha then adds: 'They engineered a psychopath to kill you.' This is a reference to the circumstances of River's birth, as seen in 'A Good Man Goes to War'. Although not explicitly stated, it was presumably through their influence over River that the Kovarian Chapter blew up the TARDIS, as she was on board the ship when the explosion occurred.

- The Silents, established in Series Six as creatures that can be remembered only so long as they are observed, are now revealed by the Doctor to be creatures of the Church of the Papal Mainframe: 'Confessional priests. Very popular. Genetically engineered so you forget everything you told them.' This explains why they repeatedly tell Clara to 'Confess.'

- The people of Christmas are seen at one point being entertained by a Punch and Judy-type show in which puppets are used to depict the Doctor fending off a Monoid – one of the monocular creatures featured in the classic-era story 'The Ark' (1966). The Doctor also shows the townsfolk how to do the dance that he first demonstrated to a group of young wedding guests when Amy and Rory got married in 'The Big Bang' (2010). The dance is named here as the Drunk Giraffe – a term previously used only behind the scenes.

- The children of Christmas give the Doctor gifts of numerous drawings that he displays on a pillar and the walls in his adopted home in the clock tower. The drawings depict him, the TARDIS and various alien creatures.

- Clara at one point finds herself transported from Earth to Trenzalore on the outside of the TARDIS, as the ship dematerialises while she is in the act of inserting the key into the lock. When she tells the Doctor that she was in space, he corrects her: 'Well, you were in the time vortex. She must have extended the forcefield. No wonder … no wonder she's late, dragging you around.' Captain Jack Harkness was previously carried through the time vortex clinging onto the outside of the TARDIS at the beginning of 'Utopia' (2007).

- The Church of the Papal Mainframe eventually falls to the Daleks, who convert everyone on board into the same type of 'puppets' as seen in 'Asylum of the Daleks'. The strong-willed Tasha is eventually able to resist their conditioning – but not before she has told them about the Doctor, all record of whom was deleted from their telepathic web at the end of that earlier episode.

- Tasha is able to pilot the TARDIS. When Clara expresses surprise at this, Tasha tells her, 'Flying the TARDIS was always easy. It was flying the Doctor I never quite mastered.' This confirms earlier indications that she and the Doctor have a long mutual history.

- 'The Deadly Assassin' (1976) established that Time Lords can normally regenerate only 12 times, meaning that they can normally have a maximum of 13 incarnations. This is reiterated here. It is also confirmed that the eleventh Doctor is not the eleventh incarnation of this particular Time Lord but the thirteenth: the extra two incarnations are accounted for by the War Doctor, as seen in 'The Day of the Doctor', and the tenth Doctor's second lease of life, following his aborted regeneration at the cliffhanger junction of 'The Stolen Earth'/'Journey's End' (2008). 'The Five Doctors' (1983), however, established that the Time Lords have the ability to grant members of their race a whole new regeneration cycle; an offer that they made to the Master on that occasion as an incentive for him to assist them. This is a gift they bestow upon the Doctor at the end of 'The Time of the Doctor'. Although not explicitly stated, it would seem therefore that the twelfth Doctor is the first of a potential additional thirteen incarnations. This would explain the existence of the Curator incarnation, which was left somewhat vague in 'The Day of the Doctor'.

- The unusual circumstances of the Doctor's regeneration may explain the huge outpouring of energy with which he is able to destroy the alien fleets attacking Trenzalore. Alternatively, given that his previous regeneration, in 'The End of Time' Part Two (2010), was also accompanied by an unusually large release of energy, sufficient to wreck the TARDIS interior, it is possible that Time Lords always experience increasingly violent regenerations as they approach the end of their lives.

- The unusual circumstances of the Doctor's regeneration may also account for the fact that he temporarily 'resets' to his familiar, relatively youthful appearance before the transformation completes, as nothing similar has been seen on previous occasions (e.g. when the War Doctor regenerated into the ninth Doctor in 'The Day of the Doctor').

- The averting of the eleventh Doctor's death on Trenzalore rewrites history, and gives that planet a different future. This means, amongst other things, that the TARDIS will not now grow to giant size and become the Doctor's tomb as seen in 'The Name of the Doctor'. However, when history is rewritten, this does not remove the negated events from the timestreams of those time travellers who have already lived through them, or completely erase them from their memories. This was established in the minisode 'Good Night' (2011) and the episode 'The Wedding of River Song' (2011), and seen more recently when first the Doctor and then, later, Clara recalled the negated events of 'Journey to the Centre of the TARDIS'. In this instance, therefore, the rewriting of history will not have changed the fact that Clara was splintered throughout the

Doctor's timestream in 'The Name of the Doctor', as this is something they both experienced in the old version of events.

PRODUCTION NOTES

- 'The Time of the Doctor' was made as a one-off Christmas special. It had the distinction of being the eight-hundredth transmitted Doctor Who episode.

- The sequences of the Doctor, Clara and the TARDIS outside the block of flats where Clara lives were taped on 10 September 2013 at Lydstep Flats, Lydstep Crescent, Gabalfa, Cardiff. A large military training facility called Sennybridge Training Area (SENTA) in Sennybridge, Powys, was used for the Christmas town exteriors, which were shot on 11, 12, 15 and 16 September. 17 and 18 September saw the crew relocate to Park Davies in Mamhilad Park Industrial Estate, Pontypool, for taping of scenes set at the top of the town's clock tower. Concluding the special's location work, the sequence where the Doctor and Clara first arrive in a wood on the surface of Trenzalore, to find themselves menaced by a number of Weeping Angels that emerge from a snowdrift, was recorded on 19 September at Puzzlewood, Coleford, Gloucestershire. Studio recording took place at BBC Roath Lock on various dates between 8 September and 5 October. Model filming was carried out between 14 and 16 October at Halliford Film Studios in Shepperton, Middlesex.

- Shortly after the special's Christmas Day transmission, BBC America released on its YouTube channel a 34" duration video of a deleted scene, comprising an exchange of dialogue between Clara and the Doctor as they leave the TARDIS and head for her flat, after taking her Christmas turkey into the ship to cook. This was later included as an extra on the 50th Anniversary Collector's Edition DVD and Blu-ray box set.

- This story was originally intended to feature River Song, but actress Alex Kingston was unavailable to appear, so Steven Moffat slightly rewrote her part and renamed the character Tasha Lem. Some sequences ultimately deleted from the script would have given

Tasha more backstory, including a description of how she initially met the Doctor when he was in his first incarnation, travelling with his grand-daughter Susan.

- The poem 'Thoughts on a Clock' by Eric Ritchie Jn, of which Clara finds an extract contained in one of her Christmas crackers, is a fictional one devised by Steven Moffat for his script. The extract reads, 'And now it's time for one last bow, like all your other selves. Eleven's hour is over now, the clock is striking twelve's.' The words 'eleven's hour' refer back to the title of the first Matt Smith episode, 'The Eleventh Hour' (2010).

- Karen Gillan's cousin Caitlin Blackwood, who had previously portrayed the young Amelia Pond, had grown up too much to reprise the role in this special, so her part was taken by another, uncredited child actress in the short sequence where the Doctor sees a vision of Amelia running around the TARDIS console room. Her face was kept out of shot to disguise this fact.

- Matt Smith wore various hairpieces during recording of the special, as his own hair had recently been shaved off to give him a skinhead look for his appearance in the movie Lost River (2014). This allowed for the production crew to achieve the humorous scene where the Doctor himself is at one point revealed to have shaved off his hair and been wearing a wig, and made it easier to realise the later sequences where he is seen to have aged by several hundred years, for which extensive prosthetic make-up was used. Karen Gillan had also recently had her head shaved for her performance in the movie Guardians of the Galaxy (2014), so she too wore a wig, made of her own hair, for the sequence where the Doctor sees a brief vision of the adult Amy Pond in the TARDIS console room.

- Matt Smith suffered an injury to his leg while recording this special, prompting Steven Moffat to perform script rewrites to show the elderly Doctor remaining seated during certain scenes, and walking with the aid of a stick. Moffat at one stage intended to have the Doctor reveal that he had actually lost a leg in a Weeping Angel attack, and was now using a wooden one; this was omitted from the transmitted version, but the incident was later recounted in the short story collection Tales of Trenzalore (BBC Books, 2014).

- On returning to the TARDIS at the end of the action, just prior to the Doctor's transformation, Clara finds the police box's external phone dangling on its cord and replaces it behind its panel. Steven Moffat wrote this into the script in order to set up a scene for inclusion in the first episode of Series Eight, of the future Clara receiving an unexpected phone call from the eleventh Doctor. Matt Smith recorded his contribution to the latter scene during the making of 'The Time of the Doctor'.

- The closing titles give Peter Capaldi an 'Introducing ...' credit as the new Doctor.

OOPS!

- At about 8' 50" into the episode, in a shot where the TARDIS is hovering in space with the Doctor and Clara looking out at the alien spaceships gathered above Trenzalore, the left-hand side of the police box door frame is missing, so that the door with the telephone panel appears to be attached to nothing at all.

CRITICAL REACTION

- 'The big draw in this episode was of course the departure of Matt Smith, and the script gave him some juicy opportunities to demonstrate the emotional range that has made him, for my money, the most interesting occupant of the role. Smith has been so good as the ageless, sinister, childlike, loveable alien that it was almost a shame to see that expressive Easter Island head caked in make-up for the middle section of this episode, while the swelling strings and Shakespearian speechifying of the final quarter-hour seemed comically at odds with the intricate lunacy that animates his best performances.' Tim Martin, Telegraph website, 25 December 2013.

- 'This year's thoughtful Doctor Who [Christmas special] managed to combine an eight-hundredth episode with a regeneration, then tied it all up with a Christmas Day bow. For his final episode, the BBC really got their money's worth out of Matt Smith, who carried much of "The Time of the Doctor" alone, and it was a neat trick to show the youngest ever Doctor getting old. Steven Moffat ticked all necessary boxes here: he answered the regeneration question (though it made little sense to this non-devotee) and gave incoming Time Lord Peter Capaldi a suitably sizable entrance: "Do you happen to know how to fly this thing?"' Rebecca Nicholson, Guardian website, 26 December 2013.

- '"The Time of the Doctor" was, if I'm being honest, kind of a let-down as Matt Smith's final episode. It felt like it dragged a bit in the middle, and I never really cared about the town of Christmas or the Doctor being its saviour for several hundred years. To be fair, I've been building this episode up in my mind for months, and it had to follow the well-received "The Day of the Doctor". So it would have been nearly impossible for "The Time of the Doctor" to live up to expectations. And there were aspects that I enjoyed.' Kaitlin Thomas, TV.com website, 26 December 2013.

- 'Even though the date of Smith's leaving and the identity of his successor … had been known for some time, watching the episode knowing it was Smith's last kept at least one American viewer anxious and sad, with a finger on the pause button for when things got too heavy. Possibly there are still viewers, avid viewers even, who have never quite cottoned to him – Tennant continues to cast a long shadow – but I have loved his work. Elegant and heartfelt, authoritative and playful, swashbuckling and intimate, alien and familiar, Smith's acting has accommodated and, as it were, humanised every oddball, paradoxical, high-concept, low-humour passage Moffat has thrown at him. Fate drives Doctor Who – it's not just the past that creates the present, the future does as well. And so we got flashbacks and cameos and fish fingers and custard. There were Daleks, Weeping Angels, Sontarans and Cybermen … And crucially, there was Amy Pond – a vision, perhaps, but Karen Gillan, real enough – "The first face this face saw."' Robert Lloyd, Los Angeles Times website, 26 December 2013.

- 'Easily the highlight of this year's Christmas viewing, "The Time of the Doctor" not only gave Matt Smith a great send-off but also gave viewers a careful, concise and emotional hour of top-quality entertainment. And as is typical for Who, renewal and regeneration are only the start of a brand new adventure, and from his brief introduction ("Kidneys!") Peter Capaldi looks like a fine successor to take the world's favourite TV hero in a different and equally exciting direction.' Jon Cooper, Mirror website, 27 December 2013.

ANALYSIS

Despite some rather forced attempts at humour early on – chiefly the sequence where the Doctor appears naked before Clara, then puts on holographic clothes that, it transpires, cannot be seen by her other family members; and later the incident where he reveals he is wearing a wig, as he got bored and shaved off all his hair – 'The Time of the Doctor' is, overall, unusually dour and downbeat in tone for a *Doctor Who* Christmas special. While this is arguably fitting for the swansong appearance of a hugely popular star of the show – the same was also true of 'The End of Time' Part One (2009), the first half of the tenth Doctor's regeneration story – it has to be said that it does entail the eleventh Doctor bowing out in very atypical style. Matt Smith's portrayal of the Time Lord has been marked by his boundless energy, his rapid-fire delivery of dialogue – accompanied, as observed by the War Doctor in 'The Day of the Doctor', by much expressive hand-waving – and his infectious childlike enthusiasm. In 'The Time of the Doctor', by contrast, he is uncharacteristically subdued, spending much of the action as an increasingly elderly and infirm figure, walking with the aid of a stick. Even allowing for the rewrites prompted by the minor injury that Smith suffered during recording, and perhaps also for the need to afford a contrast to the frenetic pace of 'The Day of the Doctor', this seems a rather strange creative choice for Steven Moffat to have made.

In other respects, though, the story is more representative of Moffat's writing for this era of the show. In particular, it sees him once again adopt what might be described as a 'pick and mix' approach of taking memorable characters and elements from earlier episodes and re-presenting them in a kind of 'greatest hits' package. So we have here Daleks, Cybermen, the Church of the Papal Mainframe, Weeping Angels, Sontarans, Silents and Dalek 'puppets', along with voice-over narration, a gathering of spaceships, Trenzalore, cracks in time, a nursery rhyme-like poem, Gallifrey and the Time Lords; and we would have had River Song as well, but for the unavailability of actress Alex Kingston, which forced Moffat to include instead the thinly-disguised – at times, rather *too* thinly-disguised – substitute Tasha Lem, well portrayed by Orla Brady.

There is also a sense here of Moffat tying up remaining loose ends – clarifying how Madame Kovarian and the Silents fit in with the Church of the Papal Mainframe; making explicit who was responsible for the TARDIS blowing up in 'The Big Bang'; confirming that Gallifrey survives but is now trapped in another, pocket universe; bringing the cracks in time storyline full circle – and this lends a genuine and satisfying sense of closure to the eleventh Doctor's era. There is even a welcome surprise cameo appearance by Karen Gillan, as the Doctor sees a brief vision of Amy Pond bidding him an emotionally-charged farewell with the words, 'Raggedy man, good night' – the only downside to this being that it really brings home the extent to which Jenna Coleman has been living in Gillan's shadow in her first few stories as Clara. As strong an impact as Coleman has made since her debut, there is no doubt that Amy is the quintessential eleventh Doctor companion; the one who will always be most closely associated with his era. It could indeed be argued that it was a little unfair for Steven Moffat to have brought Gillan back for this cameo appearance while Coleman was still working hard to establish herself in the show. With luck, though, Clara would now be able to come more into her own, travelling alongside the twelfth Doctor.

On the subject of companions, the Doctor acquires a temporary new one in this story in the form of the severed Cyberman head that he calls Handles. This to some extent recalls his former robotic pet K-9, and perhaps even more so Tom Baker's rather frivolous suggestion, back in the late-1970s, that his Doctor ought to dispense with human companions in favour of a talking cabbage that would perch on his shoulder! Handles works surprisingly well as a character, and the scene where he eventually 'dies', after centuries of loyal service, packs a real emotional punch.

Director Jamie Payne, who made his *Doctor Who* debut on the more low-key episode 'Hide', does another good job here, including on the spectacular action sequences of the Daleks attacking Trenzalore at the end. The town of Christmas is well realised, and is one of the few overtly Christmassy elements included, by virtue not only of its name, but also of its snowy aspect and the Victorian-style local clothing and customs, which combine to give it a distinctly Dickensian feel reminiscent of 'A Christmas Carol' – both the original 1843 novella and the 2010 *Doctor Who* Christmas special of the same title. The way the Doctor takes the townsfolk under his wing is really rather charming, and the fondness he shows toward the young boy Barnable somewhat recalls his friendship with the Arwell children in the earlier Christmas special 'The Doctor, the Widow and the Wardrobe' (2011).

What the whole story is leading up to, of course, is the regeneration at the end; and unfortunately this is not handled as well as it might be. The idea of the Time Lords giving the Doctor a whole new regeneration cycle is sound enough, and neatly circumvents the nagging problem of the 12-regeneration limit established way back in 1976 in 'The Deadly Assassin'. Less satisfactory, though, is the notion that this particular regeneration is accompanied by such a huge outpouring of energy that the Doctor is able to use it to destroy the Daleks, and presumably all of the other alien forces, attacking Trenzalore. No real explanation is given for this; and if such a comprehensive victory can be achieved simply by unleashing the regeneration energy of just a single member of their race, it begs the question why the Time Lords did not feel confident to return to the universe in the first place; and, indeed, why they still do not return even at the end of the story, after the alien fleets have been wiped out – the attackers' presence having been, supposedly, what has prevented them from doing so before, for fear that it would precipitate a new Time War. Possibly the fact that the crack in time moves from inside the clock tower to the sky above it, and then snaps shut after the Time Lords have sent through the regeneration energy, is intended to indicate that, in order to help the Doctor, they have had to sacrifice their chance to return. If so, however, this is by no means clear from the on-screen action; and even if such a solution to the siege did not become viable until the Doctor was dying of old age and ready to regenerate, it does leave the viewer wondering if there really was no other way he could have avoided spending hundreds of years on Trenzalore; surely, with his formidable intelligence, and all his long experience of dealing with other alien invasion attempts, he should have been able to come up with some clever plan to end it at a much earlier stage? Of all the Doctors, the irrepressible eleventh seems perhaps the least likely of all simply to accept being stuck on one planet, indeed in one small town, for centuries on end – probably, in fact, the greater part of this incarnation's entire lifetime, which is by this point easily the longest of all the Doctors.

The other troubling thing about this sequence is that the Doctor's gleeful destruction of the Dalek attackers, celebrated with the bellicose taunt 'With love from Gallifrey, boys!', seems distinctly out of character – actually, more the type of action one would associate with the War Doctor than the eleventh. There have, admittedly, been a few other occasions when this Doctor has acted in a similarly uncompromising way – one is uncomfortably reminded of how, at the start of 'A Good Man Goes to War', he destroyed a whole Cyberman fleet simply in order to make a point – but one would have hoped that, by this late stage of his life, he would have gained the maturity to tame his ruthless streak, which in 'The Name of the Doctor' caused the Great Intelligence to refer disdainfully to his 'blood-soaked standards'. On the other hand, perhaps the events of 'The Day of the Doctor' have led him finally to accept and embrace the previously unacknowledged warrior aspect of his nature. If so, this is something we could possibly see even more of during subsequent Doctors' eras – which would be an interesting departure for the character, although not, in this author's opinion, a particularly welcome one.

Yet another issue with the regeneration is that it suffers, albeit to a lesser extent, from one of the same problems as the tenth Doctor's in 'The End of Time' Part Two; specifically, that it is overly drawn out. The ideal point for the transformation to have occurred, in dramatic terms, would have been at the climax of the elderly Doctor blasting the Dalek fleet with regeneration energy from the top of the clock tower. Instead, however, Steven Moffat has chosen to include a coda, set in the TARDIS console room, where the eleventh Doctor is for no good reason restored to his usual youthful appearance and has a final conversation with Clara before he suddenly changes into the twelfth. Had this sequence not been included, we would admittedly have been denied the poignant Karen Gillan cameo appearance – unless a way could have been found to work this in at an earlier point – and also a very well-written farewell speech, which Matt Smith delivers with his usual skill; but the way this closing section of the script is structured is far from ideal.

All told, then, 'The Time of the Doctor' concludes the eleventh Doctor's era in rather disappointing fashion. It is not a bad episode as such, but a somewhat uninspired and largely unrepresentative one that falls well short of the best of the often brilliant three series' worth of episodes that have preceded it.

Overview

The strongest part of Series Seven is unquestionably the 2012 section. The first five episodes all have a great deal going for them, despite some plot holes in 'Asylum of the Daleks' and 'The Angels Take Manhattan' and a disconcerting unevenness of tone in 'Dinosaurs on a Spaceship'. It is only with the distinctly confused and unsatisfying exit given to Amy and Rory at the end of this mini-arc that the ball is sadly fumbled. The 2012 Christmas special 'The Snowmen' is also rather let down by a weak ending, despite having a lot of positive points in its favour, but 'The Bells of Saint John' opens the 2013 run in fine style, and gives a good introduction to 21st Century Clara – although, despite Jenna-Louise Coleman's strong performance, she isn't quite as appealing a character as either of her prior *alter egos*, Oswin in 'Asylum of the Daleks' and Victoria-era Clara in 'The Snowmen'. From this point on, though, things take a downward turn. 'The Rings of Akhaten' and 'Hide' both have serious scripting issues, and 'Journey to the Centre of the TARDIS' and 'Nightmare in Silver' are two badly flawed episodes. Fortunately there are some high points amongst the disappointments, with the excellent Mark Gatiss-scripted contributions 'Cold War' and 'The Crimson Horror' and Steven Moffat's superb finale 'The Name of the Doctor' – the latter being probably the best episode of the entire series. Overall, though, Series Seven is a real mixed bag, and certainly the weakest of the three that Moffat has overseen to this point.

Although considered alongside Series Seven for the purposes of the episode guide above, 'The Day of the Doctor' and 'The Time of the Doctor' are really more correctly categorised as separate one-off productions. Transmitted just over a month apart, these two specials rounded off the celebrations for *Doctor Who*'s incredible fiftieth anniversary year and brought to an end the era of the eleventh Doctor. 'The Day of the Doctor' is a landmark story in every sense, paying homage to the past while also introducing some radical new additions to the show's mythology, most notably the previously unknown War Doctor incarnation; but it is inevitably diminished by Christopher Eccleston's non-participation and suffers somewhat from over-ambition. 'The Time of the Doctor', by contrast, is rather lacklustre, and gives the always excellent Matt Smith an uncharacteristically subdued final bow.

One especially notable aspect of the 2012-2013 stories, taken as a whole, is the way Steven Moffat has used them to complete a gradual process of unpicking almost all of the innovations brought to *Doctor Who* by his predecessor Russell T Davies. When Davies took charge of the show for its 2005 revival, he carefully tailored it to appeal to a modern audience. The Doctor was presented as a relatively young, no-nonsense figure with close-cropped hair and unostentatious working men's clothes that could pass without comment in a contemporary setting; an element of romance was introduced to the relationship between the Doctor and his down-to-earth shop girl companion Rose; the action all took place on or within sight of Earth, so that viewers could easily relate to the situations and characters depicted; Gallifrey was consigned to history, leaving the Doctor as the lone survivor of his Time Lord race; and there were few if any back-references made to the show's rich classic-era continuity, ensuring that the new stories were completely accessible even to those who had no prior knowledge of *Doctor Who*. By the end of 2013, by contrast, the Doctor has reverted to wearing a Victorian-style frock coat reminiscent of the outfits of some of his classic-era predecessors; he is back to being a decidedly eccentric character, complete with trademark bow tie and prominent quiff; the element of romance has been significantly toned down in the relationship between him and his far from down-to-earth companion Clara; the action encompasses a succession of far-flung settings in time and space; Gallifrey and the Time Lords have been brought back, albeit still currently confined to a separate universe; and the stories now revolve around the show's own continuity to an extent not seen since 'The Trial of a Time Lord' (1986). In 'The Day of the Doctor' and 'The Time of the Doctor', these developments come to their logical culmination, as the Doctor is depicted as an older man more in keeping with most of his classic-era incarnations: first in the form of the War Doctor, then in that of the greatly aged eleventh Doctor, and finally in that of the newly-regenerated Peter Capaldi version. Of course, 21st Century *Doctor Who* still differs in many ways from 20th Century *Doctor Who* – not least in its style and pace of storytelling, and in its increased emotional content. However, there is no question that, by the time the twelfth Doctor makes his sudden, startling arrival inside the TARDIS, the distinctions between the two are narrower than at any point previously.

In my analysis of 'The Day of the Doctor', I argued that, instead of devising the War Doctor, Steven Moffat would have been better advised to give the third lead role in that story to Paul McGann as the eighth Doctor. If he missed a great opportunity when he failed to do that, then arguably he and his BBC colleagues passed up an even more golden one in 'The Time of the Doctor': Matt Smith's departure at the end of the Christmas special created – in this author's opinion – an ideal opening to bring McGann back for a full starring run in the show, either as a rejuvenated eighth Doctor or as a new incarnation who simply happened to look like the eighth – a precedent for which had already been set with the Curator in 'The Day of the Doctor', and his statement that the Doctor's future incarnations would revisit some of the 'old favourites' amongst his former faces. Given McGann's proven popularity in the role, this would have been an entirely risk-free option. It is telling that, in a subsequent *Doctor Who Magazine* readers' poll, a remarkable 13% of respondents cited the McGann-starring 'The Night of the Doctor' – a seven-minute-long minisode – as their favourite thing about the entire fiftieth anniversary year, putting it in fourth place – with 'The Day of the Doctor' in first place polling only marginally better, at 16%.[93] The American literary and cultural affairs magazine *The Atlantic* even went so far as to list the minisode as one of the top television highlights of 2013. Small wonder that hundreds of fans subsequently signed an online petition calling for McGann to be given his own spin-off show.

Even after all these years, bringing in any new actor to play the Doctor is inevitably a risky business. There is always a chance that he (or, potentially, she) might fail to find favour with the viewing public. Arguably, though, in their choice of Peter Capaldi, an actor previously best known for his role as the aggressive, foul-mouthed Malcolm Tucker in the political sitcom *The Thick of It* (BBC, 2005-2012), the BBC were taking an even bigger gamble than usual. How wise that gamble was, only subsequent series would show. However, there seems little question that, with an older, seemingly spikier Doctor cast, and the stories increasingly trading on *Doctor Who*'s own complex continuity, the show was moving in a direction likely to appeal more to dedicated fans and less to casual viewers – an approach that proved fairly disastrous back in the mid-1980s.

Perhaps, though, if the amazing hoopla surrounding the fiftieth anniversary demonstrated anything at all it was that, unlike in decades gone by, *Doctor Who* fans were no longer a tiny minority of the viewing

---

[93] The results appeared in Issue 479.

audience; a mere subset of general cult TV enthusiasts. On the contrary, with millions of passionately devoted viewers around the world, the show had never been more popular. When the feature-length anniversary special was regarded as a sufficiently significant television milestone to justify a record-breaking 94-country simulcast and support numerous tie-in programmes and events – not to mention screenings in over 1,500 cinemas worldwide, doing enough business to put it into the upper reaches of many countries' box-office charts for the week, even with just that single showing – the only reasonable conclusion one can draw is that the dedicated followers had by this point come to outnumber the casual viewers; and if there was any degree of unfamiliarity with the minutiae of the show's mythology, this clearly presented no obstacle to their enjoying it.

In 2013 it seemed that finally, after fifty years, almost everyone was a *Doctor Who* fan.

PART SIX

Appendices

Appendix A
An Adventure in Space and Time

Writer: Mark Gatiss
Producer: Matt Strevens
Director: Terry McDonough

DEBUT TRANSMISSION DETAILS

BBC Two/BBC Two HD
Date: 21 November 2013

Duration: 83' 02"

CREDITED PRODUCTION TEAM

Simon Maloney (1st Assistant Director), Tom Alibone (2nd Assistant Director), Matt Jennings (3rd Assistant Director), James Metcalf, Calum Carpenter, Jennifer Golding (Floor Runners), David Robbins (Production Accountant), Simon Wheeler (Assistant Production Accountant), Pippa Suren (Production Co-ordinator), Catriona Scott (Production Secretary), Sam Donovan (Script Supervisor), Jack Thomas-O'Brien (Production Runner), Lucienne Suren (Art Director), Kate Purdy (Standby Art Director), Julian Nix (Graphic Designer), Oliver Benson (Art Department Assistant), Stuart Bryce (Prop Buyer), Colleen Macleod (Assistant Prop Buyer), Dan Crandon, Brian Quin (Construction Managers), Iain Adrian, Daniel Bishop (Camera Operators), Peter 'Skip' Howard (Focus Puller), Phoebe Arnstein, Felix Pickles (Camera Loader), Louise McMenemy (Camera Trainee), Marc Tempest (Camera Grip), Daniel Rees (Assistant Camera Grip), Alice Purser (Casting Associate), Becky Brown (Costume Supervisor), Sue Gurley (Costume Standby), Emily Thompson (Costume Assistant), Maudie Whitehead (Costume Trainee), Chloe Marsden

(Costume Construction), Ian Barwick (Gaffer), Tony Allen (Rigging Gaffer), Mathew Buchan (Best Boy), Bruno Martins, Dave Marriott, Steve Blythe, Mark Packman, Eamonn Fitzgerald (Electricians), Ricky Davis, Dan Smith (Camera Operators), Sharon Colley, Claire Burgess, Sophie Roberts, Laura Morse (Make-up Artists), Emma Collinson, Tobin Hughs (Unit Managers), Robert Judd (Prop Master), Dave Simons (Prop Chargehand), Barney Ward, Matt French (Standby Prop Hand), Tony Bandy, Pete Fentem, Scott Rogers (Dressing Prop), Paul McNamara (Prop Maker), Sarah Howe (Boom Op), Howard Peryer (In Vision Fishing Boom Op), Pablo Lopez Jordan (Sound Assistant), Paul Oakman (Standby Carpenter), Nick Martin (Unit Medic), Jenni Pain (Drama Publicist BBC), Liz Pearson, Claire McGrane (Post Production Supervisors), Adam Harvey, Matt Bate (Assistant Editors), Asa Shoul (Colourist), Des Murray (Online Editor), Nigel Squibbs (Dubbing Mixer), Tony Gibson (Sound Design), Roger Dobson (Dialogue Editor), Chris Panton (Visual Effects), Dicky Howett, Paul Marshall, Mark Jordan, Clive Sapsford (Technical Advisors), Geoff Alexander (Conductor), Toby Wood (Music Engineer), Alan Tribe, Tom O'Shea, Terry Collins, Liam Fellows (Unit Drivers), Andy Prior CDG (Casting Director), Llyr Morus, Julie Scott (Production Executives), Lindsey Alford, Richard Cooksen (Script Editors), Nick Wade (Location Manager), Simon Clark (Sound Recordist), Suzanne Cave (Costume Designer), Vickie Lang (Make-up Designer), Edmund Butt (Composer), Philip Kloss (Editor), Dave Arrowsmith (Production Designer), John Pardue (Director of Photography), Matthew Patnick (Line Producer), Mark Gatiss, Steven Moffat, Caroline Skinner (Executive Producers),

CREDITED CAST

David Bradley (William Hartnell), Ross Gurney-Randall (Reg), Roger May (Len), Sam Hoare (Douglas Camfield), Charlie Kemp (Arthur), Brian Cox (Sydney Newman), William Russell (Harry – Security Guard), Jeff Rawle (Mervyn Pinfield), Andrew Woodall (Rex Tucker), Jessica Raine (Verity Lambert), Jemma Powell (Jacqueline Hill), Lesley Manville (Heather Hartnell), Cara Jenkins (Judith Carney[94]), Sacha Dhawan (Waris Hussein), Toby Hadoke (Cyril), Sarah Winter (Delia Derbyshire), Jamie

---

[94] William Hartnell's grand-daughter Judith Carney is now better known as Jessica Carney, also the late actor's biographer.

Glover (William Russell), Claudia Grant (Carole Ann Ford), David Annen (Peter Brachacki), Mark Eden (Donald Baverstock), Ian Hallard (Richard Martin), Nicholas Briggs (Peter Hawkins), Carole Ann Ford (Joyce), Reece Pockney (Alan), Reece Shearsmith (Patrick Troughton)

CRITICAL REACTION

- 'This programme captured the spirit, wit and capacity for storytelling that was the essence of ... BBC Television Centre, with *Doctor Who* at its heart. Fifty years later ... thank goodness one of these is still going strong.' Caroline Frost, *Huffington Post* UK website, 21 November 2013.

- 'Wonderfully written and beautifully realised, this period piece crackled with the affection of a true fan. A warm glow radiated from the screen and bathed the viewer in TV magic. Bravo.' Michael Hogan, *Telegraph* website, 21 November 2013.

- 'There's a certain crackle that comes with watching the dramatisation of the creation of a popular, pervasive piece of art. *Ray* had it. *Walk the Line* had it. *Ed Wood* had it. *An Adventure in Space and Time* has it. And I can't think of a better way to pay tribute to a series that can go anywhere than by going back to its beginning.' Marc Bernardin, *Hollywood Reporter* website, 22 November 2013.

PRODUCTION NOTES

- *An Adventure in Space and Time* was a BBC America and BBC Wales co-production.

- Mark Gatiss first conceived the idea of a docu-drama about *Doctor Who*'s origins some ten years earlier, but finally got it off the ground in 2013 – fittingly, just in time to mark the show's fiftieth anniversary.

- The title was taken from the way *Doctor Who* used to be listed by the *Radio Times* in the 1960s.

- Recording began in February 2013 and took place primarily at the

Wimbledon Studios and BBC Television Centre in London. This was in fact the last drama production to be made at Television Centre before that iconic building's closure the following month and subsequent much-lamented demolition. The most prominent location recording took place on 17 February on Westminster Bridge in London, recreating a scene from 'The Dalek Invasion of Earth' (1964). Other locations used included Wimbledon Common on 4 February and a pub on Wilton Road, in the Victoria area, on 5 February.

• The drama features cameo appearances by a number of *Doctor Who*'s original stars, including William Russell, Carole Ann Ford and (uncredited, in a scene of original producer Verity Lambert's leaving party) Jean Marsh (Sara Kingdom) and Anneke Wills (Polly). 1960s script editor Donald Tosh also appears (again, uncredited, in the leaving party scene).

• In addition to the original trio of William Russell (Ian), Jacqueline Hill (Barbara) and Carole Ann Ford (Susan), a number of original *Doctor Who* companion actors were briefly portrayed in the drama by uncredited cast members: Anna-Lisa Drew as Maureen O'Brien (Vicki), Edmund C Short as Peter Purves (Steven Taylor), Sophie Holt as Jackie Lane (Dodo Chaplet), Robin Varley as Michael Craze (Ben Jackson) and Ellie Spicer as Anneke Wills (Polly).

• Also in an uncredited cameo appearance at the end of the drama is Matt Smith as the eleventh Doctor.

• The action concludes with a clip of William Hartnell's Doctor delivering his farewell speech to Susan at the end of 'The Dalek Invasion of Earth'. This same clip was also used to open *Doctor Who*'s twentieth anniversary special 'The Five Doctors' (1983).

• Mark Gatiss at one point envisaged making a cameo appearance as third Doctor actor Jon Pertwee, but this was cut.

• The opening and closing title sequences consisted of outtakes from the original *Doctor Who* opening title sequence designed by Bernard Lodge.

- The docu-drama had an audience of 2.71 million viewers. It was subsequently released on DVD, and also as part of the *50th Anniversary Collector's Edition* DVD and Blu-ray box set. The extras included Gatiss as the third Doctor, and a number of specially-recorded recreations of scenes from first Doctor episodes, performed by the docu-drama's principal cast members. Parts of these were seen on screens as the action was recorded during the docu-drama itself, but the scenes are presented 'as recorded' in the extras.

ANALYSIS

An Adventure in Space and Time is a moving, heartfelt love-letter by Mark Gatiss to the early years of *Doctor Who*, with some excellent performances and high production values. Unfortunately, as signalled by the opening monologue about 'rewriting history' – borrowing some lines from 'The Aztecs' (1964) – this is at the expense of presenting an honest picture of how *Doctor Who* really came into being. Several key contributors, including co-creator Donald Wilson and first script editor David Whitaker, are omitted altogether, and others are placed in unrealistic positions – to give just one of many examples, associate producer Mervyn Pinfield is shown as being still involved in the autumn of 1966, which was actually some two years after he had left *Doctor Who* and several months after he had died. The specifics of how the show was made in the 1960s are also wildly misrepresented, and although David Bradley gives a very strong central performance, the way William Hartnell is characterised does not get particularly close to the real man. This was never intended as a documentary, however, but as a docu-drama – and as a piece of drama, it succeeds very well indeed.

Appendix B
The Five(Ish) Doctors Reboot

Immediately after the BBC One debut transmission of the fiftieth anniversary special 'The Day of the Doctor', the humorous tie-in *The Five(ish) Doctors Reboot* became available to view via the BBC Red Button service. This had numerous former and current *Doctor Who* stars and production team members, their families and others appearing – generally as fictionalised versions of themselves – in a tongue-in-cheek storyline written and directed by fifth Doctor actor Peter Davison, who was the initiator and principal driving force behind the project.

Writer: Peter Davison
Director: Peter Davison

DEBUT TRANSMISSION DETAILS

BBC Red Button
Date: 23 November 2013

Duration: 30' 45"

CREDITED PRODUCTION TEAM

James deHaviland, Jennie Fava, Jack Wren (Assistant Directors), Michael Williams (Floor Runner), Luke Baker, Matt Andrews (Camera Operators), Cai Thompson, Gethin Williams, Sarah Jones (Camera Assistants), Dewi Jones, Tony Bell (Boom Operators), Julia Jones (Standby Props), Catrin Thomas, Ros Wilkins, Bethan Kate Harris (Make-up & Hair Artist), Katrina Aust (Assembly Editor), Joel Skinner (VFX Editor), Gary Hewson (Online Editor), Owen Thomas (Dubbing Mixer), Sam Price (Post-Production Coordinator), Nerys Davies (Post-Production Supervisor),

APPENDIX B

Derek Ritchie (Script Editor), Deian Humphreys, Wil Planitzer, Christian Joyce (Sound Recordists), Ceres Doyle, Jamie Pearson (Editors), Simon Walton (Director of Photography), Julie Scott (Head of Production), Katie Player (Production Manager), Steffan Morris (Line Producer), Georgia Moffett (Producer), Steven Moffat, Brian Minchin (Executive Producers)

CREDITED CAST (IN ORDER OF APPEARANCE)

Sean Pertwee, Olivia Coleman, Peter Davison, Louis Davison, Joel Davison, Jenna Coleman, Matt Smith, Steven Moffat, Heddi-Joy Taylor-Welch, Louisa Cavel, Lauren Kilcar, James DeHaviland, Janet Fielding, Sylvester McCoy, Colin Baker, Rhys Thomas, Georgia Moffett, Olivia Darnley, Niky Wardley, Marion Baker, Katy Manning, Louise Jameson, Carole Ann Ford, Deborah Watling[95], Sophie Aldred, Sarah Sutton, Lalla Ward, John Leeson, Anneke Wills, Lisa Bowerman, Matthew Waterhouse, Paul McGann, Jon Culshaw, Jemma Churchill, Lucy Baker, Bindy Baker, Lally Baker, Rosie Baker, Bruno Du Bois, Peter Jackson, Ian McKellen, John Barrowman, Alice Knight, Sarah Churm, Nick Jordan, Brad Kelly, David Tennant, Richard Cookson, Elizabeth Morton, Marcus Elliott, Ty Tennant, Barnaby Edwards, Nicholas Pegg, David Troughton, Nicholas Briggs, Frank Skinner, Adam Paul Harvey, Derek Ritchie, Michael Houghton, Dan Starkey, Russell T Davies, Des Hughes, Gabriella Ricci, Sandra Cosfeld, Christian Brassington

PLOT

Disgruntled former Doctor actors Peter Davison, Colin Baker and Sylvester McCoy engage in various subterfuges to try to secure appearances in the *Doctor Who* fiftieth anniversary special, and eventually succeed – on the Under-Gallery set, incognito under the white dust-sheets that the Zygons have supposedly appropriated to conceal themselves.

CRITICAL REACTION

• 'With its synth-heavy incidental music evoking '80s Who and its wry take on the show's once minimal budget ("I used to love the old wobble!"), this special was both a satisfying in-joke for

---

[95] First name misspelt 'Debora'.

Whovians and a naughty dig at the neediness of actors.' Ben Lawrence, Telegraph website, 24 November 2013.

PRODUCTION NOTES

- Peter Davison originally envisaged this as an independent project, but after he discussed it with Steven Moffat, the showrunner agreed to provide some resources and personnel, and it was made as a BBC Wales production.

- The title is a reference to that of the twentieth anniversary story, 'The Five Doctors' (1983).

- The production opens and closes with a variation on the standard eleventh Doctor title sequences, minus the image of Matt Smith's face.

- A slightly edited version of the production was later given a commercial release on the 50th Anniversary Collector's Edition DVD and Blu-ray box set.

ANALYSIS

Peter Davison had previously made a couple of short, humorous videos to be screened as treats for fans attending the annual Gallifrey One conventions in Los Angeles, USA, and *The Five(ish) Doctors Reboot* is in a similar vein, although far more ambitious, and involving many more people. The humour is beautifully observed, with lots of in-jokes for the fans to appreciate – such as John Barrowman apparently having a secret life, married to a woman and with young children; Tom Baker, voiced by impressionist John Culshaw, declining to participate, as he did in the case of 'The Five Doctors' itself; and repeated mentions of Sylvester McCoy's involvement in the *Lord of the Rings* film franchise – which lead on to its director Peter Jackson and star Ian McKellen putting in brief appearances. The production also serves as a fitting contribution to *Doctor Who*'s fiftieth anniversary celebrations by those classic-era Doctors who could not be accommodated in 'The Day of the Doctor' itself. It is a nice touch, too, that some of their family members are involved in the project – including notably Peter Davison's daughter and David Tennant's wife Georgia

Moffett, who produced, and Davison's and Colin Baker's wives and children. The Troughton and Pertwee families are also represented, with cameo appearances from David Troughton and Sean Pertwee. All in all, a thoroughly enjoyable tie-in.

Appendix C
Ratings and Rankings

This Appendix is subdivided into four sections, revealing: i) the facts of how the 16 episodes covered by this book – the 13 episodes of Series Seven proper plus 'The Snowmen', 'The Day of the Doctor' and 'The Time of the Doctor' – performed in terms of their ratings, audience shares, chart positions, appreciation index (AI) figures and other viewer reaction data; ii) the relative popularity of the 16 episodes in terms of their ratings, AI figures and fan rankings; iii) the comparative picture of how the figures for these episodes measure up to those for the previous six full series of 21st Century *Doctor Who* (omitting the 'gap year' specials of 2009/10, owing to their atypical transmission pattern); and iv) the main conclusions that can be drawn from the data presented in sections i) to iii).

i) THE FACTS

Table One below lists, for the BBC One[96] debut transmissions of each of the 16 episodes covered in this book: the estimated total number of viewers aged four and over (corrected and adjusted to include those who recorded the episode to watch within the week following transmission) in millions (RATING); percentage share of the total television audience at the time of transmission (SHARE); chart position amongst all programmes transmitted the same day on BBC One (D); overall chart position amongst all programmes transmitted the same day on all terrestrial channels (D/O); chart position amongst all programmes transmitted the same week (Monday to Sunday inclusive) on BBC One (W); overall chart position amongst all programmes transmitted the same week (Monday to Sunday) on all

---

[96] All references to BBC One include BBC One HD.

terrestrial channels (W/O); and the audience AI as a percentage.

TABLE ONE – RATINGS, AUDIENCE SHARES, CHART POSITIONS, AI FIGURES

EPISODE	RATING	SHARE	D	D/O	W	W/O	AI
'Asylum of the Daleks'	8.33	34.4	1st	2nd	3rd	6th	89
'Dinosaurs on a Spaceship'	7.57	31.9	1st	2nd	4th	9th	87
'A Town Called Mercy'	8.42	33.4	2nd	3rd	2nd	9th	85
'The Power of Three'	7.67	31.8	1st	2nd	5th	13th	87
'The Angels Take Manhattan'	7.82	32.0	1st	2nd	5th	13th	88
'The Snowmen'	9.87	38.8	4th	6th	7th	9th	87
'The Bells of Saint John'	8.44	35.8	1st	1st	2nd	8th	87
'The Rings of Akhaten'	7.45	34.8	2nd	3rd	6th	16th	84
'Cold War'	7.37	31.4	2nd	3rd	5th	15th	84
'Hide'	6.61	29.2	2nd	3rd	6th	19th	85
'Journey to the Centre of the TARDIS'	6.50	30.2	2nd	3rd	7th	21st	85
'The Crimson Horror'	6.47	31.5	2nd	3rd	6th	20th	85
'Nightmare in Silver'	6.64	27.1	2nd	3rd	9th	22nd	84
'The Name of the Doctor'	7.45	31.7	2nd	3rd	3rd	10th	88
'The Day of the Doctor'	12.80	40.9	1st	1st	1st	1st	88
'The Time of the Doctor'	11.14	30.7	2nd	2nd	2nd	3rd	83

Source for viewing figures: Broadcasters' Audience Research Board (BARB)
Source for AI figures: BBC

The full ratings statistics produced by BARB for the main BBC One transmissions (which go into too fine a level of detail to be reproduced in their entirety here) reveal that, as in previous years, *Doctor Who* consistently scored well above the average for drama programmes under a range of viewer response headings including 'It was high quality', 'It was original and different' and 'It was entertaining'. The percentage male/female split in the show's audience over the course of the series averaged 52/48 – a very slight shift toward the male from the 51/49 recorded for Series Six and the 50/50 recorded for Series Five – whereas for BBC One dramas in general it averages 40/61[97] – also a slight shift toward the male from the 38/62 for 2011 and the 36/64 for 2010. The age breakdown was much the same as for previous series. The biggest sections of the audience came in the 4-15, 35-44 and 45-54 age ranges, each of which made up just less than 20% of the total on average. The smallest section was in the 16-24 age range, which accounted for about 10% of the total on average. This means that, on average, around 70% of the show's viewers were over the age of 24. No doubt many of these would have been parents watching with children – indicating that the show was continuing to meet its family-viewing remit – although clearly, as in previous years, it also had a large adult following.

For each transmission of each television programme on the channels it covers, BARB gives not only a final ratings figure but also an initial 'overnight' figure, which is generally available the next day after the transmission. The overnight figure indicates how many viewers watched the programme on the day of transmission, whereas the final figure, which usually becomes available about eight days later, is adjusted to include also those who recorded it to watch within the same week. The difference between the overnight and the final ratings figures for a given programme thus shows how many people 'time-shifted' their viewing of that programme during the week in question.[98, 99] Table Two records what the time-shift was (in millions of viewers) for the BBC One debut transmissions

---

[97] Adds up to more than 100 due to rounding.
[98] Viewers who miss a programme's 'live' transmission but catch up with it later the same day – referred to by the statisticians as VOSDAL, or 'viewing on same day as live' – are counted within the overnight figure, even though they too have technically time-shifted.
[99] Occasionally other adjustments and corrections are made between the overnight and final ratings figures for a programme, but these are generally minor compared with the time-shift factor.

of each of the 2012/2013 run of *Doctor Who* episodes.

TABLE TWO – TIME-SHIFT

EPISODE	OVERNIGHT RATING	FINAL RATING	TIME-SHIFT
'Asylum of the Daleks'	6.39	8.33	1.94
'Dinosaurs on a Spaceship'	5.43	7.57	2.14
'A Town Called Mercy'	6.49	8.42	1.93
'The Power of Three'	5.59	7.67	2.08
'The Angels Take Manhattan'	5.86	7.82	1.96
'The Snowmen'	7.49	9.87	2.38
'The Bells of Saint John'	6.15	8.44	2.29
'The Rings of Akhaten'	5.48	7.45	1.97
'Cold War'	5.67	7.37	1.70
'Hide'	4.97	6.61	1.64
'Journey to the Centre of the TARDIS'	4.86	6.50	1.64
'The Crimson Horror'	4.61	6.47	1.83
'Nightmare in Silver'	4.73	6.64	1.86
'The Name of the Doctor'	5.45	7.45	2.00
'The Day of the Doctor'	10.20	12.80	2.60
'The Time of the Doctor'	8.29	11.14	2.85
AVERAGE	**6.10**	**8.16**	**2.05**

Source: Broadcasters' Audience Research Board (BARB)

Table Three indicates how many viewers (in millions) each episode attracted not only on its BBC One debut but also on its BBC Three repeat and through unique same-week hits on the BBC's interactive iPlayer service. This gives an overall total viewing figure – otherwise known as audience reach – for the whole period. The figures for the specials 'The

Snowmen', 'The Day of the Doctor' and 'The Time of the Doctor' are not strictly comparable to those for the other 13 episodes, and so are given separately.

TABLE THREE – TOTAL AUDIENCE REACH

EPISODE	BBC ONE DEBUT	BBC THREE REPEAT	BBC iPLAYER	ALL
'Asylum of the Daleks'	8.33	0.58	0.93	9.84
'Dinosaurs on a Spaceship'	7.57	0.59	0.76	8.92
'A Town Called Mercy'	8.42	0.31	0.68	9.41
'The Power of Three'	7.67	0.46	0.69	8.82
'The Angels Take Manhattan'	7.82	0.45	0.82	9.09
'The Bells of Saint John'	8.44	0.52	0.95	9.91
'The Rings of Akhaten'	7.45	0.43	0.90	8.78
'Cold War'	7.37	0.31	0.76	8.44
'Hide'	6.61	0.42	0.77	7.80
'Journey to the Centre of the TARDIS'	6.50	0.41	0.79	7.70
'The Crimson Horror'	6.47	0.50	0.83	7.80
'Nightmare in Silver'	6.64	0.42	0.89	7.95
'The Name of the Doctor'	7.45	0.49	0.92	8.86
Average over 13 episodes	**7.44**	**0.45**	**0.82**	8.71

EPISODE	BBC ONE DEBUT	BBC THREE REPEATS	BBC iPLAYER	ALL
'The Snowmen'	9.87	1.01	0.60	11.33
'The Day of the Doctor	12.80	0.68	2.81	16.29
'The Time of the Doctor'	11.14	0.41	1.95	13.50
Average over three specials	**11.27**	**0.65**	**1.79**	**13.71**

Source for viewing figures: Broadcasters' Audience Research Board (BARB)
Source for iPlayer figures: BBC.
BBC One includes BBC One HD

Figures for total non-unique iPlayer hits (in millions) across the duration of the whole series were as follows:

TABLE FOUR – TOTAL iPLAYER HITS

EPISODE	DAYS AVAILABLE	iPLAYER HITS
'Asylum of the Daleks'	36	2.26
'Dinosaurs on a Spaceship'	29	1.83
'A Town Called Mercy'	22	1.41
'The Power of Three'	15	1.46
'The Angels Take Manhattan'	14	1.65
'The Snowmen'	12	1.60
'The Bells of Saint John'	57	2.51
'The Rings of Akhaten'	50	2.20
'Cold War'	43	1.85
'Hide'	36	1.83
'Journey to the Centre of the TARDIS'	29	1.77
'The Crimson Horror'	22	1.71
'Nightmare in Silver'	15	1.73
'The Name of the Doctor'	14	1.90
'The Day of the Doctor'	n/k	3.10
'The Time of the Doctor'	n/k	1.96

Source: BBC

An indication of how the episodes shaped up in the estimation of dedicated fans can be gleaned from the online episode polls conducted on Gallifrey Base – the most popular *Doctor Who* fan forum on the internet – at www.gallifreybase.com. An average of 3,629 voters participated in these polls, ranging from a low of 2,981 for 'The Power of Three' to a high of 4,512 for 'The Day of the Doctor' Each episode was given a mark of between one and ten by each voter, with ten being the highest. The percentages – or 'fan AIs' – in the table below have been calculated by adding together the total number of marks received by each episode (as of 26 May 2016) and dividing by the maximum that could have been achieved if everyone who voted had given the episode a ten.

TABLE FIVE – FAN APPRECIATION INDEX

EPISODE	FAN AI
'Asylum of the Daleks'	81
'Dinosaurs on a Spaceship'	70
'A Town Called Mercy'	71
'The Power of Three'	71
'The Angels Take Manhattan'	84
'The Snowmen'	80
'The Bells of Saint John'	73
'The Rings of Akhaten'	57
'Cold War'	85
'Hide'	78
'Journey to the Centre of the TARDIS'	72
'The Crimson Horror'	75
'Nightmare in Silver'	67
'The Name of the Doctor'	87
'The Day of the Doctor'	88
'The Time of the Doctor'	69
Average	**76**

Source: Gallifrey Base

ii) RELATIVE POPULARITY

The total reach figures set out in Table Three above indicate that the ranking of the episodes from most-watched to least-watched was as follows:

TABLE SIX – RANKING BY TOTAL AUDIENCE REACH

1	'The Day of the Doctor'
2	'The Time of the Doctor'
3	'The Snowmen'
4	'The Bells of Saint John'
5	'Asylum of the Daleks'
6	'A Town Called Mercy'
7	'The Angels Take Manhattan'
8	'The Name of the Doctor'
9	'The Power of Three'
10	'Dinosaurs on a Spaceship'
11	'The Rings of Akhaten'
12	'Cold War'
13	'Nightmare in Silver'
14	'Hide'
15	'The Crimson Horror'
16	'Journey to the Centre of the TARDIS'

Based on the AI figures for the BBC One debut transmissions, the general viewing public's order of preference for the episodes, working downwards from favourite to least favourite, was:

TABLE SEVEN – RANKING BY DEBUT TRANSMISSION AI FIGURES

1	'Asylum of the Daleks'
2=	'The Angels Take Manhattan'
2=	'The Name of the Doctor'
2=	'The Day of the Doctor''
5=	'Dinosaurs on a Spaceship'
5=	'The Power of Three'
5=	'The Snowmen'
5=	'The Bells of Saint John'
9=	'A Town Called Mercy'
9=	'Hide'
9=	'Journey to the Centre of the TARDIS'
9=	'The Crimson Horror'
13=	'The Rings of Akhaten'
13=	'Cold War'
13=	'Nightmare in Silver'
16	'The Time of the Doctor'

Based on the figures in Table Five, the fans' order of preference for the episodes was:

TABLE EIGHT – RANKING BY FAN AI FIGURES

1	'The Day of the Doctor'
2	'The Name of the Doctor'
3	'Cold War'
4	'The Angels Take Manhattan'
5	'Asylum of the Daleks'
6	'The Snowmen'
7	'Hide'
8	'The Crimson Horror'
9	'The Bells of Saint John'
10	'Journey to the Centre of the TARDIS'
11	'The Power of Three'

12	'A Town Called Mercy'
13	'Dinosaurs on a Spaceship'
14	'The Time of the Doctor'
15	'Nightmare in Silver'
16	'The Rings of Akhaten'

The fan AI figure for the eighth Doctor minisode, 'The Night of the Doctor', incidentally, was 93, putting it way out in front of all the standard episodes, albeit on a relatively small poll size of 1,118 voters.

To conclude this section, set out below, for what it's worth, is this author's own ranking of the episodes, again working downwards from favourite to least favourite – although I should perhaps add that my views on this tend to change from time to time!

TABLE NINE – RANKING BY AUTHOR'S PREFERENCE

1	'The Name of the Doctor'
2	'The Crimson Horror'
3	'Cold War'
4	'Asylum of the Daleks'
5	'A Town Called Mercy'
6	'The Power of Three'
7	'The Bells of Saint John'
8	'The Snowmen'
9	'Dinosaurs on a Spaceship'
10	'The Angels Take Manhattan'
11	'The Day of the Doctor'
12	'Hide'
13	'The Time of the Doctor'
14	'The Rings of Akhaten'
15	'Nightmare in Silver'
16	'Journey to the Centre of the TARDIS'

iii) COMPARISON WITH PREVIOUS SERIES

Table Ten shows how the show's average final ratings (in millions), audience shares (in percentages) and weekly overall chart placings have changed over the course of the seven full series up to the end of 2013. (The Christmas specials and anniversary special are not included in these figures, due to their exceptional nature.)

TABLE TEN – COMPARISON OF AVERAGE RATINGS, SHARES AND CHART PLACES

SERIES	AVERAGE RATING BBC ONE	AVERAGE TOTAL REACH	AVERAGE SHARE BBC ONE	AVERAGE CHART PLACE
Series One	8.0	8.7	40	17
Series Two	7.7	8.7	41	12
Series Three	7.6	8.9	39	13
Series Four	8.1	10.5	39	10
Series Five	7.3	9.9	37	12
Series Six	7.5	9.6	33	15
Series Seven	7.4	8.7	32	14

Source: Broadcasters' Audience Research Board (BARB)

Table Eleven sets out the series-by-series comparison of AI figures for the BBC One debut transmissions. (Again, the Christmas specials and the anniversary special have been omitted.)

TABLE ELEVEN – COMPARISON OF BBC ONE AI FIGURES

SERIES	LOW	HIGH	SPREAD	AVERAGE
Series One	76	89	13	82
Series Two	76	89	13	84
Series Three	84	88	4	86
Series Four	85	91	6	88
Series Five	83	89	6	86
Series Six	85	88	3	86
Series Seven	84	89	5	86

Note: For Series One, final AI figures are available only for the first six

episodes; initial, less accurate, figures have been used for the other seven episodes.
Source: BBC

Lastly, Table Twelve gives the series-by-series comparison of fan AI figures, based on the polls conducted on the forums of Gallifrey Base and its *de facto* forerunner Outpost Gallifrey. (Christmas specials and the anniversary special are omitted once more.)

TABLE TWELVE – COMPARISON OF FAN AI FIGURES

SERIES	LOW	HIGH	SPREAD	AVERAGE
Series One	68	93	25	82
Series Two	65	93	28	82
Series Three	71	95	24	81
Series Four	72	92	20	81
Series Five	65	90	25	80
Series Six	63	89	26	77
Series Seven	57	87	30	75

Source: Outpost Gallifrey/Gallifrey Base

iv) CONCLUSIONS

The main conclusion to be drawn from the figures in Table One is that, over the course of 2012 and 2013, *Doctor Who* continued to be a hugely successful show. It was almost always BBC One's top-rated or second-rated programme of the Saturday – the main competition coming from editions of the singing talent contest *The Voice* – and invariably within its top ten-rated programmes of the week. It outstripped almost all of ITV's Saturday programming too, with only the hugely popular light entertainment show *Britain's Got Talent* consistently bettering it. Its average weekly chart position of fourteenth – with many of the higher places taken up by multiple episodes of the soap operas *EastEnders* and *Coronation Street* – also showed what a huge hit it continued to be. As in previous years, the Christmas specials had extremely good figures too, and the heavily-promoted fiftieth anniversary special, 'The Day of the Doctor', was Britain's top-rated television drama of the whole of 2013 – a remarkable achievement. Not only did large audiences watch Series Seven, but they also greatly enjoyed what they saw, as demonstrated by the average BBC One AI figure of 86, which equalled the previous two years'.[100] All in all, in Steven Moffat's third year in charge, *Doctor Who* unquestionably maintained and reinforced its position as a big-hitter in the ratings war, and one of the BBC's flagship drama productions.

For Series One to Five, the ratings followed a pattern whereby the first episode pulled in an exceptionally high number of viewers, but the figures then gradually declined as the run continued, before picking up again somewhat for the last couple of episodes. This is typical of drama series in general, and can be fairly easily explained. A proportion of the viewers who tune in for the start of any new series are bound to find it is not to their taste and drift away, producing a dip in the figures; but often some of that lost ground is recovered over the last couple of episodes – particularly where there is an ongoing element to the story – as even non-regular viewers may be curious to see how it ends. For Series Six, however, that pattern was disrupted by the introduction of the novel mid-series break. The episodes immediately before and after the break came much higher up the list of total audience reach than would normally be expected for mid-series entries. In effect, each half of the series followed the same pattern as normally seen over the series as a whole – peaks for the first and last episodes, and a dip in between. As is evident from Table One, the similarly split Series Seven repeated this pattern, with the last episode of the 2012 section – 'The Angels Take Manhattan' – and the first of the 2013 section – 'The Bells of Saint John' – both rating especially well. More difficult to account for is the extremely good figure for the mid-run episode 'A Town Called Mercy' – possibly the unusual Western theme attracted a number of viewers who would not normally have tuned in to the show.

One point illustrated by Tables Six and Seven is that whereas 'The Time of the Doctor' had the highest audience reach of all the episodes bar the exceptional 'The Day of the Doctor', it had the lowest AI figure. Again, this matches a pattern seen with most of the previous *Doctor Who* Christmas specials. The probable reason for this is simply that the large Christmas Night audiences for these specials include a proportion of

---

[100] Scores of 85 or over are officially considered 'excellent', and those of 90 or over 'exceptional'.

people who would not normally watch *Doctor Who* and who appreciate it rather less than its regular viewers. However, the 2012 offering, 'The Snowmen', proved a notable exception to the general rule, having not only the usual exceptionally high audience reach but also a mid-range audience appreciation figure.

Some caution must be exercised in comparing the figures in Table Seven with those in Table Eight, because the BBC's official AI figures in the former reflect UK audience opinion about the quality of the episodes in relation to UK television programmes in general, whereas the fan AI figures in the latter reflect worldwide fan opinion about the quality of the episodes in relation to *Doctor Who* in general – so, in other words, they are measuring slightly different things. That said, however, there can be seen to be some degree of correlation between the two sets of figures. 'Asylum of the Daleks', 'The Angels Take Manhattan', 'The Name of the Doctor' and 'The Day of the Doctor all come at or near the top in both tables, and were thus clearly the most well-received episodes of this two-year period; and 'The Rings of Akhaten', 'Nightmare in Silver' and 'The Time of the Doctor' all come at or near the bottom in both, and were thus clearly the least well-received. Judging from its relative placings, 'Cold War' seems to have been much more highly regarded by fans than by members of the general viewing public.

Table Ten shows that the episodes of Series Seven had much the same average final rating as those of Series Six, but their average total audience reach fell notably, back to the same level as for Series One and Series Two. This also meant that Series Seven continued Series Six's reversal of the previous trend of the show's BBC One debut transmission viewers making up a progressively smaller proportion of the show's total audience reach. These developments can perhaps be accounted for by the fact that the final rating and total audience reach figures count only those viewings that take place within the first seven days of the debut transmission, and more and more people are now waiting to catch up with episodes at a later date, courtesy of hard-disk recorders and – as illustrated by Table Four – services such as the BBC's iPlayer. Nevertheless, the further fall in average audience share to 32 percent, the lowest since *Doctor Who* returned to television in 2005, indicates that, in terms of live and same day viewing, the show was competing slightly less effectively than in previous years with programmes scheduled opposite it on other channels.

Taken together, the figures in Tables Ten and Eleven suggest that

Doctor Who's overall popularity with the general viewing public increased slightly over the course of Series One to Four, only to fall a little for Series Five to Seven. Series Four still has the highest average BBC One viewing figure, total audience reach, weekly chart placing and BBC One AI figure; the equivalent figures for Series Five to Seven all dropped back to around the same level as they were for Series Three. It would thus be fair to say that – leaving aside the 'gap year' specials of 2009/10, and the anniversary special 'The Day of the Doctor' – Series Four represents the peak of *Doctor Who's* general audience popularity to date.

Table Twelve, on the other hand, suggests that, as far as the dedicated fans are concerned, Series One and Two still stand as the best so far of 21st Century *Doctor Who*, and there has been a slow decline since then, with Series Seven being the least popular of all. Indeed, 'The Rings of Akhaten' earned an all-time-low fan poll score of 57, indicating that it was even less liked than previous holders of that dubious record, 'The Curse of the Black Spot', which scored 63, and 'Fear Her' (2006) and 'Victory of the Daleks' (2010), which both scored 65. Series Three's 'Human Nature' and 'The Family of Blood' remain the fans' favourites, having gained impressive poll scores of 94 and 95 respectively – over 35 points higher than 'The Rings of Akhaten'.

The fans' relatively low opinion of Series Seven is, nevertheless, a rare negative in what the statistics otherwise show to have been, all things considered, another excellent year for *Doctor Who*. And 'The Day of the Doctor' was, by any standards, a hugely successful and highly appreciated milestone.

Appendix D
Original Novels

During 2012 and 2013, BBC Books published a further six eleventh Doctor novels and novellas: two more of the 'Quick Reads' paperbacks designed to promote literacy; a third in the new series of special hardback books by acclaimed mainstream authors; and three more titles (nos. 49 to 51) in the ongoing range of hardback *Doctor Who* novels commonly referred to as New Series Adventures.[101] Summary details are as follows.

MAGIC OF THE ANGELS

Publication date: 2 February 2012
Writer: Jacqueline Rayner
Editorial Director: Albert DePetrillo
Editorial Manager: Nicholas Payne
Series Consultant: Justin Richards
Project Editor: Steve Tribe
Cover Design: Lee Binding
Production: Rebecca Jones

PUBLICITY BLURB

'No one from this time will ever see that girl again ...'
    The Doctor, Amy and Rory round off a sight-seeing tour round London with a trip to the theatre. That's when things start to go wrong.
    The Doctor wonders why so many young girls are going missing from the area. When he sees Sammy Star's amazing magic act, he thinks

---

[101] The three New Series Adventures were published in paperback rather than hardback in the USA.

he knows the answer. Sammy's glamorous assistant disappears at the climax of the act – but this is no stage trick.

The Doctor and his friends team up with residents of an old people's home to discover the truth. And together they find themselves face to face with a deadly Weeping Angel.

Whatever you do – don't blink!

A thrilling all-new adventure featuring the Doctor, Amy and Rory, as played by Matt Smith, Karen Gillan and Arthur Darvill in the spectacular hit series from BBC Television.

NOTES

• A 'Quick Reads' book.

S3: DARK HORIZONS

Publication date: 5 July 2012
Writer: J T Colgan
Editorial Director: Albert DePetrillo
Editorial Manager: Nicholas Payne
Series Consultant: Justin Richards
Project Editor: Steve Tribe
Cover Design: Lee Binding
Production: Rebecca Jones and Alex Goddard

PUBLICITY BLURB

'We need to reach out. We need to continue the line ...'

On a windswept northern shore, the islanders believe the worst they have to fear is a Viking attack. Then the burning comes. Water will not stop it. It consumes everything in its path – yet the burned still speak.

The Doctor encounters a people under attack from a power they cannot possibly understand. They have no weapons, no strategy and no protection against a fire sent to engulf them all. The islanders must take on a ruthless alien force in a world without technology; but at least they have the Doctor on their side ... Don't they?

A thrilling adventure starring the Doctor, as played by Matt Smith.

NOTES

- Also released by AudioGo as an unabridged audiobook read by Neve McIntosh, as a download on 5 July 2012 and as a six-CD set on 3 December 2012.

- A paperback edition was published on 4 July 2013.

THE SILURIAN GIFT

Publication date: 1 February 2013
Writer: Mike Tucker
Editorial Director: Albert DePetrillo
Editorial Manager: Nicholas Payne
Series Consultant: Justin Richards
Project Editor: Steve Tribe
Cover Design: Lee Binding
Production: Alex Goddard

PUBLICITY BLURB

'My new Fire-Ice will solve all the problems of the planet!'
The world is on the brink of crisis. As fuel runs short, society begins to break down. One man seems to have the answer. But is it too good to be true?
The Doctor arrives at an old oil refinery near the South Pole, concerned by claims about this new form of energy. He soon discovers something huge and terrifying is stalking the refinery. It brings death and destruction in its wake.
The battle has begun for planet Earth.
A thrilling, all-new adventure, featuring the Doctor as played by Matt Smith in the spectacular hit series from BBC Television.

NOTE

- A 'Quick Reads' book.

49: PLAGUE OF THE CYBERMEN

Publication date: 11 April 2013
Writer: Justin Richards
Editorial Director: Albert DePetrillo
Series Consultant: Justin Richards
Project Editor: Steve Tribe
Cover Design: Lee Binding
Production: Alex Goddard

PUBLICITY BLURB

'They like the shadows. You know them as Plague Warriors.'
    When the Doctor arrives in the 19th Century village of Klimtenburg, he discovers the residents suffering from some kind of plague – a 'wasting disease'. The victims face a horrible death – but what's worse, the dead seem to be leaving their graves. The Plague Warriors have returned …
    The Doctor is confident he knows what's really happening; he understands where the dead go, and he's sure the Plague Warriors are just a myth. But as some of the Doctor's oldest and most terrible enemies start to awaken he realises that maybe – just maybe – he's misjudged the situation.
    A thrilling, all-new adventure as played by Matt Smith in the spectacular hit series from BBC television.

NOTES

• Also released by AudioGo as an unabridged audiobook read by David Warner, with Nicholas Briggs as the voice of the Cybermen, as both a download and a six-CD set, on the same date as the hardback.

50: THE DALEK GENERATION

Publication date: 11 April 2013
Writer: Nicholas Briggs
Editorial Director: Albert DePetrillo
Series Consultant: Justin Richards
Project Editor: Steve Tribe

Cover Design: Lee Binding
Production: Alex Goddard

PUBLICITY BLURB

'The sunlight worlds offer you a life of comfort and plenty. Apply now at the Dalek foundation.'
Sunlight 349 is one of countless Dalek Foundation worlds, planets created to house billions suffering from economic hardship. The Doctor arrives at Sunlight 349, suspicious of any world where the Daleks are apparently a force for good – and determined to find out the truth. The Doctor knows they have a far more sinister plan – but how can he convince those who have lived under the benevolence of the Daleks for a generation?
But convince them he must, and soon. For on another Foundation planet, archaeologists have unearthed the most dangerous technology in the universe ...
A thrilling, all-new adventure featuring the Doctor as played by Matt Smith in the spectacular hit series from BBC Television

NOTES

• Also released by AudioGo as an unabridged audiobook read by Nicholas Briggs, unabridged audiobook read by Neve McIntosh, as a download on 11 April 2013 and as a six-CD set on 3 June 2013.

51: SHROUD OF SORROW

Publication date: 11 April 2013
Writer: Tommy Donbavand
Editorial Director: Albert DePetrillo
Series Consultant: Justin Richards
Project Editor: Steve Tribe
Cover Design: Lee Binding
Production: Alex Goddard

PUBLICITY BLURB

23 November 1963.

It is the day after John F Kennedy's assassination – and the faces of the dead are everywhere. PC Reg Cranfield sees his deceased father in the mists along Totter's Lane. Reporter Mae Callon sees her late grandmother in a coffee stain on her desk. FBI Special Agent Warren Skeet finds his long-dead partner staring back at him from raindrops on a window pane.

Then the faces begin to talk, and scream ... and push through into our world. As the alien Shroud begins to feast on the grief of a world in mourning, can the Doctor dig deep enough into his own sorrow to save mankind? are trademarks of the BBC.

A thrilling, all-new adventure featuring the Doctor and Clara as played by Matt Smith and Jenna-Louise Coleman in the spectacular hit series from BBC Television

NOTES

- Also released by AudioGo as an unabridged audiobook read by Frances Barber, as a six-CD set on 4 July 2013 and a download on 5 July 2013.

Appendix E
Original Comic Strips

During 2012 and 2013, there were three different regular comic strip series presenting new eleventh Doctor *Doctor Who* stories for fans to enjoy. These appeared in, respectively: Panini's *Doctor Who Magazine*, which (under various different titles) had been home to a *Doctor Who* comic strip since 1979; *Doctor Who Adventures*, a comic aimed at a pre-teen audience, published by BBC Magazines[102]; and *Doctor Who*, a US-only comic book, published by IDW.[103] Details are given below.[104] In all cases, the publication dates quoted are the cover dates or official publication dates and do not necessarily accord with when the issues actually went on sale. (The *Doctor Who Magazine* cover dates in particular went somewhat awry during this period.) For information about comic strips included in *Doctor Who – the Official Annual 2013* and *Doctor Who – the Official 50th Anniversary Annual*, and of the graphic novel *The Dalek Project*, see Appendix F.

---

[102] Each issue of *Doctor Who Adventures* generally included another, one-page comic strip that was essentially just an extended cartoon, intended purely for laughs, and so is not covered here.

[103] IDW also published from time to time series of *Doctor Who Classics* comic books featuring stories of earlier Doctors reprinted, with newly-added colour, from earlier incarnations of *Doctor Who Magazine*. In 2012, there was a six-issue run of sixth Doctor issues, published monthly from February, plus a 100-page 'Spectacular' featuring the fourth Doctor, published in July; and in 2013, there was a five-issue ran of seventh Doctor issues, published irregularly from March.

[104] The details provided here are a little more concise than in previous books in this range. This is for reasons of space, owing to the sheer number of comic strip stories published during the period in question.

DOCTOR WHO MAGAZINE

In 2012 and 2013, *Doctor Who Magazine* published nine, generally multi-part comic strip stories in its four-weekly issues.[105] All of these (along with some others) were later reprinted across the three graphic novel collections 'The Chains of Olympus' (Panini, 2013), 'Hunters of the Burning Stone' (Panini, 2013) and 'The Blood of Azrael' (Panini, 2014).

THE CHAINS OF OLYMPUS

Story: Scott Gray
Art: Mike Collins
Colours: James Offredi
Letters: Roger Langridge
Editors: Tom Spilsbury and Peter Ware
Publication: Issue 442-Issue 445; December 2011 to April 2012

PLOT

The TARDIS brings the Doctor, Amy and Rory to ancient Greece, where an alien entity masquerading as the god Zeus is wreaking vengeance on its blasphemous people.

STICKS & STONES

Story: Scott Gray
Art: Martin Geraghty
Colours: James Offredi
Letters: Roger Langridge
Editors: Tom Spilsbury and Peter Ware
Publication: Issue 446-Issue 447; May 2012

PLOT

The Doctor, Amy and Rory come up against an alien graffiti artist named Monos – a Necrotist, whose people believe that death is the highest form

---

[105] A tenth story began in the December 2013 issue, but continued into 2014, so is not covered here.

of art. Monos attacks London, turning its inhabitants into living names, or Leximorphs.

THE CORNUCOPIA CAPER

Story: Scott Gray
Art: Dan McDaid
Colours: James Offredi
Letters: Roger Langridge
Editors: Tom Spilsbury and Peter Ware
Publication: Issue 448-Issue 450; June to September 2012

PLOT

Attempting to reach Rio de Janeiro, the Doctor, Amy and Rory arrive instead on the planet Cornucopia, which at first sight appears civilised but is actually ruled by powerful crime lords, who dispense the only form of justice.

THE BROKEN MAN

Story: Scott Gray
Art: Martin Geraghty
Colours: James Offredi
Letters: Roger Langridge
Editors: Tom Spilsbury and Peter Ware
Publication: Issue 451-Issue 454; October 2012 to Winter 2012/2013

PLOT

In Prague, 1989, the Doctor, Amy and Rory get caught up in an adventure involving an undercover British spy named Patrick Lake and his family.

IMAGINARY ENEMIES

Story: Scott Gray
Art: Mike Collins (pencils) and David A Roach (inks)
Colours: James Offredi
Letters: Roger Langridge

Editors: Tom Spilsbury and Peter Ware
Publication: Issue 455; January 2013

PLOT

In their home village of Leadworth, the young Amy Pond and Rory Williams and their friend Mels have an encounter with an alien, Krampus, and his goblins, while preparing for their school nativity play.

NOTES

This was the final *Doctor Who Magazine* comic strip story to feature Amy and Rory, though as children rather than as adults travelling with the Doctor.

HUNTERS OF THE BURNING STONE

Story: Scott Gray
Art: Martin Geraghty (pencils) and David A Roach (inks)
Colours: James Offredi
Letters: Roger Langridge
Editors: Tom Spilsbury and Peter Ware
Publication: Issue 456-Issue 461; February to July 2013

PLOT

The Doctor is reunited with his former companions Ian Chesterton and Barbara Wright, and they have another encounter with the Tribe of Gum, who have undergone an extraordinary transformation since last seen in the Stone Age.

NOTES

- This story reveals that it was the eleventh Doctor who broke the TARDIS's chameleon circuit, causing the ship to become stuck in the shape of a police box, prior to its departure from 1963 London in '100,000 BC' (1963)

A WING AND A PRAYER

Story: Scott Gray
Art: Mike Collins (pencils) and David A Roach (inks)
Colours: James Offredi
Letters: Roger Langridge
Editors: Tom Spilsbury and Peter Ware
Publication: Issue 462-Issue 464; August to October 2013

PLOT

The TARDIS arrives in the wake of a sandstorm in the Iraqi desert in 1930. There the Doctor and Clara meet celebrated aviator Amy Johnson, currently engaged in her bid to become the first woman to fly across the world. But they soon find themselves menaced by a powerful alien insect called Koragatta ...

NOTES

• This story marked Clara's *Doctor Who Magazine* comic strip debut.

WELCOME TO TICKLE TOWN

Story: Scott Gray
Art: Mike Collins (pencils) and David A Roach (inks)
Colours: James Offredi
Letters: Roger Langridge
Editors: Tom Spilsbury and Peter Ware
Publication: Issue 465-Issue 466; November to December 2013

PLOT

The Doctor and Clara take a trip to Tickle Town, an amusement park, where Clara meets her cartoon hero, while the Time Lord uncovers the terrible secrets at the heart of the deceptively happy place after crossing paths with a desperate mother and daughter.

JOHN SMITH AND THE COMMON MEN

Story: Scott Gray
Art: David A Roach
Colours: James Offredi
Letters: Roger Langridge
Editors: Tom Spilsbury and Peter Ware
Publication: Issue 467; November 2013

PLOT

The Doctor has forgotten who he is and believes he is just an ordinary man called John Smith who leads a routine life working in the Department of Commonality, fearful of breaking the law or of being noticed, and annoyed by a clock that is always five minutes slow ...

DOCTOR WHO ADVENTURES

Tailored to their young target readership, the *Doctor Who Adventures* comic strips presented simplistic stories, typically involving the Doctor and his companions thwarting an attack by a large, garishly-coloured monster-of-the-week – or, from June 2013, monster-of-the-fortnight, as the magazine then changed its frequency of publication. The Doctor was accompanied by Amy and Rory until Issue 289 in October 2012, then from Issue 293 in November 2012 by the reader-created reptilian companion Decky Flamboon, and finally from Issue 314 in April 2013 by Clara. The story 'Time Trick' in Issue 333, marking *Doctor Who*'s fiftieth anniversary, was notable for including an appearance by the first Doctor and his grand-daughter Susan.

VENGEANCE OF THE ATOMON
Words: Christopher Cooper
Art: John Ross
Colouring: Alan Craddock
Publication: Issue 251; 5 January 2012

PICTURE IMPERFECT
Words: Oli Smith
Art: John Ross
Colouring: Alan Craddock
Publication: Issue 252; 19 January 2012

THE STAR SERPENT
Words: Trevor Baxendale
Art: John Ross
Colouring: Alan Craddock
Publication: Issue 253; 26 January 2012

THE HOME STORE
Words: Eddie Robson
Art: John Ross
Colouring: Alan Craddock
Publication: Issue 254; 2 February 2012

COLD COMFORT
Words: Steve Lyons
Art: John Ross
Colouring: Alan Craddock
Publication: Issue 255; 9 February 2012

FASTER THAN LIGHT!
Words: Trevor Baxendale
Art: John Ross
Colouring: Alan Craddock
Publication: Issue 256; 16 February 2012

THE FAIREST OF THEM ALL
Words: Craig Donaghy
Art: John Ross
Colouring: Alan Craddock
Publication: Issue 257; 23 February 2012

NEW AND IMPROVED
Words: Craig Donaghy
Art: John Ross

Colouring: Alan Craddock
Publication: Issue 258; 1 March 2012

MALTHILL WAY
Words: Craig Donaghy
Art: John Ross
Colouring: Alan Craddock
Publication: Issue 259; 8 March 2012

THE DEMONS OF REPTON ABBEY
Words: Christopher Cooper
Art: John Ross
Colouring: Alan Craddock
Publication: Issue 260; 15 March 2012

THE PUNCH AND JUDY TRAP
Words: Christopher Cooper
Art: John Ross
Colouring: Alan Craddock
Publication: Issue 261; 22 March 2012

BUY, BUY, BABY!
Words: Steve Lyons
Art: John Ross
Colouring: Alan Craddock
Publication: Issue 262; 29 March 2012

GHOSTS OF THE NEVER-WERE
Words: Steve Lyons
Art: John Ross
Colouring: Alan Craddock
Publication: Issue 263; 5 April 2012

THE PARASITES
Words: Steve Lyons
Art: John Ross
Colouring: Alan Craddock
Publication: Issue 264; 12 April 2012

DOOMLAND
Words: Eddie Robson
Art: John Ross
Colouring: Alan Craddock
Publication: Issue 265; 19 April 2012

BUYING TIME
Words: Trevor Baxendale
Art: John Ross
Colouring: Alan Craddock
Publication: Issue 266; 26 April 2012

ISLAND OF THE CYCLOPES
Words: Steve Lyons
Art: John Ross
Colouring: Alan Craddock
Publication: Issue 267; 3 May 2012

TROUBLE ON THE ORION EXPRESS
Words: Luke Paton
Art: John Ross
Colouring: Alan Craddock
Publication: Issue 268; 10 May 2012

DUMMY RUN
Words: Glenn Dakin
Art: John Ross
Colouring: Alan Craddock
Publication: Issue 269; 17 May 2012

FINDERS KEEPERS
Words: Eddie Robson
Art: John Ross
Colouring: Alan Craddock
Publication: Issue 270; 24 May 2012

THE MIRROR WAR
Words: Eddie Robson
Art: John Ross

Colouring: Alan Craddock
Publication: Issue 271; 31 May 2012

GHOST TRAIN
Words: Steve Lyons
Art: John Ross
Colouring: Alan Craddock
Publication: Issue 272; 7 June 2012

I SCREAM
Words: Christopher Cooper
Art: John Ross
Colouring: Alan Craddock
Publication: Issue 273; 14 June 2012

LE TOUR DE DEATH
Words: Christopher Cooper
Art: John Ross
Colouring: Alan Craddock
Publication: Issue 274; 21 June 2012

THE SKY IS FALLING!
Words: Trevor Baxendale
Art: John Ross
Colouring: Alan Craddock
Publication: Issue 275; 28 June 2012

THE TIME GALLERY
Words: Glenn Dakin
Art: John Ross
Colouring: Alan Craddock
Publication: Issue 276; 5 July 2012

THE CLIFF FACE
Words: Eddie Robson
Art: John Ross
Colouring: Alan Craddock
Publication: Issue 277; 12 July 2012

BUMBLE OF DESTRUCTION
Words: Eddie Robson
Art: John Ross
Colouring: Alan Craddock-
Publication: Issue 278; 19 July 2012

THE LIGHT CATCHER
Words: Christopher Cooper
Art: John Ross
Colouring: Alan Craddock
Publication: Issue 279; 26 July 2012

DUNGEON OF THE LOST
Words: Eddie Robson
Art: John Ross
Colouring: Alan Craddock
Publication: Issue 280; 2 August 2012

THE INTERGALACTIC TRIALS
Words: Luke Paton
Art: John Ross
Colouring: Alan Craddock
Publication: Issue 281; 9 August 2012

24-HOUR NEWS INVASION
Words: Glenn Dakin
Art: John Ross
Colouring: Alan Craddock
Publication: Issue 282; 16 August 2012

THE PANIC ROOM
Words: Glenn Dakin
Art: John Ross
Colouring: Alan Craddock
Publication: Issue 283; 23 August 2012

TERROR FROM THE SWAMP
Words: Trevor Baxendale
Art: John Ross

Colouring: Alan Craddock
Publication: Issue 284; 30 August 2012

THE PLANET THAT SLEPT
Words: Trevor Baxendale
Art: John Ross
Colouring: Alan Craddock
Publication: Issue 285; 6 September 2012

PLANET OF THE RORYS
Words: Craig Donaghy
Art: John Ross
Colouring: Alan Craddock
Publication: Issue 286; 13 September 2012

DAWN OF TIME!
Words: Trevor Baxendale
Art: John Ross
Colouring: Alan Craddock
Publication: Issue 287; 20 September 2012

TV HELL!
Words: Christopher Cooper
Art: John Ross
Colouring: Alan Craddock
Publication: Issue 288; 27 September 2012

PONDNIUM!
Words: Craig Donaghy
Art: John Ross
Colouring: Alan Craddock
Publication: Issue 289; 4 October 2012

BITE OF THE MORPHUSE!
Words: Christopher Cooper
Art: John Ross
Colouring: Alan Craddock
Publication: Issue 290; 11 October 2012

GARBAGE DAY!
Words: Glenn Dakin
Art: John Ross
Colouring: Alan Craddock
Publication: Issue 291; 18 October 2012

THE GREEDY GULPER
Words: Steve Lyons
Art: John Ross
Colouring: Alan Craddock
Publication: Issue 292; 25 October 2012

METEORITE MEETING
Words: Craig Donaghy
Art: John Ross
Colouring: Alan Craddock
Publication: Issue 293; 1 November 2012

TOWER OF POWER
Words: Craig Donaghy
Art: John Ross
Colouring: Alan Craddock
Publication: Issue 294; 8 November 2012

THE SHARK SHOCKER
Words: Craig Donaghy
Art: John Ross
Colouring: Alan Craddock
Publication: Issue 295; 15 November 2012

THE TOYBOX
Words: Eddie Robson
Art: John Ross
Colouring: Alan Craddock
Publication: Issue 296; 22 November 2012

THE RUNAWAY BOGEY
Words: Simon Guerrier
Art: John Ross

Colouring: Alan Craddock
Publication: Issue 297; 29 November 2012

ON THE CARDS
Words: Eddie Robson
Art: John Ross
Colouring: Alan Craddock
Publication: Issue 298; 6 December 2012

DECKY THE HALLS
Words: Craig Donaghy
Art: John Ross
Colouring: Alan Craddock
Publication: Issue 299; 13 December 2012

SNOWBALL!
Words: Moray Laing
Art: John Ross
Colouring: Alan Craddock
Publication: Issue 300; 28 December 2012

MUSEUM PIECE
Words: Steve Lyons
Art: John Ross
Colouring: Alan Craddock
Publication: Issue 301; 4 January 2013

ALL CHANGE!
Words: Simon Guerrier
Art: John Ross
Colouring: Alan Craddock
Publication: Issue 302; 10 January 2013

AN ILL WIND
Words: James Hill
Art: John Ross
Colouring: Alan Craddock
Publication: Issue 303; 17 January 2013

THE WATER WORLD
Words: Moray Laing
Art: John Ross
Colouring: Alan Craddock
Publication: Issue 304; 24 January 2013

PET PANIC
Words: Glenn Dakin
Art: John Ross
Colouring: Alan Craddock
Publication: Issue 305; 31 January 2013

SPACE RACE
Words: Steve Lyons
Art: John Ross
Colouring: Alan Craddock
Publication: Issue 306; 7 February 2013

LOVE IS IN THE AIR
Words: Craig Donaghy
Art: John Ross
Colouring: Alan Craddock
Publication: Issue 307; 14 February 2013

TOOTHACHE!
Words: James Hill
Art: John Ross
Colouring: Alan Craddock
Publication: Issue 308; 21 February 2013

TERROR IN THE TAJ MAHAL
Words: Craig Donaghy
Art: John Ross
Colouring: Alan Craddock
Publication: Issue 309; 28 February 2013

EYE SPY
Words: Craig Donaghy
Art: John Ross

Colouring: Alan Craddock
Publication: Issue 310; 7 March 2013

COLOSSUS OF THE COLOSSEUM
Words: Craig Donaghy
Art: John Ross
Colouring: Alan Craddock
Publication: Issue 311; 14 March 2013

THE TAIL OF DECKY FLAMBOON
Words: Craig Donaghy
Art: John Ross
Colouring: Alan Craddock
Publication: Issue 312; 21 March 2013

THE EGG HUNT
Words: James Hill
Art: John Ross
Colouring: Alan Craddock
Publication: Issue 313; 28 March 2013

THE MYSTERY OF THE MOULD
Words: Craig Donaghy
Art: John Ross
Colouring: Alan Craddock
Publication: Issue 314; 4 April 2013

THE PLANET THAT WENT BACKWARDS
Words: Moray Laing
Art: John Ross
Colouring: Alan Craddock
Publication: Issue 315; 11 April 2013

TEACHER'S PET
Words: Christopher Cooper
Art: John Ross
Colouring: Alan Craddock
Publication: Issue 316; 18 April 2013

CORAL MAZE
Words: Glenn Dakin
Art: John Ross
Colouring: Alan Craddock
Publication: Issue 317; 25 April 2013

SANDBLASTED
Words: Steve Lyons
Art: John Ross
Colouring: Alan Craddock
Publication: Issue 318; 2 May 2013

TUNNEL TERRORS!
Words: James Hill
Art: John Ross
Colouring: Alan Craddock
Publication: Issue 319; 9 May 2013

NOVA
Words: Rik Hoskin
Art: John Ross
Colouring: Alan Craddock
Publication: Issue 320; 16 May 2013

LINE OF BATTLE
Words: Eddie Robson
Art: John Ross
Colouring: Alan Craddock
Publication: Issue 321; 23 May 2013

THE CURSE OF THE GIBWYN
Words: Craig Donaghy
Art: John Ross
Colouring: Alan Craddock
Publication: Issue 322; 4 June 2013

GUMFIGHT
Words: Glenn Dakin
Art: John Ross

Colouring: Alan Craddock
Publication: Issue 323; 19 June 2013

THE HAT TRICK
Words: James Hill
Art: John Ross
Colouring: Alan Craddock
Publication: Issue 324; 3 July 2013

GNOME GUARD
Words: Glenn Dakin
Art: John Ross
Colouring: Alan Craddock
Publication: Issue 325; 17 July 2013

STRICTLY FIGHT MONSTERS
Words: Simon Guerrier
Art: John Ross
Colouring: Alan Craddock
Publication: Issue 326; 31 July 2013

PLANET VOID
Words: Christopher Cooper
Art: John Ross
Colouring: Alan Craddock
Publication: Issue 327; 14 August 2013

REPROGRAMME
Words: Rik Hoskin
Art: John Ross
Colouring: Alan Craddock
Publication: Issue 328; 28 August 2013

SHIPWRECKED
Words: Steve Lyons
Art: John Ross
Colouring: Alan Craddock
Publication: Issue 329; 11 September 2013

EYE OF THE STORM
Words: Eddie Robson
Art: John Ross
Colouring: Alan Craddock
Publication: Issue 330; 25 September 2013

WHALE TALE
Words: Glenn Dakin
Art: John Ross
Colouring: Alan Craddock
Publication: Issue 331; 9 October 2013

FACEACHE
Words: Simon Guerrier
Art: John Ross
Colouring: Alan Craddock
Publication: Issue 332; 23 October 2013

TIME TRICK
Words: Craig Donaghy
Art: John Ross
Colouring: Alan Craddock
Publication: Issue 333; 6 November 2013

DRAGON ATTACK
Words: James Hill
Art: John Ross
Colouring: Alan Craddock
Publication: Issue 334; 27 November 2013

THE HOLLY AND THE IVY
Words: Simon Guerrier
Art: John Ross
Colouring: Alan Craddock
Publication: Issue 335; 11 December 2013

BY THE BOOK
Words: Eddie Robson
Art: John Ross

Colouring: Alan Craddock
Publication: Issue 336; 31 December 2013

DOCTOR WHO

In addition to its generally monthly 'Ongoing' series, in 2012 IDW published a one-off special, plus the eight-issue mini-series *Star Trek – The Next Generation/Doctor Who* crossover 'Assimilation²' – the first ever official cross-over of any kind between the two celebrated franchises; and in 2013 they published another one-off special, plus an untitled comic book sold exclusively as part of a US-only *Doctor Who* Blu-ray box set, plus the 12-issue multi-Doctor anniversary mini-series 'Prisoners of Time'. As in previous years, each issue came in a choice of variant covers, which in 2012 and 2013 were more numerous than ever before.[106] All of the stories were subsequently collected in graphic novel form, often more than once.

This was IDW's last two years of publishing *Doctor Who* comics, as their licence expired at the end of 2013.

ONGOING SERIES

AS TIME GOES BY

Story: Joshua Hale Fialkov
Art: Matthew Dow Smith
Colours: Charlie Kirchoff
Lettering: Shawn Lee
Edited by: Denton J Tipton
Publication: Issues 13 to 16 1; January to April 2012

PUBLICITY BLURB

1941. Casablanca. Murder. Sound familiar? It does as well to the Doctor, Amy, and Rory, who revel in being in the setting for the classic film. That is until they uncover a world-domination plot hatched not by Hitler, but the Silurians. Eisner Award-nominated writer Joshua Hale Fialkov and

---

[106] For reasons of space, full details of the all the different variant covers have been omitted on this occasion.

artist Matthew Dow Smith bring you the noir thriller, 'As Time Goes By'.

HYPOTHETICAL GENTLEMAN

Story: Andy Diggle
Art: Mark Buckingham
Colours: Charlie Kirchoff
Lettering: Shawn Lee
Edited by: Denton J Tipton
Publication: Issues 1 and 2[107]; September and October 2012

PUBLICITY BLURB

The Doctor is back! New York Times bestselling writer Andy Diggle joins Eisner Award-winning artist Mark Buckingham as a shadow being emerges from a machine used to view alternate realities, stealing time from those he touches in order to become 'real'. Can the Doctor save the Hypothetical Gentleman's latest victim?

THE DOCTOR AND THE NURSE

Story: Brandon Seifert
Art: Philip Bond and Ilias Kyriazis
Colours: Charlie Kirchoff
Lettering: Shawn Lee and Tom B Long
Edited by: Denton J Tipton
Publication: Issues 3 and 4; November and December 2012

PUBLICITY BLURB

Writer Brandon Seifert and artist Philip Bond collaborate on a story. The Doctor and Rory, on a boys' night out gone wrong, leave Amy to face the Silence on her own!

THE EYE OF ASHAYA

---

[107] The numbering of the Ongoing series was reset at this point, to mark the start of a new run of stories.

Story: Andy Diggle
Art: Josh Adams (pencils), Marc Deering and Josh Adams (inks)
Colours: Charlie Kirchoff
Lettering: Shawn Lee and Tom B Long
Edited by: Denton J Tipton
Publication: Issues 5 and 6; January and February 2013

PUBLICITY BLURB

In 'The Eye of Ashaya', Andy Diggle and Craig Hamilton bring you a tale of the Doctor, Amy and Rory on a luxury star-liner for some R&R. But as the Doctor crosses paths with a thief from his past, any thoughts of peace go right out the porthole.[108]

SPACE ODDITY

Story: Andy Diggle
Art: Horacio Domingues with Andres Ponce (pencils), Ruben Gonzalez (inks)
Colours: Adrian Salmon
Lettering: Shawn Lee
Edited by: Denton J Tipton
Publication: Issues 7 and 8; March and April 2013

PUBLICITY BLURB

When a cosmonaut attempts the first space walk in 1965, the rest of his crew watches in horror as he's swallowed whole by shadow. Only the Doctor can save the spacecraft and the historically important mission.

SKY JACKS!

Story: Andy Diggle and Eddie Robson
Art: Andy Kuhn (art), Ruben Gonzalez (inks)

---

[108] This – like most of the other publicity blurbs given here for the IDW comics – is taken from the graphic novel edition. It is unclear why artist Craig Hamilton was mentioned in the publicity for 'The Eye of Ashaya', as he was not credited on the story itself.

Colours: Charlie Kirchoff
Lettering: Shawn Lee
Edited by: Denton J Tipton
Publication: Issues 9 to 12; May and August 2013

PUBLICITY BLURB

The TARDIS has recently been on the fritz, but now it has gone completely out of control and the Doctor is nowhere to be found! Meanwhile, white holes have been forming throughout time and space, sucking in everything around them. Now Clara must find the Doctor and help him figure out what is going on.

DEAD MAN'S HAND

Story: Tony Lee
Art: Mike Collins
Colours: Charlie Kirchoff
Lettering: Shawn Lee
Edited by: Denton J Tipton
Publication: Issues 13 to 16; September to December 2013

PUBLICITY BLURB

The Doctor and Clara cross paths with Oscar Wilde and Calamity Jane in the frontier town of Deadwood as they pay their respects to the recently passed Wild Bill Hickok. But soon they discover the grave is empty and that the town is being plagued by a masked gunman who shoots his victims with nothing but a finger!

MINI-SERIES

ASSIMILATION[2]

Story: Scott and David Tipton with Tony Lee (Issues 1 to 4), Scott and David Tipton (Issues 5 to 8)
Art: J K Woodward (Issues 1, 2 and 5 to 8); J K Woodward and the Sharp Brothers (Issue 3); J K Woodward (colours) and Gordon Purcell (pencils) (Issues 4 to 8)

Lettering: Shawn Lee and Robbie Robbins (Issues 1); Shawn Lee (Issues 2 to 6), Tom B Long (Issues 7 and 8)
Edited by: Denton J Tipton (Issues 1 to 8); Jacen Smith (editorial assists) (Issues 6 to 8)
Publication: eight issues; May to December 2012

PUBLICITY BLURB

When the Federation's most terrifying enemy strikes an unholy alliance with one of the Doctor's most hated antagonists, the result is devastation on a cosmic scale! Spanning the ends of space and time itself, Captain Jean-Luc Picard and the crew of the USS *Enterprise* find themselves joining forces with the Doctor and his companions, with the fate of the galaxy hanging in the balance!

PRISONERS OF TIME

Story: Scott and David Tipton
Art: Simon Fraser (Issue 1); Lee Sullivan (Issue 2); Mike Collins (Issue 3); Gary Erskine with thanks to Mike Collins (Issue 4); Philip Bond (Issue 5); John Ridgway (Issue 6); Kev Hopgood (Issue 7); Roger Langridge (Issue 8); David Messina (pencils) and Georgia Sposito (inks) (Issue 9); Elena Casagrande (Issue 10); Matthew Dow Smith (Issue 11); Kelly Yates (Issue 12)
Colours: Simon Caldwell (Issue 1); Phil Elliot (Issue 2); Charlie Kirchoff (Issues 3 to 8, 11 and 12); ScarletGothica (Issue 9); Arianna Florean (Issue 10)
Lettering: Tom B Long
Edited by: Denton J Tipton
Publication: 12 issues; January to December 2013

PUBLICITY BLURB

November 23, 1963: A day that changed the world forever. That day saw the broadcast debut of *Doctor Who*, which was to become the longest-running science fiction series on television. And now, fifty years later, we pay tribute to one of the greatest pop-culture heroes of all time with this special series, which tells an epic adventure featuring all 11 incarnations of the intrepid traveler through time and space known simply as ... the Doctor.

ONE-OFFS

SPECIAL 2012

This special, published in August 2012, included four stories.

PUBLICITY BLURB

The eleventh Doctor returns in this all-new Annual! This oversized issue contains three complete stories by an all-star line-up, featuring legendary writer-editor Len Wein, *Doctor Who* novelist Richard Dinnick, and writer Tony Lee, with art by Matthew Dow Smith, and Mitch Gerads. Also included is a prelude to the next Ongoing series by series writer Andy Diggle and superstar artist Mark Buckingham!

IN-FEZ-STATION

Story: Len Wein
Art: Matthew Dow Smith
Colours: Adrian Salmon
Lettering: Shawn Lee
Edited by: Denton J Tipton

TIME FRAUD

Story: Richard Dinnick
Art: Josh Adams
Colours: Charlie Kirchoff
Lettering: Shawn Lee
Edited by: Denton J Tipton

ESCAPE INTO ALCATRAZ

Story: Tony Lee
Art and Colours: Mitch Gerards
Lettering: Shawn Lee
Edited by: Denton J Tipton

EAGLE OF THE REICH

Story: Andy Diggle
Art: Mark Buckingham
Colours: Charlie Kirchoff
Lettering: Shawn Lee
Edited by: Denton J Tipton

BLU-RAY EXCLUSIVE

BIRTHDAY BOY

Story: Matthew Dow Smith
Art: Horacio Domingues (pencils), Rudolfo Buscaglia (layouts), Ruben Gonzalez (inks)
Colours: Phil Elliot
Lettering: Tom B Long
Edited by: Denton J Tipton
Publication: with *Complete Series 1-7* limited edition Blu-ray gift set; November 2013

SPECIAL 2013

The 2013 special, published in December 2013, was comprised of a single story, marking the end of IDW's licence to publish *Doctor Who* comics.

THE GIRL WHO LOVED *DOCTOR WHO*

Story: Paul Cornell
Art and Colours: Jimmy Broxton
Lettering: Shawn Lee
Edited by: Denton J Tipton

PUBLICITY BLURB

In this special one-shot story celebrating the fiftieth anniversary of *Doctor Who*, a strange force flings the TARDIS and the Doctor into our own universe! Once here, the Doctor encounters a ten-year-old girl who happens to be a huge fan of the *Doctor Who* TV show. The Doctor grapples with being a fictional character and monsters lurking at the girl's school on the way to coming face-to-face with the actor who portrays him, Matt Smith!

Appendix F
Other Original Fiction

In addition to the novels and comic strip stories covered in the preceding Appendices, there were a number of other places where original, officially-sanctioned new series *Doctor Who* fiction could be found during the course of 2012 and 2013. Details are given below.

DOCTOR WHO AUDIOBOOKS

In 2012 and 2013, BBC Audiobooks released a further seven single-CD talking books of eleventh Doctor stories exclusive to the audio medium. These were as follows.

THE ART OF DEATH

Release date: 5 January 2012
Written by: James Goss
Read by: Raquel Cassidy
Project editor: John Ainsworth
Music and sound effects by Simon Hunt
Doctor Who theme music by Murray Gold

PUBLICITY BLURB

Raquel Cassidy reads this exclusive audio adventure featuring the eleventh Doctor, Amy and Rory as they encounter one of the wonders of the universe.

Don't be alarmed! the Doctor cried through gritted teeth, *It's simply sucking the life out of me. Nothing to worry about* ... When the Doctor falls through a crack in time he finds himself in the Horizon Gallery. But it's no ordinary art gallery, because this one has the best view of the most impossible wonder of the universe – the Paradox. Tour parties are eager to see this stunning, hypnotic portion of sky that's beyond description, and it's Penelope's job to stop people staring up at it for too long. For the Paradox's beauty drives people mad. The Doctor, Amy and Rory are about to discover that the Paradox also contains a giant and frightening creature with a taste for death ...

Written specially for audio by James Goss, 'The Art of Death' features the Doctor, Amy and Rory as played by Matt Smith, Karen Gillan and Arthur Darvill in the acclaimed hit series from BBC Television. It is read by Raquel Cassidy, who played Miranda Cleaves in the 2011 TV episodes 'The Rebel Flesh' and 'The Almost People'.

NOTES

- This audiobook was also issued simultaneously as part of a two-CD set with the 2011 title 'Blackout'. It was reissued by Chivers on 7 May 2012 in a three-CD set under the umbrella title *Thrilling Adventures: Volume 3*, also containing 'Blackout' and 'Darkstar Academy'. It is due to be reissued once more on 6 October 2016 as part of *The Eleventh Doctor Adventures* box set.

DARKSTAR ACADEMY

Release date: 8 March 2012
Written by: Mark Morris
Read by: Alexander Armstrong
Reading produced by Neil Gardner
Project editor: John Ainsworth
Music and sound effects by Simon Hunt
Doctor Who theme music by Murray Gold

PUBLICITY BLURB

When the TARDIS is buffeted by 'time slippage', the Doctor experiences a terrible vision of the end of everything. Tracking the source of the disruption, he takes Rory and Amy to what appears to be an English public school in the 1950s. But the friends discover that there are some very unusual things about Darkstar Academy. For a start the prefects carry guns, and then there is the strange force field that surrounds the perimeter. Not to mention the foot-long, crab-like creatures with spiny, armoured bodies ... The Doctor discovers that the whole place is in terrible danger, but with a swarm of carnivorous creatures on the loose, what can he, Amy, and Rory do to help prevent a terrible disaster?

Written specially for audio by Mark Morris, 'Darkstar Academy' features the Doctor, Amy, and Rory as played by Matt Smith, Karen Gillan, and Arthur Darvill in the acclaimed hit series from BBC Television. It is read by Alexander Armstrong.

NOTES

• This audiobook was reissued on 10 July 2012, as part of a two-CD set with 'Day of the Cockroach', and again by Chivers on 7 May 2012 in a three-CD set under the umbrella title *Thrilling Adventures: Volume 3*, also containing the 2011 title 'Blackout', and 'The Art of Death'. It is due to be reissued once more on 6 October 2016 as part of *The Eleventh Doctor Adventures* box set.

DAY OF THE COCKROACH

Release date: 1 May 2012
Written by: Steve Lyons
Read by: Arthur Darvill
Reading produced by Alec Reid
Project editor: John Ainsworth
Music and sound effects by Simon Hunt
Doctor Who theme music by Murray Gold

PUBLICITY BLURB

Arthur Darvill reads this exclusive audio adventure featuring the Eleventh Doctor, Amy, and Rory.

The TARDIS materialises in a pitch-dark tunnel, where the Doctor, Amy, and Rory stumble on the dead body of a soldier. Questioned by his superior officer, Colonel Bowe, they learn that they're inside a British nuclear bunker, in the middle of an atomic war – in 1982. Amy and Rory weren't even born then, but they know the bomb didn't drop that year, and so does the Doctor. The friends also know they had nothing to do with the death of Sergeant Trott – so who, or what, was the killer? And why does the Doctor's psychic paper not work on the Colonel? The Doctor, Amy, and Rory soon learn that something else is lurking in the shadows. Something deadly …

Written specially for audio by Steve Lyons, 'Day of the Cockroach' features the Doctor, Amy, and Rory as played by Matt Smith, Karen Gillan, and Arthur Darvill in the hit series from BBC Television.

NOTES

• This audiobook was reissued on 10 July 2012, as part of a two-CD set with 'Darkstar Academy'. It is due to be reissued once more on 6 October 2016 as part of The Eleventh Doctor Adventures box set.

THE NU-HUMANS

Release date: 5 July 2011
Written by: Cavan Scott and Mark Wright
Read by: Raquel Cassidy
Reading produced by Mary Price
Project editor: John Ainsworth
Music and sound effects by Simon Hunt
Doctor Who theme music by Murray Gold

PUBLICITY BLURB

The Doctor, Amy, and Rory are awe-struck by their first sight of Hope Eternal, a super-Earth bigger than Earth itself with heavy gravity, volcanoes and a crust loaded with mineral deposits. But their wonder is cut short when they discover a body dumped on the ground – a huge figure with extraordinarily long arms covered in thick, purple scales. Yet the corpse is not alien: he's human, albeit unlike any human Amy and Rory have ever seen. The Nu-Humans have adapted their genes to fit their new environment, and formed a thriving colony. But now they are facing a terrible threat. Can the Doctor find out who is killing Nu-Humans and why – before he, Amy and Rory are themselves tried for murder?

Written specially for audio by Cavan Scott and Mark Wright, 'The Nu-Humans' features the Doctor, Amy, and Rory as played by Matt Smith, Karen Gillan, and Arthur Darvill in the acclaimed hit series from BBC Television.

NOTES

• This audiobook was reissued on 13 November 2012, as part of a two-CD set with 'The Empty House'. It is due to be reissued once more on 6 October 2016 as part of The Eleventh Doctor Adventures box set.

THE EMPTY HOUSE

Release date: 6 September 2012
Written by: Simon Guerrier
Read by: Raquel Cassidy
Reading produced by Jo Palmer
Project editor: John Ainsworth
Music and sound effects by Simon Hunt
Doctor Who theme music by Murray Gold

PUBLICITY BLURB

Thrown off course by a howling storm, the TARDIS lands in a bleak, desolate stretch of countryside. The Doctor deduces that it has arrived in Hampshire in the 1920s and, sniffing the air, he smells a distinct odour of sulphur – indicating that a spaceship has crashed in the area. While Rory goes to fetch an umbrella, Amy and the Doctor brave the rain to find the stricken craft. It is huge, shiny, silvery-blue – and completely empty. A set of footprints leads to a cosy-looking, old-fashioned cottage: but the house, too, is deserted. However, the Doctor and Amy can distinctly hear people talking – and one of the voices sounds like Rory's. How could he be in the cottage when he was last seen heading back to the TARDIS? Where are the residents of the empty house? And what has happened to the inhabitants of the spaceship?

Written specially for audio by Simon Guerrier, 'The Empty House' features the Doctor, Amy and Rory as played by Matt Smith, Karen Gillan and Arthur Darvill in the acclaimed hit series from BBC Television. It is read by Raquel Cassidy, who played Miranda Cleaves in the 2011 TV episodes 'The Rebel Flesh' and 'The Almost People'.

NOTES

• This audiobook was reissued on 13 November 2012, as part of a two-CD set with 'The Nu-Humans'. It is due to be reissued once more on 6 October 2016 as part of The Eleventh Doctor Adventures box set.

SLEEPERS IN THE DUST

Release date: 1 November 2012
Written by: Darren Jones
Read by: Arthur Darvill
Reading produced by Lindsey Melling
Project editor: John Ainsworth
Music and sound effects by Simon Hunt
Doctor Who theme music by Murray Gold

PUBLICITY BLURB

The TARDIS touches down on Nadurniss, a planet under quarantine. A joint Nadurni/human mission has recently landed on the planet to survey it for possible re-colonisation. Two millennia have passed since the Nadurni Empire fell at the end of the Prokarian War, and Nadurniss seems to be a lifeless, barren world – but a mysterious illness is infecting the Nadurni, and now the whole team is in danger. The nature of the infection becomes clear when the sickest Nadurni dies and an amorphous creature emerges from its dried-up body. A shambling mound of bacteria, acting as one being – a Prokarian – it has been on the planet all along, sleeping in the dust. As the Prokarians attack, Amy is infected. The Doctor can do nothing to help her – until he realises that the cure could lie in the past. He and Rory must travel back more than 2000 years to try and save her life …

Written specially for audio by Darren Jones, 'Sleepers in the Dust' features the Doctor, Amy and Rory, as played by Matt Smith, Karen Gillan and Arthur Darvill in the acclaimed hit series from BBC TV.

NOTES

- This audiobook was reissued on 29 January 2013, as part of a two-CD set with 'Snake Bite'. It is due to be reissued once more on 6 October 2016 as part of The Eleventh Doctor Adventures box set.

TIME OF THE DOCTOR

SNAKE BITE

Release date: 6 December 2012
Written by: Scott Handcock
Read by: Frances Barber
Reading produced by Neil Gardner
Project editor: John Ainsworth
Music and sound effects by Simon Hunt
Doctor Who theme music by Murray Gold

PUBLICITY BLURB

Dr Elehri Mussurana has spent a lifetime on her work. She's guarded her pet project close to her chest, letting only one person share her secret – her husband and lab partner Ernst Wharner. As their experiment reaches its final, glorious fruition, they watch in awe as sparks fly in a sealed chamber and specks of sapphire light begin to join together into a shining haze. A wormhole in time and space is being created ... But then something unexpected appears inside the swirling vortex: a tall blue box with the words 'POLICE PUBLIC CALL BOX' on the side. The TARDIS has arrived in the far future, in a scientific research facility – just as reality is ripped at the seams and the universe tears in two ...

Written specially for audio by Scott Handcock, 'Snake Bite' features the Doctor, Amy and Rory as played by Matt Smith, Karen Gillan and Arthur Darvill in the acclaimed BBC TV series. It is read by Frances Barber, who played Madame Kovarian.

NOTES

- This audiobook was reissued on 29 January 2013, as part of a two-CD set with 'Sleepers in the Dust'. It is due to be reissued once more on 6 October 2016 as part of The Eleventh Doctor Adventures box set.

SUMMER FALLS AND OTHER STORIES

Published by BBC Books in paperback on 22 October 2013, the omnibus *Summer Falls and Other Stories* put into print for the first time the previously released *Doctor Who* e-books and audiobooks *Summer Falls* by

James Goss, *Angel's Kiss* by James Goss and *The Devil in the Smoke* by Justin Richards,[109] together with two new pieces of Goss-written text: an introduction, supposedly by Amelia Williams (aka Amy Pond); and 'The Girl Who Never Grew Up', a fictional 1969 magazine interview-cum-profile of Amelia.

11 DOCTORS 11 STORIES

Between January and November 2013, Puffin Books issued a series of 12 *Doctor Who* e-books, one per Doctor, by noted mainstream authors. These were collected together in an omnibus edition under the title *11 Doctors 11 Stories*, published in both paperback and audiobook form on 21 November 2013. The audiobook was available for download only, a CD version having been announced but then cancelled. Details of the eleventh Doctor entry in the series are given below.

NOTHING O'CLOCK

E-book release: 21 November 2013
Writer: Neil Gaiman
Audiobook version read by: Peter Kenny

PUBLICITY BLURB

Eleven Doctors, eleven months, eleven stories: a year-long celebration of *Doctor Who*! The most exciting names in children's fiction each create their own unique adventure about the time-travelling Time Lord.

Thousands of years ago, Time Lords built a Prison for the Kin. They made it utterly impregnable and unreachable. As long as Time Lords existed, the Kin would be trapped forever and the universe would be safe. They had planned for everything ... everything, that is, other than the Time War and the fall of Gallifrey. Now the Kin are free again and there's only one Time Lord left in the universe who can stop them!

Author Neil Gaiman puts his own unique spin on the Doctor's amazing adventures through time and space in the eleventh and final

---

[109] See the 'Episode Guide' entries on 'The Bells of Saint John', 'The Angels Take Manhattan' and 'The Snowmen' respectively for further details of the three stories.

story in the bestselling fiftieth anniversary series!

<u>NOTES</u>

- Later adapted by Neil Gaiman into a non-Doctor Who story for inclusion in his collection Trigger Warning: Short Fictions and Disturbances (Headline, 2015), also issued as an audiobook, read by Gaiman himself.

2-in-1 BOOKS

In 2011, Penguin's BBC Children's Books imprint began publishing a new range of '2 in 1' books for younger readers. As the name implies, two separate stories were included in each book. Two further titles were published in 2012. Details of these are given below.

5: MONSTROUS MISSIONS

Containing the stories: 'Terrible Lizards' and 'Horror of the Space Snakes'

Publication date: 17 February 2012
Writer: 'Terrible Lizards': Jonathan Green; 'Horror of the Space Snakes': Gary Russell
Cover Illustration: Kev Walker and Paul Campbell

<u>PUBLICITY BLURB</u>

One time travelling Doctor – two monstrous missions.
    In 'Terrible Lizards', the Doctor and his companions join a group of explorers on a Victorian tramp steamer in the Florida Everglades. The explorers are searching for the Fountain of Youth, but neither they nor the treasure they seek are quite what they seem!
    And in 'Horror of the Space Snakes', people are mysteriously disappearing on Moonbase Laika. They return with strange bite marks and no idea where they have been. Can the Doctor get to the bottom of what's going on?

NOTES

- 'Horror of the Space Snakes' was originally to have been called 'Snakes on a Base!', the change of title coming so late that the publicity blurb issued to retailers still referred to it as such.

- Both stories are due to be reissued as separate stand-alone books in 2016.

6: STEP BACK IN TIME

Containing the stories: 'Extra Time' and 'The Water Thief'

Publication date: 2 February 2012
Writer: 'Extra Time': Richard Dungworth; 'The Water Thief': Jacqueline Rayner
Cover Illustration: Kev Walker and Paul Campbell

PUBLICITY BLURB

One time travelling Doctor – two historic adventures.
    In 'Extra Time', the Doctor and his friends head to the 1966 World Cup final. While the Doctor and Amy discover that the Time Lord isn't the only alien visiting Wembley, Rory finds himself playing a crucial role in this historic England versus West Germany football match …
    An ancient artefact awakes, trapping one of the Doctor's companions on an archaeological dig in Egypt. The only way to save his friend is to travel hundreds of years back in time to defeat 'The Water Thief'.

NOTES

- Both stories are due to be reissued as separate stand-alone books in 2016.

- Due to a minor change in the publishing schedule, this sixth book in the series was actually issued just over a fortnight earlier than the fifth.

THE DALEK PROJECT

Following on from 2010's *The Only Good Dalek*, 6 September 2012 saw BBC

Books publish in hardback and e-book form another full colour *Doctor Who* graphic novel featuring the Daleks.

Writer: Justin Richards
Artist: Mike Collins
Colour: Kris Carter with Owen Jollands
Lettering: Ian Sharman
Script editor: Clayton Hickman
Commissioning editor: Albert DePetrillo
Editorial manager: Nicholas Payne
Series consultant: Justin Richards
Cover design: Mike Collins and Two Associates
Design: Lee Binding
Production: Phil Spencer

PUBLICITY BLURB

1917. The Great War is at its fiercest and most terrible. But things are about to get even worse. Armaments manufacturer Lord Hellcombe has a new secret weapon he believes will win the war. But when the Doctor witnesses the final demonstration he begins to realise how much danger everyone is in: Lord Hellcombe claims to have invented the Dalek! Except, of course, that nothing is quite what it seems. Now, the Doctor and his new friends must draw on every type of early 20th Century technology and every element of human ingenuity and bravery if they are to discover the truth – and survive – to prevent the entire Western Front of World War One from becoming part of the Dalek Project!

NOTES

• Publication of this graphic novel was originally mooted for 2011, but delayed as the plot was considered coincidentally similar in some respects to that of the 2010 television story 'Victory of the Daleks'.

DESTINY OF THE DOCTOR

Aside from the titles detailed above, 2013 saw the release of an additional eleventh Doctor audiobook as part of the 'Destiny of the Doctor' series, which consisted of 12 linked stories – one per Doctor – produced for

Audiogo by Big Finish to tie in with the fiftieth anniversary celebrations. Similar in style to Big Finish's own 'Companion Chronicles' range, these stories came out at the rate of one per month, beginning in January. The release of the eleventh Doctor entry was almost thwarted by AudioGo going into administration at the end of October, but fortunately Big Finish were able to rescue it.

THE TIME MACHINE

Release date: 1 November 2013 (download), 7 November 2013 (CD)
Written by: Matt Fitton
Directed by: John Ainsworth
Read by: Jenna Coleman
Supporting cast: Nicholas Briggs, Michael Cochrane

PUBLICITY BLURB

23 November 2013. In an Oxford laboratory, Alice Watson helps Professor Chivers assemble the final pieces of an impossible machine. The Creevix are coming, seeking control of time itself. Can the key to saving the future lie in the Time Lord's past lives?

NOTES

• Also released by Big Finish as part of a 'Destiny of the Doctor' CD box set in December 2013, delayed from 7 November.

DOCTOR WHO – THE OFFICIAL ANNUAL 2013

The Official Annual 2013, published by Penguin's BBC Children's Books imprint on 22 November 2012, was a rather more meagre offering than the previous year's equivalent. Once again it included two comic strip stories, but this time, instead of three pieces of prose fiction, there was only one. The rest of the pages were filled with factual features on the television show and its characters plus puzzles and the like.

THE ZENTRABOT INVASION

Written by Jason Loborik. Drawn by John Ross. Coloured by James Offredi.

PLOT

Doctor visits two children, Abby and Danny, on Christmas morning, and saves the Earth from an attack by Zentrabots – alien maintenance drones disguised as toys.

THE TOMB OF SHEMURA

Written by Jason Loborik. Drawn by John Ross. Coloured by James Offredi.

PLOT

The Doctor takes his young friends Abby and Danny on a trip in the TARDIS, and they end up on an alien planet where they defeat the tyrannical Queen Semura with the aid of a tusked, grey-skinned creature named Alaban.

LORNA'S ESCAPE

Written by Jason Loborik

PLOT

The Doctor saves the young girl Lorna Bucket and her fellow villagers from an attack by a huge monster with leathery wings.

NOTES

• This story briefly recounts an incident mentioned in the television episode 'A Good Man Goes to War' (2011).

DOCTOR WHO – THE OFFICIAL 50th ANNIVERSARY ANNUAL

Doctor Who's fiftieth anniversary was acknowledged in the title of the 2014 annual, published by Penguin's BBC Children's Books imprint on 19 September 2013. Like the previous year's edition, it contained two comic strip stories and one short piece of prose fiction. As usual, the rest of the pages were filled with factual features on the television show and its characters plus puzzles and the like.

THE DOOR TO A WINTER LONG AGO

Written by Moray Laing. Drawn by John Ross. Coloured by James Offredi.

PLOT

Ethan and Annie, two kids from 2014, find a connecting door to 1964, where they encounter the Doctor and Clara. The Doctor admits that he has accidentally created a time corridor between the two years. He eventually manages to put things right, and in the process repel some malevolent shadow creatures from another dimension.

NIGHT LIGHT

Written by Moray Laing. Drawn by John Ross. Coloured by James Offredi.

PLOT

While in flight, the TARDIS is struck by a beam of green light that then deflects to a house on Earth, where it possesses the toy dog of a sleeping young boy named Tom and appears to transform it into a huge, snarling hound. The Doctor tells Clara that they are within Tom's nightmare. They manage to wake the boy, and back in the real world, the Doctor traps the beam creature inside the TARDIS's roof lamp.

THE FIFTY-YEAR DELAY

Written by Moray Laing.

PLOT

A young man named Ryan Goodman encounters the Doctor in a London tube station. There seems to be a fifty year delay in the train service, due to the influence of an ancient, brightly-coloured time bird, but when the bird flies into the TARDIS through the open door, everything is restored to normal.

OFFICIAL WEBSITE STORIES

Since the end of 2009, the official *Doctor Who* website has published an irregular series of original short stories featuring the current Doctor with (in most cases) specially-created companions. Over the 2012 to 2013 period, there was just one of these, 'Houdini and the Space Cuckoos', released in December 2012 as part of the annual Adventure Calendar feature.

HOUDINI AND THE SPACE CUCKOOS

Publication date: December 2012 (four parts; first part released on 15 December 2012, final part released on 25 December 2012)
Writer: Joseph Lidster

PLOT

The Doctor recalls a time when he enlisted the aid of famous escapologist Harry Houdini in New York City, 1920, to thwart an invasion attempt by a race of aliens called the Cuculus, who possess people to do their bidding and then infect them with a deadly virus in the hope of wiping out humanity. The Doctor sets things to rights with the aid of his sonic screwdriver and a special crystal obtained by Harry from the Cuculus spaceship.

About the Author

Stephen James Walker became hooked on *Doctor Who* as a young boy, right from its debut season in 1963/64, and has been a fan ever since. He first got involved in the series' fandom in the early 1970s, when he became a member of the original *Doctor Who* Fan Club (DWFC). He joined the *Doctor Who* Appreciation Society (DWAS) immediately on its formation in May 1976, and was an attendee at the first ever *Doctor Who* convention in August 1977. He soon began to contribute articles to fanzines, and in the 1980s was editor of the seminal reference work *Doctor Who – An Adventure in Space and Time* and its sister publication *The Data-File Project*. He also became a frequent writer for the official *Doctor Who Magazine*. Between 1987 and 1993 he was co-editor and publisher, with David J Howe and Mark Stammers, of the leading *Doctor Who* fanzine *The Frame*. Since that time, he has gone on to write, co-write and edit numerous *Doctor Who* articles and books – including *Doctor Who: The Sixties, Doctor Who: The Seventies, Doctor Who: The Eighties, The Doctor Who Yearbook 1996, The Handbook* (originally published in seven separate volumes) and *The Television Companion* – and he is now widely acknowledged as one of the foremost chroniclers of the series' history. He was the initiator and, for the first two volumes, co-editor of Virgin Publishing's *Decalog* books – the first ever *Doctor Who* short story anthology range. More recently, he has edited the three-volume *Talkback* series of *Doctor Who* interview books and written *Inside the Hub: The Unofficial and Unauthorised Guide to Torchwood Series One* and *Something in the Darkness: The Unofficial and Unauthorised Guide to Torchwood Series Two*. *Time of the Doctor* is the sixth book he has written in Telos Publishing's acclaimed series of annual guides to *Doctor Who*. He has a BSc (Hons) degree in Applied Physics from University College London, and his many other interests include cult TV, film noir, vintage crime fiction, Laurel and Hardy and an eclectic mix of soul, jazz, R&B and other popular music. Between July 1983 and March 2005 he acted as an adviser to successive Governments, latterly at senior assistant director level, responsible for policy on a range of issues relating mainly to individual employment rights. His working time is now taken up by his writing projects and by his role as co-owner and director of Telos Publishing Ltd. He lives in Kent with his wife and family.